Who Speaks for Plato?

Who Speaks for Plato?

Studies in Platonic Anonymity

Edited by
Gerald A. Press

ROWMAN & LITTLEFIELD PUBLISHERS, INC.
Lanham • Boulder • New York • Oxford

ROWMAN & LITTLEFIELD PUBLISHERS, INC.

Published in the United States of America
by Rowman & Littlefield Publishers, Inc.
4720 Boston Way, Lanham, Maryland 20706
http://www.rowmanlittlefield.com

12 Hid's Copse Road
Cumnor Hill, Oxford OX2 9JJ, England

British Library Cataloguing in Publication Information Available

Library of Congress Cataloging-in-Publication Data

Press, Gerald A. (Gerald Alan), 1945–
    Who speaks for Plato? : studies in Platonic anonymity / Gerald A.
Press.
        p.   cm.
    Includes bibliographical references and indexes.
    ISBN 0-8476-9218-3 (alk. paper). — ISBN 0-8476-9219-1 (pbk. :
alk. paper)
    1. Plato. Dialogues.   I. Title.
B395.P74 2000
184—dc21   99-14796
                                                                CIP

Printed in the United States of America

♾™ The paper used in this publication meets the minimum requirements of
American National Standard for Information Sciences—Permanence of Paper
for Printed Library Materials, ANSI/NISO Z39.48-1992.

Contents

Who Speaks for Plato?

Introduction

Gerald A. Press

The modern interpretation of Plato's dialogues has been dominated by two assumptions: that what the dialogues contain is what many interpreters are seeking, namely the philosophic doctrines of their author, Plato, and that in the discovery of Plato's doctrines little or no systematic attention need be paid to the fact that the dialogues are dialogues rather than treatises. An essential presupposition of this approach, and the theme of the present volume, is that the words, arguments, and apparent doctrines of the leading speaker in each dialogue are those of Plato himself.

This way of reading the dialogues goes back to antiquity. Aristotle, the most famous student of Plato's Academy, often states as Plato's views positions taken by Socrates or other leading speakers in the dialogues.[1] It is stated explicitly by Diogenes Laertius: "[Plato's] own views are expounded by four persons— Socrates, Timaeus, the Athenian Stranger, and the Eleatic Stranger—even when Socrates and Timaeus are the speakers it is Plato's doctrines that are laid down."[2] The second century C.E. *Didaskalikos*, whether it be by Albinus or Alcinus,[3] is, according to its first sentence, a summary of Plato's principal doctrines as is Diogenes Laertius's discussion at 3.67–109. There was also the contrary but related ancient tradition of Platonic skepticism, characteristic of the "New Academy" of Arceilaus (316–242 B.C.E.) and Carneades (214–129 B.C.E.), well

---

1. The passages are collected and discussed in Harold Cherniss, *Aristotle's Criticism of Plato and the Academy* (Baltimore: Johns Hopkins University Press, 1944).

2. καὶ τὰ Σωκράτους καὶ τὰ Τιμαίου λέγων Πλάτων δογματίζει; D.L. 3.52; tr. by Hicks (Loeb).

3. The point is in dispute in recent scholarship. Reginald E. Witt, *Albinus and the History of Middle Platonism* (Cambridge, Cambridge University Press 1957) attributed the book to Albinus as does *The Platonic Doctrines of Albinus*, tr. by Jeremiah Reedy (Grand Rapids: Phanes Press, 1991). Jaap Mansfeld, *Prolegomena: Questions to be Settled before the Study of an Author or a Text* (Leiden: Brill, 1994), like John Dillon, *Alcinous: The Handbook of Platonism*, tr. by John Dillon (New York: Oxford University Press, 1993) follows Whittaker and Louis, eds., *Alcinoos: Enseignement des doctrines de Platon* (Paris: Budé, 1990) in attributing the work to Alcinoos or Alcinous.

known to Cicero and Augustine.[4] Some ancient interpreters certainly were aware of literary aspects of the dialogues.[5] And, as Harold Tarrant argues later in this volume, there was an ancient tradition of reading the dialogues for their contribution to one's own search for truth, rather than for the purpose of finding out simply what Plato may have thought the truth was.

There are several variations and specifications on these widespread assumptions. One variation is reading a subset of the dialogues as sources, not for the doctrines of Plato, but for those of a Socrates who may or may not be identical with the historical Socrates.[6] Much more widespread is Platonic developmentalism, the view that the differences and contradictions among the claims apparently put forward in various dialogues evidence the evolution of Plato's doctrines.[7] Obviously, an essential aspect of a developmental view is an arrangement of the dialogues in their compositional order, a Platonic chronology, and this, in turn, has come to be based primarily on stylometry.[8]

Since the 1950s, however, a new Plato scholarship has been developing— a new kind of Platonism—that is defined by sharing in varying combinations and to varying degrees two nontraditional orientations: suspicion of the dogmatic approach to the dialogues, and belief that literary and dramatic matters are important (even essential) to proper understanding of the dialogues and Plato's philosophy as found in them.[9] Earlier writers commented on the

---

4. Cicero, *Academica* and Augustine, *Contra Academicos* are, for quite different reasons, critical of the skeptical academics. See Harold Tarrant, *Skepticism or Platonism? The Philosophy of the Fourth Academy* (Cambridge: Cambridge University Press, 1985).

5. See, e.g., Proclus' comments about the dramatic setting, characters, style, and the significance of Plato's preludes; *Proclus' Commentary on Plato's Parmenides*, tr. by Glenn R. Morrow and John M. Dillon (Princeton: Princeton University Press, 1987), pp. 20–46. Diogenes Laertius is also aware of various literary features (3.37, 63–65).

6. This is the approach of Gregory Vlastos, his students and associates. See, e.g., Vlastos' originating book, *The Philosophy of Socrates* (Garden City, NY: Anchor Books, 1971) and his final statement, *Socrates: Ironist and Moral Philosopher* (Ithaca: Cornell University Press, 1991); Thomas C. Brickhouse and Nicholas D. Smith, *Socrates on Trial* (Princeton: Princeton University Press, 1989) and *Plato's Socrates* (New York: Oxford University Press, 1994); Hugh Benson has collected many of the decisive papers in this "Socratic philosophy" genre in *Essays on the Philosophy of Socrates* (New York: Oxford University Press, 1992).

7. See E. N. Tigerstedt, *Interpreting Plato* (Stockholm: Almquist and Wiksell, 1977). The original version of developmentalism in Hermann's *Geschichte und System der Platonischen Philosophie* (Heidelberg: Winter, 1839; repr. New York: Arno Press, 1976) and widely disseminated in Hans Raeder's *Platons' philosophische Entwicklung* (Leipzig: Teubner, 1905) was intended to save the picture of a Platonic system of philosophic doctrine from the implications of such contradictions.

8. The earliest stylometric analyses, of Lewis Campbell, *The Sophistes and Politicus of Plato* (Oxford: Clarendon Press, 1867) and W. Lutoslawski, *The Origin and Growth of Plato's Logic, with an Account of Plato's Style and of the Chronology of his Writings* (London: Longmans, Green, 1897), have been transformed of recent years into computerized statistical analyses. See Gerard R. Ledger, *Re-counting Plato: A Computer Analysis of Plato's Style* (Oxford: Oxford University Press, 1989) for the statistical analysis and Leonard Brandwood, *The Chronology of Plato's Dialogues* (Cambridge: Cambridge University Press, 1990) for an account of some important earlier stylometric analyses.

9. For a more detailed account of recent developments, see my article, "The State of the Question in the Study of Plato," *The Southern Journal of Philosophy* 34 (1996): 507–532. Now reprinted in *Plato: Critical Assessments*, ed. Nicholas D. Smith. Vol. I, pp. 309–332 (New York: Routledge, 1998). Some publications that belong with the "new Platonism" but were not mentioned there are: Thomas H. Chance, *Plato's Euthydemus: An Analysis of What Is and What Is Not Philosophy*

interpretive problem posed by the fact that, in the dialogues, only characters speak, while Plato remains silent, absent, and distanced from the words spoken by his characters, but only recently has the problem gained more widespread attention. [10]

Although the new Platonism has been increasing in influence, scholarship, at least in the English language, has been dominated by these dogmatic and nonliterary orientations for more than a century. But times are changing. Some scholars previously committed to a more doctrinal interpretation have begun to see things less dogmatically[11] and others have begun to take an interest in the dialogue form.[12] Developmentalism, chronology, and stylometry have come under severe criticism[13] and scholars increasingly retreat from reliance on them.[14] The implicit assumption that the dialogues are, on the whole, serious and didactic texts has also been challenged.[15] Interpretations

---

(Berkeley: University of California Press, 1992); Bernard Freydberg, *The Play of the Platonic Dialogues* (New York: Peter Lang, 1997); Amihud Gilead, *The Platonic Odyssey: A Philosophical-Literary Inquiry into the Phaedo* (Amsterdam: Rodopi, 1994); Thomas Prufer, "The Dramatic Form of the *Phaedo*," *Review of Metaphysics* 39 (1986): 547–51; Robert Sternfel and Harold Zyskind, "Plato's *Parmenides*: The Drama and the Problem," *Revue internationale de philosophie* 40 (1986): 140–56; Michael C. Stokes, *Plato's Socratic Conversations: Drama and Dialectic in Three Dialogues* (Baltimore: Johns Hopkins University Press, 1986).

10. On this "Platonic anonymity," see the classic studies by Philip Merlan, "Form and Content in Plato's Philosophy," *Journal of the History of Ideas* 8 (1947): 406–30; Ludwig Edelstein, "Platonic Anonymity," *American Journal of Philology* 83 (1962): 1–22; Paul Plass, "Philosophic Anonymity and Irony in the Platonic Dialogues *American Journal of Philology* 85 (1964): 254–78 and "'Play' and Philosophic Detachment in Plato," *Transactions of the American Philological Association* 98 (1967): 343–64. More recently, L. A. Kosman, "Silence and Imitation in the Platonic Dialogues," pp. 73–92 in *Methods of Interpreting Plato and His Dialogues*, ed. Klagge and Smith, *Oxford Studies in Ancient Philosophy Supplement*, 1992.

11. See, e.g., John Cooper's "Introduction" to the recent *Plato. Complete Works*, ed. John M. Cooper and D. S. Hutchinson (Indianapolis: Hackett, 1997).

12. Christopher Gill and Mary Margaret McCabe, eds., *Form and Argument in Late Plato* (Oxford: Oxford University Press, 1996) show an increased interest in dialogue form among "analytic" Plato scholars to whom the volume is limited. However, see Gonzalez' critical review in *Journal of the History of Philosophy* 36 (1998): 311–13.

13. The comprehensive undermining of Platonic chronology by Holger Thesleff, *Studies in Platonic Chronology* (Helsinki: Societas Scientiarum Fennica, 1982) is updated in his "Platonic Chronology," *Phronesis* 34 (1989): 1–26. The argument is carried forward and applied to the "Socratic philosophy" school by Debra Nails, *Agora, Academy, and the Conduct of Philosophy* (Dordrecht: Kluwer, 1995). Further support for the antistylometry and antichronology position is found in Jacob Howland, "Re-reading Plato: The Problem of Platonic Chronology," *Phoenix* 45 (1991): 189–214; T. M. Robinson, "Plato and the Computer, *Ancient Philosophy* 13 (1993): 375–82; and Charles M. Young, "Plato and Computer Dating," *Oxford Studies in Ancient Philosophy* 12 (1994): 227–50.

14. E.g., Richard A. McNeal, *Law and Rhetoric in the Crito* (Frankfurt: Peter Lang, 1992): 46–57 and T. K. Seung, *Plato Rediscovered: Human Value and the Social Order* (Lanham, MD: Rowman & Littlefield, 1996): xvii finds Platonic chronology not only unsubstantiated but unhelpful in the pursuit of their otherwise very different interpretive goals. Perhaps more significant is that John Cooper, in the "Introduction" to the new *Complete Works of Plato* that he edited for Hackett Publishing Co., has largely abandoned stylometry, chronology, and developmentalism, and has come to consider literary and dramatic aspects of the dialogues important for understanding their philosophic import.

15. E.g., by Straussians, by the Tübingen school or by followers of F. J. E. Woodbridge. For a brief account of these approaches, with bibliography, and the criticisms that have been brought against each, see my "State of the Question," 513–14.

that attempt to unify philosophical and literary readings have increased and diversified.[16] One recent interpreter has written, "It is becoming increasingly difficult to argue that the dramatic context or action of a dialogue is simply incidental to its philosophical importance,"[17] but there are still scholars who seem to find no such difficulty.[18]

Perhaps because their differences are matters of principle rather than of conclusions reached, direct confrontations between the traditional and the new Platonism have not been frequent or productive. Several recent collections make the attempt. The first, by Charles L. Griswold,[19] is often mentioned in discussions of different approaches to Plato. It contains some direct confrontations,[20] but focuses on the methodological question of how to read the dialogues and on the general question of why Plato wrote dialogues. A supplement volume to the *Oxford Studies in Ancient Philosophy*[21] contains some attempts to confront traditional approaches to Plato but is tilted toward that tradition and weak on scholarship. Similarly, a special issue of *Apeiron*[22] tries to find a middle ground between philosophy and literature by focusing on Plato's awareness of the difficulties of pursuing philosophical inquiry in the sort of language that will be understandable to those who lack the philosopher's knowledge. An earlier book that I edited touches on a variety of methodological issues and in-

16. See Mitchell Miller, *The Philosopher in Plato's Statesman* (The Hague: Martinus Nijhoff, 1980), and *Plato's Parmenides: The Conversion of the Soul* (Princeton: Princeton University Press, 1984); Victorino Tejera, *Plato's Dialogues One by One* (New York: Irvington, 1984); James A. Arieti, *Interpreting Plato* (Lanham, MD: Rowman & Littlefield, 1991); E. de Strycker and S. R. Slings, *Plato's Apology of Socrates: A Literary and Philosophical Study* (Leiden: Brill, 1994); Kenneth M. Sayre, *Plato's Literary Garden: How to Read a Platonic Dialogue* (Notre Dame: University of Notre Dame Press, 1995); Richard B. Rutherford, *The Art of Plato* (Cambridge: Harvard University Press, 1995); and Albert Cook, *The Stance of Plato* (Lanham, MD: Littlefield Adams Books, 1996). Also interesting in this regard, and also not mentioned in my "State of the Question," are the works of W. Thomas Schmid, *On Manly Courage: A Study of Plato's Laches* (Carbondale: Southern Illinois University Press, 1992), and *Plato's Charmides and the Socratic Ideal of Rationality* (Albany: State University of New York Press, 1998), who employs careful attention to dramatic and literary matters to expose "Socratic" arguments and ideas.

17. Gerald M. Mara, *Socrates' Discursive Democracy: Logos and Ergon in Platonic Political Philosophy* (Albany: State University of New York Press, 1997).

18. E.g., Mary Margaret McCabe, *Plato's Individuals* (Princeton: Princeton University Press, 1994); Thomas A. Blackson, *Inquiry, Forms, and Substances: A Study in Plato's Metaphysics and Epistemology* (Dordrecht: Kluwer, 1995); and Stephen Menn, *Plato on God as Nous* (Carbondale, IL: *Journal of the History of Philosophy Monograph*, 1995). Particularly egregious in this respect is Richard A. Kraut, ed., *The Cambridge Companion to Plato* (Cambridge: Cambridge University Press, 1992), who writes with near complete disregard for orientations other than the traditional one. A more ingenious solution is that of Melissa Lane, who simply *assumes* the point at issue: "I take the liberty of identifying the Eleatic Stranger's arguments with Plato's, in the spirit of identifying what the arguments are on their own terms rather than seeking clues that they are to be disregarded or minimised." M. S. Lane, *Method and Politics in Plato's 'Statesman'* (Cambridge: Cambridge University Press, 1998): 8.

19. Ed., *Platonic Writings, Platonic Readings* (New York: Routledge, 1988).

20. Chs. 10–15.

21. James Klagge and Nicholas Smith, eds., *Methods of Interpreting Plato and His Dialogues* (Oxford Studies in Ancient Philology Suppl. Vol. 1992). See my review, *Journal of the History of Philosophy* 34 (1996): 135–136.

22. Andrew Barker and Martin Warner, eds., *The Language of the Cave* (Apeiron 25:4 [1992]).

terpretive approaches along with their applications to specific dialogues, but does not attempt to confront a specific issue.[23] A 1995 volume edited by Francisco Gonzalez attempts to find an alternative to the dogmatic and skeptical orientations that have dominated most of the history of Plato scholarship.[24] A recent volume on "The Dialogical Approach" to Plato offers a collection of non-traditional interpretations, but, like the other volumes mentioned here, does not attempt to confront traditional Platonism on a single and crucial particular issue.[25]

The chapters in this book attempt just this: to confront the traditional approach to Plato's dialogues on a specific issue that is crucial to the viability of either approach, namely the idea—more accurately, the methodological assumption—that the words and arguments of some character in a Platonic dialogue can be taken to state Plato's (or the historical Socrates') own beliefs and arguments. Less felicitously, but more plainly, the question is whether some character is to be taken as Plato's mouthpiece. When we read what Socrates says as the leading speaker in most of the dialogues, are we entitled to suppose that the claims apparently being made and the arguments being set forth are those of Plato himself? And when we read the words of the Eleatic Stranger, Parmenides, Timaeus, Critias, and the Athenian Stranger in the dialogues in which they are the leading speakers, are we entitled to take their claims and arguments as Plato's own?

The issue involves both the literary-dramatic interests and the nondogmatism of innovative Plato interpreters. As many contributors note, Plato's dialogues are dramas, not treatises; and in interpreting dramas it is simply inappropriate to attribute a character's words and ideas directly to the author. Moreover, looked at as literary texts the dialogues are 'dialogical' in Bakhtin's sense; i.e., texts in which different characters see the world and speak from their own well grounded point of view rather than being controlled by the 'monological' point of view of their author. That Plato wrote dialogues of this sort, when he might have written treatises, suggests to many of the contributors that he did not intend a direct communication of doctrine, of his own (even temporarily) settled philosophical knowledge or beliefs. Perhaps this was because he did not believe that he had knowledge to communicate; either that he had not reached that point as yet or that such knowledge was unattainable by humans. Or perhaps it was because, although he did have such knowledge, he preferred to communicate it—or thought it was only communicable—orally and intended the dialogues to serve rather as incitements or inducements to readers to pursue philosophy. Or perhaps he thought that the specifically philosophical sort of knowledge is such that it cannot be stated in propositional form. Or perhaps the dialogues were intended to

---

23. Gerald A. Press, ed., *Plato's Dialogues: New Studies and Interpretations* (Lanham, MD: Rowman & Littlefield, 1993).

24. Francisco Gonzalez, ed., *The Third Way: A New Direction in Platonic Studies* (Lanham, MD: Rowman & Littlefield, 1995).

25. Richard A. Hart and Victorino Tejera, eds., *Plato's Dialogues: The Dialogical Approach* (Lewiston, NY: Edwin Mellen Press, 1997).

function—as, indeed, they have functioned for more than two millennia—as examples and dialectical exercises from which readers can learn how to philosophize, rather than what philosophical conclusions they ought to hold. There are many ways to see the dialogues as nondogmatic if one does not treat any single character as uniquely stating Plato's own philosophy.

The issue, however, is exceedingly consequential for the present and future of Plato studies. If most contributors to this volume are correct in believing that no single character in a dialogue should be taken to be Plato's mouthpiece, then a very great deal of scholarship is logically flawed, methodologically inappropriate, or just plain wrong. It is logically unjustified to assume without proof what is in dispute: that Socrates or the Eleatic Stranger, for example, speaks for Plato in a given dialogue, and it is methodologically inappropriate to interpret a dialogue as if it were a treatise. But many books and articles about Plato's epistemology or ethics or metaphysics, Plato's theory of Forms or method of dialectic or political theory or doctrine of love depend on just this transition from character to author as an implicit premise in their arguments. But if one of the premises is false, then, however valid the author's argument may be, its conclusion is not necessarily true.

The contributors to this book do not share an intellectual orientation or method; nor do we share a single, positive view of the inferences to be drawn from Platonic anonymity. What most of us share is the belief that it is unjustified and inappropriate to attribute the words and arguments of Plato's characters directly to Plato himself. If we are right in denying the validity of these interpretive moves from character to author, then it will be necessary to reexamine, as several contributors to this volume do, some other common assumptions made by Plato scholars about the nature of philosophy and of knowledge along with that of the purposes for which Plato wrote the dialogues.

The book is divided into three parts. Part I takes a general and theoretical look at the question of whether it is reasonable or appropriate to attribute the words and arguments of Plato's characters to Plato himself. The chapters by Nails and Press criticize the unjustified assumption that it is. Debra Nails, in "Mouthpiece Schmouthpiece" argues that the question "Is Socrates Plato's mouthpiece?" may be of literary or historical interest, but that it is not a philosophical question, however much it may interest philosophers. After considering a number of possibilities she concludes that the possible "yes" answers to the question are all patently false, ridiculously jury-rigged, and/or philosophically useless.

My own chapter looks closely at "The Logic of Attributing Characters' Views to Plato." The important difference between the statements (1) "Socrates says that justice is minding your own business" and (2) "Plato says that justice is minding your own business" is that (1) is true and (2) is false. The logical question is, Can (2) be inferred from (1)? I argue first that the prima facie reasons against the view that any character is Plato's mouthpiece lead to the conclusion that the burden of proof is on an interpreter who wants to use that view as a premise in an interpretation. There are reasons why, nevertheless, many interpreters assume it or believe it to be true, but none of these reasons is sufficient. Certain types of evidence would render the view plausible or justify it, but none of these types of evidence is actually available to us. Finally, I consider the view first articulated by Mulhern in 1971 that interpretive arguments that include premises of the form "Character X is Plato's mouthpiece" inevitably involve a *petitio principii.*

Joanne Waugh also attacks the mouthpiece assumption by focusing on the kind of text Plato wrote and on the differing views of philosophy and language that lead many modern interpreters to underestimate its significance. In "Socrates and the Character of Platonic Dialogue," Waugh argues that those who assume that Socrates speaks for Plato must explain why Plato chose to write dramatic dialogues in which no speaking character is his namesake and in which the dominant speaker is so often Socrates. Scholars who assume that Plato did not choose to write dialogues for philosophical reasons are not treating Plato differently from other philosophers, she observes, for scholars typically assume that the style in which philosophy is written, or if it is written, is of no philosophic significance. Waugh claims that this view of philosophy rests on mistakenly viewing written language and not speech as the model of language. But a text stands in for a speaker. A speaker, Waugh points out, conveys meaning not just by words, but also by intonations and phrasing, gestures and movements *to those with whom or to whom he speaks.* Determining the text's meaning(s) thus depends, Waugh argues, on knowing not just the language in which the text was written, but also the context in which it was produced and is read, the literary history of which it forms a part, and the interpretative communities to which it is addressed. When she examines the historical and cultural contexts in which Plato wrote his dialogues, Waugh finds that citizenship in the *polis* is identified with one's participation in its public discourse, and that this public discourse stands in contrast to the character Socrates who contests "in what he says and in what he is" the established belief that one becomes virtuous by engaging in the traditional forms of Athenian public discourse.

In Holger Thesleff's, "The Philosopher Conducting Dialectic," seven arguments for supposing that no character in the dialogues speaks for Plato are first presented and then opposed by nine counterarguments for believing that Plato's views are somehow expressed in the dialogues. Two rebuttals to these counterarguments are given. Then an attempt is made to construct an explanation that integrates both the positive and negative arguments on the basis of the philological and contextual evidence.

Where Nails, Waugh, Thesleff, and I are concerned with current arguments for the view that Socrates or some other character speaks for Plato, Harold Tarrant, "Where Plato Speaks: Reflections on an Ancient Debate," looks instead at earlier points of view. He shows that to ancient commentators on Plato—e.g., various introductions to the reading of Plato, Plutarch, Cicero, the *Anonymous Commentary on the Theaetetus,* Olympiodorus, Aulus Gellius—who speaks for whom is much less important than who speaks for the common notions and for the truth that they ultimately contain. The key question for them is rather, How will truth emerge? The answer is, Through dialogue between speakers who are both intelligent and free from preconceptions that obscure their natural insights into reality. The commentator was not seeking Plato's preconceptions, his personal views that could be seen in isolation from the views of others. He was seeking Plato's company and guidance in a living dialogue that continued into his own day and beyond it into ours; and the object of that dialogue was the discovery of common truths of which all human beings have at least a glimmer in their own minds.

Where the chapters in Part I consider Platonic anonymity and inferences from character to author in a theoretical and historical perspective, the chapters in Part II reconsider the use of that approach in the interpretation of particular dialogues. Often, for example, scholars studying the *Laches* seek Plato's doctrine of courage in Socrates' words. Eugenio Benitez takes a different approach in his "Cowardice, Moral Philosophy, and Saying What You Think." Plato uses in the *Laches* a single, pervasive anticonventional image: the image of fighting in armor. Benitez shows first how the image of the battle-armed hero (and later the hoplite) was customarily linked to an opinion about courage as standing one's grounds. Then he argues that Plato is breaking with convention by setting the image in a novel and unattractive context. This anticonventional image of fighting in armor is then expanded so that the actions of the main characters, especially Nicias, are shown to be cowardly by its standard. Plato's use of this image in the *Laches* supports and complements Socrates' dialectical arguments. Plato also makes an independent philosophical point, however: images are always derivative, dependent for their proper sense on the originals of which they are the images. Absent an apprehension of the original, the viewer of an image is in no position to see what is right or true about it. In that case, the image is liable to be misunderstood; it can even be perverted to represent the opposite of what it appears to represent.

Like many interpreters, Elinor West ("Why Doesn't Plato Speak?") is interested in what Plato's dialogues may reveal about the character Socrates; but unlike most of them, she approaches the dialogues as oral interactions that, unlike the dramas they resemble in many other ways, do not end. By *not* concluding his dialogues, West argues, Plato is able to help us reexperience in the present what it felt like to talk with Socrates. By provoking us to rediscover and explain the various gaps built into his temporal structures, we are able to learn how to witness Socrates probing Euthyphro's beliefs. If so, then one can similarly grasp how others who will live on after us can likewise reexperience the sorts of questions Socrates put to a respondent and the kinds of arguments he favored. By making a place for us within his texts Plato insures that the sounds of Socrates' talking do not cease, even though his accusers would have had it otherwise.

In modern scholarship, Plato's *Republic* has been considered the most important of the dialogues, as giving not only his doctrine of the ideal state but also a view of his entire doctrinal system.[26] This, of course, involves taking the words of Socrates as expressing the ideas and arguments of Plato. Two contributors discuss the *Republic* without making Socrates Plato's mouthpiece or the dialogue a matter of settled doctrine. P. Christopher Smith, "Not Doctrine, but 'Placing in Question': The "Thrasymachus" (*Rep.* I) as an *Erôtêsis* of Commercialization," examines the first book of the *Republic* as

26. G. Press, "Continuities and Discontinuities in the History of *Republic* Interpretation," *International Studies in Philosophy* 29 (1996): 61–78.

exemplifying Aristotle's distinction between dialectic and demonstration. He argues that in the "Thrasymachus" no supposed doctrines of Plato's are assumed and argued for by any of the protagonists. Rather, what "justice" and "the just" are, is placed in question. From the start it is not assumed either that "'Justice' is x" or that "'Justice' is not x." Rather it is asked, in entertaining both sides of a contradiction simultaneously, both whether "'Justice' is x" and whether "'Justice' is not x." Thus the argument has the form not of a demonstration in support of a doctrine, but of a questioning. What is being placed in question at a deeper level, Smith argues, are the devastating effects of commercialization on a community based in the *philia* (kinship, loyalty) felt by its members for each other.

Where Smith focused on Book 1 of the *Republic*, Ruby Blondell, "Letting Plato Speak for Himself: Character and Method in the *Republic*," looks at books 2–10 in contrast with Book 1. Like any literary artist, Blondell believes Plato speaks to his audience in a variety of ways. Since his preferred form is that of the dramatic dialogue, some of these ways of "speaking" resemble those of a dramatist who airs a range of views through a variety of characters, without being committed to any of them while remaining free to suggest approval or disapproval of various points of view by means of such "literary" features as characterization and dramatic structure. Thus Plato "speaks" to us through the choices he makes in his use of dramatic form and characterization.

The *Republic* provides an exceptional vehicle for exploring the significance of such choices, because of the marked shift in tone, style, use of dialogue form, characterization, and representation of philosophical method that occurs after Book 1. Blondell argues that the style and method of books 2–10 embody a critique of the "early" Socrates and his method, as portrayed in Book 1. This critique further implies a self-criticism by Plato of his own literary and philosophical methods as practiced in Book 1. The net result, however, is not (as is often claimed) a newly dogmatic Plato. It is rather a Plato who offers us new a paradigm for philosophical exploration without committing himself to the ideas that emerge from such exploration, or even to the effectiveness of the new methodological paradigm itself.

Diotima's speech in the *Symposium* is usually interpreted as Plato's theory of love. However, in "Eros as Messenger in Diotima's Teaching," Gary Alan Scott and William Welton show that Diotima's speech frames a tension—that persists throughout Plato's dialogues—between two very different images of philosophy. On one, philosophy ends in Socratic ignorance; on the other, philosophy leads to a grasp of transcendent Forms. This tension emerges through Diotima's discussion of Eros, for Eros aims at immortal Beauty while remaining in-between the mortal and immortal realms. Scott and Welton first consider the significance of this tension for reading Plato, arguing that the dialogues deliberately reflect the in-between character of Eros and that this tension has helped to give rise to the interpretive debates in Platonic scholarship. They conclude that both the form and the content of Diotima's speech supply ample evidence for holding that the juxtaposition of Socratic ignorance with the theory of Forms is integral to Plato's strategy and is not merely the result of a transitional phase in his development. Diotima is not simply a mouthpiece for Plato's presentation of doctrine, they maintain, but is one element in a delicate drama that serves to exhibit the tension of Eros.

That the Eleatic Stranger is Plato's mouthpiece in the *Sophist* and *Statesman* is considered by most scholars to be so obvious as to need no justification. In "The Eleatic Stranger: His Master's Voice?" however, Francisco Gonzalez seeks to show that this view is actually quite implausible. For one thing, it ignores the presence of Socrates, who, through both his silence and his few but decisive words, exposes fundamental limitations in the Stranger's method and conclusions. In the *Sophist*, the Stranger's pretense of ethical neutrality and his conflation of philosophy with theoretical wisdom result in his failure to distinguish the Socratic philosopher from the sophist. In the *Statesman*, the Stranger recognizes only two alternatives between which his discussion vacillates: a godlike, unattainable, and purely theoretical knowledge of statesmanship, and the practical expediency of a rule by law that outlaws independent inquiry into the good. Thus, Gonzalez argues, the Stranger fails to grant humans their distinctive dignity and philosophy its proper place in human life. Specifically, the only realizable state described by the Stranger is one in which Socrates would *necessarily* be sentenced to death. But why would Plato write a dialogue in which the main interlocutor presents so thorough a philosophical condemnation of Socrates? Gonzalez replies that this reveals genuine limits to Socratic philosophizing *and* to the nature of philosophy. Thus *neither* the Stranger *nor* Socrates is Plato's "mouthpiece."

Just as the Eleatic Stranger is usually taken to be the spokesman for Plato in the *Sophist* and the *Statesman*, so Timaeus and Critias are taken to be his spokesmen in the dialogues named after them. Accordingly, Hayden Ausland ("Who Speaks for Whom in the *Timaeus-Critias*?") focuses attention on the problems created for attributing a character's words to Plato both by the diversity of characters and contexts in the dialogues and by the peculiarity of shifting (alleged) spokesmen. He views the *Timaeus* and the *Critias* in conjunction with the *Republic*, with which Plato may have intended it to be linked, and a dialogue called *Hermocrates* that, like the *Philosopher*, Plato seems never to have written. Ausland maintains that neither Timaeus nor Critias nor Socrates nor the mysterious, missing fourth person should be considered simply and univocally as Plato's spokesman. Instead, he argues, the peculiar structure of the trilogy or tetralogy—a presupposed first conversation and a missing fourth—itself suggests the *Timaeus*' idea of mathematical growth in three dimensions as applied to the political concerns of *Republic*, but stopping short of the fourth stage in which solids are set in motion; for that, in the nature of the case, requires living individuals who have both knowledge of the "true" state and the practical ability to bring it about. And that remains an open question.

Part III returns to a more synoptic perspective on the question, Who Speaks for Plato? Lloyd Gerson, "Plato *Absconditus*," offers criticisms of the positions presented earlier in the volume. To the extent that contributors depend on passages in the *Phaedrus* and the *Seventh Letter*, Gerson argues that those texts are misused in supporting a claim that no character really speaks for Plato. He also argues that use of the analogy between Plato's dialogues and dramas is misleading because philosophical arguments are unlike dramatic speeches in important respects. And overall, he maintains the denial that the principal interlocutors in the dialogues are Plato's mouthpieces results in a Plato who is hidden from view behind the dialogues but is based on premises that beg questions about Plato's intentions.

Like Lloyd Gerson, Erik Ostenfeld believes that it is possible to discover Plato's views from what characters say in the dialogues. But where Gerson argues, against many contributors to this volume, that the traditional approach of taking a particular character's words as Plato's is justifiable, Ostenfeld's position is, "Who Speaks for Plato? Everyone!" That is, not only Socrates and the other leasing speakers, but everyone. Insofar as the views resulting from the dialogues are *homologiai* of the parties to the discussion, Ostenfeld argues that we have Plato debating with himself and his resulting view. More generally, the dialogue is an artistic whole composed by Plato, and in that sense too represents his views. This applies also to the "middle" dialogues where Socrates still has interlocutors who resist his questioning. The "late dialogues," however, in Ostenfeld's opinion, are didactic, virtually monologues (anticipated by *Republic* 2–10) that leave us with the main speaker (generally not Socrates) as the undisputed mouthpiece. The element of irony and play (in the myths) and warnings against the written word do not prevent a well informed contemporary like Aristotle from referring to the dialogues as Plato's views.

The late twentieth century has been a time of considerable ferment in Plato studies.[27] As the author of one of the earliest papers to focus on the problem of attributing the words and arguments of Plato's characters to Plato himself,[28] J. J. Mulhern is well positioned to look back at the development of Platonic scholarship on this particular interpretive question. In "Interpreting the Platonic Dialogues: What Can One Say?" Mulhern assesses some basic points about the condition of interpretive technique in today's Platonic scholarship—including some contributions to this volume—in comparison to the technique of a quarter-century ago. He first describes the "impasse" Plato studies had reached by 1970 and his own opposition at the time to two interpretive principles: that an author should be assumed to mean what he says and assumed to say all that he means. The technical and logical criticisms that he made at the time have begun to receive wider acceptance. Then he examines at some length Constance Meinwald's work on the *Parmenides* as an example of current interpretive technique and finds that the mainstream of contemporary Plato scholarship continues to make some of the mistakes of twenty-five years ago. His argument—and this book—concludes with "A Modest Program for Improvement."

---

27. In addition to my "State of the Question," see my "The Dialogical Mode in Modern Plato Studies," pp. 1–28 in *Plato's Dialogues: The Dialogical Approach*, ed. Richard E. Hart and Victorino Tejera.

28. "Two Interpretive Fallacies," *Systematics* 9 (1971): 168–72.

Part I

Theory and History

1

Mouthpiece Schmouthpiece

Debra Nails

Who is Jane Austen's mouthpiece in her novels? Is it, as is widely believed, the lively Elizabeth Bennet of *Pride and Prejudice*? Or, as Miss Austen herself implies, the intractable eponymous heroine of *Emma*?[1] And what about the sensible Elinor Dashwood of *Sense and Sensibility,* so very like the author's own sister? If we could answer these questions with certainty, we might gain a richer understanding of the writer's craft, her ingenious mixing of biography and imagination, and—since we know the dates of composition of her works—her talent's development during her productive lifetime. Is this the kind of question we should be asking about the Platonic dialogues? I concede, of course, that the dialogues are great literature even while I deny, as most of us would, that Plato neatly distinguished "biography" from "fiction": those terms refer to modern genres and are imposed on Plato only anachronistically.[2]

Who is Thucydides' mouthpiece in *The Peloponnesian Wars*?[3] It has often been imagined that the speeches of Pericles, describing a city as ideal as it is possible to convey in words, express the views of the historian himself. Yet the death of Pericles shortly after the beginning of the war leaves the author to demonstrate a vision of Athens that goes far beyond the lines that Pericles is given to speak. The question is of historical importance because seeking to distinguish the views of Pericles from those of Thucydides is a legitimate enterprise in the service of greater understanding of the causes and character of the events of that crucial period. Pericles was not *only* a character in Thucydides' *Peloponnesian Wars,* after all. But is this the kind of question

---

1. Austen-Leigh 1870.
2. Cf. Havelock 1983: 157.
3. "Readers of Thucydides love Athens, and so tend to take the funeral oration as expressing Thucydides' own love of Athens" (Introduction to Woodruff's 1993 translation of Thucydides, p. xxi). Woodruff denies that Thucydides has any mouthpiece in his history, although the most likely candidate would have to be the verdict of the five thousand. Thucydides, *On Justice, Power, and Human Nature: The Essence of Thucydides' History of the Peloponnesian War.* Tr. by Paul Woodruff. Indianapolis: Hackett, 1993, (p. xx).

we should be asking about the Platonic dialogues? Paul Woodruff suggests a similarity between Platonic and Thucydidean interpretation when he says that, "Some scholars . . . cannot read Thucydides as a whole because, in their eyes, the book breaks down into sections that were written at different stages, and each of these must be taken on its own. I shall not deal with the developmental hypothesis here, except to say that it must be a last resort" (1993: xxv).[4] Plato's dialogues are and have always been treated as sources for the historical personages, events, and daily life that they describe, a practice that makes their author more of a historical realist than is perhaps appropriate; for "historical realism" is another of those modern concepts that should remind us to be wary of anachronism. Even so, I concede of course that the dialogues provide grist for the mills of the historians.

If a 'mouthpiece' is a spokesman, a character whose philosophical views and methods are those of the author, then who is Plato's mouthpiece in the dialogues? Insofar as the question is legitimate, it is a biographical and historical question that cannot be settled definitively on the existing evidence. Its proposed answers may impinge on the history of philosophy, may interest philosophers, and may influence interpretation by privileging one voice over others. But these considerations are distinguishable from, and secondary to, the philosophical version of the question, Is Socrates Plato's mouthpiece?—to which the answer is No. Who speaks for Plato? The dialogues do, irreducibly. The dialogue form provides a means of encouraging readers and listeners to reason dialectically to defensible positions of their own, rather than to treat Plato's words—or those of his Socrates—as so authoritative as to obviate the necessity for intellectual labor.

The strategy of this chapter is to consider variations of several different "yes" answers to the question whether Socrates is Plato's mouthpiece in an attempt to eliminate the patently false, jury-rigged, and/or philosophically useless. This winnowing process, the reader might profit to know in advance, shares virtually all the assumptions and most of the conclusions of Lloyd Gerson's "Plato *Absconditus*,"—itself a *defense* of the mouthpiece hypothesis appearing near the end of this book. His position cannot be accused of the excesses I have just mentioned, and my *non-mouthpiecer* position is not subject to Gerson's arguments against *antimouthpiecers*. To place my own view in the useful initial framework he provides, we agree about "the uncontentious points that development is not provable and that, logically speaking, there is no direct inference from the words of the character Socrates to the mind of Plato." At the end of the day, having adduced what evidence he can to undermine their plausibility, it remains these considerations that lead Gerson to use the mouthpiece hypothesis only with wise caution, while leading me to refrain altogether from using it, even as an interpretive tool of last resort. For I go on to agree with two views Gerson attributes to his opposition: I am a skeptic about "our ability to read off a development within the dialogues," and I deny that there are "conclusive grounds for inferring from the words of any character in any dialogue

---

4. Interestingly for Plato studies, Woodruff advises reading Thucydides "with care as a whole."

what their author thinks."[5] Where the issue is joined is in our estimation of what it means for Plato to claim authority about such knowledge as he may have believed he had, an issue that I will take up in its place later.

I begin with a naïve mouthpiece view—*yes*, Socrates speaks for Plato—of the sort that students sometimes develop: (i) The Greeks loved myths, and Socrates, if not simply invented by Aristophanes to represent sophists generally, was used by Plato and other authors for whatever views they wished to express. This was repeated with Jesus and the gospel writers, much as anyone nowadays might indifferently frame the argument of John Q. Public or Jane Doe. If Socrates were a pure invention, however, as the nameless Eleatic guest-friend may be, it still would not *follow* that he were Plato's mouthpiece: an invention can be put to a variety of purposes; some other character or characters could still represent Plato; and the character Socrates could still present the interesting views of someone else, or no one in particular, or the best arguments Plato could devise, regardless of his own beliefs about their ultimate soundness.

What we do not have uncontested in Plato, which we do have for Hume's *Dialogues Concerning Natural Religion,* for example, is an explicit statement that such and such a character expresses the author's philosophical positions and exhibits his methods. An explicit statement would be useful, but it is vain to hope that even that would put an end to the dispute: after all, we have an explicit statement to the contrary already in the *Second Letter* (314c), "I myself have never yet written anything on these subjects, and no treatise by Plato exists or will exist, but those that now bear his name belong to a Socrates become fair and young."[6] Thus, we may well suppose that if somewhere Plato were to tell us that his character Socrates is his mouthpiece, we would go on to wonder (as do some Straussians) whether the statement had been crafted to throw the uninitiated off the track, and (analogous to the controversy surrounding the letters generally) whether the statement itself was genuine—especially since such a claim would be incompatible with what the more probably genuine *Seventh Letter* says about there being no treatise expressing Plato's own views (341c-d) on the issues being addressed.

Yet it is also possible to read the *Second Letter* as *declaring* the mouthpiece thesis: I, Plato, never write in my own voice because it would be dangerous to do so. That is Gadamer's ground for saying, "In Socrates' name and *persona,* as 'a young Socrates become beautiful', Plato practices his apolitical education—in both writing and live discussion" (1980: 76). I will come back to that interpretation later. Ultimately, we have no uncontroversial statement from Plato that Socrates is his mouthpiece; we have only this ambiguous statement from a spurious source, claimed by both sides.

---

5. Specifically, for the former position, I argue in Nails 1995, chs. 4–7, and for the latter in ch. 2. Like Gerson, I argue that the *Phaedrus* passages on writing have been widely misinterpreted; although his penetrating critique is textual and mine is historical (Nails: 232–233), both tolerate the same range of interpretive conclusions. While I deliberately avoid discussion of the *Seventh Letter* because the question of its authenticity makes its use in argument precarious (Nails: 10 n. 3), I have no quarrel with Gerson's account.

6. Bury, tr. Loeb Classical Library. London: Heinemann, 1929. The *Second Letter* is generally considered spurious, in part because it repeats and elaborates an important passage from the *Seventh Letter.*

(ii) A less radical "yes" answer is that the *character* Socrates is nothing but *the* mouthpiece of Plato in the dialogues; every utterance by the character Socrates expresses Plato's own doctrines regardless of whether the historical Socrates held those doctrines; every methodological move made by the character Socrates is the very move Plato would have chosen in similar circumstances; and Plato has no *other* mouthpieces. The so-called biographical project, the effort to extract a coherent Socratic doctrine and methodology for the *historical* Socrates from Plato's dialogues, usually supplemented with other sources, is irrelevant to this version of the answer to whether Socrates is Plato's mouthpiece—irrelevant because what is at issue is the *character* Socrates in Plato's dialogues. This answer, though still extreme, is not impossible, but at least two things have made it seem highly implausible.

First, Socrates unarguably says and does *some* things in the dialogues of Plato that he says and does in the extant dialogues and fragments of other writers of the Socratic *logoi* genre: Aischines of Sphettus and Xenophon, for example.[7] So there is at least a minimal sense in which Plato's character is *either* true to the historical Socrates *or* deliberately constructed in response to the Socrates of the popular imagination. Whatever the scope of any of that, Socrates cannot be nothing but the mouthpiece of Plato. Or perhaps he can: suppose I concede that the either-or I have just constructed is a fallacious bifurcation, that some things about Socrates were just so impressive or convincing that Plato and other writers picked those up themselves, easily accounting for the overlap. That is, Plato *agreed* with his mentor Socrates about some things, as did others; this would be no surprise: true statements are true, and productive methods produce, regardless of who states or practices them. And in just those cases, I wonder that we do not say more accurately that Plato is Socrates' mouthpiece, giving voice to certain of the historical Socrates' views and methods for posterity. But if Plato is Socrates' mouthpiece in just and exactly those cases where Socrates is not Plato's mouthpiece, it is hard to see how the mouthpiece metaphor can be very helpful here, for further criteria are then required to determine which case is which, and those further criteria tend to be highly suspect, as we shall see, diverting us from the philosophical questions raised in the dialogues. That is, unless I have gotten it wrong *again:* What if the character Socrates is the mouthpiece of Plato who is the mouthpiece of the historical Socrates? Everybody goes home a winner. We are back to the case in which it is *all* Socrates, and Plato was a dumb recorder—a view I take to be false.

The second thing that has always made this view—that the character Socrates is nothing but *the* mouthpiece of Plato—so unattractive is the great variety of doctrines and methods exhibited throughout the corpus from, let us say, *Phaedrus* to *Phaedo*, or *Laches* to *Laws* (although Socrates does not appear in the *Laws*, Aristotle's lapse on the matter notwithstanding). Who is Plato's mouthpiece when someone else's arguments are stronger, or in passages that

---

7. There were numerous authors of Socratic *logoi*, leading Aristotle later to refer to these dialogues as a genre (*Poetics* 1447b9 ff.). Cf. Field (1948: 146–152); Thesleff (1982: 59–60 n. 22); and Vlastos (1991: 52). Comic poets including at least Aristophanes and Ameipsias used the character Socrates on stage.

purport to be autobiographical of Socrates? Why does Socrates sometimes exhibit the very philosophical behavior he elsewhere criticizes, giving in to longwinded expositions and browbeating his interlocutors? If Socrates sometimes is, and sometimes is not, Plato's mouthpiece, we are back to requiring further criteria, an independent external perspective from which to judge what are, and what are not, the views and methods of Plato (and Socrates).

The issues raised by these questions go a long way toward proving false the all-out yes answer that the character Socrates simply is, and is only, the mouthpiece of Plato. And if an overall clear and certain yes is not achievable, leaving us all struggling to find further criteria for determining exactly when Socrates is Plato's mouthpiece, why not give up the quest and ask ourselves instead whether this or that particular argument is sound, whether this or that particular philosophical position is meaningful or productive? The reason we do not all give it up, I suppose, is that attaining the objective still seems promising to some, so let me not lose sight of the goal: if it were possible to establish that the character Socrates is Plato's mouthpiece in the dialogues, it would follow that there is an identifiable subset of statements and techniques that could be tested against one another for consistency and coherence and effectiveness—not to mention truth. Another subset of statements and techniques would presumably fall outside this domain. Such an objective promises to be related directly to the philosophical success of the dialogues insofar as internal or even intramural consistency is sought. Thus, such problems as we have so far encountered have prompted two further and more defensible yes answers, this time rather popular ones, to which I now turn. The one common among philosophers with a more continental leaning, holds that (iii) Because each dialogue is a coherent literary whole, the mouthpiece question must be asked, if it is to be asked at all, for each dialogue separately. The other, associated with contemporary Vlastosians, and which I shall call 'developmentalist,' contends that (iv) Socrates becomes Plato's mouthpiece as Plato *develops* into an independent philosophical thinker.[8]

The literary approach to Plato often provides stunning and provocative interpretations of individual dialogues. There is something disarming, for example, in Gadamer's insistence that his studies of Plato are 'hermeneutical' essays: we need not accept his assumptions to be delighted when some part of the interpretation occasions philosophical insight, much as a Platonic image might and I am as charmed as anyone else when that happens.[9] But to assume the mouthpiece metaphor—as when Gadamer asserts that Plato practices in Socrates' *persona*—is precisely to cast one's anchor outside the text, to seek an extrinsic mooring, to break the hermeneutic circle, and to destroy its analogy to an axiomatic system. To make matters worse, a literary interpretation may take the mouthpiece metaphor as a premise, and yet shield itself from criticism by pleading a hermeneutic warrant; interpretation in that vein is not what Plato meant

---

8. The developmentalist literature has always been with us, but I am controlling the scope of this glance at the issue by limiting myself to current views.

9. When this happens, one goes on to question and elaborate the insight, to find its usable boundaries—a procedure only somewhat different from one's approach to an argument in a text.

by 'philosophy' if how he described it and how he conducted it are to serve as examples.[10] Nothing philosophical is less hermeneutically sealed than a Platonic dialogue, both the initial assumptions and conclusions of which are perpetually open to scrutiny and assault. What I call the double open-endedness of Plato's dialogues is what is most admirable about Plato's conduct of philosophy: by adamantly refusing to treat philosophical discussion as closed, he avoids casting himself as the authority on any philosophical issue, leaving authority to arise from sound arguments. I have already said the dialogues are great literature, but I have no examples to offer of cases where philosophical progress depends on a particular literary interpretation of a passage. Call me recalcitrant, but the truth is no truer when uttered by Socrates.[11] Thus I find the literary interpretive approach, when harboring the mouthpiece metaphor, philosophically useless.

The very position that I have just stated in opposition to Gadamer's assuming the mouthpiece metaphor is what I must now emphasize in light of Gerson's contribution to this volume. One of his most rhetorically effective moves is to describe the antimouthpiecer as making Plato into either a sophist deliberately misleading his readers or a skeptic indifferent about the conclusions they reach. In contrast, Gerson supplies a Plato who wrote dialogues "to reveal his own mind." That could account for why Plato wrote, but not for why he wrote *dialogues* or established the Academy. No doubt there are philosophers who write to reveal their own minds, but others write to draw fire, thereby continuing the dialectical process. No doubt there are philosophy teachers who advocate their own beliefs, and others who devise arguments for and against a variety of incompatible positions to draw their students to philosophy; some may even refuse to own up to their own views when asked, but that does not mean they have no views. Citing Frede's (1996) view that Plato wrote in dialogue form to avoid authoritarian pronouncements on philosophical matters, Gerson comments, "But making claims and arguments is not equivalent to claiming authority." Yes it is, and almost unavoidably, when one is the head of the Academy, if *particular* claims and arguments can be identified as those of the master.

What links the literary approach to the developmentalist one is the shared belief that sometimes when Socrates is speaking, Plato is dropping a very big hint that this is what his listeners and readers should believe and how they should act—*because* Socrates is Plato's mouthpiece. The difference is that, whereas the literary approach allows the mouthpiece metaphor to be assumed, analytic developmentalists usually defend the view with arguments; and whereas the former typically proceeds one dialogue at a time, Vlastos's work has made many philosophers comfortable with spreading the assumption across the corpus.[12]

---

10. I have in mind especially the descriptions of philosophy and the philosophical life in the *Republic*, the *Apology*, and the *Theaetetus*, and Plato's practice of writing dialogues rather than treatises—all of which are so controversial that consensus about their "points" has never been reached. And I take the literary critical parts of the *Protagoras* as an excellent counterexample to the conduct of philosophy.

11. Cf. *Symposium* 201c–d; *Gorgias* 473b.

12. My two immediate problems with that, as I have implied already, are the dialogues' inconsistencies and the implication that Plato sets himself up as the jack-in-office of the dialectic—but let me not get ahead of myself.

Developmentalists, concerned to isolate the Socratic from the Platonic elements in the dialogues, have seriously considered both the general types of criticism mentioned above of the *universal* claim that Socrates is Plato's mouthpiece and have ingeniously sought the appropriate criteria for narrowing the claim. Is Socrates Plato's mouthpiece? Sometimes yes, sometimes no. *Exactly when* is Socrates Plato's mouthpiece? Well, one begins with the fertile assumption that variety and contrariety in the dialogues are explained by an evolution in Plato's own thinking, then one proceeds by weighing the various kinds of evidence that can be consulted; and if all or most of it points in the same direction, one ought not to resist the conclusion—which was one's assumption—that Plato's views evolved. The evidence consulted in this process is, first, stylometry for confirmation of the order of composition of the dialogues along which Platonic development is mapped; second, the texts of contemporaries such as Xenophon and Aristophanes, and those of later writers such as Aristotle;[13] and third, evidence internal to the dialogues: not only the perceived philosophical sophistication of various arguments and positions, but even the perceived evolution of Socratic irony. This is the famous bootstrapping maneuver that looks so suspiciously like jury-rigging to an outsider. I am an outsider, and although I have argued at some length elsewhere against the use of each of these three props, I shall assume here that there is nothing wrong in principle with these three lines of investigation, concentrating on the *result* of using them, a result that looks makeshift to me.[14]

Developmentalists have settled on an account that goes like this: "As Plato changes, the philosophical persona of his Socrates is made to change, absorbing the writer's new convictions, arguing for them with the same zest with which the Socrates of the previous dialogues had argued for the views the writer had shared with the original of that figure earlier on."[15] The words are those of Vlastos (1991: 53), but the picture is familiar, in fact pervasive, and the mouthpiece interpretive strategy is easily identified as its natural child.[16] Whereas Vlastos represents it as a hypothesis and seeks to strengthen it, for others it has become dogma. Kraut, for example, is rather like a soldier planting his flag on the hill, asserting that one *must begin* with the assumption that Socrates is Plato's mouthpiece, for all other assumptions with which one might begin are "hazardous."[17]

---

13. McPherran continues to recommend Aristotle in this context, as if that testimony were unambiguous, but I fall back on my original assessment (Nails 1995: 21–22). Kahn (1996: 79–87) repeats his earlier negative assessment of Aristotle as an historian of philosophy.

14. Nails 1995, chs. 2, 4–7.

15. McPherran worries that those, including me, who are skeptical of the mouthpiece methodological thesis are too quick to use the term 'doctrine', and he offers 'commitment' as a substitute. I admit I have accused the developmentalists of turning Plato into a doctrinaire thinker, but I have no special attachment to the term. Vlastos sometimes uses it of the historical Socrates (1991, thesis IV), but the point is the same when he uses the word 'views'–as he does here–since he refers explicitly in the same passage to "the truth of Socrates' teaching."

16. Cf. derivative accounts in Penner 1992: 130–131, and Kraut, ed., 1992: 26–27.

17. He belittles Tigerstedt (1977) for his "assumption that because of internal conflicts in every dialogue we cannot take Socrates to be a mouthpiece for Plato's views" (Kraut, ed., 1992: 29, 49 n. 73); and he also belittles the Tübingen school for assuming an exaggerated importance for lost oral doctrines (1992: 24). Why Kraut cannot see that his own developmentalism is a hazardous and exaggerated assumption escapes me.

Even Gerson, whose developmentalism is minimal, fears that antidevelop-mentalism will prevent the search for *philosophical* reasons for contrariety among dialogues, will cut off dialogue between author and reader—a perplex-ing view, given that developmentalism is a purely biographico-historical hy-pothesis. Recourse to developmentalism is *non*philosophical, inviting the reader not to consider which of two arguments is stronger, but merely which came later, or which was held by whom. Gerson's willingness to resort to de-velopmentalism is linked to a goal he approves, "trying to know the mind of the philosopher who wrote the dialogues." Such a goal, however, is neither philo-sophical nor realizable; and the substitution of that goal for genuinely philo-sophical ones—trying to know how one ought to live, or what is real, or the na-ture of knowledge—is to idealize a *person,* the all too common result of which is to enshrine as his *doctrine* what is rather a vital corpus with contemporary power to aid our making philosophical progress on a number of fronts. It is to defer to the imagined mind of Plato, in short, to treat his words as authoritative.

Vlastos, whose developmentalism is grand, suggests a simple interpretive rule that I shall use to test his version of the mouthpiece theory: "If we believe that in any given dialogue Plato puts into the persona of Socrates only what at the time he himself considers true, we must suppose that when that persona discards the elenchus as the right method to search for the truth this occurs be-cause Plato has now lost faith in that method himself" (1988: 373).[18] The rule, then, is that Plato assigns to Socrates only such views and methods as Plato sin-cerely believes at the time of writing. And its implication in brief: Socrates is Plato's mouthpiece in the dialogues. Combining the implication with the quo-tation at the beginning of this paragraph, it is necessary to add that although Socrates was Plato's mouthpiece all along (the character always spoke for the author), the very *essence* of the mouthpiece function was altered after the 'early' period. The pressing question whether Socrates was Plato's mouthpiece only arises to accommodate the popular interpretive strategy of dividing up the dissimilar views and methods encountered in the dialogues between the two philosophers, a strategy that demands Plato's views evolve beyond those of Socrates. Whatever one may think of the claim that Socrates is Plato's mouth-piece all along, while the two are said have the same views, there is no mouth-piece *problem.* Thus I shall limit the remainder of the developmentalist dis-cussion to the problematic assertion that Socrates is Plato's mouthpiece in the dialogues after the 'early' period.

There immediately arises the problem that there is no consensus among an-alytic philosophers about which dialogues to include in any period except the 'late' one, a problem that has only become more acute since Vlastos extracted a set of so-called transitional dialogues between what had been the 'early' and the 'middle' ones. Naturally, there is vast and fascinating literature on the sub-ject, the details of which are inappropriate to this context.[19] I would like to as-sume for the sake of argument the most charitable possible interpretation of

---

18. Cf. Vlastos 1991: 117, and n. 50.
19. Cf. Nails 1995, ch. 6, for references to the literature.

the analytic position, but that puts me in a bind: if I only discuss the three 'middle' dialogues about which there is unanimity, it will seem that I am attempting to minimize the influence of the mouthpiece hypothesis; but if I throw in all the dialogues for which any of my six contemporary analytic sources argue, it will appear that I am generating controversy by playing on internecine squabbles.[20] I have settled on eight dialogues for which the mouthpiece hypothesis ought to hold; that is, one should be able to say with confidence that Socrates speaks for the mature Plato in (alphabetically) the *Cratylus, Parmenides, Phaedo, Phaedrus, Philebus, Republic, Symposium,* and *Theaetetus.*

But we cannot. All these dialogues include passages that are exceptions to the hypothesis that Socrates is Plato's mouthpiece, if the Vlastosian rule is observed. The first exception, *unless someone else is Plato's mouthpiece,* costs us two dialogues: the characters Parmenides and Diotima are Plato's mouthpieces at *Parmenides* 126a–136e and *Symposium* 203b–212b, respectively (Vlastos 1991: 73–74, 117, n. 50). It is legitimate to point out that, after Vlastos, some of his followers, Kraut (1992: 29) for example, amended the earlier position so that the 'principal interlocutor' of a dialogue, rather than only Socrates, was to be considered Plato's mouthpiece. And one might then point out that in 1991 when Vlastos named Parmenides and Diotima as Plato's mouthpieces, he was already implicitly conceding that his earlier position had been rather too strong. One might quibble about Diotima's role as principal . . . but never mind. Since I adduce independent arguments addressing the *Parmenides* and *Symposium,* I would not bicker if the first exception were ignored. Those who wish it to dis-

---

20. Those who have committed themselves on the issue are unanimous about the *Phaedo,* the *Symposium,* and the *Phaedrus.* Everyone (Guthrie 1975: 50; Irwin 1977: 291–293; Vlastos 1991: 46–47; Kahn 1981–1988; Kraut, ed., 1992: xii, 46 n. 57; and Fine 1992: 215 n. 1) agrees that at least most of the *Republic* is also 'middle', though there is disagreement whether Bk. I is 'early'. The *Phaedrus* and the *Republic* are stylometric nightmares, however: the "Lysias speech" of the former looks unplatonic by stylometric tests; and the *Republic* has passages typical of early, middle, and late writing that disappear into the averaging process. Four dialogues isn't much, but even if I include majority agreement among the six analytic sources who have taken a stand, only the *Cratylus* is added; so there are five dialogues from the 'middle' period to consider, to which we are allowed to add from the 'late' period the *Philebus* because of the *elenchus* conducted there. We also add the *Theaetetus* and the *Parmenides* (since they're unanimously considered *either* 'middle' or 'late') for a grand total of eight. The *Parmenides* is another bugbear for stylometricians, and has recently become more controversial than ever. Tradition has it that the *Parmenides* is 'late-middle', just before the obvious and undeniable onset of the consistent (and turgid) style evident in the *Sophist* and *Timaeus* groups, and in the *Laws.* The *Parmenides* must be so late, the argument goes, because Plato there criticizes a version of the theory of forms that he had elsewhere (meaning 'earlier') defended. Harold Tarrant, using raw data provided by Ledger (1989), but now refined in several useful ways suggested by Ledger's reviewers, separated the initial conversation of the dialogue from the longer portion in which Parmenides questions Aristoteles, and subjected the two portions independently to a full battery of stylometric tests. The initial conversation fits perfectly with other so-called early dialogues; and the longer portion proves what might well be called unplatonic—that is, its style is significantly unlike other examples of Plato's writing. The fact that most stylometry has measured whole texts has caused a thoroughly misleading averaging of stylometric features: the *Republic,* for instance, with sections that perfectly illustrate 'early' style, and others 'late', is thus labeled 'middle'. A similar averaging has long had an impact on the relative position of the *Parmenides.* Tarrant's printouts and early results were discussed at the 1995 International Plato Society meeting in Granada, Spain.

appear altogether may substitute 'his principal interlocutor' for 'Socrates' as they please. I leave it because it is instructive: when one's desire is to illustrate a house of cards, the amendment becomes one more datum in the history of contemporary developmentalism's use of ad hoc bolsters.

The second exception, *unless the mouthpiece disavows knowledge,* is based on the claim that whereas Socrates disavows knowledge *"at the very moment at which he has produced evidence which appears to belie it"* (1991: 85, Vlastos's emphasis), Plato is confident of his demonstrative knowledge (1991: 48). Taken seriously, this claim would require amputating *Cratylus* 384c and 391a, *Phaedo* 91b, *Phaedrus* 235c, *Theaetetus* 210c, and the single paragraph of Book I of the *Republic* (354c1–2) that Vlastos insists is *not* early (1985: 26, n. 65). In all these cases, what should be a Socrates-speaking-for-the-mature-Plato is someone who disavows knowledge in precisely the early-Socratic fashion. I happen to share Vlastos's view that *Republic* 354a11–c is in fact a later addition to Book I, but my points of agreement with the details of a great scholarly opus are irrelevant here: the fact is that the exception called for in *this* case is incompatible with the required fourth exception to follow.

Sometimes, in the midst of a dialogue in which Socrates is Plato's mouthpiece, the historical Socrates is said to emerge for a bit, as in Alcibiades' speech in the *Symposium* (215a–222c); this practice provides the third exception, unless *Plato is engaging in genuine biography.* It is particularly troubling in the *Phaedo* where there are three such biographical passages (57a–61c, 96e–99e, and 115c–118), only the first and third of which are regarded by Vlastos as proper exceptions to the mouthpiece view; the middle passage is deemed mouthpiece again (1991: 47, n. 11). That is where Socrates says that, as a youth, he was interested in the investigation of nature (contrary to what is implied by the *Apology,* which developmentalists regard confidently as 'early'); it is rejected as Socratic because it can be interpreted as serving as an introduction for the theory of forms that is off limits to nonmouthpiece characters. The *Theaetetus* suffers on the biographical see-saw too: several accepted details about Socrates himself are gleaned there (143e, 149a, and 209c), but other details are disallowed; for example, that Socrates sends philosophically inept students to Prodicus (151b), presumably because that fact would interfere with another Vlastosian rule, namely that Socrates was a philosophical populist (1991: 48) who would not dissuade any potential student. But I am guessing what the presumption might be in the absence of independent interpretive criteria from Vlastos. One of the most taxing aspects of the mouthpiece interpretive strategy is that anyone who might choose to employ it is left at a loss to determine when to use which of its subsidiary techniques.[21]

The fourth and final exception that brings into question passages from all the candidate mouthpiece dialogues except the *Phaedrus* requires more argument than I can make here.[22] In brief, Vlastos limits Socratic elenchus to the "search for moral truth" (1991: 49); and he attributes to Plato a rejection of the elenchus

---

21. Cf. Nails 1995: 84.
22. For a fuller account, cf. Nails 1995: 87–95.

in favor of the didactic and maieutic methods. But there is elenchus in the *Philebus* (11a–22b) and *Republic* (Bk. I except 354a11–c), the subject matter of which is moral-political. And arguments with the elenctic *form* conducted by Socrates on *other* subjects seem to occupy deep mouthpiece limbo: *Cratylus* 384c–391a, *Parmenides* 130e–134e, *Phaedo* 92a–e, and *Symposium* 199c–201d. The *Theaetetus* is a special case because of the many scholars who have argued, *pace* Vlastos, that the dialogue is clearly if not paradigmatically elenctic.

These four exceptions are rationalized in the literature, shored up by subsidiary and ad hoc arguments, and exceptions to the exceptions. But I have no use for a hypothesis so shot full of holes. Its holiness only further confirms my belief that such legitimacy as the question, Is Socrates Plato's mouthpiece? has, is not a philosophical legitimacy. The mouthpiece strategy is perfectly designed to resurrect and pay homage to a Socrates who is lost, a goal inappropriate to philosophy.[23] But even as biography, the thesis is not compelling, paling by comparison to a methodological unity thesis that preserves the coherent variety of doctrines and methods in the dialogues with the argument that Plato deploys views and methods, as he deploys images and myths, to create occasions for philosophizing.[24] One need not, and I do not, argue that Plato simply *had* no doctrines; and it would be absurd to argue that the dialogues have no philosophical content, that *only* the Platonic method is important. Nevertheless, I maintain that the *primary* function of the dialogues was to stir academic dialectic by illustrating exemplary philosophical discussions and by setting out complex philosophical positions for critique.[25]

---

23. For the religious connections, cf. Vlastos 1958.

24. McPherran counsels that "even a dyed-in-the-wool mouthpiecer like Kraut, ed., (1992: 27) can be found endorsing" the dialogues as "occasions for philosophizing," as if my characterization were not incompatible with the mouthpiece approach; but this is not true, as a turn of the page makes clear: Kraut, ed., (1992: 27–28) conflates the view with Straussianism and then dismisses the whole. Frede (1992) makes the finest case I have seen for the position Kraut discounts.

25. I am grateful to Mark McPherran, who disagrees with me fundamentally and vigorously, and whose SAGP comments prompted significant improvements. For more sympathetic and nonetheless useful criticism, I am grateful to William Levitan, to Gerald Press, and to the publisher's anonymous referee who suggested I meet head-on Lloyd Gerson's arguments.

WORKS CITED

Austen-Leigh, J. E. "A Memoir of Jane Austen," variously reprinted. 1870.

Field, G. C. *Plato and His Contemporaries: A Study in Fourth-century Life and Thought.* 2nd ed. London: Methuen, 1948.

Fine, Gail. "Inquiry in the Meno." In Kraut, *The Cambridge Companion to Plato* (1992: 200–226).

Frede, Michael. "Plato's Arguments and the Dialogue Form." In *Methods of Interpreting Plato and His Dialogues,* ed. James C. Klagge and Nicholas D. Smith. 201–219. *Oxford Studies in Ancient Philosophy,* supplementary vol. Oxford: Clarendon Press, 1992.

———. "The Literary Form of the *Sophist.*" In *Form and Argument in Late Plato,* ed. Christopher Gill and Mary Margaret McCabe, 135–151. Oxford: Clarendon Press, 1996.

Gadamer, Hans-Georg. *Dialogue and Dialectic: Eight Hermeneutical Studies on Plato,* tr. P. Christopher Smith. New Haven: Yale University Press, 1980.

Guthrie, W. K. C. *Plato the Man and His Dialogues: Earlier Period. A History of Greek Philosophy* IV. Cambridge: Cambridge University Press, 1975.

Havelock, Eric Alfred. "The Socratic Problem: Some Second Thoughts." In *Essays in Ancient Greek Philosophy,* vol. 2, ed. John P. Anton and Anthony Preus, 147–173. Albany: State University of New York Press, 1983.

Irwin, Terence H. *Plato's Moral Theory; The Early and Middle Dialogues.* Oxford: Clarendon Press, 1977.

Kahn, Charles H. "Did Plato Write Socratic Dialogues?" *Classical Quarterly* 31:2 (1981): 305–320.

———. "Plato's Methodology in the *Laches.*" *Revue Internationale de Philosophie* 40 (1986): 7–21.

———. "On the Relative Date of the *Gorgias* and the *Protagoras.*" *Oxford Studies in Ancient Philosophy* 6 (1988): 69–102.

———. *Plato and the Socratic Dialogue: The Philosophical Use of Literary Form.* Cambridge: Cambridge University Press, 1996.

Kraut, Richard, ed. *The Cambridge Companion to Plato.* Cambridge: Cambridge University Press, 1992.

Ledger, Gerard R. *Re-Counting Plato: A Computer Analysis of Plato's Style.* Oxford: Oxford University Press, 1989.

Nails, Debra. *Agora, Academy, and the Conduct of Philosophy.* Philosophical Studies Series 63. Dordrecht and Boston: Kluwer, 1995.

Penner, Terry. "Socrates and the Early Dialogues." In Kraut, *The Cambridge Companion to Plato* (1992: 121–169).

Thesleff, Holger. *Studies in Platonic Chronology.* Commentationes Humanarum Litterarum 70. Helsinki: Societas Scientiarum Fennica, 1982.

Thucydides. *On Justice, Power, and Human Nature; The Essence of Thucydides' History of the Peloponnesian War,* ed. and tr. from the Greek by Paul Woodruff. Indianapolis: Hackett, 1993.

Tigerstedt, Eugène Napoleon. *Interpreting Plato.* Uppsala: Almquist and Wiksell, 1977.

Vlastos, Gregory. "The Paradox of Socrates." *Queen's Quarterly* (Winter 1958). Revised as "Introduction: The Paradox of Socrates," pp. 1–21 in G. Vlastos, ed., *The Philosophy of Socrates.* Notre Dame: University of Notre Dame Press, 1971.

———. "Socrates's Disavowal of Knowledge." *Philosophical Quarterly* 35, no. 138 (1985): 1–31.

———. "Elenchus and Mathematics: A Turning-Point in Plato's Philosophical Development." *American Journal of Philology* 109 (1988): 362–396.

———. *Socrates: Ironist and Moral Philosopher.* Cambridge: Cambridge University Press, 1991.

2

The Logic of Attributing Characters' Views to Plato

Gerald A. Press

It is a fact about a very great deal of Plato scholarship that interpreters take one or another character to be the mouthpiece for Plato's own doctrines and arguments; that is, their words, arguments, conclusions, and beliefs are attributed to Plato as his own. In what are often called the "early" and "middle" dialogues (and also the "late" *Philebus*), Socrates is taken to be Plato's representative.[1] In the *Sophist* and *Politicus* it is taken to be the Eleatic Stranger; in the *Parmenides* Parmenides, in the *Timaeus* Timaeus, in the *Critias* Critias, and in the *Laws*, the Athenian. This widespread interpretive practice implies a logically prior belief. Sometimes the belief is asserted, as by Julia Annas writing "After all, Plato does put forward his views in the mouth of Socrates,"[2] or Michael Frede writing, "Sometimes we are confident that an argument . . . is Plato's argument—an argument Plato himself endorses."[3] More often it is assumed, as Nicholas White says, speaking of the conversation between Socrates and Euthyphro, "Plato does not infer simply that Euthyphro's capacities to judge such

---

1. The widespread belief in a division between early (or "Socratic"), middle (or "critical"), and late (or "constructive") dialogues is based on a Platonic chronology the foundations of which have been seriously undermined by recent scholarship. Holger Thesleff, *Studies in Platonic Chronology* (Helsinki: Societas Scientiarum Fennica, 1982) is fundamental and his "Platonic Chronology," *Phron* 34 (1989): 1–26, is not to be read apart from it, as, e.g., does Jacob Howland, "Re-reading Plato: The Problem of Platonic Chronology," *Phoenix* 45 (1991): 189–214. See also, Debra Nails, "Platonic Chronology Reconsidered," *Bryn Mawr Classical Review* 3 (1992): 314–27, "Problems with Vlastos' Platonic Developmentalism," *Ancient Philosophy* 13 (1993): 273–91, and *Agora, Academy, and the Conduct of Philosophy* (Dordrecht: Kluwer, 1995): 53–138; and Charles M. Young, "Plato and Computer Dating," *Oxford Studies in Ancient Philology* 12 (1994): 227–50.
2. Julia Annas, *An Introduction to Plato's Republic* (Oxford: Clarendon Press, 1981), 9.
3. Michael Frede, "Plato's Arguments and the Dialogue Form," in *Methods of Interpreting Plato and His Dialogues*, ed. James Klagge and Nicholas Smith, *Oxford Studies in Ancient Philology*, Suppl. Vol. 1992, 203.

matters are infallible."[4] In neither case, however, is it simply a fact about the dialogues which one is entitled, therefore, to use as a premise. One important difference between the statements (1) "Socrates says that justice is minding your own business" and (2) "Plato says that justice is minding your own business" is that (1) is true and (2) is false. The question is, Can (2) be soundly inferred from (1)?

An enormous number of books and articles profess to tell us Plato's theories and doctrines.[5] The plain fact, however, is that Plato wrote no treatises under his own name in which he expounded his theory of knowledge or metaphysics, his ethical or political doctrines.[6] Therefore, any scholar who claims to tell us Plato's theory or doctrine in any of these areas can only be deriving evidence from the dialogues, with perhaps some supplement from the *Letters*. Yet, in the dialogues there is no character called Plato who speaks; even if there were, it would only open up another variation of the same question. The question is, What justifies an interpreter in quoting or referring to the words of a named character in a Platonic dialogue and attributing the words or their meaning to Plato as his own opinion, belief, doctrine, or argument?

I am concerned here with the *logic* of this interpretive approach that has dominated Plato scholarship for much of its history as well as much of the work in our own century. Because it is so often assumed—so rarely made explicit or defended—the crucial first step is to see that there is, necessarily, an argument involved in this common interpretive practice, or at least a premise in the broader interpretive structure. Even though it is rarely made explicit, this is not a minor, but an essential step in the argument of such interpreta-

---

4. The prevalence of the presumption that one can switch from words of the character Socrates to arguments, conclusions, or beliefs of Plato is exemplified by most of the contributions to *The Cambridge Companion to Plato*, ed. Richard Kraut (Cambridge: Cambridge University Press, 1992). E.g., Fine, p. 215; Morgan, p. 237; White, p. 278 and *passim*; Richard Kraut, p. 312 and *passim*; Asmis, p. 338; M. Frede, p. 398 and *passim*; D. Frede, p. 436; Saunders, p. 464 and *passim*.

5. E.g., Paul Natorp, *Platons Ideenlehre* (Leipzig: Meiner, 1903); J. A. Stewart, *Plato's Doctrine of Ideas* (Oxford: Clarendon, 1909); W. D. Ross, *Plato's Theory of Ideas* (Oxford: Clarendon, 1951); W. J. Verdenius, *MIMESIS: Plato's Doctrine of Imitation* (Leiden: Brill, 1972); F. M. Cornford, *Plato's Theory of Knowledge* (London: Macmillan, 1957); Norman Gulley, *Plato's Theory of Knowledge* (London: Methuen, 1962); I. M. Crombie, *An Examination of Plato's Doctrines*, 2 vols. (London, 1962 and 1963);Terence Irwin, *Plato's Moral Theory* (Oxford: Clarendon, 1977); Jon Moline, *Plato's Theory of Understanding* (Madison: University of Wisconsin Press, 1981). That it is not just an older fashion in scholarship to speak of Plato's theories and doctrines can be inferred from the following: Daniel T. Deveraux, "Separation and Immanence in Plato's Theory of Forms," *Oxford Studies in Ancient Philology* 12 (1994): 63–90; Jonathan Lear, "Plato's Politics of Narcissism," pp. 137–59. ed. Terry Irwin and M. C. Nussbaum, *Virtue, Love and Form: Essays in Memory of Gregory Vlastos* (Edmonton: Academic Publishing, 1994); Graciela E. Marcos de Pinotti, *Platón ante el problema del error. La formulación del Teeteto y la solución del Sofista* (Buenos Aires: FUNDEC, 1995); Uwe Meixner, "Eine logische Rekonstrucktion der platonischen Prädikationstheorie," *Grazer Philosophische Studien* 43 (1992), 163–75; José Montserrat, *Platón, de la perplejidad al sistema* (Ariel: Barcelona, 1995); Paul Pritchard, *Plato's Philosophy of Mathematics* (Sankt Augustin: Academia Verlag, 1995).

6. "Plato is the one voluminous writer of classical antiquity whose works seem to have come down to us whole and entire. Nowhere in later antiquity do we come on any reference to a Platonic work which we do not still possess," as A. E. Taylor wrote in *Plato: The Man and His Works* (New York: Meridian, 1956), 10.

tions. If it cannot be made plausible that Plato means what Socrates or other characters say to be understood as his own beliefs and doctrines, then a good deal of scholarship is unsound because it is based on a kind of category mistake or *ignoratio elenchi*.

Again, much English-language scholarship in the twentieth century has been concerned to assess Plato's arguments and beliefs about problems of contemporary interest.[7] But before one can assess Plato's arguments, one must get them from somewhere. In practice they are taken variously from the words of the characters Socrates, Timaeus, the Eleatic Stranger, Parmenides, and so on. Like Frede, we may be "confident that an argument we are dealing with is Plato's argument," but confidence is not proof, or even evidence, that that of which one is confident is true. It is a logically essential preliminary step that I shall claim is unjustified.[8]

There are a number of prima facie reasons against the view that a particular character in any dialogue should be taken as Plato's mouthpiece. First, a point about general methodology: as has often been pointed out in recent years, a dialogue is not a treatise and the interpretive strategies appropriate to the latter are not necessarily appropriate to the former.[9] The author of a treatise ordinarily communicates to the reader directly, explicitly, and in a way that has been called monologically; that is, a single voice, as it were, speaks to the reader uninterruptedly. Even when the author considers objections to the position being defended, those objections are stated *by* the author and *within* the author's own intellectual framework. Communication by the author of genuine dialogue, however, is indirect in the sense that what the author means has to be looked for and found; it is not right there on the surface. It is implicit, suggested, rather than stated clearly and openly. And it is dialogical in the sense that the reader hears, as it were, a multiplicity of voices, each character speaking from his own intellectual framework. Thus, absent clear statements to this effect on the part of the author—deciding that some one character's words are those of the author—requires an examination of evidence and the formation of arguments. It

---

7. Thus Mary Margaret Mackenzie writes of her *Plato on Punishment* (Berkeley: University of California Press, 1981), "This book is an essay in the philosophy of punishment" (1) and the volume, *Feminist Interpretations of Plato*, ed. Nancy Tuana (University Park: Penn State Press, 1994) brings together differing views of whether Plato was a feminist.

8. The same arguments that I present here against taking various characters' words as Plato's apply to taking them as the words, beliefs, or arguments of some historical or constructive Socrates who is taken to be a person outside the world of the dialogues and independent of Plato's authorial control. In the first case the interpreter mistakes Plato's dialogues for treatises; in the second for history.

9. E.g., J. J. Mulhern, "Treatises, Dialogues, and Interpretation," *Monist* 53 (1969): 631–41; Albert W. Levi, "Philosophy as Literature: The Dialogue, *Philosophy & Rhetoric* 9 (1976): 1–20; Victorino Tejera, *Plato's Dialogues One by One* (New York: Irvington, 1984): 3–7; Charles L. Griswold, *Platonic Writings/Platonic Readings* (New York: Routledge, 1989); James A. Arieti, *Interpreting Plato: The Dialogues as Drama* (Lanham, MD: Rowman & Littlefield, 1991): 1–17; Daniel Anderson, *The Masks of Dionysos* (Albany: State University of New York Press, 1993): 1–6; Kenneth M. Sayre, *Plato's Literary Garden: How to Read a Platonic Dialogue* (Notre Dame: Notre Dame University Press, 1995): 1–32; R. B. Rutherford, *The Art of Plato* (Cambridge: Harvard University Press, 1995): 1–29; and Albert Cook, *The Stance of Plato* (Lanham, MD: Rowman & Littlefield, 1996): 1–29.

may be the case that Socrates or another character is Plato's mouthpiece; but it may not be simply assumed.

A second assumption involved in attributing characters' views to Plato is that Plato's philosophic doctrines must be embedded in the dialogues somewhere; otherwise there is no need of a mouthpiece to begin with. But to *assume* that Plato has philosophic beliefs that are so embedded is unjustified. Absent proof to the contrary, Plato may have had no philosophic beliefs or doctrines; that is, he may have thought that philosophic knowledge is unattainable.[10] Or he may have thought that the kind of knowledge that is possible or philosophically significant is not doctrinal, but knowledge of a different kind.[11] Alternatively, Plato may have philosophic doctrines that he deliberately did *not* write down in his dialogues or anywhere else.[12] I do not assert that Plato had no philosophic beliefs, nor that he thought philosophic knowledge unattainable, nor that he thought philosophic knowledge non-doctrinal. My point is, rather, that unless it is *shown* that he had philosophic doctrines that he intended to communicate by means of the dialogues, it is merely an assumption on the interpreter's part. And it is the logic of this assumption that I want to bring to the reader's attention.

---

10. This was the interpretation of the ancient "New Academy" of Carneades and Arcesilaus (third to first centuries C.E.); see A. A. Long and David Sedley, *The Hellenistic Philosophers* (Cambridge: Cambridge University Press, 1987), vol. 1, 445–49. That it was not the view of Philo of Larissa and Charmadas is argued by Harold Tarrant, *Scepticism or Platonism? The Philosophy of the Fourth Academy* (Cambridge: Cambridge University Press, 1985). The position was revived by Bruni, Vives, Melanchthon, Nizolio, and Montaigne; see E. N. Tigerstedt, *The Decline and Fall of the Neoplatonic Interpretation of Plato* (Helsinki: Societas Scientiarum Fennica, 1974), 32–36. In the twentieth century, skeptical interpretations have been propounded by thinkers as diverse as Luigi Stefanini, *Platone*, 2 volumes (Padova: CEDAM, 1932–1935); 2nd ed., (Padova: CEDAM, 1949); Richard Kraut, *Socrates and the State* (Princeton: Princeton University Press, 1984); Peter Stemmer, *Platons Dialektik* (Berlin: de Gruyter, 1992); and Rafael Ferber, *Die Unwissenheit des Philosophen, oder Warum hat Platons die "ungeschriebene Lehre" nicht geschrieben* (Sankt Augustin: Akademia, 1991).

11. Various types of non-doctrinal knowledge have been proposed. R. S. Bluck, "Knowledge by Acquaintance in Plato's *Theaetetus*," *Mind* 72 (1963): 259–63; A. C. Lloyd, "Non-Discursive Thought—An Enigma of Greek Philosophy," *Aristotelian Society Proceedings* 70 (1969–70): 261–74; Richard Sorabji, "Myths about Non-propositional Thought," in *Language and Logos*, ed. M. Schofield and M. C. Nussbaum (Cambridge: Cambridge University Press, 1982), 295–314; Gerald A. Press, "Knowledge as Vision in Plato's Dialogues," *Journal of Neoplatonic Studies* 3 (1995): 61–89; and Francisco Gonzalez, *Dialectic and Dialogue: Plato's Practice of Philosophical Inquiry* (Evanston: Northwestern University Press, forthcoming).

12. The core idea of the "Tübingen school" is that Plato's true philosophy consists in the "unwritten doctrines." See, Konrad Gaiser, *Platons ungeschriebene Lehre. Studien zur systematischen und geschichtlichen Begründung der Wissenschaften in der platonischen Schule* (Stuttgart: Klett, 1959), and *Protreptik und Paränese bei Platon. Untersuchungen zur Form des platonischen Dialogs* (Stuttgart: Tübingener Beiträge zur Altertumswissenschaft, 1959); H. J. Krämer, *Arete bei Platon und Aristoteles. Zum Wesen und zur Geschichte der platonischen Ontologie* (Heidelberg: Abhandlungen der Heidelberger Akademie der Wissenschaften, 1959). Some recent interpreters in the U.S. are finding the unwritten teachings in the written dialogues. See Kenneth M. Sayre, *Plato's Late Ontology: A Riddle Resolved* (Princeton: Princeton University Press, 1983), and Mitchell Miller, "The Choice between the Dialogues and the 'Unwritten Teachings': A Scylla and Charybdis for the Interpreter?," *The Third Way: A New Direction in Platonic Studies*, ed. Francisco Gonzalez (Lanham, MD: Rowman & Littlefield, 1995), 225–44

Third, even if we were to grant for the sake of argument that Socrates *does* speak for Plato, we would still be confronted by the fact that nearly all the dialogues end aporetically; that is, without any doctrine having been explicitly stated. By my reckoning only seven dialogues—*Republic, Symposium, Phaedrus, Timaeus, Sophist, Politicus,* and *Philebus*—could be said to offer clear answers to their central questions. Of those, two—*Symposium* and *Phaedrus*— are not concerned with what would be considered core philosophic topics by most philosophers today, although they were long among the most important philosophic topics. In four of the seven, the arguably clear answer is given by someone other than Socrates *(Symposium, Timaeus, Sophist, Politicus)*. The *Phaedo* is problematic in this respect. The question that seems to be unequivocally answered is whether the soul is immortal. As for the more philosophically interesting question about the nature of the soul—it seems to be unitary here, in contrast with the tripartite view articulated in *Republic* and *Phaedrus*—and thus to raise problems discussed later about apparent doctrinal differences. The problem can not be solved by any simple developmental explanation according to which the "later" *Republic* asserts a different doctrine from the "earlier" *Phaedo;* for the "earlier" simple soul recurs in a later book (10) of the *Republic*. Under such circumstances we will need yet another interpretive operation by which to extract the doctrine from the words of a mouthpiece that does not assert a doctrine, and this interpretive procedure, in turn, will require justification as well.[13]

Fourth, in practice interpreters who attribute characters' words and arguments to Plato in practice exercise considerable selectivity about just which of their chosen character's words are taken to express Plato's doctrines. Jokes, fables, rhetorical speeches, and interpretations of poets, for example, are usually excluded from consideration when one tries to discover Plato's doctrines in favor of passages that are more recognizably arguments.[14] But, absent a well-grounded principle for distinguishing between what are taken to be the "philosophically serious" and the "philosophically nonserious," or the "philosophical" and the "nonphilosophical" words, this practice seems just arbitrary. It is certainly arguable that myths and playful statements express serious philosophic points.[15]

---

13. The notorious disagreements among scholars about the definition of piety in the *Euthyphro* and about one's obligation to obey the law in the *Crito* are instructive. For a sampling of views on the former, see Mark McPherran, "Socratic Piety in the *Euthyphro," Journal of the History of Philosophy* 23 (1985): 283–310. Taking the variety of points of view articulated into account makes all of the solutions appear to be ad hoc.

14. E.g., Grote's comments on *Charmides* 161c, "This is the dramatic art of Plato, charming to read, but not bearing on him as a philosopher" *(Plato and the Other Companions of Sokrates.* London, 1865–67, 2.155).

15. Gavin Ardley, "The Role of Play in the Philosophy of Plato," *Philosophy* 42 (1967): 226–44; Paul Plass, "Play and Philosophic Detachment in Plato," *Transactions of the American Philological Association* 98 (1967): 343–64; H. D. Rankin, "Laughter, Humour and Related Topics in Plato," *Classica et Medievalia* 28 (1967): 186–213; Rosemary Desjardins, "Why Dialogues? Plato's Serious Play," pp. 110–125, ed. Griswold, 1988; G. J. de Vries, *Zum Spel bij Plato* (Amsterdam: North Holland, 1949); Adi Ophir, "Plato's *Republic*: Philosophy as a Serious Game," *Iyyun* 35 (1986): 3–29. More recently, Bernard Freydberg, *The Play of the Platonic Dialogues* (New York: Peter Lang, 1997).

Fifth, if, again, we accept the assumption for the sake of argument that characters speak for Plato, then the well-known differences and contradictions between the apparent doctrines of various dialogues constitute a consequent problem that will have to be solved.[16] The solution of this problem will require the machinery of some further theory, such as developmentalism and Platonic chronology, that, in turn, will have to be proved since these approaches have become more disputed in recent years than before.[17]

A version of Occam's Razor might be applied to interpretive strategies or practices of this sort: do not multiply interpretive hypotheses beyond need. The hypothesis that Plato presents his doctrines through one or more mouthpiece characters combined with recognition of the contradictions and differences of doctrines asserted necessitates the further hypotheses of developmentalism and Platonic chronology. Could we not account for the observed facts about the dialogues more simply?

Sixth, for those who accept its authenticity, the *Seventh Letter* constitutes yet another prima facie argument against the mouthpiece theory. For the implication of its so-called "philosophical passage"[18] seems to be that Plato never wrote nor intended to write what he believed most seriously.[19] If so, then perhaps *no* character in the dialogues should be taken as expressing Plato's own beliefs and arguments about these matters.

Seventh, even if we assume for the sake of argument that some character is always Plato's mouthpiece, it is arbitrary to suppose that this is Socrates in many dialogues but someone else in other dialogues, such as *Parmenides, Sophist, Politicus,* and *Timaeus,* in which Socrates is a minor or largely silent participant. A cogent explanation—that is, derivation from some well-grounded interpretive principle—is required to show why the character that functions as the mouthpiece in one dialogue does not do so in another.[20] Frequency or quantity of words spoken—that seems to explain the usual practice—hardly seems such a principle.

---

16. E.g., "minding one's own business" is said to be the essence of Justice and the principle of a just society in *Republic* (432b), but in the *Charmides* (161b-163c) Socrates describes it as an enigma (162b) and refutes it twice. In the *Phaedrus, Timaeus,* and *Republic* 4, the soul is tripartite, but in the *Phaedo* and again in *Republic* 10 the soul is simple. In the *Gorgias* and many other dialogues, rhetoric per se is considered pernicious, but in the *Phaedrus* Socrates presents what has been called a "philosophic rhetoric." In the *Meno* Socrates' final position seems to be that virtue is an unteachable divine gift (99e), but in *Republic* 4 virtue is being taught to the future rulers of the just society.

17. See the references in n. 1 *supra*.

18. In addition to the literature cited in n. 25 Margarita Isnardi-Parente, "Per l'interpretazione dell'excursus filosofico della VII epistula Platonica," *Parola del Passato* 19 (1964): 241–90. Notwithstanding the wealth of attention that has been given to the passage, Harold Tarrant has argued that it is a later interpolation, perhaps by Thrasyllus; "Middle Platonism and the *Seventh Epistle,*" *Phronesis* 28 (1983): 75–103, that also reviews earlier defenses of this hypothesis. He has reiterated the argument in his more recent *Thrasyllan Platonism* (Ithaca: Cornell University Press, 1993).

19. περὶ ὧν ἐγὼ σπουδάζω (341c) is nearly identical to wording found in the *Second Letter* and taken to have been copied from this.

20. As noted by Tejera, *Plato's Dialogues One by One*, p. 17.

These arguments need not all be accepted as true or as valid arguments against the mouthpiece theory. They are given as prima facie reasons why the mouthpiece assumption ought not be accepted as true without proof and they are intended to put the burden of proof on an interpreter who wants to use the mouthpiece theory as a premise in an interpretation. There are various reasons why, nevertheless, many interpreters assume it or believe it to be true. For one thing, it is a habit that is formed in us by our schooling and re-inforced by a good deal of scholarly reading. It is simply a fact that most of those who now teach Plato's dialogues were themselves taught Plato by in-structors who as a matter of course took the words and arguments of Socrates or the Eleatic Stranger as those of Plato (or the historical Socrates). And in practicing the craft of scholarship we find similar transitions in far the great-est part of the secondary literature.

That is to say, as a second reason, that this is a tradition in Plato interpre-tation; and it is one that demonstrably goes back to Aristotle.[21] Partly for that reason, it has long been the most popular way to read the dialogues.[22] An-other way of putting this point is to say that it is a matter of preference for many interpreters to identify some character as speaking for Plato in order to be able read Plato's own beliefs more or less directly off the words of the character so identified.

Habit, tradition, popularity, and preference, of course, are not reasons that justify philosophic beliefs or practices, and they ought not to justify the as-sumption that Socrates' words express Plato's own beliefs. But the last one mentioned suggests what might be a deeper reason why the assumption has been so long and so widely accepted: that it seems unacceptable—indeed, un-thinkable—to do without it.[23] We are reading Plato's dialogues in order to learn Plato's philosophy, are we not? But if we cannot assume that Socrates, the Eleatic Stranger, and Parmenides speak for Plato, then how can we figure out what Plato thought? In other words, assuming that a philosophy is a doc-trine or set of doctrines, the mouthpiece assumption is a *sine qua non* for knowing what Plato's doctrines are, since in Plato's dialogues only Plato's char-acters speak directly.

This pattern of (probably, usually unconscious) thinking would serve to ex-plain *why* interpreters make the mouthpiece assumption; but it will not *justify* it. None of the reasons given so far is sufficient; in fact, they are not even rele-vant. The fact that a person needs to use a certain assumption in order to reach

21. Aristotle's criticisms of Plato are so numerous as to have provided substance for Harold Cherniss, *Aristotle's Criticism of Plato and the Academy* (Baltimore: Johns Hopkins University Press, 1944). This volume, along with its companion, *Aristotle's Criticism of Presocratic Philosophy* (Baltimore: Johns Hopkins University Press, 1935) made a powerful case that Aristotle systemati-cally misrepresented the views of others, that has serious, but not widely appreciated, conse-quences for the conventional view of presocratic philosophy as well as that of Plato.

22. Tigerstedt, *Decline and Fall*.

23. As Harry Berger, Jr., has argued ["Levels of Discourse in Plato's Dialogues," pp. 75–100, ed. Anthony J. Cascardi, *Literature and the Question of Philosophy* (Baltimore: Johns Hopkins Uni-versity Press, 1987)], a dominant motivation for Plato scholarship has been to "listen to" Plato's own thoughts.

a desired conclusion is irrelevant to the truth or acceptability of that assumption. Similarly, the fact that a belief is familiar, traditional, or popular is irrelevant to whether it is true. *Argumentum ad populum* is a fallacy of relevance in logic. Bandwagon appeals and appeals to tradition are fallacious because the emotions to which they appeal are not relevant to the truth or falsity of the conclusion asserted. Thus the prima facie reasons against assuming that characters' words and arguments can be attributed to Plato suggest that a strong argument *for* it is required by those who wish to proceed in this way.

Well, then, what types of evidence would render the view plausible or justify it? The best evidence would be an explicit statement by Plato. In fact, under certain circumstances it would be sufficient proof. The statement would have to be made, however, somewhere other than in a dialogue, because otherwise taking a statement by a character, even a character called Plato, to express Plato's own views—in this case a view about how the writer Plato proceeds— would simply beg the question at issue.

This path of inquiry leads to the *Letters,* since they are the only documents in which Plato is alleged to speak directly. None but the seventh is now widely considered authentic, but in the *Seventh Letter* it is stated that Plato has never and will never write the things about which he is most serious.[24] This not only does not support the mouthpiece assumption, it tends to support the quite opposite view that Plato's own beliefs are not to be found in the dialogues at all. The Seventh Letter is actually a serious problem for those who accept its authenticity and also want to discover Plato's philosophic doctrines in the dialogues.

Another sort of possible evidence would be the testimony of Plato's students or associates that *he* said that this or that dialogical character expressed his own beliefs. But no such testimony has come down to us. Alternatively, a well-established tradition in which philosophical writers produce dialogues in which characters simply express the author's views might provide some support. But we do not have such a tradition, and even if we did that would not prove Plato followed its rules.

I have been suggesting the kinds of evidence or argument that might provide the support necessary to support the assumption that characters' words and ar-

---

24. A sampling of the extensive scholarly literature on the Letters: Frantisek Novotný, *Platonis Epistulae Commentariis Illustratae* (Brno, 1930); J. Harward, *The Platonic Epistles* (Cambridge: Cambridge University Press, 1932); R. S. Bluck, *Plato's Seventh and Other Letters* (Cambridge: Cambridge University Press, 1947); Glenn Morrow, *Plato's Epistles* (Indianapolis: Bobbs-Merrill, 1962); Ludwig Edelstein, *Plato's Seventh Letter* (Leiden: Brill, 1966); M. Levinson, A. Q. Morton, and A. D. Winspear, "The Seventh Letter of Plato," *Mind* 77 (1968): 309–25; P. Deane, "Stylometrics Do Not Exclude the Seventh Letter," *Mind* 82 (1973): 113–17; Rainer Thurnher, *Die Siebte Platonbrief* (Meisenheim: Hain, 1975); Gerhard Müller, "Die umpseudoplatonischen Brief," pp. 146–71 in *Platonische Studien,* ed. A. Graeser and D. Maue (Heidelberg: Winter, 1986); Andreas Graeser, *Philosophische Erkenntnis und begriffliche Darstelluing: Bemerkungen zum erkenntnistheoretischen Exkurs des VII. Briefs* (Mainz: Akademie der Wissenschaften und der Literatur, 1989); Kenneth Sayre, "Plato's Dialogues in Light of the Seventh Letter," pp. 93–109, ed. Griswold, *Platonic Writings/Platonic Readings*; Mauro Tulli, *Dialettica e Scrittura nella VII Lettera di Platone* (Pisa: Giardini, 1989); Harold Tarrant, "Middle Platonism and the Seventh Letter," *Phronesis* 28 (1983): 75–103.

guments can be attributed to Plato, so I should consider the one recent attempt of a sort to defend that assumption, by Richard Kraut in the introductory chapter of his *Cambridge Companion to Plato*.[25] Two general comments to begin with. First, Kraut only considers whether it is justified to take characters as Plato's mouthpiece on page 25, that is *after* he has *used* the assumption throughout the preceding twenty pages. So his argumentation as a whole has the look of rationalization rather than a rational consideration of the evidence. Second, the notes to these pages suggest that Kraut is not aware of or has chosen to omit the many scholars who have taken approaches different from his own. He mentions only three other books[26] and gives the main emphasis to Leo Strauss's widely criticized *Persecution and the Art of Writing*[27] rather than his more directly Platonic and more widely acceptable writings,[28] as if this position were the essential, prevalent, or most cogent representative of those who do not accept the mouthpiece assumption. Knocking down a straw man is not what is needed to convince us that the mouthpiece assumption is acceptable.

In the actual argumentation, Kraut makes three distinguishable points to which I would like to respond. Kraut writes:

> The comparison between Plato's dialogues and dramas is misleading in a number of ways in spite of the fact that in each genre there is dialogue among two or more characters. To begin with what is most obvious, Plato's works were not written to be entered into competition and performed at civic religious festivals, as were the plays of Greek tragedians and comedians. Plato is not assigning lines to his speakers in order to win a competition or to compose work that will be considered beautiful or emotionally satisfying by official judges or an immense audience. The dramatist does have this aim, and if it suits his purpose to have his main characters express views that differ from his own, he will do so. But if Plato's aim in writing is to create an instrument that can, if properly used, guide others to the truth and the improvement of their souls, then it may serve his purpose to create a leading speaker who represents the sincere convictions of Plato himself. The point is that, if Plato's aims differ from those of a dramatist, then he will have a reason that the dramatist lacks for using his main speaker as a mouthpiece for his own convictions (25).

In this paragraph Kraut confuses matters that ought to be kept distinct and utilizes the false dichotomy of philosophy and literature that plagues many interpretations.[29] It is true that Plato's dialogues were neither entered into the

---

25. "Introduction to the Study of Plato," pp. 1–50 (Cambridge: Cambridge University Press, 1992). The volume as a whole is striking for its exclusion of any non-traditional point of view.

26. Griswold, ed., *Platonic Writings/Platonic Readings*; Tigerstedt, *Interpreting Plato*. (Stockholm: Almquist and Wiksell, 1977); and Michael C. Stokes, *Plato's Socratic Conversations* (Baltimore: Johns Hopkins University Press, 1986).

27. Leo Strauss, *Persecution and the Art of Writing* (Glencoe, IL: Free Press, 1952).

28. E.g., Strauss "On a New Interpretation of Plato's Political Philosophy," *Social Research* 13 (1946): 326–67, *The City and Man, What Is Political Philosophy? and Other Studies* (Glencoe, IL: Free Press, 1959).

29. Rowe's accurate observation, "The distinction between literature and philosophy is certainly not one that would have interested Plato" (*Plato. Phaedo*, ed. C. J. Rowe. Cambridge: Cambridge University Press, 1993, 3) is consistent with the growing literature on the dialogues as inseparably

public religious festival competitions nor performed publicly ("official judges
... immense audience") in the way tragic and comic plays were. But that is not
the only kind of "performance" that exists, and it is a question that has been discussed by several scholars whether the dialogues were in fact performed.[30] It is
begging the question, however, to assert that Plato did not intend his dialogues
to "be considered beautiful or emotionally satisfying," and unnecessary unless
one believes in an exclusive opposition between philosophic and literary motives. Their literary brilliance and emotional impact, which has been recognized
since antiquity, can hardly be accidental.

Kraut concludes the paragraph with two conditionals of which the an-
tecedents are not established and the consequents assert only possibility: "It
may serve his purpose to create a leading speaker who represents the sincerest
convictions of Plato himself." Yes, of course, it *may*; but it does not show that it
did nor that he took the next step and actually created such speakers. "The
point is that, if Plato's aims differ from those of a dramatist, then he will have a
reason that the dramatist lacks for using his main speakers as a mouthpiece for
his own convictions." As every detective knows, having a reason to have done
something is not proof of having done it.

Next Kraut believes that the so-called "middle" and "late" dialogues display
"a high degree of collaboration among interlocutors." After discussing aspects
of the *Phaedo, Republic, Theaetetus,* and *Philebus,* he concludes, "Plato's dialogues cannot have been intended merely to dramatize conflict between op-
posing characters and to give expression to competing philosophical ideas. Nor
can they have been designed merely to give mental exercise to the reader, for
that purpose would have been much better served by simply recording as many
arguments as possible on opposite sides of a question (26)."

There certainly is collaboration among interlocutors, and not only in the dialogues Kraut has selected. But what logical or material connection exists between his evidence and his conclusion he does not say and I fail to see. Why
does such collaboration prove that the dialogues "cannot" be meant to dramatize conflict, express competing ideas, or give mental exercise? More to the
point, why must these tasks and the task of communicating philosophic doctrine be mutually exclusive? The answer is, as his repeated use of "merely" suggests, that Kraut has already decided that only the articulation of one's own doctrines is worthy of the name "philosophy" applied to a written text. For, of
course, the dialogues *could* have been intended for these other purposes as well

both philosophy *and* literature; Arieti, *Interpreting Plato*; E. De Strycker and S. R. Slings, *Plato's Apology of Socrates: A Literary and Philosophical Study* (Leiden: Brill, 1994); Rutherford 1995, Sayre 1995, Gerald A. Press, "Plato's Dialogues as Enactments," pp. 133–52 in *The Third Way: A New Direction in Platonic Studies,* ed. Gonzalez; and Cook 1996. For earlier approaches along these lines, see Julius Stenzel, "The Literary Form and Philosophical Content of the Platonic Dialogues," in Julius Stenzel, *Plato's Method of Dialectic,* tr. D. J. Allan (New York: Russell & Russell, 1964), 1–22. John Herman Randall, Jr., *Plato: Dramatist of the Life of Reason* (New York: Columbia University Press, 1970); and Phillip Merlan, "Form and Content in Plato's Philosophy," *Journal of the History of Ideas* 8 (1947): 406–30.

30. E.g., Gilbert Ryle, *Plato's Progress* (Cambridge: Cambridge University Press, 1966).

as or instead of his allegedly more serious one. The question at issue—but not properly addressed—is whether they *were*.

Finally, and revealingly, Kraut argues that the dialogues are essentially like philosophic treatises:

> When the dialogues are read in their entirety, they take on the shape we would expect . . . of works that record the intellectual development of a single individual who is struggling to express and argue for the truth as he best understands it. There is development and there is reversal, but there is at the same time the kind of continuity that indicates that Plato is using his main speaker to express his own views. And so although the dialogue form might be used by a philosopher in order to reveal the deficiencies of the views expressed by all of the interlocutors, we have strong reason for thinking that this is not in fact what Plato is doing. The dialogue form of his works should not keep us from saying that they are vehicles for the articulation and defense of certain theses and the defeat of others. Though they are not philosophical treatises, many of them share these purposes with philosophical treatises (26).

Unfortunately, Kraut does not explain what this "shape" is nor why it is "what we would expect" of someone trying to present his philosophic doctrines and arguments. The problem is that the obvious "shape" of the dialogues is precisely that, dialogues, not treatises; and that in them Plato never speaks directly. Thus the dialogue's obvious shape is *not* what we expect for the expression of one's own view of the truth. The claim that the dialogues have "the kind of continuity that indicates that Plato is using his main speaker to express his own views" is similarly ungrounded. Of what exact kind is this "continuity"? And exactly why does continuity of that kind indicate that Plato is using his characters as mouthpieces? In short, Kraut's attempt to justify the mouthpiece theory looks a lot like special pleading.

Finally, I want to consider J. J. Mulhern's view that interpretive arguments that include premises of the form "Character X is Plato's mouthpiece" inevitably involve a *petitio principii*. In an extremely interesting 1971 paper, Mulhern discusses "Two Interpretive Fallacies" frequently committed in writing about Plato's dialogues.[31] He begins from Richard Robinson's idea of misinterpretation by inference.[32] According to Robinson, arguments of the form

(1)   **c** [a character] says that **p**
        p implies **q**, therefore
        c meant **q**

are invalid since the premises may be true but the conclusion false. Mulhern doesn't think this notion has much use when dealing with interpretations of dialogues. I would think, though, that just this sort of misinterpretation by inference is to be found especially in books and articles about "Socratic philosophy" when an unjustified transition—actually a fallacy of equivocation—is made

---

31. J. J. Mulhern, *Systematics* 9 (1971), 168–172.
32. Richard Robinson, *Plato's Earlier Dialectic*, 2nd ed. (Oxford: Oxford University Press, 1962), p. 2.

from a premise stating the words of c_1, the character Socrates, to a conclusion about the meaning of c_2, some extra-Platonic Socrates who may or may not be the historical one.

However, he rightly observes that the first premise needs to be more carefully analyzed because in the literature on Plato's dialogues we often find arguments of the form

(2)   **c** says **p**
        p implies **q**; therefore
        a [the author, Plato] meant **q**.

Mulhern thus first analyzes arguments from what a character says to what Plato meant and argues that this sort of argument is a fallacy; he calls it the Plato Says Fallacy.

Then he goes on to analyze a slightly different argument form that is often encountered in the literature on Plato.

(3)   **c** says **p**
        c is Plato's mouthpiece [if **c** says **p**, then **a**, Plato, says **p**]; therefore
        Plato says **p**.

This he calls the Plato's Mouthpiece Fallacy, and he concludes,

> In the nature of the case, . . . a (PM 2) line [e.g., "**b** is **a**'s mouthpiece; i.e., if **b** says **p**, **a** says **p**"] cannot be justified without committing either a Plato Says Fallacy or a *petitio principii*. The distinctive Plato's Mouthpiece Fallacy, I suggest, is a variety of *petitio principii* (171).

That is, anyone who uses statements such as "Socrates is Plato's mouthpiece" or "The Eleatic Stranger is Plato's mouthpiece" in interpretive moves from what a character says to conclusions about what Plato says is begging the question.

I think two small revisions are necessary here. First, while such arguments are not sound, calling them a variety of begging the question might be going too far. Interpreters who either make the move from what characters say to what Plato says without discussion or state that a given character is Plato's mouthpiece without supporting that statement have certainly argued injudiciously; but, given the long tradition of Plato interpretation in which this has been done, they have probably proceeded in ignorance that there is a problem about such a premise. I hope that after such discussions as this and the others in the present book, interpreters will no longer be unaware of the problem. Having been made aware of the problem, an interpreter who still uses arguments such as (2) or (3) above, would be begging the question.

Second, to say that such a premise "cannot" be justified may go beyond the evidence. It *has* not been justified heretofore, but some Great Man may yet appear who can provide an argument for it.[33] It is to issue the call for such an argument that I have written this chapter.

---

33. *Charmides* 169A.

3

Socrates and the Character of Platonic Dialogue

Joanne Waugh

To see Socrates as Plato's mouthpiece is prima facie to discount that Plato chose not to speak in his own voice—that there was no character named Plato in the dialogues, and almost no mention at all of Plato in the dialogues.[1] This assumption is in contrast to our *not* assuming that Hippolytus, say, rather than Phaedra speaks for Euripides. In the latter case, we assume that all of these characters say what Euripides wanted them to say, and we determine what Euripides thought by looking at what the *Hippolytus* did—and meant—in fifth-century Athens. To respond that unlike Euripides, Plato wrote *philosophy* and not drama begs the question, for what is at issue is *how* Plato's dialogues present philosophy.

Assuming that Socrates is Plato's mouthpiece is not, of course, incompatible with the claim that understanding Socrates' statements—and Plato's philosophy—requires that we examine the dramatic occasion of these statements, i.e., the dialogues, or the historical context in which the dialogues were produced. Some of Plato's readers insist that although Socrates speaks for Plato, his words must be understood in the *dramatic* context in which they are uttered; on this view, the philosophical import of Socrates' statements can only be determined through reading the dialogues as literature, literature in which the character Socrates says what Plato would have said had he been a character in this drama. For these readers, there is no shortcut, as it were, to Plato's philosophy; if one does not read the dialogues as literature he or she will not understand Plato's thought.

Although few philosophers actually state that Plato's choice of the dialogue form is unrelated to an understanding of his philosophical projects, it is still difficult to find philosophers who seriously consider whether and how philosophical importance attaches to the dramatic situations, characters, and events of

---

1. Plato mentions himself at *Apology* (34a1–2) and at *Phaedo* (59b9) where it is suggested that he was absent because of sickness from this last meeting with Socrates.

the dialogues.[2] By assuming that Socrates speaks for Plato and by looking only at the arguments Socrates offers—or rather at the arguments that contemporary philosophers rationally reconstruct for him based on what he says and what they take this to logically imply—some philosophers think it possible to formulate Plato's alleged answers to the problems of philosophy, despite his apparent preference for anonymity. In so doing, they assume that Plato was providing answers to the same questions with which they as contemporary philosophers are concerned. Why Plato would have chosen to mask his answers by writing in the form of dramatic dialogues is not given much, if any, consideration. The questions or problems that contemporary philosophers think that Plato is addressing are not, it seems, the product of specific historical events occurring at a specific place and time, but are "there" (wherever "there" is) for any rational being who thinks philosophically (whatever "thinking philosophically" is). In this way, philosophical problems are timeless; it is as if they had sprung fully formed from the head of Zeus (though Aristotle is doubtless more deserving of the honor).[3] And the answers to these questions or problems, though formulated by a particular philosopher at a particular time and in a particular style of speech or writing, are capable of being formulated as propositions, that is, as statements that though grammatically tensed are logically tenseless.[4] As such their meaning is supposed to be somehow independent of the occasion of their utterance or inscription, independent, indeed, of any particular style of philosophical speaking or writing, including the Platonic dialogue.

Mining the dialogues for "philosophical texts" that can be detached from their literary and historical context and inserted into the language and problematic of contemporary philosophy is one of the species of misinterpreting Plato identified by Richard Robinson nearly a half-century ago.[5] Robinson ob-

2. Drew Hyland, "Why Plato Wrote Dialogues," *Philosophy and Rhetoric* 1 (1968): 38. Of course, there have long been scholars, e.g., Friedländer and Brumbaugh, who emphasized the importance of the dialogue form, but in recent decades have been a distinct minority. For a history of the doctrinal or dogmatic approaches to Plato's dialogues, as well as the skeptical interpretations, see E. N. Tigerstedt, *Interpreting Plato* (Stockholm Studies in the History of Literature, 17; Almquist & Wiksell International, 1979), and "The Decline and Fall of the Neoplatonic Interpretation of Plato" (Helsinki: Societus Scientarum Fennica, 1974). See also Victorino Tejera, "The Hellenistic Obliteration of Plato's Dialogism," in *Plato's Dialogues: New Studies and Interpretations*, ed. Gerald A. Press (Lanham, MD: Rowman & Littlefield, 1993).

3. Michael Morgan writes of the tendency dominant in English-language philosophy to treat Plato as if he were a contemporary philosopher writing about timeless, philosophical problems in *Platonic Piety* (New Haven: Yale University Press, 1990), 4–5. It turns out that these "timeless" problems are best analyzed using those techniques that have been refined through the course of the history of philosophy, that are, of course, the techniques of contemporary philosophy.

4. On traditional views—including those attributed to Plato on the basis of (some of) the statements of Socrates and what they logically imply, propositions are about an extraordinary kind of object, an object with characteristics or powers that compel parts of the mind or parts of the body to believe true propositions about the object. Richard Rorty provides an eloquent statement of this point in *Philosophy and the Mirror of Nature* (Princeton: Princeton University Press, 1979), 157–158.

5. Richard Robinson, *Plato's Earlier Dialectic*, 2nd ed. (Oxford: Clarendon Press, 1953), 1–4.

served that some scholars misinterpret earlier philosophers "for the sake of *insinuating the future* . . . of reading into your author doctrines that did not become explicit until later." Philosophers who reconstruct Plato's answer to the "timeless" problems of philosophy typically engage in the other species of misinterpretation identified by Robinson: *mosaic interpretation* ("The habit of laying any amount of weight on an isolated text or single sentence, without determining whether it is a passing remark or a settled part of your author's thinking"); *misinterpretation by abstraction* ("your author mentions X; and X appears to you to be a case of Y; and on the strength of that you say that your author 'was well aware of Y', or even that he 'explicitly mentions Y' "); *misinterpretation by inference* ("Plato says p, and p implies q; therefore Plato meant q"); and *going beyond a thinker's last word* ("ascribing to him not merely all the steps he took in a certain direction but the next step also, which in reality was first made by a subsequent generation").

Implicit within these species of misinterpretation one finds, again, not only the notion that philosophy consists of timeless problems, but also that it matters not how, when, or—indeed—if, the philosopher in question *wrote* philosophy. When the philosopher in question is Plato, this assumption translates into the belief that the choice to write dialogues was not philosophically motivated, and that, accordingly, they may be read as if the presence in them of a *character* named Socrates was not motivated by *philosophical concerns,* nor essential to the accomplishment of Plato's philosophical aims.

It is curious that in the century in which Anglo-American philosophy made "the linguistic turn" one finds such indifference about whether one "philosophizes" in speech or in writing, and scant discussion of the questions of how and why and in what style philosophy is written. Although the differences between written language and speech are remarked on as early as the *Phaedrus* (275d), many English-language philosophers continue to write as if philosophy were not a kind of speech nor a style of writing but a kind of language that is independent—somehow—of the occasion of its utterance or inscription. But speech does not exist independently of speakers, and although written language does appear to have a certain independence from the occasion of its inscription inasmuch as inscribed marks on an enduring substance can survive their author or inscriber, the fixity of these inscribed marks does not carry over to the meaning of the text(s) inscribed. In any case, written language cannot serve as the model for language since speech is prior to, and independent of, writing.[6]

Meaning is conveyed not just by uttering words but by uttering them with a certain intonation and phrasing.[7] It is not merely what is said that matters, but also the expression on the speaker's face and the stance of her body, and her

---

6. As Eric Havelock reminds us in *The Literate Revolution in Greece and Its Cultural Consequences* (Princeton: Princeton University Press, 1982).

7. Think of the recently ubiquitous, "yeah, right." Better yet, think of the many instances in the Platonic dialogues in which readers—and sometimes interlocutors—miss Socrates' irony precisely because they assume that his meaning is carried only by his words. Taking Socrates' statements in this way can result in one's totally missing the irony and humor of the dialogues, and in one's ascribing mistaken philosophical positions to Plato.

gestures and movements, or the lack thereof.[8] When speakers and hearers are present to each other, they can repeat and rephrase and question what is being said until it is understood. Language and meaning thus exist in the embodied actions of speaker and hearer; they are written on the body, as Foucault reminds us. But this metaphor in which the body is metaphorically a text needs to be turned around, for it is the text that stands in for an embodied speaker. We are able to communicate because we are embodied not despite it, and written texts should be viewed as standing-in for embodied creatures that negotiate meaning and not the other way around.[9]

Just as a speaker conveys meaning not just by her utterance but also by her gestures and movements, her intonation and phrasing, the expression on her face and the stance of her body, the writer of a text conveys meaning not only by adopting a "style," but also by choosing this style and these words for a certain audience at a certain time in contrast to other choices. To determine what a text "means" requires knowledge not only of the language that the inscribed marks are meant to record, but also the context(s) in which the text was produced and is being read, the literary history of which this text forms a part and which are the source of its allusions, and the interpretative communities to which it is addressed or which are engaged in its interpretation. Far from being the "autonomous" linguistic entity of "New Criticism," a text depends on an encultured reader to give it "voice" and meaning, to embody it, as it were. In other words, it requires a speaker—or reader—who is a representative of the cultural and interpretative community of which the author of that text is also a member. The reader attempts to understand what the author is trying to say through his text, just as one who hears another's words tries to understand their meaning. But while speaker and hearer can "negotiate meaning" in a shared space, a reader need not share the writer's historical and material context, and she must recover this context in order to recover the meaning of the text.

This is true of philosophical writing as well, despite its pretensions that "any rational being" could understand its meaning, that somehow this meaning is independent of cultural and interpretative community in which it is written. It is especially true of Plato, whose dialogues provide us with a picture of the cultural and interpretative community for whom he is writing.[10]

---

8. Thomas Cole, *The Origins of Rhetoric in Ancient Greece* (Baltimore: Johns Hopkins University Press, 1991).

9. Who counts as "we" or "us" is, of course, a problem, especially, as feminist philosophers have pointed out, if and when we take seriously the notion of embodiment.

10. This community presumably included citizens like himself as well as those noncitizens who might be part of a deserving audience that, given Socrates' remarks in *Republic* V, may have included women. [I have argued that *Republic* V should be taken seriously and not seen as a digression nor dismissed as humor in "Women, Citizenship, Democracy: The Challenge of the *Republic*," *Plato's Political Philosophy and Contemporary Democratic Theory: A Dialogue*, ed. Konstantine Boudouris (Athens: Center for the Study of Greek Philosophy and Culture, 1997)]. If the dialogues were used to assist in the philosophical education of students in the Academy, the audience may have been rather atypical when compared with the Athenian citizenry at large. For a discussion of the occasion of the presentation of the dialogues and their effect(s) on their audience(s), see the articles by Hershbell, Waugh, and West in *The Third Way*, ed. Francisco Gonzalez (Lanham, MD: Rowman and Littlefield, 1995).

In the late twentieth century, scholars have emphasized the importance of public speech—and the changes in its style, delivery, and authority in Greek society—and the importance of writing in the development of what we know as philosophy.[11] Vernant has argued that what we think of as "Reason" was first "expressed, established, and shaped" in Greece in the activities of politics.[12] The techniques most important to the development of rational discourse were not so much those that apply to manipulating or transforming the world as "those that give one person a hold over others, and whose common instrument is language; the art of the politician, the rhetorician, the pedagogue. Greek reason is that reason which makes it possible to act practically, deliberately, and systematically on human beings, not to transform nature, in its limitations as in its innovations. It is a creature of the city" (131–132). Indeed, Vernant claims that in Greece, for the first time, "social life became the object of conscious and deliberate research and reflection";[13] he sees as implicit in the institutions of the city, "not only a 'political' sphere of action but also a 'political' thought/theory" (181). *Ta koina,* Vernant notes, "means 'that which is common to all'" (181) and this is the expression used for the political sphere and public affairs. In the institutions of the city that appear, Vernant says, in the period between Hesiod and Anaximander:

> All things held in "common" must be the subject of free debate between those who compose the political body. They must be discussed publicly in the open, in the *agora,* and the discussion must take the form of speeches that develop arguments. Thus the establishment of the *polis* involves a process of secularization and rationalization of social life . . . so far as the citizens were concerned the affairs of the city could be decided only following public debate in which each man was free to intervene in order to develop his own arguments (181–182).

Logos becomes the "instrument" for these public debates, the word not only for "speech pronounced by an orator at the assembly," but also for reason, "the

---

11. The importance of public speech is discussed by Cole 1991, by Bruno Gentili in *Poetry and Its Public,* tr. Thomas Cole (Baltimore: Johns Hopkins University Press, 1989), and by Jean-Pierre Vernant and Marcel Detienne as noted below. Vernant also remarks on the how the development of Greek prose composition encourages a "new form of thought" that is more analytical, logical and abstract in *Myth and Society in Ancient Greece,* tr. Janet Lloyd (New York: Zone Books, 1988), 204ff. The importance of Greek alphabetic writing on the development of philosophy has been the major focus of the work of Eric Havelock, and more recently, Kevin Robb. For Havelock, see *The Greek Concept of Justice: From Its Shadow in Homer to Its Substance in Plato* (Cambridge: Harvard University Press, 1978), *The Literate Revolution in Greece and Its Consequences* (Princeton: Princeton University Press, 1981), "The Pre-Literacy of the Greeks," *New Literary History,* 8 (1977), 369–377, and *The Muse Learns to Write* (New Haven: Yale University Press, 1988). For Robb, see *Literacy and Paideia in Ancient Greece* (New York: Oxford University Press, 1994). More recent studies of ancient literacy support the notion that although writing was used for the purposes of keeping records, the oral way of doing things persisted long after the introduction of the Greek alphabet. See, for example, William V. Harris, *Ancient Literacy* (Cambridge: Harvard University Press, 1989); and Rosalind Thomas, *Literacy and Orality in Ancient Greece* (Cambridge: Cambridge University Press, 1992).

12. Jean-Pierre Vernant, *Origins of Greek Thought* (Ithaca: Cornell University Press, 1982). Further references to this work will be indicated in parentheses following the material cited.

13. J. P. Vernant, *Myth and Thought among the Greeks* (London: Routledge & Kegan Paul, 1983). Further references to this work will be indicated in parentheses following the material cited.

faculty of argumentation which defines man as being, not just an animal, but a 'political animal', a reasonable being" (182). By engaging in this free debate citizens demonstrate their standing as equals and peers *(isoi* and *homoioi).* This process by which speech becomes "secularized," to use the term employed by Vernant, Pierre Levêque and Pierre Vidal-Naquet, and Marcel Detienne, is intimately tied, then, to the developing *polis* and the emerging concept of a citizen, and what we regard as rational thought—and philosophy—is an essential part of this process and these developments.[14] Indeed, Detienne follows Vernant in finding the origins of public debate among citizens in the dialogue—speech between warriors in deliberative assemblies as depicted in the Homeric epics, and contrasts this dialogue—speech that was "secular, complemented action, operated within a temporal context, and possessed a unique autonomy that extended to one whole social group"—with the magicoreligious speech of poets, diviners, and kings of justice that was "efficacious, atemporal, and indissociable from symbolic behavior and meaning" (89). Dialogue-speech, like the distribution of booty and of funerary game prizes, was conducted *es meson,* in the middle.[15] The middle is the "single spatial model that dominates the interplay of all these institutions—deliberative assemblies, booty distributions, funeral games" (97).[16] This space was "a circular and centered space within which, ideally, each individual stands in reciprocal and reversible relationship to everything else. . . . As a commonly shared point, the *meson* is the public place, par excellence: its geographical position was synonymous with all that was public" (97). This dialogue-speech of warriors was a privilege and a sign of their equality, and as Greek society developed the privilege of public speech was extended to the citizens of the *polis.*[17] As Detienne observes, "to express one's opinion in a political assembly was to 'take one's opinion to the middle' (φερειν γνωμην ες μεσον) or 'speak in the middle' (λέγειν ἐς μέσον)"(102). These expressions are

---

14. See Vernant, *Myth and Thought,* and Pierre Levêque and Pierre Vidal-Naquet, *Cleisthène: l'Athénien* (Paris: Les Belles Letters, 1964); and Marcel Detienne, *The Masters of Truth in Archaic Greece,* tr. Janet Lloyd (New York: Zone Books, 1996). Further references to this volume will be noted in parentheses following the material cited. Vernant (*Myth and Thought,* 215) notes that Levêque and Vidal-Naquet add to their description of Cleisthenes' reforms as secular the qualification "in so far as there could be any such thing in the sixth century." Vernant concedes there is a sense in which the use of "secularization" is an anachronism. He suggests that what emerges with Cleisthenes is "a religion which is itself political" (215). In his foreword to Detienne's *Masters of Truth,* Vidal-Naquet writes that he shares with Vernant and Detienne the view that "'rational thought' arose within a specific political, economic, and social framework . . . that of the city, which itself appeared through a decisive crisis of sovereignty, and within a social space unencumbered by the dominating presence of a Minoan or Mycenaean monarch modeled after Eastern 'despots'"(8–9).

15. Detienne, *Masters of Truth,* 89 ff. Detienne and Vernant both cite the influence of Louis Gernet, *Droit et sociétè dans la Grèce ancienne* (Paris: Recueil Sirey, 1955) on their discussions.

16. Indeed Richard Martin suggests that, among other things, one of the things that distinguishes Achilles as a hero is his performance as a poetic public speaker; see *The Language of Heroes: Speech and Performance in the Iliad* (Ithaca: Cornell University Press, 1989).

17. Detienne argues that the hoplite reform was an essential ingredient in the development of the city and the new model of intellectual thought that accompanied it (103–104). Vernant cites Cleisthenes' reforms as the turning point in the development of the *polis;* for Vernant, Cleisthenes' reforms are "the inauguration of politics, the emergence of a true political dimension in the social existence of the Greeks" (*Myth and Thought,* 212).

part of the definition of a political space, the importance of which for Greek thought, Detienne reminds us, "is conveyed by the ancient formula pronounced by the herald at the beginning of the assembly: what man has good advice for the city and wishes to make it known [at the center] (τις θελει πολει χρηστον το βουλευμ' ες μεσον φερειν εχων)?"[18] The inseparability of words and actions in conveying meaning that constitutes communication, public and private, was thus especially important in archaic and classical Greece. The inseparability of public words *and* public actions that was the sign of the Homeric hero remained an important aspect of Athenian public discourse in the closing years of the fifth century. One's *sophia* was evident not only in what one said, but in how one looked and acted when speaking. The Athenians, Pericles tells us in the Funeral Oration, can philosophize without becoming soft or effeminate: *philosophoumen aneu malakias* (2.40.1). Philosophizing, then, was a matter not just of the mind, but also of the body; being *sophos* meant that one had a certain type of body—a male body—the body of a citizen.[19] For Periclean Athens, there is no incompatibility of words and deeds: a citizen is one who loves Athens, and so looks, speaks, and says what befits a citizen and a lover—he is the embodiment, as it were, of *sophia*.[20] One's body as well as one's voice needed to be trained to stand, move, and speak in a way that befitted an Athenian; thus did traditional Greek *paideia* consist, as Socrates says, of *gymnastikē* for the body and *mousikē* for the soul (Rep. 376e-3–6).

Because meaning is conveyed not only by one's words but also by one's actions, and how one appears in performing them, the public discourse of citizens was carried out not only in the agora and assembly, but also at *symposia, gymnasia,* and given the testimony of Plato's *Charmides,* at the *palestra.* Public debate was also carried out in social and cultural institutions such as the dramatic and comedic festivals. Christian Meier has argued that the public debate was a precondition for "the mental venture of politics" that was carried out via tragedy.[21] According to Meier, tragedy assumed a central political role in fifth century Athens as her successes early in the century, coupled with the growth of democracy, generated the need for "a platform for an utterly unique form of institutionalized 'discussion' of the more profound problems of a population"(42). J. Henderson has made a similar case for the political significance of Old Comedy, the authors of which saw themselves "as public voices who could, indeed were expected to, comment on, and seek to influence public thinking

---

18. Euripides, *The Suppliant Women,* tr. Frank William Jones (Chicago: University of Chicago Press, 1958) 438–439.

19. Thus I argue that for those who shared Socrates' preoccupation with questions of *paideia,* politics, and philosophy, that is, for anyone familiar with the public discourse of Greece, there could be no more direct challenge to the traditional association of *sophia,* citizenship, and public discourse than Socrates' remarks in *Republic* V. See Joanne Waugh, "Women, Citizenship, Democracy: The Challenge of the *Republic,*" ed. Boudouris (1997).

20. '*Kalokagathia*', Paul Zanker reminds us, referred to beauty at once physical and spiritual. See Zanker, *The Mask of Socrates: The Image of the Intellectual in Antiquity,* tr. Alan Shapiro (Berkeley: University of California Press, 1995), 39.

21. Christian Meier, *The Political Art of Greek Tragedy,* tr. Andrew Webber (Baltimore: Johns Hopkins University Press, 1993), 43.

about matters of major importance—the same matters that were being or might be presented to the voting *demos* in other settings and in different way, by competitors in a tragic competition, for example, or by speakers in an assembly, or by litigants in a law court."[22]

Plato's choice to write dialogues—and his conception of the activity in which philosophy must consist—needs to be viewed against this background in which what we would regard as "literary" or "stylistic" choices were, in fact, ways of extending—or contesting—the public debate that was the sign of membership in the *polis*. Until the end of the fifth century—the dramatic date of Plato's dialogues—being *sophos* meant that one had expertise in such public discourse.[23] For Greeks of the fifth and early fourth century, *"philosophein"* and its cognates signified "intellectual cultivation" in the broad sense, and a *philosophos* did not necessarily engage in what we would recognize as philosophy, let alone its timeless problems. A wide array of intellectuals—including poets and sophists— were described as practicing "philosophy" until at least the late fifth century.[24] Indeed, the characters in Plato's dialogues—leading figures of fifth-century democratic Athens, especially in its closing decades—do not recognize a difference between what they do and "philosophy," and Andrea Nightingale reminds us, the meaning of "philosophy" was still being contested in the Fourth century by Plato and Isocrates. The enterprise of philosophy is contrasted in Plato's dialogues with other "genres that have currency in classical Athens—genres which make some claim to wisdom or authority."[25] It is Plato who is the first to use the term "philosophy" to designate a specific intellectual enterprise.[26] In Greece, at least, philosophy had a history.

To understand what philosophy meant for Plato, then, we must look at what his dialogues—and the character of Socrates—do in classical Athens, how they contest the authority of the genres of speech and writing that were dominant in fifth and fourth centuries. The extant *ipsissima verba* of "philosophers" before Plato suggest that there was no conventional nor accepted style for "philosophical" writing: Xenophanes and Parmenides favored hexameter verse, while Her-

---

22. J. Henderson, "The *Demos* and Comic Competition," in *Nothing To Do With Dionysius? Athenian Drama in its Social Context*, ed. J. J. Winkler and F. I. Zeitlin (Princeton: Princeton University Press, 1990), 271–272.

23. Cf. Gentili, *Poetry and its Public*.

24. Cf. Andrea Wilson Nightingale, *Genres in Dialogue: Plato and the Construct of Philosophy* (New York: Cambridge University Press, 1995), 10–11.

25. *Ibid.*, 5. Nightingale follows G. B. Conte's notion of genre: "genre must be thought of as a discursive form capable of constructing a coherent model of the world in its own image. It is a language, that is, a lexicon and a style, but it is also a system of the imagination and a grammar of things. Genres are the expressive codification of a culture's models; indeed, they are those very models subjected to a process of stylization and formalization that gives them a literary voice" [*Genres and Readers*, tr. G. Most. (Baltimore: Johns Hopkins University Press, 1994), 132]. Originally published as *Generi e lettori: Lucrezio, L'elegia d'amore, L'enciclopedia di Plinio* (Milan, 1991). "Genres of discourse," then, refers not just to artistic forms or styles, but also to *"forms of thought,* each of which is adapted to representing and conceptualizing some aspects of experience better than others" (emphasis original) with the result that "an encounter between two genres within a single text is itself a kind of dialogue" (3).

26. According to Nightingale, *Genres* 10ff, philosophy, for Plato, consisted of a "unique set of ethical and metaphysical commitments that demanded a whole new way of living."

aclitus composed oracular pronouncements in rhythmical prose.[27] *Sokratikoi logoi* (as Aristotle called them) began in the late fifth century just before Plato began writing, but all that remains are fragments of Aeschines and the dialogues of Xenophon and Plato, and it is impossible to know the conventions, if any, of the early stage of the genre. But the dialogue bears a relation to mime and tragedy, as Diskin Clay has observed, and also interacts with comedy that, according to Clay, provides both a model and a target for the early Socratic writings.[28] Tragedy offered itself as a paradigm after Socrates' execution turned him into a famous or infamous historical figure, for "the literary Socratics who wrote after Socrates' death could exploit a resource available to the tragedian and the historian; the actors in the events they narrate or dramatize were aware of the full implications of their words and actions."[29]

Much of the dramatic power of Plato's dialogues comes from the masterful way that he exploits his audience's awareness of the full implications of the words and actions of Socrates and his interlocutors. The audience would recognize how these characters, excepting Socrates, think to display their *sophia* as they demonstrate their expertise in public discourse. The dialogues are nothing if not clashes between characters known for their expertise in various kinds of public discourse:[30] one finds Protagoras, Gorgias, Aristophanes, Alcibiades and a large cast of others who though less important historically, e.g., Meno, nonetheless consider themselves experts in public discourse.[31] Through engaging in such discourse, Meletus claims in the *Apology* (24d–28) and Anytus insists in the *Meno* (92e–94e), one becomes not only *sophos*, but also virtuous. Indeed, precisely because engaging in such talk is identified with the acquisition of virtue, Socrates is accused of corrupting the youth of Athens, despite his protestations that he has never claimed such knowledge nor the ability to pass it on to others. Even those who believe that traditional methods of acquiring expertise in public discourse can be improved upon—Protagoras, for example—assume that in teaching others how to be proficient speakers they are also making them better people and more virtuous citizens.[32]

---

27. For Heraclitus as "oracular," see Kevin Robb, "Preliterate Ages and the Linguistic Art of Heraclitus" in *Language and Thought in Early Greek Philosophy*, ed. Kevin Robb (LaSalle, IL: The Monist Library of Philosophy, The Hegeler Institute, 1983).

28. Diskin Clay, "The Origins of the Socratic Dialogue," in *The Socratic Movement*, ed. Paul Vander Waerdt. (Ithaca: Cornell, 1994), 45–6. With Nightingale (and others) I would maintain that Plato's dialogues differed from earlier *Sokratikoi logoi* in both their aim and the means by which they accomplished their aim.

29. Clay 46.

30. *Pace* Nightingale, I would suggest that Plato's dialogues were, at least initially, part of public discourse, and that the Socratic method as well as the character Socrates were put forth as models for the way in which public discourse should be conducted and by whom. Although the dialogues may have circulated as written texts among elite audiences as Nightingale suggests, this would not preclude their being recited before audiences as well. See Joanne Waugh, "Neither Published, Nor Perished" in *The Third Way*, ed. Gonzalez (Lanham, MD: Rowman & Littlefield, 1995).

31. Even Parmenides and Zeno make an appearance in the dialogues: characters whose discourse was deemed important if not exactly comprehensible by their audience.

32. The only character who does *not* profess such expertise is Socrates, who, incidentally, is not in violation of his own claim when he explicitly serves as a "mouthpiece" for Aspasia and Diotima in the *Menexenus* and *Symposium*, precisely because he is serving as a mouthpiece for those who

Within the medium of public discourse, Socratic dialogue stands in sharp contrast to the political debate that Vernant and Detienne argue was the legacy of the dialogue-speech of heroes. The way that Socrates talks is not familiar to an Athenian audience—his interlocutors repeatedly describe what Socrates says as strange and difficult; indeed, the way Socrates speaks lacks the majesty of epic, the *pathos* of tragedy, and the persuasiveness of oratory. Although his conversations sometimes take place in a quasipublic venue, and the *Apology*, of course, takes place in the courts, Socrates does not offer speeches of the sort that Athenians have come to expect. Plato's dialogues are also replete with references to Socrates' concern with how people should talk—and to their impatience with how he does talk; one thinks for example, of his spelling out just what kind of answer to his question about "holiness" he wants in the *Euthyphro;* his discussion with Protagoras about just how they will proceed; and Thrasymachus's mocking remarks to Socrates about asking questions and marking off answers in the *Republic.* Socrates' refusal in the *Apology* to give the kind of speeches that jurors have come to expect in the law courts, and his protests at speech-making in the *Protagoras* underscore just how much his way of talking differs from public discourse, as does Alcibiades defense of Socrates' way of talking as beautiful in the *Symposium.*

The events and action of the Platonic dialogue consist of talk; what unfolds dramatically is conversation, even if it is conversation about thinking and speaking itself. What is so striking about these conversations is their insistence that dialogue, whether with oneself or others, is necessary for such knowledge. The dialogue form, Ronald Hathaway suggests, is a way of solving problems that arise from internal thinking, that "no sooner is one fruitful way of talking, one line of thinking, one direction probed, than another emerges with credentials if not stronger then at least as strong as the first to crowd it out or replace it."[33] Hathaway argues that resistance to this displacement process leads "to the need to actually portray eikastically an external Dialogue in which publicly acknowledged restraints as well as permissions are imposed on the flux of inner Dialogue" (204). These public restraints and licenses are the result not only of the dialogues as conversations, but also of social concerns: "The format that 'frames' a Dialogue owes something to an imaging of background conventions as well as of persons. The important point is that Plato needed portrayal by imaging, as well as modeling, to place checks and balances on the free flow of thinking" (204). It is not clear that "external" dialogue and "inner" dialogue stand in the relation described—that internal dialogue is the model for talk that is external and public. In the *Meno* Socrates does propose that true beliefs become knowledge only through repeated questioning (85c9–d1),[34] and in the

---

as women—and foreigners—are not citizens and, consequently, are neither required nor officially permitted expertise in public discourse. How these women came by this expertise would likely be a more provocative question for Plato's audience than for a modern one, but it arises as a question for both.

33. Ronald Hathaway, "Explaining the Unity of the Platonic Dialogue," *Philosophy and Literature* 8 (1984): 195–208. Further references to this article will be noted in parentheses following the citation.

34. See Alexander Nehemas, "Meno's Paradox and Socrates as a Teacher," *Oxford Studies of Ancient Philosophy* (1985): 15–24, where he argues that "the role of questioning is crucial in bringing

Charmides what is sought through such questioning, though not found, is the "knowledge of knowledge" (165e ff.). Socrates' injunction to "know thyself" requires a questioning of oneself, and Socrates characterizes thinking *(dianoeisthai)* in the *Theaetetus* as a talk *(logon)* that the soul has with itself (189e–190b). This suggests that thinking is being modeled on external dialogue and not the other way around. One learns this sort of thinking by listening to those who are engaged in such conversations and then by engaging in them oneself. Philosophy must be public discourse, i.e., speech, before it can become private, and philosophical thinking is like other intelligent activities in that the "philosopher" is still learning because each performance is modified by its predecessors.[35] The majority of Plato's dialogues are representations of philosophical speech, discourse in which the speakers are present and indeed are *required* by Socrates to explain, rephrase and repeat in an effort to minimize or correct misunderstanding.[36] Plato's dialogues represent such speech in order that their listeners (and readers) might learn to speak and think philosophically, for there appears to be no other way in which they could learn to do this. The dialogues are dramatic examples of such speech and thinking that their audience can take in and in which they can, at least vicariously, participate. Philosophy, as characterized in the dialogues, is not independent of the dialogue; the dialogue form is necessary to show in what philosophizing consists.

It is clear that speech and not written language is Plato's prototype for philosophy, for written texts, as we are told in the *Phaedrus,* seem to be talking to you, but just keep saying the same thing over and over when you ask them something (275d–e). Moreover, there is no control over who takes up these texts; they do not know how to direct themselves to only the right people. In contrast, Socrates offers "living speech," the kind of *logoi* that goes with knowledge, but this type of speech is also "written" in the soul of the learner (276a), presumably as a result of his or her engaging in dialectic (276e). Implicit in this distinction between written texts and "living speech" is recognition of the fact that texts merely imitate the way that language—and knowledge—exist in the bodies and actions of speakers; living speech—even that "written" in the soul of the learner—is the kind of speech that can defend itself against questioning, a dialogue that it presumably invites. This kind of speech could only be represented by the kind of dialogues that Plato writes, dialogues that do not present philosophical truths, but, instead, teach others how to philosophize. That teaching how to philosophize rather than presenting philosophical doctrines is Plato's

---

about a match between what one knew that one does not know" with "what one did not know that one knows," and that "Plato's resolution of Meno's paradox is dialectical rather than logical."

35. Cf. Gilbert Ryle, *Plato's Progress* (Cambridge: Cambridge University Press, 1966), 27.

This is one reason why we err if we fail to see the difference between speech and written language, taking written language as simply a token of speech, and also err when we see philosophy as a type of language.

36. This may also explain why the *Theaetetus*, *Sophist*, and *Statesman* resemble the early dialogues in returning to the Socratic *elenchus*, though in the latter two dialogues it is not Socrates who is doing the speaking. Of course, if one does not accept the division of the dialogues into the "early," "middle," and "late" periods, and the alleged systematic development of Plato's philosophical thought—both of which are becoming increasingly problematic—then this feature of the *Theaetetus*, *Sophist*, and *Statesman* may not require explanation.

aim in the dialogues should be evident not only because of the statements in
Epistle VII that he has not written any works on such serious subjects (341c)
because a serious man would not think of writing of such matters (344c),[37] but
also because of Socrates' observation in the *Phaedrus* that one who knows what
is just, honorable and good will not write with serious intent in ink, but will
"sow his seed in literary gardens" as a means of recreation and "refreshment"
for his own memory against the day "when age oblivious comes" and *for those
who "follow in his footsteps."*[38]

Still, Socrates' desire to provide some sort of permanence for "living speech"
leads him to say that it is "written" in the soul of the learner, and thus does it
become possible for one to have a dialogue with oneself. The inscription of language allows language or thought itself to be the object of study, and, in turn,
language or thought becomes philosophical, for the metaphor of inscription
here is what permits there to be inner dialogue that resembles the dialogues
that Socrates has with his interlocutors. What has been inscribed, presumably,
is the effect on the soul of its association with objects that are not particular nor
transient, objects that are one and unseen and do not "happen." Only with such
objects could truth and meaning and virtue transcend the speaker and the body
and the present. As a consequence of this transcendence, statements about
these objects would acquire the sort of necessity that is possessed by the objects; if these objects were not contingent then neither would be the statements
that describe them. The relations between such statements would not be based
on tradition, but on logic.

Socrates, of course, exhibits a fascination with such special objects, but they
resist his attempts to talk about them; neither the Socratic question, nor any
tentative answers to it can operate within the logic of a narrative, while the dramatic dialogue must operate within this logic.[39] His interlocutors are not altogether happy with his "Socratic questions"; some seem not to recognize his re-
quests for propositions that seem not a part of their everyday speech. Those
who have better luck at formulating propositions arrive at none that can escape
scrutiny. When Socrates is not asking such questions, he is speaking of such ordinary things—cobblers and carpenters—that his aristocratic friends, like
Alcibiades, are turned away. Whatever difficulty his interlocutors may have had
with Socratic questions seems to have been overcome by Aristotle, who, instead
of in addition to exoteric dialogues, writes the kind of philosophical language

---

37. Even if one assumes that the *Seventh Letter* is not genuine, these statements should still
carry a great deal of significance; for a forgery to be successful, as Gilbert Ryle notes, it must be
quite believable. If the dialogues were presumed by Plato's audience to be a presentation of his
philosophical doctrines, *Epistle VII* would appear as an obvious forgery.

38. I discuss how and why the dialogues may have been composed as a means of teaching their
audience how to philosophize in "Neither Published, Nor Perished" ed. Gonzalez (1995).

39. Cf. Havelock: "The new 'is' syntax required a new type of subject—impersonal, nonactive,
abstracted as we might say from any particular action or transient event. This called for and encouraged a use of vocabulary that could isolate this subject in its abstraction and its unchanging uniformity." "The Orality of Socrates and the Literacy of Plato: With Some Reflections On The Historical Origins of Moral Philosophy in Europe," in *New Essays on Socrates*, ed. Eugene Kelly (New
York: University Press of America, 1984), 76–79.

with which we are familiar. Aristotle is so successful in this enterprise that philosophy becomes identified with the way in which he writes, and not with the dialogues of Plato.

But to identify philosophy with philosophizing as it is found in Aristotle overlooks the fact that *philosophia,* as portrayed in the dialogues of Plato, is the passion for and not the possession of knowledge. It is also to mistake the purpose of writing dramatic dialogues in which Socrates, whether present or absent, is the model philosopher, for the character Socrates constitutes a challenge to the notion that one becomes virtuous by engaging in the traditional forms of public discourse not only in what he says, but also in what he is.

Not an aristocrat, Socrates was renowned, we are repeatedly told, for being short, squat, and bald—a physically ugly man with a snub nose and protruding lips. His very existence is a repudiation of the notion that *sophia* is exemplified by those who are noble and beautiful and good *(kaloi kagathoi),* and that one will become a virtuous man through one's encounters—civic, athletic, and sensual—with these citizens. His existence is thus also a challenge to traditional institutions such as *sunousia,* the *gymnasium,* and the *symposium,* all of which used emotional and erotic associations to reinforce the bond among citizens and their love of Athens, and to the claim that it is through such institutions that one becomes a *philosophos.*[40]

Zanker has commented on the philosophical significance of Socrates' appearance. Echoing Alcibiades' speech in the *Symposium* in which Socrates is compared to a Silenus, which when you open it, contains a divine image, Zanker suggests that Silenus statues of Socrates be seen as an exemplar of the precept that "true philosophy recognizes the 'seemingness' of the external and leads instead to the perception of actual being," and thus "the portrait of Socrates becomes a kind of extension of Socratic discourse [or, we might say, of Platonic dialogue] into another medium."[41]

But those who participate in Socratic discourse may not become "true philosophers" as is clear from Socrates' encounters with Alcibiades—the full implications of which were, of course, known to Plato's fourth-century audience. In the *Symposium,* Alcibiades says that Socrates' effect upon those who converse with him is like that of Marsyas, but Socrates "can get just the same effect without any instrument at all—with nothing but a few simple words, not even poetry. . . ." (215c–d). Alcibiades reports that those with whom Socrates talks are "absolutely staggered and bewitched" (215d), that Pericles and the other orators never affected Alcibiades as Socrates has, that they never turned his "whole soul upside down" and left him feeling as if he were "the lowest of the low" (215e). Alcibiades also tells us that despite what Socrates says, he cares not at all about good looks, money, or any of the honors that most people care

---

40. For a discussion of how Socrates' criticisms are hostile to the traditional institution of *sunousia,* see Kevin Robb, "*Asebeia* and *Sunousia,*" in *Plato's Dialogues,* ed. Press (Lanham, MD: Rowman & Littlefield, 1993), 77–106. For a discussion of the importance of the citizens' naked bodies, their emotional/erotic bonds, public discourse and the architecture of Periclean Athens, see Richard Sennett, *Flesh and Stone: The Body and the City in Western Civilization* (New York: W.W. Norton & Company, 1994).

41. Zanker, *The Mask of Socrates,* 39.

about (216e). Of Socrates' arguments Alcibiades says they are "the only arguments in the world that have any sense to them and that nobody else's are so
godlike, so rich in images or virtue, or so peculiarly, so entirely pertinent to
those inquiries that help the seeker on his way to the goal of true nobility"
(222a). Alcibiades also tells us that his offer to exchange his "beauty" for Socrates' "beauty" was rebuffed by Socrates as an offer of bronze for gold, echoing,
Nightingale notes, the exchange of armor between Glaucus and Diomedes in
the *Iliad*: "No amount of Alcibiades' physical beauty will add up to the 'true'
beauty of Socrates" (47).

Socrates' rejection of Alcibiades offer also provides us with the Socratic response to Pausanias' views about the exchange of sex and *logoi*—which he cites
as a difference between cultured and "philosophical" Athenians and other more
boorish peoples—and to the traditional concept of *sunousia* from which this
claim proceeds. Socrates refuses Alcibiades who, like Pausanias, invokes the
practice of the *erastes* "instructing" the *erōmenos* about virtue, in exchange for
erotic pleasure.[42] For Socrates, *sophia* is different in kind from honors, power,
property, fame, and sexual pleasure, and consequently cannot be part of any
system in which knowledge is exchanged for such things. For Plato, *philosophia*
is not related to the way of life in the *polis* as it had been traditionally conceived. This is the point, Nightingale argues, on which Plato contests Isocrates'
conception of philosophy. For Isocrates, philosophy is intellectual property that
can and should be measured in monetary terms and in symbolic terms.[43] Plato's
Socrates, in contrast, rejects the notion that the value of philosophy can or
should be measured in terms of honors, power, property, fame, or sexual pleasure, and consistently refuses to be part of a system in which knowledge is exchanged for such things.

Socrates, however, claims to be an expert about love; indeed, Socrates' only
claim to expertise is made about matters of love. Through philosophy one is
transformed into desiring what is good and fine and noble; one who loves such
things might become good and fine and noble by virtue of pursuing this desire.
But though transfixed by talking with Socrates, Alcibiades is not transformed,
as his disgraceful end makes clear. Alcibiades' eloquent tribute to Socrates is
Plato's ironic reminder that there is no guarantee that Socratic discourse—or
Platonic dialogue—will make one good and fine and noble. But if it is not
through Socratic discourse and Platonic dialogue, and not through the traditional institutions of Greek *paideia* that one becomes good and fine and noble,
then how? How should the search for a good and fine and noble life be conducted? Should it take the form that Aristotle adopts in the *Nicomachean
Ethics*? Would Alcibiades have come to a different end had he read Aristotle?

---

42. According to Nightingale, Plato questions whether such a relationship differs from prostitu-
tion, for which a citizen might be punished by *atimia*, an infraction that entailed the loss not merely
of honor but also of one's "entitlement as a citizen to take part in the civic and religious life of
Athens" [David Halperin, *One Hundred Years of Homosexuality and Other Essays on Greek Love*,
(New York: Routledge, 1990), 94]. For the suggestion that this sexual relationship was a modification of the traditional association of *sunousia*—a practice that was more fundamentally "familial,
tribal, and civic, not sexual" see Robb, "*Asebeia* and *Sunousia*."

43. Nightingale, 40.

4

The Philosopher
Conducting Dialectic

Holger Thesleff

The question posed by this chapter may warrant a seemingly naive confrontation of Contras and Pros. It is easy to list points such as the following against
the view that Socrates or any other Platonic character always or even normally
stands for Plato:

CONTRA

1. Plato does not appear as a character in the dialogues.
2. Many or most of the dialogues are prose dramas, and Greek drama does
   not propagate directly the opinions of the author.
3. The views and positions of the different characters, including Socrates,
   are not in themselves consistent enough to constitute a coherent "Platonic
   philosophy."
4. Plato's only (alleged) self-testimony about his views occurs in the Letters,
   which are all (including the *Seventh*) of doubtful authenticity.
5. Disagreement in the Old Academy (including Aristotle's testimony) and in
   Platonism down to Neoplatonism suggests that the written dialogues give
   no true picture of Plato's own thought.
6. Some of the opponents of Socrates (Kallikles, Protagoras, Kritias, Plato's
   brothers and some others) express views that, considering both contents,
   context and style, are likely to be seriously meant by the author; and
   sometimes "Socrates" resorts to eristic argumentation or statements that
   neither the author nor the reader is likely to trust.
7. In the late works with their philosophically interesting (and influential)
   content, the discussion is normally led by somebody other than
   "Socrates," and the themes and views are rather far from what the Platonic Socrates used to present; yet the possibility that Plato's philosophy
   underwent fundamental changes has been seriously doubted.

Of course, it is also easy to list points in favor of the view that Socrates (or in some 'late' dialogues, another character) as a rule represents Plato's own position:

PRO

1. Plato was considered a teacher with specific views of his own at least the foundation of the Academy.
2. Aristotle owes much, implicitly and even explicitly, to what "Socrates" says in the dialogues; and he polemicizes against this Socrates as "Plato."
3. In the *Politics,* Aristotle quotes both Socrates of the *Republic* and the Athenian of the *Laws,* as "Plato."
4. The evidence we have of a 'Proto-*Republic*' suggests that the utopian "communistic" State was from the beginning thought to be Plato's, not Socrates', idea.[1]
5. There is some evidence of banter in the Academy about Plato being a "Younger Socrates."[2]
6. Plato's dialogues are not in themselves open conversations between equals: there is always one person (Socrates or his stand-in, i.e., a philosopher) who in the long run leads or manipulates the argument, the partners being brought to follow (and/or being silenced).
7. A (partial) identification of Plato with "Socrates" is understandable from biographical facts: Plato owed his method, perhaps his attitudes and many challenging questions to this Master of his youth; and there may have been psychological reasons for his preferring anonymity.[3]
8. The *Seventh Letter* is likely to give correct information, though somewhat biased by apology; and here does a rather distinct picture of Plato's philosophy take shape, conforming to the *Republic*.[4]
9. Plato's art owes more to comedy than to tragedy (though parallels with tragedy are not lacking either); and in Old Comedy, rather than in tragedy, the author habitually expressed or intimated his own views, especially via the 'parabasis'.[5]

I.

It is not so easy, however, to solve the dilemma if it is put in the above terms. Who or what is Plato's 'mouthpiece'?

---

1. Argued for by Thesleff 1982:101 ff., 1989:11 ff., 1997; Nails 1995:116 ff.
2. See n.16.
3. Cf. Thesleff 1982:22; Szlezák 1985:2 ff. and passim. Note also the probable fiasco of the "Proto-*Republic*," and of the lecture "On the Good" as interpreted by Gaiser 1980.
4. Plato's political philosophy is well motivated in the Letter, and the contents of the "digression" (342a–344d) can be interpreted as in line with the "later" dialogues, if the cryptic formulations are taken to be deliberately provocative as in "On the Good." I am not on this point convinced by Tarrant 1993:131 ff. who argues for a Thrasyllean interpolation.
5. For Comedy as a background source, see Brock 1990; Arieti 1991 (who also adduces Tragedy); Nightingale 1995:172 ff. On the whole, the emotionalism of tragedy was less congenial to Plato than the satire of comedy. As for the "parabasis"-like central sections of some dialogues, cf. Thesleff 1993.

Surely we can all, historicists and modernists alike,[6] agree that Plato's 'mouthpiece', in a general sense, is each dialogue as a whole—irreducibly, insofar as it is authentic or at least semiauthentic.[7]

It is true that the dialogues are (largely) pieces of dramatic art. Yet they do, also and indeed predominantly, present explicit philosophic reasoning. This reasoning is, and clearly is meant to be, open to intellectual understanding (analysis, interpretation). Thus methods of modern literary criticism or drama theory, though perhaps helpful, are insufficient for defining and determining the "message" of the dialogue.[8] Nor can the rules of Greek drama be applied here: the Socratic dialogue, as developed by Plato, is a unique genre.[9]

So, although a "holistic" interpretation of each dialogue and its various explicit and implicit strands is an ultimate desideratum, it is reasonable, for a start, to reduce the mouthpiece question to the level of dialogic characters and ask whether somebody in a given dialogue does, rather more than anybody else, "speak for Plato."[10]

The answer automatically given in all ages is of course: "Yes, Socrates, and in some specific cases his stand-in." At first sight there would appear to be an overwhelming evidence in support of this view: the "Pro" list above may seem to contain much of the evidence, even if not all points are accepted.

Point "Pro 6" has, however, a series of seldom-noted implications to which I want to draw special attention. A separation of the so-called 'late' dialogues from the rest is clearly warranted considering both contents and form; and it is reasonable, disregarding the chronological problems, to interpret *Parmenides* and *Theaetetus* (which together with *Parmenides* foreshadows the *Sophist-Politicus* complex) as pointing towards the late group.

In all the rest of the dialogues in the Corpus, disregarding chronology and authenticity, it is Socrates who totally dominates the discussion (as indeed he does in *Theaetetus* and *Philebus* too).[11] By "domination" I mean several things.

---

6. I have sometimes tried to make a rough distinction between "modernist" and "historicist" approaches to Plato. A modernist tends to interpret the dialogues out of his (or his "school's") own predilections and presuppositions, and with special regard to what seems interesting from today's perspective. Analytical philosophers are often modernists. The historicist considers it not only possible but necessary to try to reconstruct something of the original context and aims of the dialogues; and he/she finds it meaningful to make out how Plato proceeded and what he really "meant," primarily disregarding its eventual interest to present-day philosophy, literary theory, communication theory, etc. In Germany, notably, there is still a tradition of attempting to combine the approaches (with strong "school" adherence, however). Philologists like myself tend to be historicists of no particular "school" attachment. On these distinctions, see also Press 1996:507.

7. This general point has been made, apart from Nails (n.1.), especially by nonanalytic Continental interpreters (even before Wilamowitz and Friedländer), and, from other perspectives, by, e.g., Elinor West 1995, Kahn 1996, and Ostenfeld (chapter 14 of this book).

8. The latest large-scale contributions to this issue are, to my knowledge, Arieti 1991, Farness 1991, Nightingale 1995, and Rutherford 1995. Tejera's (esp. 1984) proximity to modern communication theories, notably semiotics, is interesting.

9. Cf. "Pro 9," p. 54. For the uniqueness of the genre, cf. Thesleff 1982:56 ff., Clay 1994 (and the other contributions to Vander Waerdt (ed.) 1994).

10. See especially Press (ed.) 1993.

11. Cf. n. 27. The separation of the "late group" is now generally accepted as a fact beyond any reasonable doubt. The perhaps implicit presence of Socrates in *Demodocus* is a specific problem.

In the dialogues here in question, Socrates not only is the central person on whom the reader's interest is focused in the long run, no matter how powerful his "opponent" appears to be, Socrates also leads the discussion, even manipulating it at times.[12] We shall have to return to this later. But above all, Plato's Socrates is the only "real" philosopher present in these discussions.

'Real' or 'true' philosophy is brought forward by Plato's Socrates in various contexts, especially in the *Republic* and *Phaedo*. No doubt Plato wants his Socrates to stand for true philosophy.[13] It is interesting, indeed highly significant, that in all dialogues except for the late group no other character can be regarded as a true philosopher in Plato's sense. They are, presumably, characters with whom Plato's original audiences could identify themselves, or whom they knew as identifiable types from their own milieu. With the exception of the slave-boy in *Meno,* who is adduced for the sake of experiment, none of them is an uneducated "anybody." This social and mental standard of the audience of Plato's Socrates is worth keeping in mind. Simmias and Kebes may look like candidates for true philosophers, but on closer inspection even they are hardly more than mere promises, like several of the young men in Socrates' environment.[14] Some of the latter are known to have later abandoned philosophy (Alcibiades, Charmides, Meno, to take the most obvious cases). Plato does have a manifest respect for some of Socrates' discussion partners, as the characterization of their persons and style suggests, notably for Kallikles, Protagoras, his own brothers, and probably for Kritias and Thrasymachus too. And for instance the colorful garland of speeches in the *Symposium,* like the objections of Simmias and Kebes in *Phaedo,* contribute very positively to the treatment of the central theme. But none of these persons is a "true philosopher." The case of Diotima is more complicated: she is a priestess and "sophist," a curiously ennobled variant of Aspasia; but she speaks through Socrates in a manner very different from, say, a Protagoras or a Thrasymachus.

The *Theaetetus,* however, introduces one exceptionally promising case of a potential 'true' philosopher, namely young Theaitetos. His teacher Theodoros does not reach the same standard.[15] It is amusing to note that Theaitetos re-

---

12. In spite of his own disavowals and protests. Cf., e.g., Sprague 1962, Szlezák (esp. 1988, 1991, not really refuted by Brisson 1995:121), Ausland 1997:382 ff. Ancient sources including Aristotle (p. 54, "Pro 2") commonly identify Socrates' reasoning with Plato's; see especially DL III 52 (cf. Dörrie 1987, "Baustein 10"). For "Socrates the Younger," see n. 16.

13. For "true philosophy," see notably *Republic* V 473d (cf. X 619d, *Seventh Letter* 326a), *Phaedo* 63e, 67de, 69d, etc.; cf. *Phaedrus* 249a and des Places 1964 s.vv. Explicitly and by implication, Socrates the Philosopher represents the five cardinal virtues "already" in the *Apology* (esp. 28b–35d); cf. also *Symposium* and *Phaedo*. In *Gorgias* (521d, not markedly ironic) he appears as the only true politician.

14. In particular their circumspect doubts make them "promising"; cf. Plato's brothers in *Republic* II.

15. Theodoros is intellectually lazy and inclines towards Protagoras' "phaenomenology "; cf. Thesleff 1990:153, 159. It is interesting that both Hermogenes and Kratylos, with whom Plato is said to have also "studied" (DL III 6), appear in the *Cratylus* as similarly unable to produce very constructive arguments. But the Megarian Eukleides of the frame dialogue of *Theaetetus* was probably a philosopher to Plato's liking (cf. notably DL II 106 f.).

sembles Socrates even physically; and it can be argued that the "Younger Socrates" who now turns up in his company stands for Plato.[16] Although Theaitetos probably died young and never was a member of Plato's Academy,[17] it is clear that the *Theaetetus* (somewhat like *Phaedo*, in fact) prefigures the 'late' dialogues also in the sense that all of the central characters at least are what we would call "philosophical minds." But Socrates stands out in his uniqueness.

The general inference to be drawn from this is the not very surprising one that Plato identified himself with much of what he makes Socrates say or do or "represent." This is what made him a "Younger Socrates." But then, in the 'late' dialogues, Socrates withdraws. I have suggested before, and I now consider it even more probable, that Socrates' withdrawal is a sign of Plato's allowing his friends in the Academy to produce in written form their own contributions to, comments on, and criticism of his philosophy.[18] If this is the case, the reappearance of Socrates as the dialogue leader in *Philebus* indicates that we are here particularly close to old Plato's personal convictions.

Obviously, however, Plato does not totally identify himself with Socrates. In many dialogues, and of course in the *Apology,* there are clear biographic traits that cannot apply to Plato. Thus some of the arguments and positions presented in the dialogues by Socrates can, theoretically, be expected to belong to the historical Socrates, but not to Plato. Such cases would be interesting if sources that are certainly independent of Plato prove them to be genuinely Socratic positions, and if at the same time there are signs of Plato not being in sympathy with them. I wonder whether there exist such cases. I can see several reasons why Plato sometimes chose to take the mask of Socrates the "Aristophanic sophist," leaving the possible disapproval to his readers; and the only explicit disapproval of Socrates that remains unanswered in the dialogue, the *Clitopho,* is likely to apply to Plato as well. The whole complex of the very old and very vexed problems of Plato's relations to the historical Socrates, has received new dimensions in recent years as we have begun with the help of new approaches to free ourselves from the traditional developmentalist ballast and from theories of Plato's "Socratic period."[19] At any rate there is ever more backing for the claim that the views and methods of Plato's Socrates are also Plato's own, whatever changes they might have undergone. But what about the other characters?

---

16. See *Theaetetus* 144d–147d. "Socrates the Younger" (who is first mentioned at 147d and reappears in the *Sophist* and notably in the *Politicus*) is likely to represent a "variant" of Plato (as does the "Young Socrates" of *Parmenides*, and as does, perhaps, the reference to "Socrates the Younger" in Aristotle, *Metaphysics* VII 11.1036b25). Later traditions erroneously made him an independent historical person. See Jatakari 1990.

17. Thesleff 1990.

18. Thesleff 1989:7 ff., 23 f.; Nails 1995:126 f.

19. See especially Nails 1995. For the notorious problems of the historical Socrates, see also Montuori 1992 (and elsewhere), Brickhouse & Smith 1994 (with references), Vander Waerdt (ed.) 1994, Rutherford 1995:39–63, Kahn 1996:1–35.

II.

It is time to construct a new overall theory to explain as many as possible of the anomalies and of Plato's Socratic pushes and moves. I would propose the following general frame, taking as a start Gerald Press's hypothetically antidogmatist position[20] and Debra Nails's hypothesis of Plato's 'doubly open-ended' conduct of philosophy in the Academy.[21]

Socrates became early Plato's ideal as a philosopher.[22] His methods, and his (probably) central problem "How to live?" always haunted Plato. Since *philosophia*, as Plato wanted to understand it (to judge from, notably, *Phaedo, Symposium* and the *Republic*), implies an orientation towards supposedly stable truths but at the same time a conviction that no human being can possess full knowledge of such truths, a philosophic discourse at its best is a dialogue between a 'real' philosopher (who is aware of these conditions) and more "ordinary" people (yet preferably intelligent and educated individuals who represent commonly accepted or influential views).

Plato calls this process 'dialectic'.[23] But contrary to Zenonian (or Protagorean or *Dissoi Logoi*) eristics, and to the more common later use of the term (propagated by Aristotle), Platonic dialectic is not a series of antilogies proceeding via thesis and antithesis. It is a dialogic argument conducted by a philosopher, either destructively (elenctically) or constructively, either synthetically ('synoptically') or analytically ('diacritically', 'dihaeretically'), an argument where the partner's task is to provide commonsense objections, comments, or (especially in the 'late' dialogues) mere consent.

Thus, although in Platonic dialectic the leader "knows more" than the partner, he lacks full knowledge (and makes a point of this lack); and the partner, on the other hand, may provide quite important contributions: think again of Kallikles, Protagoras, or Glaukon and Adeimantos. Sometimes we encounter here very difficult problems of allusive play and irony. Most of them can probably never be satisfactorily solved, but on the whole it can be stated that Plato's play and irony is always somewhat ambivalent, even ambiguous,[24] and that his logic is often of an associative kind that is difficult to fit into Aristotelian patterns. There is normally "something in" what even apparently foolish or conceited partners say, and there is some backing in whatever shortcomings, eccentric thought-play, or limping logic Socrates may produce. Plato's Socrates is

---

20. Cf. Press (ed.) 1993, 1996, and elsewhere.
21. Nails 1995.
22. Cf. above, p. 54, "Pro 7–8."
23. In the enormous literature on Plato's notion of dialectic (Goldschmidt 1971 is still important), I have not seen much notice taken of the simple fact that in Platonic writings *dialegesthai* and its derivatives (and *elenkhos*) mean, basically, a dialogue led by a philosopher in cooperation with an intelligent (but rather more passive) partner; cf. *Meno* 75d, *Euthydemus* 290c, *Phaedrus* 266c, 276e, *Cratylus* 390d, and especially *Republic* VII 533c ff. Recently Gill 1996 (esp. 280 ff.) has made some good points about Plato's "collaborative" dialectic.
24. A much-debated issue, cf. Press 1996: 510, 512, 516 and (e.g.) Rowe 1989. It seems to me that Tejera's (1984 and elsewhere) laudable awareness of humor tends to overstress the satirical aspect at the expense of the implicit ambivalence. But an assessment of this is largely subjective.

never a real "authority"—this often-forgotten fact ought to make Plato more sympathetic to many of his bewildered or irritated readers. It is important, however, to realize that none of Socrates' 'antagonists' has won over him when the dialogue is ended (the situation is not that of sophistic antilogies; Clitopho may be an exception); and if powerful protests to Socrates' argument or position recur (as in the case of Kallikles and Thrasymachus), they are refuted by this same Socrates.[25]

We are gradually approaching the crucial question of Plato's personal commitment to what he makes his characters say.

To understand a Platonic dialogue as a 'two-level' process, as well as a 'doubly open-ended' one, makes sense to me. There is always some sort of interaction between the levels, though the philosopher's level is on the whole the dominant one, the more active one, and the productive one. This was presumably the impression Plato had of Socratic *elenchoi*. Socrates' avowal of ignorance was ambivalently ironic, and his partner's common-sense position was useful in many respects. The refutations were not merely destructive, in spite of a first feeling of "narcosis." The questioning led by Socrates always "led somewhere," though never to definite positions. We may pretty safely accept that Plato felt himself to be a new Socrates, continuing the search that his Master had begun.[26] If so, his personal anonymity is as easily explicable as are the two levels and the openness of his dialogue technique. No mysticism is needed to explain this.

But Plato's philosophy is not just method. Can we ever reach Plato's own beliefs and convictions (or the tenets to which the indirect traditions refer) within this doubly or triply open pattern of dialogue moves where no point, not even chronology, is a priori certain?[27] To be able to deal with these vexed problems in a somewhat new manner, I would expand the above theory with a theory of Plato's 'two-level vision' the details of which have to be discussed elsewhere.[28]

It can be reasonably argued that Plato had formed for himself, at an early date and from all Presocratic and Socratic traditions known to him, an ontological view of the world that can be termed a 'two-level model'. This was not a pointedly dualistic model. It can be reduced to pairs of asymmetric contrasts, such as 'divine/human', 'soul/body', 'light/shadow', 'unity/plurality', 'knowledge/opinion',[29] where the first ('upper') member is felt to be more prominent, lead-

---

25. In fact, extensively in Books II–X of the *Republic*. The situation is slightly different with the silent Socrates of the "late" dialogues beginning with the *Parmenides*. For Szlezák's concept of "Aussparung," see n. 38.

26. Cf. *Apology* 39d. I am now more definitely convinced than I was in 1982 (22 f., also 1989: 4) that Plato soon after Socrates' death felt himself as the latter's only true follower. Cf. also n. 16.

27. Nails 1995 and Press 1996 have rightly seen that my chronological studies of 1982 (cf. 1989) were meant to be primarily critical, not constructive (in spite of a very tentative new model that I suggested). Among recent refutations of the traditional tenets about Platonic chronology, note especially Howland 1991.

28. Cf. Thesleff 1993 and my *Studies in Plato's Two-Level Model* (Helsinki: Scientiarum Fennica, 1999).

29. This could be schematically illustrated for instance as follows:

one	same	stable	divine	soul	leading	intellect	truth	knowledge	defined
many	different	changing	human	body	being-led	senses	appearance	opinion	undefined

ing, and in all senses primary, but the second ('lower') is also a necessary pre-requisite for the world as we have it. If the upper level is 'good', the lower is not simply 'bad', but 'less good'; and the lower may be said to be 'oriented' towards the upper level. The not-very-early simile of the Divided Line in the center of the monumental *Republic* illustrates rather well some aspects of Plato's two-level model (here subdivided into four levels), but all dialogues are more or less clearly based on the model.[30]

It has to be emphasized once for all that this 'two-level model' certainly was no more than an intuitive vision, a way of looking at the world, a frame for thought and thought-experiment. It invited one to speculation, reflection, crit-icism, analogical reasoning, and construction of more or less consistent theo-ries. No fixed doctrines would automatically emerge from it.

Plato's true philosopher seems to operate 'above' the ordinary human level, with a better orientation towards the upper level than other humans have. The simile of the Cave illustrates this beyond further comments. So does the *Phaedo*.[31] But even the Philosopher is not a god; at most, he has the powers of an intermediate being, a daimon (cf. *Symposium* 202d ff., 215a ff.). By means of his dialectic he is able to clarify and explicate details of the interrelations of the ontological levels to sufficiently gifted and trained individuals, and so help humanity to a better life. I find it important to note that the dialectic that is con-ducted by the Philosopher always, in each Platonic dialogue, moves between the two levels, often with glimpses of more stable truths in the center rather than on the periphery.[32]

The complicated changes of the dialectic patterns within and between the different dialogues, ought to be analyzed and studied much more systematically than has been done so far. It might be possible to detect constants or trends not seen before. For my part, I believe the 'upper-level' orientation of the dia-logue's Philosopher will turn out to be one useful clue among many others, in spite of all the variations found.

We can see in many dialogues how similar thought patterns take shape within the two-level model and combine in different ways. Take, for instance, the con-frontation of the Philosopher with orators (*Gorgias, Phaedrus, Menexenus*), with sophists (*Protagoras, Euthydemus, Hippias Minor, Hippias Major*), with poets and other influential people (*Symposium, Charmides, Meno, Euthyphro, Ion, Laches,* etc.). In spite of all his shortcomings, the Philosopher is always

---

30. *Republic* VI 509d–511e. The central place of the simile within the "pedimentality" of this work (that is likely to have received its final shape rather late, and primarily for an Academic audi-ence; cf. Thesleff 1993:27 ff.) is highly significant. New openings to the much-discussed problems of the interpretation and symbolism of the Line have recently been made by N. D. Smith 1996 and Nails (in an unpublished paper read at a Society for Ancient Greek Philosophy meeting, 1996). I would draw particular attention to the fact that the geometric proportion suggests a complex in-volvement of the "more important" with the "less important." There is no *khorismos* (a problem to the Eleatics, cf. *Parmenides* 130b, rather than to Plato).

31. The Cave, *Republic* VII 514a ff. As for the *Phaedo*, I would again point out the pedimental structure emphasizing Socrates' significant aporias and silence at the centre (84b ff., 95e, cf. 88c ff.); Thesleff 1993:25 f.

32. See in general Thesleff 1993.

better equipped than others for finding a way to human excellence. He sees something of stable truth; he sees it even when hiding behind a smile or a grimace (as in *Menexenus* or *Protagoras* or *Hippias Minor*). The Philosopher sees the true implications of *arete*. From the surrounding appearances, the Philosopher is rising toward truth (however unreachable this may be), even by 'extrapolating' (cf. *Republic* VI 509b ff.). For instance, the Philosopher seeks what is always the 'same' behind different appearances;[33] this is one of the beginnings of the theory of Forms.[34]

I see no reason to deny that Plato, through the mouth of Socrates, presents different varieties of the theory of Forms, or that he makes Socrates present the Philosopher's positive uniqueness among human beings, or the pre-eminence of his dialectic method for the search of truth beyond appearances. He makes his Philosopher advance several other views looking like 'doctrines'. It seems that the 'doctrine' of the Philosopher's State was an early thought experiment within the two-level model that remained a utopian, pointedly theoretical ideal to Plato throughout his life.[35] A reasonable criterion for a Platonic 'doctrine' is to be repeatedly, in different reasoning contexts, brought forward by Plato's Philosopher. But a Platonic doctrine need not be more than a theory or a thought experiment.

The relative importance to Plato of a certain 'doctrine', and the degree of his personal commitment to it, can probably be to some extent inferred from the tone and context of what is said. A reported dialogue or story usually reveals more nuances to judge by than purely dramatic contexts: it is easier to extract Plato's view of *to kalon* from the *Symposium* than from *Hippias Major*. The idea of retribution after death occurs, however repeatedly, only in myths, which suggests that it is no real 'theory' but a poetic vision. On the other hand, for instance, the tripartite soul with its two main levels (*Republic* IV 434c ff., *Timaeus* 69b ff., cf. *Phaedrus* 246a ff.) and the power of sublimated love (*Symposium* 201e ff., cf. *Phaedrus* 249d ff., *Alcibiades* I, *Theages*) also occur in pieces of *logos*.

An interesting example of a later Platonic doctrine is what can be called General (Two-Level) Categories: namely 'Being', 'Sameness/Otherness', 'Rest/Movement', and 'One/Many' (Number). They occur explicitly as basic constituents of all that is in *Parmenides* (especially 129c ff.), *Timaeus* (especially 34c ff.) and the *Sophist* (254c ff., here called *megista gene*; cf. *Laws* X 893b ff.). Their connection with the two-level model can hardly be doubted. Although they extend over the entire universe (cf. *Sophist* 255e, etc.), there is surely

---

33. Cf., e.g., *Meno* 75ab (and 72a ff., 75e), *Laches* 191e ff., *Amatores* 138b, *Lysis* 222bc, also *Apology* 26a ff., and (with some ironical play) *Gorgias* 482a ff. (cf. 473a, *Symposium* 221e).

34. Note the fact that Greek *to auto* and *auto to* easily associate. The higher status of value Forms (apparently taken as a group) in relation to other *eide* seems to become illustrated by the two "upper" segments of the Divided Line. But the entire theory may be just an elaboration of some aspects of Plato's ever-present "higher level" (in relation to the "lower"). Most modern attempts to distinguish stages of development in the theory of Forms (before the "late period") are biased by traditional developmentalist hypotheses. The importance of the theory for Plato himself has probably been overstressed (due to Aristotle's criticism of it).

35. Cf., n. 1.

more of True Being, Sameness, Rest, and Unity on Plato's upper level, and more of apparent being, otherness, movement, and plurality on the lower level. In spite of the looseness of Platonic terminology here as elsewhere (and the fact that the Form of 'likeness' is taken as the starting point for the presentation at *Parmenides* 129a; cf. *Phaedo* 74c), it seems rather clear to me that these Classes, qua Categories, have little to do with the metaphysical Value Forms that culminate in *to agathon*.[36] The remarkable thing is that they are systematized in *Timaeus* and *Sophist* (and the *Laws*) by philosophers other than Socrates; in the Eleatic context of *Parmenides* they are rather unexpectedly and provocatively introduced by "Young Socrates," and in *Theaetetus* something like them is 'extracted' by Socrates from that young philosopher-apprentice, Theaitetos (185c–186d). It is also interesting that in the *Philebus*, the Platonic "Socrates" at first vaguely and somewhat disparately operates with Forms and Categories (12c–16a), but then (16c) introduces the Pythagorean contrast *peras/apeiria (apeiron)* that later takes the function of two-level Categories (cf. 23b, etc.). Perhaps we may infer that the doctrine of General Categories, though originally an idea of Plato's, was developed by his friends and then accepted by Plato as an elaboration of his two-level vision.

To anticipate what will be argued elsewhere,[37] Plato's controversial "unwritten tenets" concerning the First Principles, *Hen* and *Ahoristos Duas* (with its infinitely varying Great-and-Small), and the even more vexed traditions about 'ideal numbers' are more easily explained as a pythagorizing extension of the theory of two-level Categories than, directly, as a variant of the theory of Forms. These issues concern us here mainly as examples of allegedly esoteric Platonic doctrines not reaching explicit written communication. What seemed particularly problematic here, to Plato and to his critics, was the interrelation of Plato's two levels and the interconnections of Forms and phenomena (intimated by the symbolism of the Divided Line): the theories of two-level Categories and Principles gave useful help. Oral debates about these and other problems obviously continued in the Academy after Plato's death. It is probably a hopeless task for us to distinguish exactly Plato's position from his friends' in the case of Categories and Principles: here it can be said that the Academic debate as such represented Plato's voice. I cannot see, however, that anything of this was really

---

36. There is a considerable literature on the *megista gene* (some references in Fine 1993). Most interpreters take them to be, simply, Forms; but there are notable exceptions, beginning with Peck 1952 (see also McCabe 1994, esp. 224 ff.). I can agree with the Tübingenite classing of the *megista gene* close to the First Principles (see notably Krämer 1959: 430 ff.) but I would keep them apart from Value Forms (cf. below). What is sometimes called "Platonic Categories" (i.e. "substance," "relation," and "opposition," e.g., Krämer 1959: 282 ff.) seems to be rather a specific development of the contrast "sameness/otherness."

37. See n. 28. Today's "Tübingen" position is presented by Szlezák 1991 (German version 1993); cf. the contributions to the 1993 volume of *Méthexis* (see Szlezák) and the criticism, in various connections, by Isnardi Parente, Brisson, and several Anglo-Saxon scholars such as Sayre (cf. Miller 1995). The fullest collection of the ancient evidence is Gaiser 1988. Krämer's *mega biblion* of 1959 is a cornerstone to be studied carefully and critically. Much of it will stand firm in spite of some necessary modifications. It is unavoidable, for instance, to try to understand "esoterism" differently (see below) and to distinguish the rather late theories of Categories and First Principles from the theory of Forms.

"secret." For the aging Plato himself, 'esoterism' hardly implied very much more than a "reluctance" arising from the difficulty of communicating 'true philosophy' and pythagorizing dogmata to larger audiences (a difficulty that the lecture "On the Good" is said to have proved).[38]

III.

Considering the all-importance to Plato of philosopher-conducted dialectic, it seems quite natural that he wrote dialogues with Socrates as the protagonist and hero. By choosing personal anonymity, he was free to let his idealized Dialogue Leader make very different pushes and moves, even act as a "quasi-authority" at times. And he may well have accepted later the substitution of his Socrates with other types of philosophers popular in the Academy, with whom he was largely in agreement.[39]

But for whom were the dialogues written? This question, often overlooked, is certainly relevant to interpretation.

There is much to suggest, and nothing to contradict, that Early Academic philosophy in the guidance of Plato covered much more than what became explicitly written down in the dialogues and other documents that have come down to us. Few deny this, though there is little agreement on what was not published or not preserved, what to read between the lines of preserved texts, and whether such reading is methodically allowable.

I find it worth noting that, with the probable exception of the *Apology*,[40] the dialogues can hardly have been written for a totally anonymous general public—as epic, drama, and oratory (and probably historiography) were normally produced in classical Athens. Narrated ("reported") dialogues may have been originally intended for a somewhat wider circulation than the directly dramatic type.[41] All dialogues, however, had a specific, rather sophisticated, philosophically interested audience in view. They are not prima facie understandable, or even enjoyable (like Greek drama), to a general public. Though parts of most dialogues could be amusing or suggestive to unphilosophical minds, the dialogues as a whole were surely not written for "anybody." The general public could not possibly appreciate most of their niceties and allusions and, more significantly, would have become ever more convinced that Socratic philosophy as presented by Plato is a silly and useless business.[42] Plato is likely to have

---

38. Cf. Gaiser 1980 and the "provocative" philosophical digression in the *Seventh Letter* (342a ff.). A similar reluctance to enter on complex problems is sometimes manifest in the dialogues ("Aussparungsstellen," Szlezák 1990, 1996).

39. Here I on the whole disagree with Tejera (1984 and elsewhere) who prefers to see pointedly un-Platonic features in the Elean Guest, Timaios, and the rest.

40. And obvious forgeries such as *Axiochus* and *Alcyon*.

41. Argued in detail by Thesleff 1982:53 ff. But cases such as *Theaetetus* and the *Republic* suggest a change to a more esoteric audience.

42. Argued by Thesleff 1993:37 ff. Is, say, Kallikles convinced by Socrates' protreptic, even if the Corinthian farmer of the well-known story (Themistios 23.296bc, probably from Aristotle) happened to be so? The "On the Good" issue (see n.38) illustrates the fact that it was not Plato's habit to give public lectures.

written for his friends and for their friends (and for different groups of such people), and to have taken for granted that there were well-informed persons present at the reading performances to provide explication, comments, and perhaps a continuation of the discussion. The 'late' dialogues seem to have been primarily written for internal Academic use (though the final posthumous *Laws* must again have had a wider audience in view). This assumption about the intended readership would on the whole explain the general character of the dialogues, the fact that so much is left unsaid or implicit in them, and also the fact that many of the short ones are not so 'primitive' on closer inspection, but rather focus the elenchus method on some narrow problem of a certain philosophic significance.[43]

Even if the 'semiauthentic' and also the 'late' dialogues represent various sliding scales of proximity to Plato, they all illustrate the pushes and moves towards truth by philosopher-conducted dialectic.[44] But even the Philosopher is not fully 'informed': it is in cooperation with his partners and friends that progress is made. This cooperation is particularly evident in the late group of dialogues, and indeed with the *agrapha*.

IV.

To sum up, then. The answer that the above sketch seems to give to the question of "Who Speaks for Plato?" is: the Philosopher of the authentic and semiauthentic dialogues (and, I believe, Plato of the *Seventh Letter*). That is, in principle, Plato's Socrates or (with a somewhat varying degree of commitment on Plato's part) his stand-in. The Philosopher's discussion partners do not speak for Plato (unless they are philosophers themselves),[45] but their views, their protests, and their comments are a necessary part of the progress of the argument. Plato was convinced that there exists a higher level of truth and reality to which only the Philosopher may have some access, but the openness of the dialogues[46] precludes the presentation of any fixed dogmas. It is doubtful, I think, whether Plato had any dogmas apart from his general, loosely intuitive 'two-

---

43. Whether authentic or "semiauthentic," at least the following can be regarded as written for training elenchus about a specific topic: *Hippias Minor, Alcibiades* I, *Hipparchus, Ion, Amatores, Theages, De Justo, De Virtute, Minos* (and *Demodocus*). A special case is the much-discussed *Crito*: what if the covert theme is *peithein* (note the possibly ironic reference to corybantic music at the end)?

44. Almost all of the dialogues in the Corpus were probably written in Plato's lifetime or very soon after his death (Thesleff 1989:8 with references), and only *Eryxias* and *Axiochus* (and *Alcyon*) have no obvious bearing on Plato's philosophy. In addition to the *Seventh Letter* (that I consider basically authentic), at least Letters 2–4, 6, 8, and 13 seem to have originated in Plato's close environment.

45. This becomes normal in the late dialogues except for *Philebus*. But Plato is certainly in sympathy with Glaukon, Adeimantos, Simmias, Kebes, and Theaitetos; and perhaps nostalgically with his uncle Charmides (rather than Kritias? note Apatouria in *Timaeus* 21b, and *Seventh Letter* 325a).

46. Even of the *Philebus*, the most systematically composed dialogue in the Corpus, and of the *Seventh Letter*.

level vision'. Particular views and positions that are repeatedly argued for, or intimated by the Philosopher, may be called 'Platonic doctrines' (such are the theory of Forms, the tripartite soul, or the sublimating force of Eros). But it is good to remember that such 'doctrines' cannot be proved to be part of any consistent systematic philosophy, and that most alleged lines of doctrinal development before the late period can be seriously disputed.

WORKS CITED

Arieti, J. A. *Interpreting Plato. The Dialogues as Drama.* Lanham MD, Rowman & Littlefield, 1991.

Ausland, H.W. "On Reading Plato Mimetically." *American Journal of Philology* 118 (1997): 371–416.

Brickhouse, T. C., and N. D. Smith, *Plato's Socrates.* New York: Oxford University Press, 1994.

Brisson, L. "Premises, Consequences, and Legacy of the Esotericist Interpretation of Plato." *Ancient Philosophy* 15 (1995): 117–134.

Brock, R. "Plato and Comedy." In *Owls to Athens, Essays on Classical Subjects presented to K. J. Dover,* ed. E. M. Craik, 39–49. Oxford: Oxford University Press, 1990.

Clay, D. "The Origin of the Socratic Dialogue." In Vander Waerdt, 1994:23–47.

Des Places, É. *Lexique de la langue philosophique et religieuse de Platon. Plato, œuvres complétes,* T.XIV:1–2. Paris: Les Belles Lettres 1964.

Dörrie, H., and M. Baltes, eds. *Der Platonismus in der Antike.* Bd. I. Stuttgart: Fromann-Holzboog, 1987.

Farness, Jay. *Missing Socrates. Problems of Plato's Writing.* University Park, PA: Pennsylvania State University Press, 1991.

Fine, Gail. *On Ideas. Aristotle's Criticism of Plato's Theory of Forms.* New York: Oxford University Press, 1993.

Gaiser, K. "Plato's Enigmatic Lecture 'On the Good'." *Phronesis* 25 (1980): 5–37.

———, ed. *Supplementum Platonicum,* I. Stuttgart: Fromann-Holzboog 1988.

Gill, C. *Personality in Greek Epic, Tragedy, and Philosophy. The Self in Dialogue.* Oxford: Clarendon Press, 1996.

Goldschmidt, V. *Les dialogues de Platon. Structure et méthode dialectique.* 3me éd. Paris: Presses universitaires de France, 1971.

Gonzalez, F. J. (ed.). *The Third Way. New Directions in Platonic Studies.* Lanham, MD: Rowman & Littlefield, 1995.

Howland, J. "Re-reading Plato. The Problem of Platonic Chronology." *Phoenix* 45 (1991): 189–214.

Jatakari, Tuija. "Der jüngere Sokrates." *Arctos* 24 (1990): 29–45.

Kahn, C. H. *Plato and the Socratic Dialogue. The Philosophical Use of a Literary Form.* Cambridge: Cambridge University Press, 1996.

Krämer, H. J. *Arete bei Platon und Aristoteles. Zum Wesen und zur Geschichte der platonischen Ontologie.* Abhandlungen der Heidelberger Akad. d. Wiss., Phil.-hist.Kl. 1959, 6. Heidelberg. Winter 1959.

McCabe, Mary M. *Plato's Individuals.* Princeton: Princeton University Press, 1994.

Miller, M. H. "The Choice between the Dialogues and the 'Unwritten Teachings': a Scylla and Charybdis for the Interpreter?" In Gonzalez (ed.), 225–244. 1995.

Montuori, M. *The Socratic Problem.* Philosophica IV. Amsterdam: J. C. Gieben, 1992.

Nails, Debra. *Agora, Academy, and the Conduct of Philosophy.* Philosophical Studies Series 63. Dordrecht: Kluwer, 1995.

Nightingale, Andrea Wilson. *Genres in Dialogue. Plato and the Construct of Philosophy.* Cambridge: Cambridge University Press, 1995.

Peck, A. L. "Plato and the *megista gene* of the *Sophist.*" *Classical Quarterly* 46 (N.S.2) (1952): 32–56.

Press, G. A. (ed.). *Plato's Dialogues. New Studies and Interpretations.* Lanham, MD: Rowman & Littlefield, 1993.

———. "The State of the Question in the Study of Plato." *The Southern Journal of Philosophy* 34 (1996): 507–532.

Rowe, C. J. "Plato's Use of Irony: A Case Study." In *Sprachaspekte als Experiment,* hrsg.v.T.Viljamaa al., Annales Univ. Turkuensis B 187, Turku 1989, 83–97.

Rutherford, R. B. *The Art of Plato. Ten Essays in Platonic Interpretation.* London: Harvard University Press, 1995.

Smith, N. D. "Plato's Divided Line." *Ancient Philosophy* 16 (1996): 25–45.

Sprague, Rosamond Kent. *Plato's Use of Fallacy. A Study of the Euthydemus and Some Other Dialogues.* London: Hackett, 1962.

Szlezák, T. A. *Platon und die Schriftlichkeit der Philosophie. Interpretationen zu den frühen und mittleren Dialogen.* Berlin: de Gruyler, 1985.

———. "Gespräche unter Ungleichen. Zur Struktur und Zielsätzung der platonischen Dialoge." *Antike und Abendland* 34 (1988): 99–116. Slightly expanded in G. Gabriel & Chr. Schildknecht (eds.), *Literarische Formen der Philosophie.* Metzler, 1990: 40–61.

———. *Come leggere Platone.* Milano: Vita e Pensiero, 1991.

———. "Zur üblichen Abneigung gegen die Agrapha Dogmata." *Méthexis* 6 (1993): 155–174.

———. Review of G. Cerri, *Platone sociologo della communicazione* (Milano, 1991). *Gnomon* 68 (1996): 589–593.

Tarrant, H. *Thrasyllan Platonism.* Ithaca: Cornell University Press, 1993.

Tejera, V. *Plato's Dialogues One by One. A Structural Interpretation.* New York: Irvington, 1984.

Thesleff, H. *Studies in Platonic Chronology.* Commentationes Humanarum Litterarum 70. Helsinki; Societas Scientiarum Fennica, 1982.

———. "Platonic Chronology." *Phronesis* 34 (1989): 1–26.

———. "Theaitetos and Theodoros." *Arctos* 24 (1990): 147–159.

———. "Looking for Clues. An Interpretation of Some Literary Aspects of Plato's 'Two-Level Model'." In Press (ed.) 1993:17–45.

———. "The Early Version of Plato's *Republic.*" *Arctos* 31 (1997): 149–74.

Vander Waerdt, P. A. (ed.). *The Socratic Movement.* Ithaca: Cornell University Press, 1994.

West, Elinor J. M. "Plato's Audiences, or How Plato Replies to the Fifth-Century Intellectual Mistrust of Letters." In Gonzalez.1995:41–60.

5

Where Plato Speaks

Reflections on an Ancient Debate

Harold Tarrant

INTRODUCTION

Many major issues confronting Plato's readers today have arisen before; sometimes there is evidence of early debate, often there are only traces. Sometimes we can learn from it, sometimes it puts our own endeavors in perspective. There are special reasons for going back to see how *antiquity* interpreted Plato: first, Greek was still the normal medium for philosophical discourse, and Greeks and Romans could respond to the text as living (if now somewhat formal) language; second, they had knowledge of the conventions of "Socratic" dialogue out of which Platonic literature grew, for they still possessed early dialogues by other Socratics. Their position was thus privileged, compensating for the comparative infancy of interpretative theory.

Furthermore the earliest interpreters were straightaway confronted with issues so basic that we today can easily forget to address them, leaving us content to work within a tradition that regards such issues as resolved, irrelevant, or too difficult. These basic questions are now attracting attention again: should we approach the dialogues as drama or as philosophy, is there direct teaching within them, and do we read the lines or between the lines? Again, is the corpus a unified whole, which dialogues are best read in sequences, should we distinguish some that offer lessons from others involving polemic or mental exercise, and if so on what criteria? All these issues had arisen by the second century A.D. One such issue is whether certain characters could be relied upon to speak for Plato.

I. ANCIENT SPOKESPERSON-THEORY
IN INTRODUCTIONS TO READING PLATO

If figures within the dialogues speak for Plato, then Plato must have something to say: something to affirm or to deny. He must have views, whether mundane or sophisticated. Those who seriously thought Plato had no message, in ancient times as now, could have little use for the idea of Platonic spokespersons.[1] Thus, in the best-known ancient passage to tackle this issue, discussion of spokespersons arises from consideration of whether Plato communicates doctrine. In Diogenes Laertius's unusually extended treatment of Plato's works (3.48ff.) we soon meet the question of whether Plato 'dogmatized' (3.51).[2] This issue is said to be keenly disputed, a situation that presumably applied at the time of Diogenes' ultimate source.[3]

At 3.52 Plato is said to reveal his position and to refute falsehoods where he has a cognitive grasp, but to suspend judgment on issues that are unclear. Thus a distinction can be made among dialogues where Plato reveals a view, those where he refutes others, and those in which no positive or negative conclusions are reached. Though no such distinction is spelled out at this point, we have recently encountered a classification of dialogues in which such classes are easily detected.[4] Distinctions might similarly be made *within* dialogues, and it is clear from what follows that *Republic* I is thought of as an exercise in refutation just like the *Gorgias*, *Protagoras*, *Euthydemus*, and *Hippias* dialogues: for Thrasymachus is designated as one of the characters employed for purposes of refutation.

To 'reveal one's position' *(apophainesthai)* implies openness, and that suggests that the meaning will not be concealed—it will be directly expressed by some character. It is unsurprising that we are now told Plato reveals "that which seems so to him" through four characters: "Socrates," "Timaeus," and the Athenian and Eleatic Strangers.[5] On the other hand he uses "Thrasymachus," "Gorgias," "Protagoras," "Euthydemus," "Hippias," *and others like them* as victims of his refutations. In effect we have a list of "goodies" and "baddies" in Plato's dialogues, a list that leaves out mainly those characters who are Socrates' close acquaintances.

Consider the list of spokespersons, and the belief that Plato (in some dialogues) requires spokespersons to reveal doctrines. At first glance the Athenian Stranger is an obvious choice, since he is a representative of Athens as opposed

1. Five arguments for the view that Plato was a skeptic are recorded in anon. Prolegomena to Plato's Philosophy 10. In Cicero's *Academica* the position taken by antidogmatists is that Plato has (and expresses) opinions but not dogmata. They speak of what Plato "thought" in relation to the *Timaeus*, what "certain persons believe Plato is saying in the *Timaeus*," what "was pleasing to Plato" in the *Republic*, and what Plato "wanted," 2.118, 123, 124, 142. They do not refer to what Plato said. At 1.46 we are told that in Plato "nothing is affirmed, both sides are debated, everything is investigated, and nothing certain stated." At 2.74 Plato employs "Socrates" because he approves of Socrates' profession of ignorance. "Socrates" is close to, but does not speak for Plato.

2. We should not read too much into this word (see my *Scepticism or Platonism?* [New York: Cambridge University Press, 1985], 62–65). Diogenes asserts that "dogmatizing" is the laying down of doctrines in the same way that lawgiving lays down laws.

3. I argue that Diogenes follows Thrasyllus (d. A.D. 36) here (*Thrasyllan Platonism* [Ithaca, New York: Cornell University Press, 1993], 17–30), but a later source is possible.

4. The hyphegetic dialogues of 3.49 correspond roughly to those where Plato allegedly expounds doctrine, the agonistic subclass would involve the refutation of falsehood, and most of the gymnastic subclass seem to suspend judgment.

5. I enclose in single inverted commas any references to Plato's characters based on historical philosophers, sophists etc. (including Timaeus).

to Sparta or Crete. That "Timaeus" should be considered a spokesperson is expected, as he uninterruptedly expounds his theories, and the fact that his doctrine was Pythagorean (in the eyes of many) does not preclude the possibility that it was also Platonic.[6] The Eleatic Stranger's inclusion follows naturally from the *Sophist* and *Politicus* being regarded as works with positive doctrine (3.50), and this leaves the Platonic "Socrates" as the remaining spokesperson. There is no implication that he is *always* such a spokesperson, but that in any dialogue featuring "Socrates" and none of the others, then, if it expounds doctrine, it does so through "Socrates." This has interesting implications for the *Parmenides,* seen as a work of instruction at 3.50, since "Parmenides" is not included among spokespersons. Is "Socrates" here too a spokesperson, though an unsuccessful one?[7]

Another oddity is that the Athenian Stranger, although regarded as a vehicle for Platonic doctrine, is not seen simply as a mask for Plato; nor is the Eleatic Stranger identical with Parmenides. Diogenes' source sees both Strangers as unnamed Platonic inventions, distinct from Plato and from Parmenides; they are vehicles for Plato's doctrine *without* their *standing for* Plato. How is it that the Athenian is a mouthpiece for Platonic doctrine without his actually representing Plato? Is he assigned the task of arguing for Plato without being characterized as Plato? Is he *philosophically* inseparable but *dramatically* distinct?

While such explanations are tempting—literary issues being clearly a consideration—it seems to me that Diogenes' source, like many of us today, has uncritically adopted the earlier mouthpiece theory and then had qualms about applying it rigidly. Radical mouthpiece theory would make the Athenian Stranger the thinnest of disguises for Plato, and might plausibly make his Eleatic counterpart the thinnest of disguises for Parmenides (assuming that Plato were in agreement with Parmenides on relevant issues). That position would seem to be that of *Oxyrhynchus Papyrus* no. 3219 (fragments of a seemingly earlier, more drama-oriented introduction to the dialogues).[8] Fragment 1 of this work discusses the alleged precedents for Plato's 'direct' or 'dramatic' dialogues, accepting that Sophron was a model but denying that Alexamenos was.[9] The first column of fr. 2 then reads something like this: "Protagoras [is among] those being refuted in his works. But he reveals what seems to him to be the case through [4] characters, Socrates, Timaeus, the Athenian Stranger, the Eleatic Stranger; the Eleatic Stranger and the Athenian Stranger are Plato and Parmenides, but because he constructs his dialogues to be dramatic right through [...] and creates an imaginary unnamed Athenian."[10]

---

6. Cicero dedicated his translation of the monologue of "Timaeus" to a Pythagorean; Ps.-Timaeus Locrus, *On the Soul of the World and on Nature*, was sufficient to suggest to early imperial Platonists that Plato was following this Timaeus closely. The Pythagoreans Nicomachus and Numenius use the *Timaeus's* cosmology as a Pythagorean document. For evidence that the popular view regarded it as Pythagorean one may refer to Lucian, *Vit. Auct.* 2.

7. Again, how the *Critias, Clitophon,* and *Menexenus* fit is unclear.

8. I associate this introduction with the school of Aristophanes of Byzantium; see below.

9. Material on Aristotle's mention of Alexamenos's dialogues overlaps with D.L. 3.48.

10. Possibly "he conceals Plato." What follows is likewise conjectural.

As we see, the same four characters are singled out as the vehicles through which Plato expresses his view, and the wording is more or less identical with that of Diogenes, signifying at very least a common source. But in the case of the papyrus-work the unknown author has gone on to claim quite simply that the Athenian and the Eleatic represent Plato and Parmenides. For this author the need to achieve a plausible drama is the only reason why Plato thinly disguised the Strangers' identities. Here the absence of Parmenides from the list of spokesmen is even more striking, because the Eleatic does have spokesman status and is identical with Parmenides!

Returning to Diogenes, the indications are that his own source has been following an earlier introduction to Plato's works closely related to our papyrus; but he has refused to accept that the Strangers are masks for historical philosophers, and therefore felt obliged to deny this view, which he attributed simply to "certain persons." The spokesperson theory belongs to an introduction to Plato that the papyrus followed more faithfully. The papyrus contained a lot of material relevant to drama, and Diogenes' source argues against "certain people" who have divided the dialogues into 'narrative' and 'dramatic' and 'mixed' works, dividing *tragikôs*, 'theatrically', rather than philosophically (3.50).[11] The papyrus seems to make such a division.[12] Material relevant to tragedy surfaces at 3.56, with prominence given to Thrasyllus's notion that the dialogues were promulgated like tragedies in tetralogies; at 3.61 however a dissenting voice is again observed—Aristophanes of Byzantium, who had constructed Platonic *trilogies*. I have therefore argued that Diogenes' source is arguing with some consistency *for* a broadly Thrasyllan position *against* details of Aristophanes' treatment; the papyrus is related to Aristophanes' tragedy-related approach.[13]

Accordingly the list of four spokesmen in both the papyrus and Diogenes is ultimately Aristophanes of Byzantium's list. Hence it includes all those who might be reasonably regarded as spokespersons *from the fifteen works which Aristophanes arranged into trilogies;*[14] no candidates from outside the works included in the arrangement are present; "Parmenides" is not included, perhaps because the work in which he speaks had not been present.[15] At any rate the

---

11. It investigates origins of "dramatic" dialogue in fr. 1, and examines Plato's use of characters in fr. 2, including his varying the principal character (2 ii, 5–8); Dionysus and acting are mentioned in fr. 3.2–3, perhaps Sophocles in fr. 4.4, tragedy in fr. 5.4, drama (?) in fr. 6.

12. It deals specifically with "dramatic" dialogues in fr. 1.

13. *Thrasyllan Platonism*, 103–107.

14. "Socrates" from *Republic, Cratylus, Minos, Theaetetus, Euthyphro, Apology, Crito, Phaedo;* Timaeus from *Timaeus;* the Eleatic Stranger from *Sophist* and *Politicus;* and the Athenian Stranger from *Laws* and *Epinomis.* No spokesman is needed for the *Epistles* and the remaining work is the *Critias* of which what was written does not include philosophic doctrine.

15. The critic will observe that Protagoras is apparently mentioned in the papyrus among those who are employed for refutation, but the *Protagoras* was excluded from the arrangement. Apart from the fact that Protagoras features also in the *Theaetetus*, if not in person, one may here observe that it was in general difficult to find characters against whom Plato polemicizes from within the fifteen works, Thrasymachus being the only other clear example. If one were to admit that Aristophanes was interested in works outside the fifteen in some contexts, it is entirely possible that he did not think that Plato's voice was heard directly in any works that had not been included. The most important of these were *Gorgias, Symposium, Phaedrus,* and *Philebus.*

omission of *Parmenides* from Aristophanes' select corpus probably means one of the following two things: either this work was too puzzling to be well known at the time, or too puzzling to be thought to include any character expounding doctrine.

Both Diogenes and the Papyrus confirm that some kind of 'spokesperson' theory was perfectly normal among those who detected strong positive messages in the works of Plato. In both cases the material derives from introductions to the reading of Plato, and consequently very many who encountered the dialogues would have come to them with the expectation of learning from the words of a single respected character.[16] In each case Introductions to the reading of Plato would have incorporated this spokesperson theory from the period of Aristophanes of Byzantium in the early second century until at least the flurry of Plato scholarship in the second century C.E.

II. WHERE PLATO SPEAKS IN EARLY EXEGESIS

If we examine the earliest datable extant works of Platonic exegesis, Plutarch's *Quaestiones Platonicae* and *De Animae Procreatione,* we find a strong tendency to talk as if Plato employs spokesmen for his views, even though Plutarch does not treat Plato as one who speaks forth openly in the manner of a Stoic or Epicurean. His nodding allegiance to New as well as Old Academy has not been enough to counter the attractions of reading many expressions of belief from "Socrates" and "Timaeus" as Plato's views.[17] In the *Quaestiones* Plutarch generally writes as if Plato speaks through "Timaeus" in the *Timaeus;*[18] through the Eleatic Stranger in the *Sophist* (1009b); and through "Socrates" in *Republic* VI (1001c, e, 1006e),[19] *Symposium* (1002e), and *Phaedrus* (1008c). Nevertheless he is not comfortable about applying spokesman theory to all works. In the first *Quaestio* he begins by carefully speaking of the words that Plato attributes to "Socrates" in the *Theaetetus,* and concludes by denying that Socrates *taught* anything (999d, 1000e). A "Socrates" who never taught anything but operated rather as a midwife or memory jogger (1000d–e) cannot be the mouthpiece for doctrine. We must therefore suppose that Plutarch recognized certain works in which "Socrates" operated in a more authentically Socratic manner, not as a mouthpiece for Plato. Perhaps these would have included most of the works

---

16. O. Gigon, "Das Dritte Buch des Diogenes Laertios," *Elenchos* 7 (1986): 136–37; Tarrant, *Thrasyllan Platonism,* 17–21; "Introducing Philosophers and Philosophies," *Apeiron* 28 (1995): 152–54; J. Mansfeld, *Prolegomena: Questions to Be Settled before the Study of an Author or a Text.* (Leiden: Brill, 1994), 58–107.

17. I have benefited from Jan Opsomer, *In Search of the Truth: Academic Tendencies in Middle Platonism* (Brussels: Koninklijke Academie voor Wetenschappen, Letteren en Schone Kunst, 1999). My reading of Plutarch should emerge from *Scepticism or Platonism?*

18. Nos. 2, 4, 5, 7, and sometimes 8. Plutarch does not always mention Plato by name, though it is usually clear that he means Plato. He actually says "Plato himself demonstrates" in 5 at 1004a, again names Plato in 7 at 1004d and 1006a, and in 8 at 1007c-d; but 8 actually begins with a reference to what "Timaeus" says at 42d (1006b).

19. And seemingly *Republic IV* (1007e).

often labeled "Socratic" in modern times, along with the *Theaetetus* itself. Relevant here is the early division of the dialogues into 'expository' and 'inquisitive', known from Albinus *(Prologus* 3) and from Diogenes (3.49, etc.), for the 'inquisitive' class originally included both aporetic discussions with young men (including Theaetetus) and polemical works.[20] The 'expository' dialogues on the other hand were precisely those in which Plato was widely thought to be trying to teach us something.[21] Certainly *De Animae Procreatione* treats most of these as works in which Plato himself speaks. Plutarch speaks of *what Plato says* in the *Phaedo, Republic, Phaedrus, Sophist, Politicus, Philebus, Laws,* and of course *Timaeus.*[22] Only at one point does he mention the characters through whom Plato allegedly speaks, and this is an interesting case. At 1017c he supports his view that the creation-process in the *Timaeus* must be taken literally by appealing to what "Timaeus" says in *Critias,* what the "Parmenidean Stranger" says in *Politicus,* and what "Socrates" says in *Republic* VIII. It appears that he is showing how no fewer than three of Plato's spokespersons agree in referring to a (temporal) creation in dialogues other than the *Timaeus.* Is he perhaps suggesting that caution *may* lead us to doubt that *one* accurately reflects Plato's views, but we *cannot* doubt that *all three* do?[23]

Plutarch's position on Plato's voices within the dialogues is shaped by the kind of interpreter he is. Never one to thoughtlessly retail the views of any predecessor, he specializes in finding ways in which he can make philosophic texts and religious practices harmonize with his own experiences. He forges links in his own mind between a variety of interpretations of the world, finding consistency within traditions that to us seem irreconcilable. We might call this approach 'creative syncretism', and it is applied within philosophies as well as between them. Hence in tackling Plato he tries to understand all dialogues that give instruction *as a unity.* Exegesis involves finding consistency within dialogues, between them, and among respected thinkers generally. Hence he must find *messages* within dialogues that are important to him, generally those dialogues mentioned above; but the words of the chief speakers do require *interpretation* before meaningful messages can be placed before the reader and reconciled with messages elsewhere.[24]

---

20. Though both Albinus and Diogenes are later than Plutarch, it was probably already well known. So Tarrant, *Thrasyllan Platonism,* 46–57; T. Goeransson, *Albinus, Alcinous, Arius Didymus* (Studia Graeca et Latina Gothoburgensia: Göteborg 1995), p. 81, but contrast Mansfeld, *Prolegomena* 89–97. Alcinous knew the distinction too, *Didasc.* 6, cf. Quintilian 2.15.26 (elenctic and dogmatic dialogues).

21. The distinction is implied by Sextus Empiricus's use of a division into "gymnastic" (=aporetic) and dogmatic dialogues (PH 1.221).

22. *Phaedo* 1013d, *Republic* 1029c, *Phaedrus* 1013c, 1016a, 1026d, *Sophist* 1013d, *Politicus* 1015c-d, *Philebus* 1014d, *Laws* 1013e-f, 1015e, *Timaeus* passim.

23. The tactic of Plutarch is rejected by his successor Taurus (text 23B.44–48 Lakmann = Philop. Aet. 6.21), who denies that other dialogues such as *Critias* and *Politicus* can tell us anything about the meaning of "generated" in the *Timaeus.*

24. *Cratylus* is a possible addition to the list. Two more passages that are heavily indebted to Plato will here be used for comparison: (i) the attempt to reconcile Isis & Osiris with Platonism in

After Plutarch, because it is difficult to claim Plato's authority without indicating where his voice is to be found, evidence suggests that spokesperson theory is not wholly lost. One indication is the repeated use of expressions such as "he says" in commentaries, where the reader is entitled to some confusion over whether the subject is "Socrates" or Plato.[25] Even in a late Neoplatonic commentary that generally speaks of what "Socrates" says, there is a tendency to talk of what Plato says in dialogues other than that being interpreted.[26] However, this may be a lack of precision rather than a commitment to any simple version of spokesperson theory, for a degree of sophistication in interpreting the Platonic "Socrates" was emerging.

III. TRUTHS IN THE MOUTHS OF THE FALLIBLE

Just as many of us today sympathize with the words of characters certainly not intended by Plato as spokesmen, so too in the ancient world a number of lessons were derived from what *opponents* of "Socrates" said. Strictly speaking, if Plato has a 'spokesperson', then that character ought to be in agreement with everything Plato thinks right, and any of this character's opponents, *qua* opponents, could only make such contrary points as Plato thought mistaken. Whenever such figures as "Gorgias," Callicles, "Hippias," and "Protagoras" make valid points against "Socrates," then this last is not unambiguously a spokesperson. Even where less-sophisticated characters who are not direct opponents are advancing the argument, the lessons that emerge from the whole drama amount to more than the line pushed by a single approved character. With this in mind I look at passages where an *opponent* was thought to be conveying an important lesson, and go on to consider cases where such lessons are found in the words of more genial nonspokesmen.

---

the *De Iside* (370f-383a), and (ii) the attempt to detect some special interest in the number five on Plato's part in the E. Delph. (389f-391d). The former passage makes use of *Timaeus*, *Republic*, *Laws*, *Politicus* (376b-c), *Theaetetus* (371a, cf. 176a), *Symposium*, *Phaedrus* (382b, d, 383a), *Phaedo* (382f-83a, cf. 80d, etc.), and *Cratylus*, and the latter of *Timaeus*, *Sophist*, *Philebus*, and *Cratylus*. I have not included references where allusions are noted in Roger Miller Jones, *The Platonism of Plutarch* (Garland reprint, London & New York, 1980), 109–153. Jones's tables suggest that the dialogues of Plato most frequently alluded to, in descending order: *Timaeus*, *Republic*, *Laws*, *Phaedrus*, *Symposium*, *Phaedo*, *Georgias*, *Theaetetus*, then (roughly equal) *Sophist*, *Cratylus*, *Apology*, *Politicus*, *Philebus*, and *Meno*.

25. E.g., *anon. Theaetetus* 23.15, 51.35, 57.16 (a reference to Socrates in the *Symposium*, as 57.24 shows, but strictly it is Diotima who was speaking!), 67.41; the reader experiences some ambiguity also in Olympiodorus In Grg. 4.5, 8.6, 10.4, 14.1, 18.4, 24.3, 27.7, 30.1, 30.8, 33.2, 39.2, 39.8, 41.11, 41.13, 466-7, 48.10, 49.3; references are usually to what "Socrates" says, but in this commentary there is a tendency to speak of what Plato says (i) when speaking of other dialogues, (ii) in the context of Aristides' criticisms of Plato, 1.13, 36.4-5, 41.11, and (iii) in the context of the myth (lectures 46-50).

26. Olympiodorus. *In Gorgias* has Plato rather than the "Socrates" of other dialogues speaking at proem 9, 3.10, 5.2, 10.3, 37.2, 41.9, 44.3, 46.5 (contrast what "Socrates" says in *Crito*, 25.23, and *Phaedrus*, 44.7), and Plato rather than the Athenian Stranger at 21.5, 24.3, 33.4-5, 36.5, 38.3, 40.3.

IV. GELLIUS'S "KALLIKLES"

An impressive discussion of a Platonic passage occurs in Aulus Gellius's *Noctes Atticae* 10.22. Gellius gives an interpretation of Kallikles' attack on mature-age philosophizing in the *Gorgias* (484c–485e); and while he is reading the Greek for himself, and can form his own view of its correct interpretation, what he offers us is sufficiently sophisticated to suggest the influence of his Platonist mentor Taurus.[27]

In Gellius's eyes Kallikles' invective against mature aged persons studying philosophy is a valid criticism when applied to certain types of intellectual pursuit: he has a skewed idea of what philosophy is, but he correctly identifies a problem concerning what he supposes philosophy to be. Gellius acknowledges that Kallikles is "not a weighty or desirable character" (1) and that he had undesirable qualities (24), but sees in him both common sense and commendable frankness. Hence there will be lessons for us here too—if Kallikles is depicted as knowing, and if he openly expresses his knowledge, then Kallikles too may here be functioning as a Platonic mouthpiece. What Gellius says about the *Gorgias* is related to contemporary prejudices, but it also owes much to a close reading of the text. Plato's "Socrates" had credited Kallikles with knowledge *(episteme)* at 487a. "Socrates" takes the frankness theme from the description of Kallikles at 487a–b. So the alleged spokesperson "Socrates" is painting a picture of the nonspokesperson that allows the reader to think of Kallikles' opinions as (i) right, and (ii) faithfully expressed! Can we ignore what "Socrates" says about Kallikles? Certainly spokesperson-theorists cannot simply explain this away as 'Socratic irony', for if they do they are imputing a certain lack of frankness to their vehicle of Platonic doctrine—with the result that all that "Socrates" says has to be assessed for sincerity!

It is thus unlikely that Gellius could subscribe to any simple spokesperson theory, such as that of Diogenes, when interpreting the *Gorgias*. He has shown a willingness to find truth behind the words of morally dubious interlocutors much as we might show a willingness to find falsehoods behind the words of their morally impeccable questioners. It is clear that in this case he was correct to do so. The lesson agrees well with Plato's *Euthydemus*, where two sophist brothers spend their aging days (not to mention the youth of their hapless pupils) in trivial, indeed juvenile sophisms without any potential for improving one's life. Any astute reader, seeking truth behind Kallikles' words and asking himself whether Plato knew people who had grown old in philosophic trifles, would immediately think of Euthydemus and Dionysodorus—and remember that their pursuit too was called "philosophy" (304e7–307b7).

So Gellius thoughtfully derives from Kallikles a lesson that is confirmed elsewhere, showing that we sometimes need to dig a little deeper into Plato to find the true meaning of the text. He thinks that we are being brought to "gradually realize" the warning *(sensim moneri intellegamus*, 10.22.2), because it is Kalli-

---

27. Tarrant, "Platonic Interpretation in Aulus Gellius," *Greek, Roman and Byzantine Studies* 37 (1996): 173–193.

kles *when interpreted* that is of value. Kallikles is not turned into a spokesperson just because his words contain a lesson, for the real lesson involves a *slight variation* on what he said. If Gellius is right—if Kallikles does say something of value whose message is only gradually perceived—then how does Kallikles differ in this respect from "Socrates"? Does not "Socrates" too demand a degree of interpretation? Perhaps our reason for denying spokesperson status to Kallikles also means that we must deny it to "Socrates"!

V. TRUTHS FROM "GORGIAS" AND "PROTAGORAS"

Gellius finds important moral messages even in the words of Kallikles; this has a partial parallel in the traditions of *Gorgias* interpretation, in that Olympiodorus in his *Commentary on the Gorgias* can find messages in the character Gorgias's own words; take 8.12 on 458d7 for example: Then Gorgias says, "If everyone wishes to hear me, it would be base not to engage in discourse. For I undertook to give answers to everyone. So since they wish it I must do what I undertook." Here we have an ethical lesson, that if you give an undertaking you must fulfill it and not be found to have spoken falsely, but in every way bring it to completion.[28]

Here "Gorgias" is found to be making a moral observation that is considered to be quite valid. Much the same applies a few lines above (8.7): "But perhaps we ought to have thought of these people here too (458b5–6): for it is a mark of someone who loves himself to be concerned for himself alone and not for those with him. For we ought to be concerned that everyone should benefit." Olympiodorus finds similar observations in the words of "Socrates,"[29] but what is the difference of status between these and lessons from "Gorgias"? Spokesperson theory should have an answer for this; indeed Olympiodorus did have an answer of a general kind. Socrates is 'divine', but the pro-rhetorical lobby suffers from various faults.[30] Kallikles is insensitive to the "common notions," the vital underpinnings of moral theory; Polus is aware of some, but not of others; "Gorgias" is generally aware of the common notions, but has somehow become "misguided" *(diastrophos)*.[31] This awareness of the common notions explains why moral lessons can come from "Gorgias," while Kallikles is considered barren. Moral lessons, though, are one thing, while genuine insights are another, and only Socrates is 'divine' and 'intellective'. This gives him increased stature, but not stature *as Plato's mouthpiece*: more *as the mouthpiece of some god*, a status in which he is Plato's equal.

The value of the comment of "Gorgias" at 458b, about the need to consider how the spectators are feeling, is also appreciated by Plutarch, who alludes to

---

28. Translations of 8.12 and 8.7 from K. R. Jackson, K. Lycos, H. Tarrant, *Olympiodorus: On Plato's Gorgias* (Leiden: Brill, 1998).
29. In *Gorgias* 3.4, 11.3, 12.3, 15.9, 17.6, 19.1, 23.2, 24.9.
30. 8.4. As proem 8 establishes, "Socrates" somehow stands for "the intellective and knowledgeable."
31. For Polus and Kallikles see 11.2, 20.2, 21.1-2, 6, 25.1, 28.4, 31.4; for Gorgias 27.2, proem 8.

the passage twice in the *Quaestiones Conviviales*.[32] So Plutarch too derives lessons from the opponents of "Socrates." A partial parallel for doctrine in the mouth of an opponent is found in *On Chance* (*Mor.* 98d). Here the account by "Protagoras" of the creation of humans (*Protagoras* 321c) is seemingly regarded as Plato's. Indeed the status of the sophist's long rhesis is much debated today, and can plausibly be thought to conceal *either* much truth *or* much deception. Furthermore, while it is indeed doubtful whether Plato intended us to take seriously the words of "Protagoras," whether in the long rhesis, or the literary digression, or at key points of the argument such as 350c–351b, the same can be said of "Socrates" in this work. Is his argument based on hedonistic values to be taken seriously? If so what of his other arguments that mostly seem less substantial? And what of *his* part in the literary digression—is that not quite as contentious as anything that "Protagoras" says? The conclusion of the work (361a–c) shows both protagonists to have been adopting inconsistent positions. How can one of them be seen as a spokesperson in preference to the other? Plutarch is in this case simply being evenhanded, and using from Plato what he finds helpful. We have already found evidence (section ii) that he saw no spokespersons operating in the 'inquisitive' dialogues, including *Protagoras* and similar polemical works.

VI. TRUTHS IN THE LESSER SPEECHES OF THE *SYMPOSIUM*

We now return to Gellius's *Noctes Atticae,* to 17.20.4–6 where Gellius depicts Taurus as finding much to commend in the speech of Pausanias at *Symposium* 180e. While the ancients, like us, often supposed that the distinction between two Aphrodites and two Erotes encountered there is of wider importance for Plato, Pausanias is clearly not meant to have the same authority as "Socrates" in this work.[33] While it is not surprising that Taurus admired the artistry of the passage, he also commended Pausanius's technique of argument (4). Above all, his warning at 17.20.6 that Gellius should proceed to "the very recesses of Plato and the gravity and worthiness of the matters themselves" implies that there is much value and seriousness beneath the surface *even here*, though gravity is hardly a quality associated with Pausanias. So it is Taurus's method, recognized by Gellius, to look for deep meaning in the words of a variety of Plato's characters: the same surprisingly modern technique that Gellius applied to Kallikles in the passage discussed earlier.

---

32. 613d, 634a; see Jones, *The Platonism of Plutarch,* p. 116.

33. E.g., Plut. *Erot.* 752b, 764b. Another example from a second-century Platonist is Apul. *Apologia* 12: *mitto enim dicere alta illa et divina Platonica, rarissimo cuique piorum ignara, ceterum omnibus profanis incognita: geminam esse Venerem deam.* . . . The bipartition, however, is probably not Apuleius's preferred division of Eros (though E. J. Kenney, "Psyche and her Mysterious Husband," in D. A. Russell, ed., *Antonine Literature* [Oxford: Oxford University Press, 1990], 175–98, makes much of its role in the *Metamorphoses*), as can be seen from the tripartition in *De Plat.* 2.14, and this again suggests that the need was felt to look deeper than Pausanias for guidance.

VII. THE INTERLOCUTORS AND THE EMERGENCE OF TRUTH IN ANON. *IN THEAETETUM*

I now move to consider our earliest substantial example of Platonic commentary, the anonymous *Commentary on the Theaetetus*, dating from no later than the mid-second century A.D., the age of Taurus and Gellius, possibly from earlier.[34] The commentary does indeed detect important lessons in the *Theaetetus*, and regards Plato, and his "Socrates," as having *dogmata*.[35] The only passage from the *Theaetetus's* prologue that attracts a regular comment is 142d1–3, Euclides' reminiscences of Socrates' inspired prophecies concerning Theaetetus. Hence one begins with the impression that Socrates' words have some special status for the writer, and demand special attention. Yet the commentator does not ignore the words of either Theaetetus or Theodoros, both of whom are seen as making comments much deeper than would now be suspected.

To begin with Theodoros, his words at 143e7–9 and 144a3–b7 attract detailed comment (8.45–12.20). At 144a3–6 he is seen as operating with at least two of the three Platonic faculties of soul, and apparently as recognizing that the innate good qualities (like gentleness and bravery here) can often impede each other even though the mature excellences go hand in hand. At 144b3–5 he is seen as offering worthwhile insights into the correct attitude for a young man to adopt in the course of inquiries, not as proceeding in leaps and bounds, nor as getting upset by obstacles. Such lessons were probably regarded as important for the Platonists' own pupils.[36] Similarly the commentator remarks on Theodoros's words at 144d1–4 about his pupil's liberality: another quality a teacher likes to discover in a pupil![37] The continuing strategy is to discover in Theodoros an appreciation of qualities desirable for learning, and to harmonize this with Platonic theory; the underlying assumption is that Plato chose even the words of the interlocutors so as to pass on genuine insights.

What applies to Theodoros applies all the more to Theaetetus. It is not hard for us to assume that, in telling "Socrates" about his mathematical definitions (147c–148b), the youth is giving genuine lessons to readers. "Socrates" approves at 148b, and, if "Socrates" were a Platonic spokesperson, we should have to take this approval seriously. The commentator certainly does so, and thinks Plato indicates how an investigation should proceed (44.43–50). This hardly makes Theaetetus into a spokesperson himself, but it does highlight the extent to which lessons can emerge in a dialogue through *interaction* between questioner and interlocutor.

The next contribution of Theaetetus that receives much attention from the commentator is his attempt to define knowledge in terms of perception at 151e.

---

34. The work may now be consulted in the edition of Guido Bastianini and David N. Sedley, *Corpus dei papiri filosofici greci e latini, iii: Commentari* (Firenze: Olschki, 1995), 227–562. On the author and date see particularly 246–56.

35. See 47.37, 47, 48.8, 55.5, 10.

36. Cf. Olympiodorus In *Gorgias* 2.10, 5.12, 6.4, 8.1, 42.3, 43.2.

37. That a pupil should be generous is stressed at Olympiodorus In *Gorgias* 43.2. Some dialogues of Lucian, e.g. Piscator, Eunuchus, satirize concern for income among philosophers. Compare Taurus on philosophers who go searching for rich pupils at *NA* 7.10.5.

The commentator believes that the young man is being wittingly or unwittingly sophisticated in equating knowledge with perception "as appears now at least" (e2), and assumes that "perception" here signifies any act of observation (59.40–49). Again he takes note of praise from "Socrates" (e4–5), which he relates to Theaetetus's judging (like a Pyrrhonist) by the impression of the moment, but being willing (unlike a Pyrrhonist) to express himself (59.1–46). Implicit in the young man's words were the equation of what appears to one (*phainetai*) with what one perceives (*aisthanetai*), which is brought out explicitly by "Socrates" at 152b9–c2, and which the commentator regards as Plato's own contribution to an otherwise Protagorean theory (66.34–43). The commentator did not believe that Plato thought the equation true, but that he advances the argument by employing a plausible premise. He sees this advance emerging as "Socrates" draws out the implications of what Theaetetus has said. It is a joint effort, not the gift of one privileged speaker.

When one thinks in general terms about the encounter between "Socrates" and Theaetetus one can see that philosophy moves forward through this interaction between two vital characters, one offering a natural succession of ideas, the other putting them to the test. This may not always be the case in a Platonic dialogue, but the midwifery paradigm employed in the *Theaetetus* has been chosen with a view to the dramatic separation of the theory-generating and theory-analyzing elements in the process of learning, both of which will be necessary if knowledge is to be approached. *In his role with young men* "Socrates" acts primarily as a facilitator who brings ideas to birth, and as a friendly critic exposing their inadequacies (149c–151c); but nothing can be brought to birth without the "pregnancy" of his patients. We are thus expecting a huge contribution from interlocutors without full awareness of how they are contributing, and the eliciting and testing of this contribution by "Socrates." Anything that emerges, and even in the most aporetic of dialogues much of value can emerge, is necessarily the result of this joint production team. In the discussion between Theodoros and "Socrates" the midwifery model is abandoned, and "Socrates" looks on occasion remarkably like a Platonic spokesperson (171d–177c) or like an agent of Platonic refutation (177e–179b); but midwifery returns as soon as Theaetetus resumes (184a7–b2).

Sadly we miss the commentator's evaluation of wider philosophic and dramatic issues, since the papyrus leaves off around 158a, but that "Socrates" is no simple spokesperson for Plato has certainly not escaped him. Commenting on the fact that the "midwife" is banned from agreeing to falsehood or obscuring the truth (151d2–3), he tells us that in his 'inquiries' "Socrates" questions and does not declare his view, so that he proposes neither truth nor falsehood: "But to those familiar with his method he reveals his preferred view imperceptibly" (59.12–21). As we see from 56.2–10, 'inquiries' here embrace all applications of the method of midwifery: it is there that "Socrates" is allowed no "discovery or psychical offspring" of his own (150d1–2). A little earlier, at 54.38–43, the 'inquiries' seem to signify Socratic interrogations in general: "When I ask people questions, I do not declare any view (of my own), but listen to them; this happens because I have no wisdom for that kind of instruction" (54.23–26).

The commentator holds that this method is not constantly employed, and that doctrine can often emerge, even within the *Theaetetus*. He criticizes those who believe that *Plato* is an antidogmatist on account of passages where Socrates disclaims knowledge, and says it is already possible to grasp that Plato both has doctrines and reveals them with confidence. Here he is referring to the theory of midwifery itself, which, along with the theory of recollection, is important for his own epistemology. In saying that *Plato's* views are confidently revealed, he implies that Plato is in full agreement with views attributed here to "Socrates." It is equally evident that some of what "Socrates" has said in the *Meno* is viewed as what Plato himself is saying.[38]

The overall impression is that "Socrates" is treated in this commentary as *intermittently* akin to a Platonic spokesperson, though it is far from clear whether "Socrates" is held to be speaking for Plato in these passages or Plato for Socrates: either will explain why there is occasionally confusion in the reader's mind as to whether "Socrates" is referred to or Plato.[39] At certain times "Socrates" is *not even his own spokesman,* but an attendant who assists others to explain their beliefs, and whose views emerge not *in the text* of what he says, but *in the course* of his questioning. The *cooperative role* of the investigation is recognized, and lessons in the words of both Theodoros and Theaetetus are commented upon. The commentator recognizes that philosophy frequently advances in ways dependent upon the drama depicted. We do not have to assume that he saw the views that imperceptibly emerge as any different from Plato's views, but we cannot in these cases pinpoint anything in "Socrates'" words that can be identified with Plato's view.[40]

How did the commentator cope with the familiar problem of distinguishing where "Socrates" is being a direct Platonic voice and where he is not? We have discussed in section II the possibility that Plutarch expected to find Platonic spokespersons in the 'expository' but not in the 'inquisitive' dialogues, but now we are confronted with a distinction between exposition and inquiry *within* a dialogue. How can the lines ever be reliably drawn, even supposing the distinction to be valid? The commentator has seemingly adopted a middle line, and avoided the twin absurdities of having a Plato who goes unheard everywhere and having a writer of dialogues who intends just one voice to be heard. But the middle line seems unhelpful to us unless the key distinction can be applied.

Fortunately the commentator had one advantage over ourselves: it was not so much the authority of Plato or of Socrates that he sought, but the authority of the "common notions," those fundamentally reliable truths which he supposed to be the objects of recollection (46.43–48.11). For him Plato had access to truths, and in his dialogues depicted his own teacher as another with such access. Who speaks for whom is much less important than who speaks for the common notions and for the truth that they ultimately contain. The key ques-

---

38. The commentator finds Plato's definition of "simple knowledge" at *Meno* 98a (15.19-23), and he may be thinking of Plato himself as expounding the theory of recollection there (56.26-31).

39. See n. 25.

40. It is far from certain whether 59.12-21 refers to the message of "Socrates" or of Plato being imperceptibly appreciated!

tion is the one of how truth will emerge. The answer is through dialogue between intelligent speakers who are free from preconceptions that obscure their
natural insights into reality. The commentator was not seeking Plato's preconceptions, his personal views that could be seen in isolation from the views of
others. He was seeking Plato's company and guidance in a living dialogue that
continued into his own day and beyond it into ours, and the object of that dialogue was the discovery of common truths of which we all have some trace in
our minds. Plato is used as a guide to transcending Plato. This Platonist *did not
need* Platonic spokesmen. Neither should we.

Part II
Research on Specific Dialogues

6

Cowardice, Moral Philosophy, and Saying What You Think

Eugenio Benitez

> The lowest animal's got more courage than man.
> —Edward G. Robinson in *The Red House*[1]

I. WHO SPEAKS FOR PLATO?

No one in the dialogues is Plato's mouthpiece except insofar as she or he expresses ideas or makes arguments that Plato sometimes considered important. The doctrines of Plato are not to be found in his writings. There are many reasons for this, some that are discussed in other chapters of this book. The one I shall discuss is restricted to moral philosophy (so it only *contributes* to the argument that no one is Plato's mouthpiece). Virtue is acquired, in part, through correctly internalizing lessons exhibited in virtuous deeds. To do this one must become skilled at identifying, in deeds performed, seen, or recounted, what is essential to virtue and what is not. Plato does not tell his readers what the essential is (to do so would not help), but forces them constantly to reflect on difficulties involved in identifying it. I take the *Laches* as paradigmatic, for I think it shows the point clearly.

Images can deceive, no less when the deceit stems from ignorance than when it is intentional. The *Laches* shows how traditional icons of courage, like the heavily armed soldier, can deceive when beheld by those ignorant of what courage is. To show this Plato depicts fighting in armor so that it acquires the look of cowardice rather than the look of courage. This depiction involves more than anticonventionalism—the association of fighting in armor with cowardice

---

1. This is an allusion to *Laches* 196d9–197c4.

challenges readers to distinguish the essentials of courage from its accidentals.[2] Cowardice is as much the theme of the *Laches* as is courage.

The philosophical point of associating fighting in armor with cowardice has been missed in most accounts of the *Laches*. Analytic philosophers focus more or less exclusively on the dialogue's arguments about what courage is.[3] Such accounts limit the dialogue to lessons in moral epistemology, and in so doing expose Plato to charges of intellectualism.[4] Some recent interpretations examine the dialogue for its depictions of courageous deeds.[5] The idea is that the *Laches* supplements moral epistemology with moral education, by showing us what the courageous person does. This is a step in the right direction, but it is still too limited. Although the *Laches* points to no fewer than seven specific examples of courage,[6] and displays what may be courage in some of its characters,[7] these "showings" only recommend a pattern of behavior. The sort of education they provide is rudimentary Aristotelian habituation.[8] Moreover, Plato supplies all the examples of courage. No matter how subtle the drama is, the exercise of poring over its deeds to resolve the aporia about courage just amounts to determining what is *Plato's* conception of courage. Unless we make the unwarranted assumption that Plato's conception is authoritative, this cannot be an exercise in moral philosophy, any more than is analyzing the arguments.

I presume the *Laches* was designed to be a work of moral philosophy.[9] But to become such a work, it must force its readers to obtain wisdom about courage for themselves, and it can do this best if the aporia is sustained (if

---

2. I follow Sokolowski (1994) on two points. First, speaking of essentials and accidentals helps to avoid treating an essence as "a substantial object in its own right" (691). The *Laches* does not treat courage as an independent Platonic essence (see Penner [1973]). The second point concerns the relation between essentials and accidentals: "We could not receive the *per se* just by itself, without playing it off against the *per accidens*" (693). The *Laches* does just this: it plays off the *per se* against the *per accidens*.

3. See Hoerber (1968), Santas (1969), Penner (1973, 1992), Devereux (1977, 1992).

4. By "ethical intellectualism" I mean the belief that having the correct analysis of ethical concepts entails possession of the corresponding ethical traits. See Burnyeat (1980), Irwin (1995), Brickhouse and Smith (1994).

5. See Griswold (1986), Stokes (1986), and Gould (1987). Compare Blitz (1975), Umphrey (1976a).

6. These are: (1) Athenian bravery at Marathon, called to mind by the mention of the great deeds of Aristides the Just (179c), (2) Socrates' (and Laches') bravery in the retreat from Delium (181a–b, 189b, 194e), (3) the legendary bravery of the Scythian cavalry (191a–b), (4) the bravery of Aeneas (and his horses) in the fight with Diomedes (191a, cf. *Iliad* V.223), (5) the bravery of the Spartans at Plataea (191c), (6) the bravery of the Spartans at Mantinaea, implied at 193a, where the conditions described by Socrates correspond exactly to those of the battle (compare Thucydides, *History of the Peloponnesian War*, V.65–73), and (7) The bravery of the sow of Crommyon in its stand against Theseus (196e). The reference to Mantinaea in *Laches* 193a is identified and discussed by Schmid (1992:13–15).

7. For example, Laches' resolve to say what he thinks and admit his own ignorance (193c, 194a), or Socrates' endurance in the criticism of his own beliefs (194c ff.).

8. I say "rudimentary" because Aristotle thinks moral habituation requires more from the student than following the pattern; it requires appreciation of the goodness of the pattern. See Kosman (1980).

9. Kahn (1986:11) argues that the *Laches* is part of "a vast protreptic to the philosophic life," that was "designed to initiate the reader into ... the life of philosophical study and discussion."

Plato's personal authority underwhelms) in *both* word and deed. In this sense no one in the *Laches* speaks for Plato, or rather it is a mistake to be preoccupied with who speaks for Plato. The point of the *Laches*—the one that stems from the theme of fighting in armor—is to help us to choose and appraise actions on the basis of what is essential rather than what is accidental. It does not help us by telling or showing what the essential is, but by making us consider how the accidental affects our judgment of moral examples and moral experience. This is not sufficient for moral virtue, but learning to distinguish the essential from the accidental is part of moral philosophy—it is requisite for practical wisdom.

II. IMAGES OF COURAGE AND COWARDICE

I have suggested the *Laches* uses the image of fighting in armor to represent cowardice. This suggestion initially strikes one as unattractive. It seems perverse of Plato to use the image this way. Ordinary Athenians just did not think of heavily armed soldiers as cowards. As Schmid has pointed out, the traditional Greek conception of courage was militaristic, rooted in the Homeric model of the hero-warrior.[10] In the fifth century the military conception was updated on the model of hoplitic bravery.[11] For Plato to associate the hoplite with cowardice seems ridiculous.

The military model might only be pushed so far of course. Not anyone could become courageous by donning armor—take Thersites—but anyone brave would appear more daunting if he had the right armor. The essential and the accidental are intimately connected. The essential is a control on how the accidental appears to us, but the accidental directly influences our grasp of the essential. In the usual course of things, for most people, accidentals predominate. In the *Iliad,* for example, the Trojans quake to see Patroclus driving forward in Achilles' armor.[12] When the gear is lost to Hector, Achilles requires even more formidable armament before entering battle, armor so terrifying that "none dared to look straight at the glare."[13]

When the connection between essentials and certain accidentals is long established, accidentals may begin to tyrannize. This was the case with the military conception of courage. The armor, particularly the shield of the soldier, which is accidental to military courage was so magnified in the ordinary person's perspective that it occluded the essentials. We can see how tyrannical these accidentals were by looking at them from another perspective—the perspective of one who recognizes, but does not hold the military conception. Consider Archilochus: "Some barbarian is waving my shield, since I was obliged to leave

---

10. See Schmid (1985:113, and the references at 124n2, esp. *Iliad* XII.310–28).
11. Ibid., (1985:113). The transition from hero to hoplite is partly a result of changes in warfare (as Schmid notes), but it is also associated with the rise of democracy. For more on hoplites and democracy see Snodgrass (1965) and Detienne (1968).
12. *Iliad* 16.326–331.
13. *Iliad* 19.17–18, tr. Fagles.

that perfectly good piece of equipment behind under a bush. But I got away, so what does it matter? Let the shield go; I can buy another one equally good."[14]

Imagine how these words might strike his contemporaries. They seem to praise a coward who values life before honor. This man does not speak of terror that made him run. And despite his "obligation," his action was not involuntary, but intentional, perhaps even on purpose: he had time to leave his shield under a bush. The loss of one's shield is something the ordinary man would find shocking. The shield was an icon of courage: a brave soldier returned from battle "with it or on it." For the ordinary man the shock value of Archilochus's poem lies in its praise of cowardly action. Its rejection of the military conception of courage goes unnoticed.

It seems clear, however, that Archilochus did reject the military conception, and the fragment makes better sense if we read it that way.[15] We can distinguish in it what Paul Redding has called "indexical and referential moments."[16] The fragment is indexically centered on the ordinary man's perspective; it uses conventional language and imagery. The speaker leaves this "pattern of indexicality" intact, but abruptly "reverses the evaluative polarity" of the ordinary man's perspective: what matters to the ordinary man does not matter to him. The reversal of polarity constitutes the fragment's referential moment; we move from sharing the ordinary man's perspective to a 'negative meta-evaluation' of it. Whether the speaker has a different conception of courage is not elaborated, though we may infer something from his resolve to speak plainly. But it is crucial that we do not confuse the referential moment with a recommendation to adopt any first-level conception of courage. The fragment suggests that what is accepted without reflection as essential (the connection between courage, the shield, and standing one's ground) can be seen from a higher perspective to be only accidental. Archilochus instructs by leading us from one perspective to the other; in this respect the indexical moment is indispensable. For some the shock of seeing their own perspective turned inside out will provoke a reexamination of their beliefs.

Whether this is the right understanding of Archilochus or not, it illustrates what takes place in Plato's *Laches*. The military conception of courage was tyrannized by accidentals, so much so that fighting in armor seemed to be the essence of cowardice. The *Laches* turns the military conception of courage inside out, beginning with the conventional perspective, that is overtly the perspective of Lysimachus and Melesias.

III. FIGHTING IN ARMOR IN THE *LACHES*

The *Laches* approaches courage in a way similar to Archilochus. The discussion of fighting in armor begins from a conventional perspective. The referential

---

14. Archilochus, fr. 6, in Diehl (1936). tr, Lattimore.

15. Schmid (1985:113, 125 n.6) cites frs. 1 and 118 for Archilochus's rejection of the military conception, but does not mention fr. 6. The images of a man disarmed and exposed effectively oppose the image of a heavily armed soldier backed to the wall; they undermine the connection between courage and fighting in armor.

16. See Redding (1990:80–81).

moment comes in Laches's appraisal of fighting in armor: we are made to see that arming one's body against others is perfectly compatible with cowardice. Plato takes matters further than Archilochus does, however. After Laches's appraisal we learn that "fighting in armor" is a practice not just of the body but of the soul as well. This practice involves concealing one's motives from others, and using the armor of public opinion and rhetoric to secure one's private advantage. This sort of "fighting in armor" could not be publicly approved, nor could it be openly associated with courage, but privately many people did approve these tactics and did count themselves manly for seeking their own advantage. Lysimachus, Melesias and Nicias all practice this covert, psychical fighting in armor, and the *Laches* shows that arming one's soul against others is perfectly compatible with cowardice, just as is arming one's body against them.

The *Laches* opens with a meeting in which two aristocrats—Lysimachus and Melesias—seek the opinions of two generals—Nicias and Laches—about having their sons trained in armored combat: "hoplitics." The meeting follows a display of hoplitics by Stesilaus. Socrates has come along with the generals, we are not told why or how. On the surface, the meeting seems innocent. Lysimachus and Melesias are concerned, as any fathers might be, about the education of their sons. Although a peace holds between Athens and Sparta, there has been war and there is likely to be more. Lysimachus openly admits that he and Melesias are ashamed of their own military training; they now want what is best for their sons.

Plato casts doubt on the value of hoplitics from the beginning, however. When Lysimachus says he is concerned about the "training and improvement" of his son (179b), we suspect that Socrates takes this to be a concern for virtue (the suspicion is borne out at 186c). We wonder whether Stesilaus is a sophist, like Euthydemus or Dionysodorus, who were also expert at fighting in armor (*Euthydemus* 271d). The dialogue encourages this speculation when, in connection with the question about what sort of teaching improves young men, Nicias mentions Damon (180d), an accomplished musician and sophist.[17]

Just as the sophists were represented as the purveyors of new arts and ideas, the *art* of fighting in armor is represented as something newfangled. There is no evidence for the art of hoplitics outside of Plato. The adjective ὁπλιτικόν (the word that appears in the *Laches* 182d8; cf. 191b6, d1; cf. τὰ ὁπλιτικά ἐπιτεδεύειν 183c4) is unusual. It is used by Thucydides seven times and by Xenophon fourteen times, but never in connection with an art of fighting in armor. For Thucydides and Xenophon the sense is always "the hoplitic (part of the army)."[18] The name ἡ ὁπλιτικὴ τέχνη is original to Plato.[19] The setting of the *Laches* makes the conventional image of fighting in armor dispensable by transposing it from the realm of veneration to innovation.

The worth of hoplitics is never explicitly determined, primarily because each of the generals differs in his opinion of it. Nicias praises it; Laches con-

---

17. At 197d Socrates warns Laches that Nicias has learned "wisdom" from Damon, who "is always with Prodicus." See also 200a–b.
18. See Thucydides, *History* IV.73§4.7, Xen. *Hell.* IV.2§7.2.
19. See *Republic* 333d, *Alcibiades* 127a1, cf. *Republic* 374d. Plato is the first author to use the feminine adjective ὁπλιτικὴ (source: *Thesaurus Linguae Graecae* database).

demns it. We are supposed to believe that the generals are equally compe-
tent evaluators (186d), so their disagreement brings about an impasse.
Socrates refuses to cast the deciding vote (184d–e); Lysimachus refuses to
judge the issue for himself (189d); Melesias remains mute. Nevertheless, if
it is intrinsic worth we are after, it is hard to see how Laches's speech is not
decisive. He suggests that if the art were really valuable, the Spartans, who
know everything connected with warfare, would have either invented it
themselves or would welcome teachers in it. But, he says, "these fighters in
armor regard Lacedaemon as sacred inviolable territory, which they do not
touch with the point of their foot" (183b2–5).[20]

Furthermore, Laches speaks about hoplitics from experience (183c1–2).
None of its practitioners has ever distinguished himself in battle, and Stesilaus,
whose demonstration they have just observed, once made a ridiculous spectacle of himself. From this episode, which presents us with the most vivid images
in the dialogue, we may surmise that Stesilaus is not just inept, but also a coward. And "if the professor of this art be a coward," says Laches, "he will be likely
to become rash, and his character will be only more clearly revealed" (184b).
This episode makes a striking contrast with the well-known Homeric account
of Ajax's courage as he fought with his long spear, leaping from deck to deck
when the Trojans had forced the Greeks back to their ships.[21] Plato has turned
a classical image of courage on its head.

My point, however, is not that Plato believed fighting in armor is essentially
cowardice. The *Laches* shows it is coherent to invert the conventional image;
the episode of Stesilaus on the ships shows this clearly. But the important question is not, "What does Plato think these images mean?" or even "What do these
images mean?" but rather, "Given that there are images consistent with both
virtue and vice, how do I recognize what is essential?" The *Laches* puts a reflective reader in the position to ask this question.

At any rate, by this point in the dialogue the apparent "main question" has
been answered: the art of fighting in armor is a sham. It does not conduce to
courage, since even the expert is a coward. Why, then, after Laches's speech, is
Lysimachus in doubt as to whether his son should be trained by Stesilaus? His
indecision makes sense only if his concern is not with the intrinsic value of hoplitics, but some instrumental value. His concern with hoplitics was pretentious.
There is more to his interview with the generals than he let on in his 'open' appeal to them. Lysimachus armed himself with deceptive speeches.

At this point we begin to see Plato's deeper attack on the convention of
fighting in armor. Let me clarify by analogy with a point about courage.
Some characters in the *Laches* display a sort of "courage of conversation."[22]
For example, Socrates speaks of the need to "endure and persevere in the

---

20. Unless otherwise indicated, all translations of Plato in this chapter are taken from Hamilton
& Cairns (1963). In notes hereafter I will only mention the translator's name. Here the translation
is Jowett's.

21. See *Iliad* 15.780 ff.

22. Note the principle that word and deed should harmonize (188d–e).

inquiry," so that "courage will not laugh at our faintheartedness in searching for courage, which after all may frequently be endurance" (194a). This sort of 'philosophical courage' is a far cry from anything seen on the battlefield.[23] But philosophical courage is easily expressed in military terms: the philosopher's enemy is ignorance, the danger is exposing one's flank on matters of the greatest importance, etc. Earlier in the dialogue, Socrates used battle metaphors in just this way to describe courage of the soul: "I meant to ask you about . . . not only who are courageous in war, but who are courageous in perils by sea, and who in disease, or in poverty, or again in politics, are courageous, and not only who are courageous against pain or fear, but *mighty to contend against desires and pleasures, either fixed in their rank or turning upon their enemy*" (191b, my emphasis).

Immediately he adds: "Some are cowards under the same conditions." There is a counterpart for philosophical courage, a philosophical cowardice, for which the sham-art of fighting in armor is an apposite metaphor. Courage to examine oneself means letting defenses down, allowing oneself to be stripped naked.[24] Fighting in armor is a way of covering up, protecting but at the same time not revealing oneself. The philosophically courageous interlocutor will say what he really thinks: "Why, Socrates, what else can a man say?" (193c). The philosophical coward conceals his ignorance. This cowardice of the soul is always more common than military cowardice. Most people will obey orders, even face death, but few ever submit willingly to Socratic examination. Some, like Lysimachus, will not submit at all. Others, like Nicias, say they are fond of Socratic conversation, but they often do not mean what they say.

As we move to the remaining part of the dialogue we can see why inverting the conventional image of courage is important. Even if that image tends often not to express genuine physical bravery (so that it is with difficulty made compatible with cowardice), it does not sit easily with courage of the soul. Yet if courage is essentially the same on the battlefield and in conversation, it becomes clear that the conventional image of fighting in armor may not capture the essentials. Plato follows through with inversion of the conventional image of courage by showing that intellectual fighting in armor is compatible with intellectual cowardice. In the last part of this section I suggest that Melesias, Lysimachus, and Nicias all show cowardice (are all depicted metaphorically as fighting in armor) in their conversations and dealings with others. The case against Melesias is circumstantial, so I will not hang anything on it. But the case against Lysimachus is stronger, and the one against Nicias is, I think, convincing. Once we have examined their displays of intellectual cowardice, we can return to the philosophical point of dramatizing this theme.

---

23. The term "philosophical courage" is Griswold's (1986:187, 189–93). I think the term is apposite. Military and philosophical courage differ mostly in respect of the thing threatened: in battle the body, in philosophical contexts, the psyche.

24. The metaphor of "stripping" the soul is common in Plato. See, e.g., *Charmides* 154e, *Protagoras* 352a, and *Gorgias* 523c–524a.

Melesias

About Melesias we know little.[25] He and Lysimachus operate jointly (178a–179b), but whether by prior agreement or for some other reason, Melesias allows Lysimachus to do the talking. Melesias never speaks on his own initiative, but only in direct answer to Socrates' questions. His longest reply is five words. Melesias's armor of silence is almost impenetrable. Yet in his brief exchanges we notice an opposition to democracy: the opinion of one expert is worth more than that of four nonexperts, because a good decision is based on knowledge, not on numbers.

Lysimachus

Though he was the son of a prominent Athenian, Aristides "the Just," we know comparatively little about Lysimachus. In the *Meno*, Socrates says Lysimachus had the best education in Athens, but then adds ironically, "you know him, I think, and can say what he is like" (*Meno* 94a; tr. Guthrie). What he is like becomes clear in the *Laches*. In his first speech Lysimachus claims twice that he will be open with Nicias and Laches (178a, 179c). The other side of his openness with Nicias and Laches, of course, is reserve towards others. Lysimachus and Melesias have set themselves apart from most Athenians through their practice of *sussitia* (179b). Lysimachus describes the concerns of Athens as the concerns of others (179d). His family and Melesias's comprise a community (180a5) that they invite Nicias and Laches to join. The κοινωνία is in opposition to the polis. Lysimachus is not, in general, open with others.

Moreover, Lysimachus is not frank with Nicias and Laches. His feigned openness hides a bold conspiracy. Lysimachus and Melesias plotted to obtain Nicias's and Laches's help, and had them brought along on false or uncertain pretences. They are determined to go through with their plan (178a, 179e), but are vague about what their plan is. Lysimachus does not seem so concerned that his son learn a skill to make him safe, as one that will bring him repute. He wants his son to "grow up to honor" (179d). Does he speak to Nicias and Laches in their special capacity as generals or because of their influence as prominent citizens?

Lysimachus says that he and Melesias are ashamed of their parents, but tell their sons only of the grandparent's great and noble deeds. (179c–d). They are ashamed of themselves, but they are loath to let their children know this (179c). "Someone" recommended they have their sons trained by

---

25. In the *Meno*, Socrates says that Melesias and his brother Stephanus became the best wrestlers in Athens, but that they never acquired virtue (94c). Melesias' father, Thucydides, was related by marriage to Cimon, and was thus associated with the aristocrats. According to Thucydides, Melesias was one of three ambassadors who sought peace with Sparta, and who was prominent in the overthrow of the democracy. Plutarch (*Life of Aristides*) suggests that both Lysimachus' and Melesias' families were antidemocratic, but many historians discount this.

Stesilaus (we do not learn who). Why not count that someone as an expert whose view is to be trusted? Lysimachus must either think that the recommendation is of no value (but then why does he pursue the suggestion?), or he means to use Nicias and Laches for a different purpose: he may be concerned primarily with the appearance hoplite training would convey, especially with the respect it might generate. If he thought Nicias was expert in the education of the young, why not send his son to Damon (180d), to whom Nicias sends his son? Or why not ask Socrates, since Socrates was the "expert" who advised Nicias? In fact Lysimachus does not even acknowledge Socrates' presence. Indeed, it appears that he intentionally ignores Socrates. He knew Socrates' father well, and had heard his son mention Socrates often, yet he does not approve of his son's activities when left to do as he pleases (179a, 180e). Lysimachus is a man who likes to command others rather than comply with them (180e, 181c, 187d, 189c, 201c); his covert attempts to gain control amount to a kind of fighting in armor.

Nicias

We get a good idea of Nicias's character from descriptions in Thucydides. When Thucydides tells of the events leading to a temporary peace with Sparta, the "peace of Nicias," he writes: "Nicias, while still happy and honored, wished to secure his good fortune, to obtain a present release from troubles for himself and his countrymen, and hand down to posterity a name as an ever successful statesman. He thought the best way to do this was to keep out of danger and trust as little as possible to fortune, and that peace alone made this possible."[26]

A passionate desire to avoid risks is characteristic of Nicias. When he led the Athenian expedition to Syracuse caution was his downfall.[27] In the *Laches,* Nicias adopts a cautious stance, one that makes him look ridiculous and ultimately provokes him to rashness. For example, take his advice to Lysimachus about fighting in armor. Lysimachus has been careful about seeking advice: "Some people," he says, "guess at the wishes of the person who asks them and answer according to his, and not according to their own opinion" (178b). Nicias is such a person. He is so concerned to avoid disagreement that he does not advise according to his own opinion, but in words he thinks Lysimachus wants to hear.

As a politician and peacebroker Nicias learned a great deal about speech-making. When the Athenian troops were in retreat on Sicily he was able to make one of those speeches that "with little alteration can be made to serve on all occasions alike."[28] The same may be said of his speech in the *Laches* about

---

26. Thucydides, *History* V.16 (tr. Livingstone).
27. For example, he refused to attack when he had a tactical advantage, and waited for reinforcements, giving the Spartans time to aid Syracuse. During an eclipse he refused to attack, though he was not personally superstitious, because he was concerned about how his troops might respond.
28. Thucydides, *History* VII.69 (tr. Livingstone).

fighting in armor: it could be made, with little alteration, in praise of philosophy, or rhetoric, or political expertise, or any activity. As evidence, I present five
brief excerpts from the speech:[29]

(a) "the acquirement of this art is in many ways useful to young men. It is an
advantage to them that instead of the favorite amusements of their
leisure hours they should have one which tends to improve their bodily
health" (181e1–5).

(b) "this and the art of riding are of all arts the most befitting a free man"
(182a1–2).

(c) "for they who are thus exercised in the use of arms are the only persons
being trained for the contest in which we are engaged, and in the ac-
complishments which it requires" (182a2–5).

(d) "Certainly he who possessed the art could not meet with any harm"
(182b2–3).

(e) "this sort of skill inclines a man to pursuit of other noble lessons"
(182b4–5).

Excerpt (a) marks the opening of Nicias' speech. It sets the tone for everything that follows. Although we understand that "this art" refers to ὁπλιτικήυ,
the statement is entirely general. It could be claimed by the advocates of any
learning that their accomplishment was "useful"; that it was to their "advantage" and "improved" them. The only significant specification in the excerpt is
the restriction to "bodily" health, but that is an "alteration" that can be made to
suit the occasion. If he were speaking in praise of philosophy, he could replace
"bodily" with "psychic"; no further alteration would be necessary. Excerpt (b),
with its reference to riding, appeals to the aristocratic prejudices of Lysimachus. It is gratifying for advocates to hear hoplitics described as befitting the
free man. This is the summit of praise, the sort Plato elsewhere reserves for
philosophy (*Sophist* 253c). Excerpt (c) suits the context well—we understand
"the contest in which we are engaged" to mean the war with Sparta. But remove the reference to weapons and you have the vague sort of remark made
about education in so many commencement addresses. Excerpt (d) is remarkable: does Nicias really think that hoplitics provides complete protection
against death or injury? He seems to be playing to Lysimachus's apparent concern for his son's safety. Hoplitics was not the only practice to hold out the
promise of safety. Socrates thought virtue was such a practice when he said in
his trial: "Nothing can harm a good man, either in life or after death" (*Apology*

---

29. Anyone who reads the full speech carefully will notice how general and gratifying it is. Two
points in translation deserve comment here. First, Nicias nowhere uses the term τέχνη, that one
naturally suspects from the translations "art" and "skill." He uses μάθημα/μάθειν and ἐπιστήμη/
ἐπίστασθαι, that are somewhat more general. Second, throughout the speech Nicias speaks of
fighting in armor as a γυμνάσιον (181e5, 182a2, 3, 5). This is peculiar, but Jowett's "weak" translations—"training," "exercise"—are correct. Hoplitics must have been training for the *fully armed*
foot soldier. I suggest that Plato wanted to convey Nicias' lack of familiarity with hoplitics, and to
remind readers of the opposition between ὁ ὁπλίτης and ὁ γύμνης.

41d; tr. Tredennick). Excerpt (e) treats hoplitics as propaideutic. It goes without saying that many practices fit this description. In the *Republic*, Socrates claims that mathematics inspires the philosophic soul to the love of more noble lessons. These excerpts are all too general to count as recommendations of hoplitics. And the fact that most of Nicias's claims are applied to philosophy in other dialogues suggests that here Plato is treating Nicias ironically.

I mentioned that Nicias says what he thinks Lysimachus wants to hear. That can be inferred partly from his general praise of hoplitics. But Nicias also responds on two specific points to concerns of Lysimachus's. First, Lysimachus is resolute that his son should not do as he pleases. Nicias proposes that hoplitics will put a stop to that. Young Aristides presently spends his time conversing with Socrates. Nicias claims the amusement of Aristides' leisure ought to be replaced with one that conduces to bodily health. I doubt that Nicias himself believes this (or he would not have sent his own son to Damon the Sophist to be educated), but he may think that Lysimachus will believe it. Lysimachus, after all, has revealed himself to be less musical and more military than Nicias, by disclosing that he and Melesias adopted the Spartan practice of *sussitia*. Second, Lysimachus had said that he wants Aristides to "grow up to honor" (179d). In response Nicias says, "there is no difficulty in seeing that the knowledge and practice of other military arts will be honorable and valuable to a man" (182c).

In his speech to Lysimachus, then, Nicias uses words that belie what he thinks. No wonder Laches twice accuses Nicias of "decking himself out in words" (κόσμει λόγοις 196b, 197c). [30] Nicias even adopts the armor of "logoi" for his battle against Socrates. Despite saying he has no fear of Socratic dialogue, he shows no desire to enter the conversation. At 188b he says, regretfully, "I was fairly certain all along that where Socrates was, the subject of the discussion would soon be ourselves." Nicias was careful not to hasten that eventuality. (1) *He* did not introduce Socrates into the discussion (Laches did). (2) He warned the others what Socratic conversation would be like (187e–188c): [a] Anyone close will be drawn into argument, [b] He will continually be carried round in circles, [c] Socrates will not let him go until he has thoroughly sifted him. (3) Finally, unable to persuade the others, he waited until Socrates had finished with Laches before entering the discussion. By then he has thought up a defense as he says: "I have been thinking" (194c).

What Nicias has been thinking about is an impregnable defense against Socrates. He will engage him armed with words taken from Socrates' own lips. What risk in that could there be? Apparently Nicias does not suspect that Socrates has greater fear of ignorance than he does of being proved wrong. Socrates has the courage to attack his own convictions. When Nicias fails at defending Socrates' "logoi" against Socrates, he does not look within himself for understanding. Instead he says, "if the treatment has been inadequate, that may be rectified with the help of Damon" (197d, 200b). Nicias

---

30. Plato's choice of words suggests irony. The verb κοσμέω ordinarily refers to governing (what Nicias does) particularly governing an army (see LSJ, κοσμέω I and *Iliad* 14.379), whereas Socrates' use here—"to adorn, embellish"—was applied usually to women (see LSJ κοσμέω III, and *h. Hom*.6. 11, Hes. *Op*.72).

will get armor from the Sophists rather than investigate the question himself. "I think you are very much in want of knowledge" (200a) he tells Laches, but that is his own situation.

Recall that Nicias said fighting in armor would lend one "a more impressive *appearance* at the right time, that is to say, at the time when his appearance will strike terror into his enemies" (182c). He failed to recognize, as Socrates and Laches do, that the appearance of courage is worthless without the reality, that when the time comes, the coward's character is revealed.

It seems clear, then, that Nicias, Lysimachus, and Melesias are represented in the dialogue as fighting covert battles, whether in the armor of "logoi," or deception, or silence. These characters are revealed as lacking virtue and understanding. Thus, the *Laches* associates fighting in armor, in both the literal and the metaphorical sense, with cowardice. We may proceed to ask the reason for this.

IV. IMAGES, CONVENTIONS AND MORAL PHILOSOPHY

Why should Plato associate fighting in armor with cowardice? Is he just opposed to the military conception of courage? Does he want to supplant that with another conception? It is typical of Plato to pervert conventional images. Certainly the claim that philosophers should be kings would have sounded as preposterous in the fifth century B.C.E. as it does today—in conventional usage 'philosopher' was a pejorative term, virtually equivalent to 'sophist'.[31] Or consider the passage of the *Gorgias* in which Socrates speaks about how best to harm ones enemies: "You must see to it that your enemy be not sentenced and punished, but that, if he has robbed others of a large sum of money, he shall not pay it back but shall keep it and squander it, in defiance of god and man, upon himself and his friends; and if his crimes are worthy of death, that, if possible, he shall never die but live forever in wickedness, or, if not this, shall at any rate live as long as possible in this character" (481a; tr. Woodhead). In the *Gorgias* as in the *Laches*, the point of standing a convention on its head is to provoke the reader to consider whether and how much that convention conveys the essentials of courage, or justice, or some other virtue. A passage from the *Protagoras*, thematically connected with our discussion of courage and cowardice, will help to illustrate. Socrates is musing about a saying of Pittacus (a Spartan): "hard it is to be noble." In order to

---

31. See *Laches* 200c. Nicias calls Laches ignorant and suggests that the sophist Damon will have an impregnable definition of courage, whereupon Laches replies, derisively, "You are a philosopher Nicias, of that I am aware." See also *Charmides* 161b. Charmides defines σωφροσύνη as "doing ones own," whereupon Socrates replies, "You wicked boy! ... this is what Critias or some other philosopher has told you." See also *Phaedo* 64b–c, where Simmias remarks that most people think "death would serve the philosophers right" (tr. Tredennick). Small wonder that Adeimantus says in *Republic* VI that those who devote their lives to philosophy are cranks (ἀλλοκότους), rascals (παμπονήρους), or totally useless (ἀκρήστους) to society (487d).

defend Pittacus, Socrates describes the Spartans as wise and sophisticated:

> The most ancient and fertile homes of philosophy among the Greeks are Crete and
> Sparta, where are to be found more Sophists than anywhere on earth. But they
> conceal their wisdom like the Sophists Protagoras spoke of, and pretend to be fools
> so that their superiority over the rest of Greece may not be known to lie in wisdom,
> but seem to consist in fighting and courage.... By this disguise they take in the pro-
> Spartans in other cities, who to emulate them go about with bruised ears, bind
> their hands with thongs, take to physical training, and wear short cloaks under the
> impression that these are the practices that have made the Spartans a great power
> in Greece (342a–343b; tr. Guthrie).

There is much irony in this passage. But a serious point Plato wants to make
is the importance of distinguishing between the accidental and the essential.
The Spartans are not the wisest of Greeks, but they claim preeminence in fighting and courage. Yet all the cauliflower ears and short cloaks in the world will
not a Spartan make. The Spartophile mistakes accidental appearances of typically courageous men for the essentials.[32]

It is a common human failing to emulate superficially those we admire. But
in ethics the mistaking of πάθος for οὐσία can be a source of serious confusion.
The *Laches* shows this by exposing the accidentality of the military image of
courage. The ordinary person, steeped in Homeric images such as Ajax fighting
by the ships, does not see that the armor is accidental to Ajax's courage. The depiction of Stesilaus as cowardly in similar circumstances is a small corrective.
Plato's more extensive attack on the connection between fighting in armor and
cowardice reveals how pervasive that connection had become. But there is danger in his Socratic approach that refuses to say what courage is essentially. A
person who is fixed in the ordinary perspective may not ever get beyond criticism of conventional associations. He will not see Socrates as exposing inadequacies in the conventional image of courage; he will not be provoked to consider what courage is. Such a person would be unlikely to find any value in
Socrates. Others might even take him to be rejecting courage as a value. In
fifth-century Athens many were prepared to reject it.[33] "Courage" one might
have said, "is no vice, but it may sometimes be little more than foolishness."[34]
This way of taking Socrates' criticisms tended to confuse him with the sophists.

A. W. H. Adkins once claimed that the source of the Athenian 'turmoil of
values' was a shift in emphasis from competitive to cooperative excellences.
But Plato, if I am right, spied an additional source.[35] The sophist's way of

---

32. A good contrast to the Spartophile is Socrates in retreat from Delium (see *Symposium*
221b). It was not Socrates' armor that frightened the enemy, but only the same "lofty strut and side-
ways glance" that he plied about Athens (tr. Joyce). Unlike the cauliflower ear and short cloak, these
appearances are not manufactured; they are not κατὰ συμβεβηκός. They are unalterable outward
expressions of Socrates' character.

33. See Adkins (1973:4). Adkins account of Greek ethics has been called into question (e.g. by
Williams [1993]), but his point about the turmoil of values and the tension between competitive
and cooperative virtues stands.

34. Take Thrasymachus in *Republic* I. He will not call justice a vice, but he will call it "high-
minded foolishness" (348c).

looking at things leaves conventional images of courage and justice intact, while changing the appraisal of these images. The warrior who dies fighting in armor is still called courageous, but we are now made to wonder whether courage is worthwhile. The law-abiding citizen is still called just, but when the laws do not benefit him, we wonder how advantageous justice is. In the twentieth century there are many who will not go so far as to say that piety is a vice, but who have little time for piety themselves. They still associate piety with a set of outward behaviors, but they no longer hold those behaviors to be worthwhile.

For Plato it is true *a priori* that virtue is a good and vice an evil. If people come to believe that practicing injustice shows good sense (σωφροσύνη; *Protagoras* 333c1 ff.), they are mistaken about what justice or good sense is. If willingness to go to war is called courage, but is rightly not praised, then it was not really courage after all (*Protagoras* 359c). Conventional ethics goes wrong by reposing in accidentals, rather than in essentials. Courage may sometimes require fleeing from battle (*Laches* 193c–d); justice may require breaking the law.[36] It is part of Plato's instruction to break the connection between the virtues and their common images, even if he must later restore that connection in some measure.[37] This insight of Plato's is stated with precision by Hegel in the *Philosophy of Right*:

> [The] concept, as it actually is in its truth may not only be different from our common idea of it, but in fact must be different from it in form and outline. If however, the common idea of it is not false in content also, the concept may be exhibited as implied in it and as essentially present in it. In other words, the common idea may be raised to assume the form of the concept. But the common idea is so far from being the standard or criterion of the concept … that it must derive its truth from the latter, adjust itself to it, and recognize its own nature by its aid.[38]

Let me summarize my chapter about the *Laches* in Hegelian terms. The image of the battle-ready soldier expresses the common idea of courage. But the common idea must be distinguished from real courage as πάθος is distinguished from οὐσία. Πάθος and οὐσία are intimately related however, so the common idea may be able, on occasion, to exhibit or represent the actuality of courage. But the common idea hovers freely over one representation and another: it may represent boldness, or confidence, or willfulness. Its representation of courage will be adequately intelligible only in terms of a prior grasp of the essentials of courage. Absent that understanding we have no guide—in Platonic terms, no tether—to secure for us what is right and true about courage in

---

35. His diagnosis is similar to the one Nietzsche offers in *The Genealogy of Morals*, when he talks about the slave morality that replaced the aristocratic pair Good/Bad with the pair Good/Evil. See Nietzsche (ed. Kaufmann, 1968), 463–475.

36. See *Apology* 32c–d. The thirty commanded Socrates to extradite Leon of Salamis. Socrates' refusal could have earned him the death penalty. Socrates' principle that it is better to suffer wrong than to do wrong compels him to violate any law that commands unjust action.

37. The requirement of restoring the connection with conventional accounts is clear enough in the *Republic*.

38. Hegel (tr. Knox, 1952). Introduction, §2¶3.

the common idea. If we are to appreciate the image of courage, then, we must first break with it, and the most decisive way to do that is to see that the image is compatible with the very opposite of courage—cowardice.

WORKS CITED

Adkins, A. W. H. "ἀρετή, τέχνη, Democracy and the Sophists." *Journal of Hellenic Studies,* 93 (1973): 3–12.

Blitz, Mark. "An Introduction to the Reading of Plato's *Laches.*" *Interpretation* 5 (1975): 185–225.

Brickhouse, T., and N. Smith. *Plato's Socrates.* New York: Oxford University Press, 1994.

Buford, Thomas O. "Plato on the Educational Consultant: An Interpretation of the *Laches.*" *Ideal Studies* 7 (1977): 151–171.

Burnyeat, Myles. "Aristotle on Learning to be Good," In Rorty, Amélie O., *Essays on Aristotle's Ethics.* Berkeley: University of California Press, 1980.

Cooley, Kenneth W. "Unity and Diversity of the Virtues in the *Charmides, Laches,* and *Protagoras.*" *Kinesis* 1 (1969): 100–106.

Detienne, M. "La phalange: problémes et controverses." J. P. Vernant, ed. *Problémes de la guerre en Grece Ancienne.* Paris: La Haye, Mouton, 1968.

Devereux, Daniel T. "Courage and Wisdom in Plato's *Laches.*" *Journal of the History of Philosophy* 15 (1977): 129–141.

———. "The Unity of the Virtues in Plato's *Protagoras* and *Laches.*" *Philosophical Review* 101 (1992): 765–789.

Diehl, E., ed., *Anthologia Lyrica Graeca,* 2nd ed., vol. 1. Leipzig: Teubner, 1936.

Fagles, Robert, tr. Homer. *The Iliad.* New York: Penguin Books, 1990.

Gould, Carol S. "Socratic Intellectualism and the Problem of Courage: An Interpretation of Plato's *Laches.*" *History of Philosophy Quarterly* 4 (1987): 265–279.

Griswold, Charles. "Philosophy, Education, and Courage in Plato's *Laches.*" *Interpretation* 14 (1986): 177–193.

Hamilton, E., and H. Cairns. *Plato: The Collected Dialogues.* Princeton: Bollingen, 1963.

Hegel, G. W. F., tr. *Philosophy of Right,* tr. Knox. Oxford: Clarendon Press, 1952.

Hinske, N. "Zur Interpretation des platonischen Dialogs *Laches.*" *Kantstudien* 59 (1968): 62–79.

Hoerber, R. G. "Plato's *Laches.*" *Classical Philology* 63 (1968): 95–105.

Irwin, Terence. *Plato's Ethics.* New York: Oxford University Press, 1995.

Kahn, Charles H. "Plato's Methodology in *Laches.*" *Revue Internationale de Philosophie* 40 (1986): 7–21.

Kosman, A. "On Being Properly Affected." In *Essays on Aristotle's Ethics.* Berkeley: University of California Press, 1980.

Livingstone, Richard, tr. Thucydides. *History of the Peloponnesian War.*

McKeon, R., ed. *The Basic Works of Aristotle.* New York: Random House, 1941.

Mills, M. J. "The Discussions of *Andreia* in the *Eudemian* and *Nicomachean Ethics.*" *Phronesis* 25 (1980): 198–218.

Nietzsche, F., tr. *Basic Writings.* Ed. W. Kaufmann. New York: Modern Library, 1968.

O'Brien, M. J. "The Unity of the *Laches.*" *Essays in Ancient Greek Philosophy,* vol. 1, ed. Anton and Kustas, 303–316. Albany: State University of New York Press, 1983.

Penner, Terence M. "The Unity of Virtue." *Philosophical Review* 82 (1973): 35–68.

———. "What Laches and Nicias Miss—and Whether Socrates Thinks Courage Merely a Part of Virtue." *Ancient Philosophy* 12 (1992): 1–28.

Redding, Paul. "Nietzschean Perspectivism and the Logic of Practical Reason." *The Philosophical Forum* 22 (1990): 80–81.

Santas, Gerasimos. "Socrates at Work on Virtue and Knowledge in Plato's *Laches.*" *Review of Metaphysics* 22 (1969): 433–460.

Schmid, Walter Thomas. "The Socratic Conception of Courage." *History of Philosophy Quarterly* 2, (1985): 113–130.

———. *On Manly Courage: A Study of Plato's Laches.* Carbondale: Southern Illinois University Press, 1992.

Snodgrass, A. M. "The Hoplite Reform and History." *Journal of Hellenic Studies* 85 (1965): 110–122.

Sokolowski, Robert. "Knowing Essentials." *Review of Metaphysics* 47 (1994): 691–709.

Stokes, Michael C. *Plato's Socratic Conversations: Drama and Dialectic in Three Dialogues.* Baltimore: Johns Hopkins University Press, 1986.

Umphrey, Stewart. "On The Theme of Plato's *Laches.*" *Interpretation* 6 (1976): 1–10.

———."Plato's *Laches* on Courage." *Apeiron* 10 (1976): 14–22.

Williams, Bernard. *Shame and Necessity.* Berkeley: University of California Press, 1993.

Woodruff, Paul. "Expert Knowledge in The *Apology* and *Laches:* What a General Needs to Know." (Add. comm. by M. McPherran, 116–130.) *Proceedings of the Boston Area Colloquium in Ancient Philosophy* 3 (1987): 79–115.

7

Why Doesn't Plato Speak?

Elinor J. M. West

> Perhaps someone might say, Socrates can you not go away from us and live quietly, without talking?
>
> —Plato, *Apology* 37e

Suppose one or another of us had lived in ancient Athens. Then face-to-face with Plato, one could have asked him a question like the one that Priscilla, centuries later, asked of John Alden. Indeed, upon hearing him request her hand on behalf of Myles Standish, Priscilla inquired, "Why not speak for yourself, John?" How lovely it would be if Plato could tell us in his own voice or person why he, like John, does not speak for himself in the dialogues. The name Plato of course is heard: first at *Apology* 34a in a list of persons, willing to testify to not having been corrupted by Socrates; second, at 38b in a list of those willing to help pay Socrates' fine; and lastly, at *Phaedo* 59c, where Plato is said to be sick and unable to be present at Socrates' final conversation. Yet so impersonal are such lists that Plato resembles that painter who has put a likeness of himself into his *Last Judgment* but will not be recognized as present unless the viewer happens to know what Michelangelo looks like. Besides, even if his name is mentioned, Plato is voiceless.[1] Could it be better for him to say nothing? Perhaps so, for only then will it be possible for us to philosophize with his Socrates and for Plato's enigmatic conversations to continue.[2]

---

1. Those of us living in literate cultures sometimes forget that in an oral culture it is not the look of a man's signature but the sound of his voice that marks his identity. See William Harris, *Ancient Literacy* (Cambridge: Harvard University Press, 1989): 72–3, and n.38 where Harris notes that even in the mid-fourth century after an individual's signature had been recognized as distinctive, it was still the oral way of doing things that everyone understood.

2. Paul Friedländer adopts an oral thesis, Plato I, tr. Hans Meyerhoff (New York: Bollingen Foundation, 1958): 165–6, "For the written dialogue transmits its dialogical ... dynamics to the reader. To him is addressed every question raised by Socrates." Kenneth Sayre more recently argues that our relation to Plato develops out of Plato's oral relation to the historical Socrates. That Plato, even though writing, hopes to produce a similar effect in us. *Plato's Literary Garden* (Notre Dame: University of Notre Dame Press, 1995): 25–6. For how my position differs, see ns. 11, 20, 27, 29, and 35.

Later it will be plain how this chapter is at odds with traditional ways of reading 'Plato' but in order to underscore its idiosyncrasies, one must first go
through what is taken for granted when reading the dialogues. Since far from
treating Plato as a reluctant speaker, scholars more often than not celebrate him
as among the world's greatest authors. Hence Plato and Socrates are traditionally distinguished not as speaking or not speaking but as speaking or writing.

Time and again each is imagined as painted by Jacques Louis David in of *The
Death of Socrates*. There within an ornate frame, separate from a three-di-
mensional reality is a two-dimensional image of Socrates speaking with griev-
ing friends. With the index finger on his left hand pointed upward, Socrates alludes to the journey about to be taken and reaches out with his other hand for
a cup of hemlock. Near the foot of the couch where Socrates is half seated is a
second old man. His head is bowed in resignation. His back is turned toward
Socrates. Despite his white beard, one sees through the years to recognize
Plato. For under his chair are inks, pens, and scrolls. That what David illustrated has been inspired by Plato's *Phaedo* is clear enough not simply from the
placement of Socrates' legs but from a conversation David had with a priest
named Adry before creating this image. Indeed, it was Adry who suggested that
Plato, even though sick, be painted as present. Hence it is not Plato's facts that
are depicted but rather, as FitzPatrick points out, our own way of preserving the
past.[3] For it is we who separate the two by equating Plato with something we
read long after Socrates' death. Indeed, it is we who disagree over how what we
read is to be interpreted.

I. A MOUTHPIECE THEORY

Few scholars will agree that Plato's reluctance to use his own voice is of any real
philosophical significance. On the contrary, the vast majority has skirted the
issue of Plato's anonymity, by insisting that just as John speaks for Myles Standish so Socrates speaks for Plato. Many recent philosophers find two Socrate-
ses in Plato but only one of them is treated as a mouthpiece.[4] Such an individ-
uation depends upon reconstructing Plato's corpus. So what is stipulated first is
that after Socrates' death, Plato developed his own philosophy, or that the theories found in Plato's later writings contain doctrines or follow methods significantly different from those earlier adopted by Socrates.[5] Hence, the best way
of tracing Plato's philosophical development is to track down a date of composition for each dialogue or failing that, grouping each according to the rough
age of its author—asking, that is, whether it is early, middle or late 'Plato'.

---

3. Consult P. J. FitzPatrick, "The Legacy of Socrates" in *Socratic Questions*, ed. Barry Gower
and Michael Stokes (London and New York : Routledge, 1992):198.

4. See Gregory Vlastos, *Socrates: Ironist and Moral Philosopher* (Ithaca: Cornell University
Press, 1991): 45–80. Also, Benson's introduction to *Essays on the Philosophy of Socrates* (Oxford:
Oxford University Press, 1992), 4 ff.

5. David Sedley, "The Dramatic Personae of Plato's *Phaedo*," *Philosophical Dialogues*, ed. Tim-
othy Smiley (Oxford: Oxford University Press, 1996): 3–22. Sedley argues that Plato handles doubt
differently than Socrates did.

Many scholars, adopting this interpretive strategy, equate the Socrates who speaks in early 'Plato' with the historical Socrates.[6] The Socrates who speaks in middle or late 'Plato' is the mouthpiece. Or to paraphrase Vlastos: The proper noun Socrates E is shorthand for a theory belonging to the historical Socrates but the proper noun Socrates M or L is shorthand for a theory belonging to Plato. If one adopts this interpretive method, the problem of Plato's anonymity is resolved. But it has been made to disappear by embracing a concept popularized during the nineteenth century, which stipulates that everything in the universe, including Plato, develops or evolves. Here then is a second case of saying at least as much about ourselves as Plato when interpreting his works.[7] Nor will we recognize ourselves in what is stipulated by alluding to what we have reconstructed as 'the voice of the author'.[8]

In addition to such questionable usage, there is the difficulty of establishing precise compositional dates, a problem thoroughly discussed by Thesleff and Nails.[9] Yet what speaks most loudly against this theory is what has not been satisfactorily resolved, i.e., why so many of Plato's readers just as Socrates' respondents are left in aporia or greatly perplexed over how to answer Socrates' questions.[10] Besides, given the fact that Socrates wrote nothing and Plato who may provoke the questions we ask without giving answers (except perhaps in letters whose authenticity is questioned), it turns out to be Plato who is inadequately represented when identified with a set of dated theories.[11]

One might of course enjoy being permitted to abstract the essence of something Socrates said just as if it were a 'voiceless' statement or to test the logic of his definition by artlessly upgrading ancient ways of talking so they resemble our own ways of philosophizing. But Priscilla did not ask John to write for himself but to 'speak' for himself instead of Myles Standish. Nor would she have said what she did unless she had been face to face with John and discerned his reluctance to act as a mouthpiece. The fact that Socrates did not write but chose instead to talk philosophically may turn out to be a powerful reason for rejecting any mouthpiece theory of interpretation—not simply because it equivocates between writing and speaking but especially because it undercuts the give and take of those conversations still to be heard in such dialogues as *Symposium*, *Phaedo*, *Phaedrus*, and *Republic*.[12] Who, for instance, would be persuaded to dismiss the

---

6. Vlastos treats the figure of Socrates in early Plato as historical. Charles Kahn does not in "Did Plato Write Socratic Dialogues?" *Classical Quarterly* 31 (1981): 305–320.

7. John Herman Randall, *Plato: Dramatist of the Life of Reason* (New York: Columbia University Press, 1970), 34.

8. For this concept of "authorial voice," see Sedley (1996), 4–5 and n.2.

9. Holger Thesleff, *Studies in Platonic Chronology*. Commentationes Humanarum Litterarum 70 (Helsinki: Societas Scientiarum Fennica, 1982). Debra Nails, *Agora, Academy and the Conduct of Philosophy* (Dordrecht: Kluwer, 1995).

10. For a penetrating analysis of such perplexity, even in the middle dialogues, see Michael Frede, "Plato's Arguments and the Dialogue Form" in *Oxford Studies in Ancient Philosophy*, Suppl. Vol., ed. James C. Klagge and Nicholas D. Smith (Oxford: Clarendon Press, 1992), 201–219.

11. My case for Plato's oral sensitivity will be rooted in Hellenic culture and epic poetry; Sayre's (1995:10–17) is based on what Plato says in his *Seventh Letter* regarding the difficulty of communicating.

12. For *Republic* as conversation, Diskin Clay "Reading the Republic," in *Platonic Writings, Platonic Readings*, ed. Charles Griswold, Jr. (New York: Routledge, 1988), 19 ff. For *Symposium*, see n. 22.

questions of a respondent as close to Plato as his brother Glaucon by labeling his bright elder sibling as a "yes-man" or devising a methodological reason for crediting Plato as author rather than his elder brother?[13] Besides, what is blocked from view when adopting language such as 'mouthpiece' or "yes-man" is our own longing for a neat system or foolproof method instead of a messy conversation. Or more explicitly put, rather than making oneself sensitive to Plato's open-ended recreation of philosophical discourse, Plato's conversations are closed off from the world. Nor do we hear how he recreates the personal character of a Socrates' elenchus as characterized in Plato's early-middle *Gorgias.*

What is said to Polus by Socrates at 471d–472d not only explicates what is meant by the personal character of an elenchus but suggests why a word like mouthpiece might mislead a modern reader through confusing one of Socrates' cross-examinations with what is heard in a law court. For just as one says mouthpiece when naming a part of the telephone so mouthpiece is used when speaking of a lawyer, who is hired not simply to speak for his client but often in place of him. Indeed, how frequently one hears of a defendant actually advised against taking the stand or personally responding to a prosecutor's questions because being unskilled at how such question-and-answer operates, he, even though innocent, may end up incriminating himself. So just as Socrates distinguishes his search for the truth from a lawyer's search for victory, so one must clarify why the authority that Socrates will not recognize is the vote of a majority. Or to listen to how he presents his arguments.

Polus, who has been acting as questioner, is puzzled over why Socrates, who has been acting as respondent, is not refuted. He is told that as questioner he has failed to refute the opinions of his respondent. Socrates' own art of cross-examination depends upon finding premises believed by the respondent and then showing how these beliefs actually imply the opposite of what was at first said. Yet Polus has not done this. By basing his refutation instead upon what most people believe, Polus has brought false witnesses against Socrates. Indeed, that is why Polus would make a good lawyer. For the witnesses whom Polus uses aim at victory through counting up numbers of votes but with an elenchus, only one vote counts: that of the respondent. For he is the authority. Hence, if he will not agree that he is wrong, it is irrelevant how many others will.[14] Thus to cast Socrates as a mouthpiece or his respondent as a yes-man is at odds with the spirit of Socrates' elenchus. This is my reason for insisting that an enigmatic Plato not be treated as a maker of systems or even an author of theories but as one who makes use of alphabetical script to recreate the oral relation of Socrates to any given respondent. Later, we can ask how in spite of writing Plato can pass on to us the oral spirit in which Socrates philosophized, or how the problem of Plato's anonymity is a function of Socrates' historicity. Why, that is, no other 'principal interlocutor' is akin to Socrates whose idiosyn-

---

13. Gregory Vlastos, "The Socratic Elenchus," *Oxford Studies in Ancient Philology* 1 (1983): Appendix 57–8. Also, Richard Kraut's introduction to *The Cambridge Companion to Plato* (Cambridge; Cambridge University Press, 1992), 26.

14. I owe a debt of gratitude to Richard Robinson for his excellent account of the personal character of the elenchus in *Plato's Earlier Dialectic* (Oxford: Clarendon Press 1953), 15–19.

cratic influence on Plato will not to be recaptured when one construes him as one bloodless character among others who exist only on a rolled up papyrus or the pages of a lettered book?[15]

II. DOES PLATO CREATE PHILOSOPHICAL DRAMAS?

A second group of scholars, more sensitive to the spoken word, is deeply committed to interpreting what Plato creates as philosophical conversation rather than philosophical theory. Indeed, explicitly denying that one can abstract sentences from a conversation, Leo Strauss shows why a statement in Shakespeare would be inappropriately removed from the mouth of his character to be ascribed to its author. To use his example without directly quoting his words: it is not Shakespeare who defines life as a tale told by an idiot full of sound and fury and signifying nothing. It is we who, after watching Macbeth violate the sacred laws of civilization, have little difficulty in recognizing such a world as reflecting Macbeth. How then is Macbeth Shakespeare's mouthpiece?[16] Which of course does not imply that Socrates is Macbeth but only that Strauss has chosen to argue by analogy so that those who read Plato's dialogue will no longer be deprived of what can be discovered by thinking of Plato as authoring dramas. On this view, for example, one's attention will be drawn not only to Plato's mimicry of men's characters but also to how Socrates' questions can lay bare the world as seen by his respondent. Yet since our concern is dramatic philosophizing, why not ask how a seeming ornament, such as a crown, may say a great deal more about the fifth-century world of an Alcibiades, whether Plato's dialogues turn out to be open-ended structures like Homer's epics or dramas like Sophocles' tragedies.

Did Alcibiades come drunk, late, and uninvited to an actual party at Agathon's who in 416 B.C.E. was celebrating the victory of his first tragic drama? Were others like Phaedrus and Eryximachus actually there? Indeed, is Plato alluding, as is sometimes thought, to the fact that all three names were to appear some months later on lists of men allegedly having parodied the sacred Eleusinian mysteries in the presence of uninitiated persons at a private dinner party? For this real-life scandal had cast suspicion on Alcibiades, just before he was to sail for Sicily as commander in chief of Athenian forces.[17] Indeed, in view of the hysteria over this and the mutilation of the *Hermes*, Alcibiades who had been formally accused demanded to be tried before sailing. He was refused. So when he was recalled to stand trial after reaching Sicily, he deserted to Sparta where the enemy was given the sort of military advice that ultimately resulted not only in Athens losing the war but in her decline.[18] Since Plato's ancient readers

---

15. Eschewing the anonymity issue, Kraut (1992) calls everyone who leads a conversation a "principle interlocutor."

16. Leo Strauss, *The City and The Man* (Chicago: University of Chicago Press, 1964), 59.

17. Our ancient sources are *Thucydides* Bk. IV, Andokides' *On the Mysteries*, and Plutarch, n.25.

18. The date of Agathon's party is 416 B.C.E. but the date of Apollodorus' conversation with Aristodemus, is 400 B.C.E. Since in 400 B.C.E. Andokides is again brought up on charges of impiety and reviews evidence he had earlier provided about these 415 B.C.E. sacrileges, Apollodorus may be correcting gossip that has grown out of Andokides' trial.

would have known such facts, it is far from inappropriate for scholars to ask again today whether his *Symposium* contains allusions to these sacrileges, especially when his reader only listens indirectly to what is said at Agathon's. Indeed, a few scholars locate Plato's readers among one group of listeners who crowd around Appollodorus after he is asked twice in as many days to tell what he knows about Agathon's party. These are things one overhears reiterated only months before Socrates is tried for impiety and corrupting young men's morale—one of whom gossips may have identified as Alcibiades.[19]

Then even if it is not possible to prove that Plato is recreating events in the late fifth century, surely it is relevant to ask historical questions. For with such things in mind, one discerns why it is the date of Socrates' conversation rather than the date of Plato's composition that is of more significance for those who would ground Plato's conversations in fifth-century realities.[20] Besides, even if Plato's characterizations are in part imaginative, his depiction of Alcibiades is consistent with what is known from elsewhere of this young military genius who was notorious not only for his good looks but for his love of power and Socrates.

Supported by flute girls and crowned with ivy and violets, a drunken Alcibiades arrives at Agathon's door late that evening. Observing that all are sober, Alcibiades will honor Agathon and leave unless they consent to drink with him. Everyone agrees, and Alcibiades appoints himself leader of the drinking until everyone is intoxicated. Yet before settling down beside Agathon, he removes the wreath from his own head to transfer it to the poet's head but when holding it in front of his own eyes, he is prevented from seeing Socrates who is also sitting there. Invited to make the third on the couch, Alcibiades all at once recognizes Socrates (213 a–b)!

Why does Plato introduce Alcibiades wearing a crown of violets and ivy? Does it symbolize his recent election as commander in chief of Athenian forces? Violets have long been associated with Athens and may, as Nussbaum indicates, suggest Alcibiades's love of his native city.[21] Another, recalling his demand that Agathon share some of his ribbons with Socrates, is puzzled over why Socrates also should be crowned.[22] Helen Bacon relates her puzzlement to the *aporia* at the close of the *Symposium* and suggests that Socrates is crowned for knowing more about the unity of tragedy and comedy than either the tragic poet Agathon or the comic poet Aristophanes. For each is forced to agree with Socrates' par-

---

19. Although I explain the point of such talking differently, Martha Nussbaum is well aware of it as gossip. See her "The Speech of Alcibiades," *Philosophy and Literature* 3 (1979): 135–8.

20. Since in any given dialogue, I treat Plato as recreating Socrates' oral relation with his respondent (not merely Plato's own oral relation with the historical Socrates), I, unlike Sayre (1995), 2 ff., find dramatic dates helpful.

21. Nussbaum (1979): 162–3.

22. Helen Bacon, "Socrates' Crowned," *Virginia Quarterly Review* 35 (1959): 415: "Why is the last word in this dialogue about love given not to Eros but to Dionysus…?" Others who puzzle over this *aporia* are Diskin Clay ("The Tragic and Comic Poets of the Symposium," *Essays in Ancient Greek Philosophy* II, ed. John Anton and Herbert Preus [Albany: State University of New York Press, 1983], 186 ff.), Stanley Rosen (*Plato's Symposium* [New Haven: Yale University Press, 1968]), and Richard Patterson ("The Platonic Art of Tragedy and Comedy," *Philosophy and Literature* 6 [1982]: 76 ff).

adox that the two forms of poetry are one and the same before falling asleep. Hence the ivy in the crown symbolizes Socrates' Dionysian knowledge.[23]

Yet how beautifully this crown has been deployed in showing not only Alcibiades's character but also the sort of life he values is best confirmed not only by attending to the materials from which it is made but observing how it functions. For if Alcibiades loves being honored, he loathes being dishonored. Hence, Alcibiades upon seeing Socrates once more sarcastically asks why he is not sitting beside a joker or lover of jokes like Aristophanes instead of the "best looking man there." Indeed, Socrates is grudgingly crowned for conquering everyone, including Alcibiades, in conversation. Later, Socrates will also be blamed for dishonoring Alcibiades for disdaining his sexual advances after leading him on like some hubristic satyr. Yet in the process of talking about Socrates, Alcibiades confesses that when he is no longer with Socrates, his own love of popularity gets the better of him. So when seeing him again he can not help but recall admitting that he neglects himself to do the business of the Athenians, and then feeling ashamed of what he had confessed. Hence the crown in front of his eyes not only adumbrates the life that he has already chosen but confirms why he is not lying about his relationship with Socrates.[24] Nor is what Alcibiades says at all inconsistent with how he behaves when hearing in Sicily that he has been tried and condemned to death by the Athenians in absentia. For then it was a dishonored Alcibiades who before turning up in Sparta had declared: "I'll show them I'm alive."[25]

That the ambivalent loves of this brilliant young man would lead not only to personal tragedy but to tragedy for Athens was already known by those listening to Apollodorus tell the story of Agathon's party, half a decade after Athens had been defeated by Sparta. What was not known is what might happen to Socrates as a result of his friendship with Alcibiades. For the Athenians unlike ourselves were far from esteeming either Socrates or his talking and so it is little wonder that Alcibiades's love of popularity had long since led him to look elsewhere for the honor he so craved. Yet, if the fate of Socrates is unsettled when he declares tragedy and comedy to be one and the same, did Plato leave what he had composed open or did he complete it? If the unity of those arts to which Socrates alludes actually refers to the structure of Plato's Symposium, then our relation to Plato as author may exhibit that logographic necessity that Strauss describes as complete and hence radically different from Socrates' oral relation with his respondent.[26] Yet, if Plato's use of this crown forces us to rethink Alcibiades' relationship with Socrates then his dialogue has been left open so that these events will be relived and retold in the future.[27] Hence my question is this: Is Plato's text an organic unity, complete with beginning, middle and

---

23. Bacon concludes that in the judgment of Dionysus, Socrates-Eros is the greatest of all poets and therefore wins the crown of tragedy and comedy from Agathon and Aristophanes.

24. Nussbaum detects how Alcibiades' actions are based on his hatred of losing (1979), 131–2.

25. Plutarch's *Lives* IV, Alcibiades, xix–xxii.

26. Strauss connects his concept of "logographical necessity" with organic unity (1964), 52–3.

27. Taking Diotima's relation to Socrates as his paradigm, Sayre instead argues (1995:esp. 124–5) that Socrates has fallen short of Diotima and therefore failed with Alcibiades. Indeed, where Sayre conceives of Plato as increasingly willing to express reservations about Socrates' philosophical skills, I would cite Plato's allusion to Alcibiades at *Republic* 494a–d as substantiating my interpretation.

end, like that appropriately ascribed by Aristotle to Sophocles' *Oedipus Rex,* or
is our relationship to Plato merely analogous to Socrates' oral relation with his
respondent? My own position will be clarified by analyzing the function of
Plato's dramatic settings.

III. HOW ARE WE RELATED TO PLATO?

Burger studies the text of the *Phaedo* as a dramatic dialogue, and points out
how it is split exactly in half by a central episode during which Socrates takes a
break from the argument and takes the occasion to warn his friends against mis-
ology.[28] She then inquires if this "interlude" happens by chance, i.e., can it be
omitted from the text on the grounds that it unlike the arguments is unnecessary? Burger thinks not. She insists that it has been made necessary by the onslaught of Simmias and Cebes on Socrates' prior arguments for the soul's immortality. Phaedo and his friends are so upset over the failure of Socrates' proofs
that they have lost all faith in the value of talking about these proofs in particular and all future proofs in general. Their faith in reason must be restored before Socrates can answer the objections of Cebes and Simmias. Yet what Burger
treats as artistically necessary is also philosophical.

By taking Phaedo as his respondent, Socrates exorcises his fear that Socrates
may not survive because his proofs for the soul's immorality seem to have
"died." By implicitly showing how predicates such as death and life are not
equally applicable to both men and arguments, Phaedo can be freed from his
fears by being taught how to think differently about arguments and men. Mir-
roring Phaedo's language, Socrates makes him aware of what he had believed
and changes his attitude so Phaedo need not cut his hair in memory of dead arguments. Hence, this "interlude" is not a rest from philosophizing but only a
break from the arguments of Simmias and Cebes.

But what, then, of Plato's prologue? Being staged in the mountains of the
Peloponnese, is it properly characterized as background material framing
the main conversation that is staged in a prison in Athens?[29] Or more significantly, is our relation to Plato as author correctly characterized as differing
from Socrates' oral relation to his respondent as what is written differs from
what is said? Or do we as Plato's respondents act as both readers and listeners? If so, then our relation to Plato may be analogous to Socrates' oral relation with his respondent.

Consider in the first place, then, how Phaedo has already been addressed before we join in. Before Plato's conversation ever commences the sound of talk-

---

28. Ronna Burger, *The Phaedo: A Platonic Labyrinth* (New Haven: Yale University Press, 1984),
4–5 and 23. Burger who adopts Strauss's contrast between chance and necessity has some difficulty
clarifying "logographic necessity," 3, 4, 20, and 220, n.15.

29. Friedländer, *Plato* III, 52: writes: "Uneasiness spreads even onto the *frame* conversation"
(my italics). Perhaps Burger (1984, 23), has been influenced by Friedländer's language. In any case,
she speaks of 'outermost frames' and 'internal frames' and even moves toward 'frames of reference'
when speaking of the prologue as supplying "background materials."

ing is already heard.[30] Hence, unlike David's ornately framed two-dimensional image of Socrates talking with friends, what Plato creates is not separated from the world. Indeed, even as we do not directly hear the guests talking at Agathon's but only Apollodorus reiterating the words of Aristodemus, so we are not present when Socrates drinks the hemlock. We only hear about that event second hand when Echecrates who had not been there asks Phaedo months later in the little village of Phlius to tell him how Socrates died. So by thinking of Phaedo's conversation with Echecrates as a frame dialogue, we forget how its temporal unification depends upon our reexperiencing in the present something said or felt at a specific time in the past. By introducing dramatic elements like frames, scenes, and prologues into his compositions when no such divisions are in Plato's original, we become insensitive to time. We fail to observe how he carefully leaves open what we reduce to written text.

To confirm Burger's sensitive observation that this interlude splits Plato's text in half, then, is not therefore to argue that the mistrust of reason felt by Phaedo and his friends proves so dangerous that it spreads to the 'frame dialogue' as well. Since emotions are probably not spread in space like butter on bread or rolls but passed down to others instead through time and in association with similar attitudes taken toward something heard or read earlier. What is to be explained, then, is not how similar emotions appear in two different places in Plato's written script, but how in the future Echecrates again feels emotions similar to those felt months earlier by Phaedo and his friends in an Athenian prison only hours before Socrates drank the hemlock. This "interlude" is not simply at the center of a text, but it also takes place in time. Hence emotions felt in the past—far from spreading to a different place in a two-dimensional text—are transmitted through time to be picked up in the present by Plato's listener or reader. Nor is it likely that the jolt delivered to Socrates' proofs by the objections of Simmias and Cebes will stop without affecting others after first shaking up Echecrates and ourselves. For others will come after us also to listen with Echecrates as Phaedo explains how Socrates had responded to their criticisms. In view of Plato's apparent sensitivity to how conversations take place in time, it is important to consider rather carefully why he has deliberately decided not to close up his 'script'. Or how he can convey what it felt like to be there with Socrates even as Phaedo conveys it to his listeners in Phlius.

When Phaedo mentions, for instance, that strange mixture of pain and pleasure that he first felt clearly initially discerned when witnessing the death of his friend and reports that other witnesses had the same strange mixture of feelings, one recognizes how those of us who sympathize with Phaedo are led to feel as though we too were there, especially after Echecrates says: "You will have listeners who feel as you feel." [31] Yet there is no requisite that each one of

---

30. John Burnet, on 57a1: "We seem to be breaking in on a conversation already begun; for ἤκουσας has no expressed object." Also see Diskin Clay, "Plato's First Words: Beginnings in Classical Literature," *Yale Classical Studies* 29 (1992): 113–129. Clay points out, rightly as it seems to me, where the *Phaedo* ought to begin if it were that sort of unity and beginning, advocated by Aristotle at *Poetics* 1450b.

31. *Phaedo* 58e "you will have listeners (ἀκουσομένους) who feel as you do."

us will experience exactly the same intensity of pain or pleasure as an Apollodorus.[32] Nor does Plato merely recreate a 'Proustian' structure of remembrance. On the contrary, in addition to tactile mixtures of pain with pleasure that Socrates reports when the chains are removed from his legs, one also hears of arguments that not only excite pleasure and pain but thereby show how this conversation will be picked up and continued in the future.[33]

Consider how Echecrates' youthful fascination with the theory of the soul as a harmony is brought home to him immediately after Simmias has suggested why Socrates' concept of the soul as a harmony is incompatible with his belief that the soul is immortal.[34] Or how that theory that had once so pleased the young Echecrates is again shaken up, not of course at the same time that Phaedo becomes overwrought by Simmias's challenge to this theory, since it is long after Socrates' death that Echecrates interrupts Phaedo because he must know at once how Socrates responded to the onslaught on his arguments. Was Socrates shaken up too or did he calmly respond to the objections put to his argument? Hence even as Echecrates assures Phaedo of listeners who feel as he feels, so Plato may have listeners who feel as Echecrates feels when he admits his earlier attraction to this theory but recognizes why he must begin all over again with a fresh examination.

But notice how this theory is not abstracted from place or time. Nor has it for that matter been preserved as a voiceless statement on paper forever removed from time and the world. On the contrary, it is brought back to life for each one of us when Echecrates associates it with present, past, and future. For not only does he mention reexperiencing that "familiar" fascination but he also recognizes his need to reexamine what he had believed in the future. Hence what is left open for Plato's listener-readers to feel or not feel is not only that strange mixture of pain and pleasure that is so very unfamiliar but the choice of which of the many arguments gone through is attractive enough an examination for the future. This 'interlude' is the future. To treat the written word, then, as different from or more fundamental than an oral communication (as is common in literate cultures) is to close up what Plato has left open; and it is to forget how he would convey Socrates' oral spirit not simply to us in the present but to all of "us" in the future. Indeed, this is my own reason for not identifying Plato with a logographic necessity or treating his written works as autonomous. On the contrary, how could we question what has been left unresolved or reexamine what he structures seeking answers to the questions we

---

32. The intensity of Apollodorus' response at 117d when Socrates is about to drink the hemlock shows not only how fond Apollodorus is of Socrates but how important an influence Socrates has been in his life. But then it is easy for us to belittle him and his emotions, for we do not share his attachment for Socrates. Virtue however is a function of controlling the emotions one feels and not of seeming to be virtuous because one has no emotions to feel.

33. Burger (1984, 16) fights strenuously against entering into a conversation by sharing the emotions felt by Phaedo or Echecrates.

34. *Phaedo* 88d: "For the doctrine that the soul is a kind of harmony has always had (and has now) a wonderful hold on me, and your mention of it reminded me that I had myself believed it before. Now I must begin all over again and find another argument."

put to his dialogues? Could this be why Plato will not speak but remains anonymous? Or more significantly, is this the reason why no one can speak for Plato, not even Socrates or John? Yet since Plato's silence assures us of his preference for the spoken word, what may have been recovered is an ancient Greek attitude, so distinct from our own that it will be helpful to document what these ancient people believed about the world. For in light of it one can better acknowledge Plato's dialogues as idiosyncratic contributions to the history of Western philosophizing and living monuments to the oral spirit in which Socrates had and will continue to philosophize.[35]

IV. WRITING AND REMEMBERING

Even as David adumbrates a heavenly direction for Socrates' soul when he paints a left index finger pointing upward, so one often finds carved on early American tombstones stylized images of hands with a thumb or index finger pointing up or down. Yet it is not simply in conjunction with one or two such "digital directives" but a host of such images that the epithet cut into W. C. Fields's tombstone proves far from grave: namely, "Better here than in Philadelphia." For in addition to Fields's rejection of hell as anywhere but the "city of brotherly love" one laughingly recalls how Fields had spent the better part of his own life making us laugh.

Whether what is discerned on an ancient Greek stone monument will prove as fitting a memorial may depend, however, not simply on our forgetting that Christian metaphysics to which Fields so dismissively alludes but our remembering why eternity for an ancient Hellene is not conceived as something forever the same or unchanging but as time without beginning or end.[36] Indeed, this idea fits ever so appropriately with the function of an oral bard in those centuries before the Greeks had acquired an alphabetic script. For the bards as servants of the Muses composed as they sang to preserve by word of mouth for future generations what was worthy of every one remembering about their ancestors. Such indeed is the task of Homer's Phemis who plucks the strings of his instrument to sing songs of heroes not in order to make Phemis famous but to keep memories of the past alive in the hearts of his listeners. So Pindar too composed songs celebrating Olympic heroes but his works are called "lyrics" not because such poetry embodied Pindar's emotions (which is our reason for using the word "lyric") but because his words have been fashioned to be sung by a chorus to the sounds of a lyre.

---

35. Realizing that the questions we are provoked to ask by Plato are very significant, Sayre (1995, 27 ff.) does not conceive of their effect as something idiosyncratic in the history of philosophy. Perhaps that is because he thinks of the seeds planted by Plato as preparing future minds for knowledge but not of Plato as transmitting the oral spirit in which Socrates had philosophized to us.

36. For orality as endlessness, Walter Ong, *Orality and Literacy* (London and New York: Routledge, 1988), 37–8 and his discussion of the logic of "and."

Nevertheless, scholars have wondered why Pindar who had lived after the Greeks acquired letters should have explicitly denied that his poetry resembled sculpture as is said in his fifth *Nemean:*

> I am no maker of statues
> who fashions figures to stand unmoved
> on the self-same pedestal.
> On every merchantman, in every skiff
> Go sweet song, from Aigina
> And spread the news that Lampon's son
> . . . has won the wreath.[37]

When composing these lines, did Pindar consider putting written copies of his text aboard those vessels he speaks of as sailing from Aigena? Or was he thinking of those who had seen the victory of this athlete and heard a chorus boarding such ships singing his lyrics to spread the news of this man's victory to others? Or more prosaically, were Pindar's words put on board as written cargo or carried there in the hearts of those excited to disperse what they had heard by word of mouth?[38] The fact that Pindar speaks of his poetry as neither fixed nor unmoving like a piece of sculpture, opts against our own preferences for what is written in stone. Then perhaps one might discover in the relation of a poet to his listeners, a model for Plato's own relation to his listeners or readers. For it is not insignificant that the sounds of oral philosophical discourse had in antiquity been classified by Aristotle as well as spoken of excitedly by Alcibiades not as literature (for that word is Latin) but as bare words or verbal sounds no longer accompanied by music.[39]

Yet in order to become aware of how our own preference for what is written overshadows not only the questions we ask but the conclusions we draw, let us not insist with Kraut that if Plato had really preferred the spoken to the written word, he would have stopped writing after completing *Phaedrus.*[40] Rather than making this inference, based on our own presumptions about Plato's chronology, let us ask instead whether we correctly assume that orality is incompatible with literacy and so Plato had to choose whether to write or speak after completing it.

In *Phaedrus,* of course, the king of the Egyptians expresses his own fear to the inventor of letters that what he has fathered may not, as predicted, improve men's memories but produce forgetting instead. Hence in light of

---

37. Pindar, *Nemean* 5 was composed about 485 B.C.E. I quote Bowra's translation of 1–5.

38. A. Burns conceives of Pindar as putting numerous written copies on board in his "Athenian Literacy in the Fifth Century B.C.," *Journal of the History of Ideas* 42 (1981): 379. Rosalind Thomas, on the other hand, thinks of the news of such victory as spread by word of mouth, *Literacy and Orality in Ancient Greece* (Cambridge: Cambridge University Press, 1992), 114–5.

39. At *Poetics* 1447b Aristotle explicitly notes how his native Greek lacks a name for an art that imitates by means of "bare words alone" (μόνον τοῖς λόγοις ψιλοῖς); G.M.A. Grube has titled this section of his translation: "No Greek Word for Literature." At *Symposium* 215 c–d when comparing Socrates with a flute playing satyr, Alcibiades speaks of him as different only in so far as Socrates produces his enchantment with bare words (ψιλοῖς λόγοις) unaided by instruments.

40. Kraut (1992), 21.

those ancient oral preferences, only just sketched, one may well confirm something earlier suggested regarding Plato's reasons for leaving so many dialogues unresolved. For if each dialogue were autonomous or complete with a beginning, middle, and end how could we by asking questions breathe life back into those marks, left behind for us? Perhaps Plato's conversations survive because we combine letters with remembering when interpreting how his conversations are structured. When Plato leaves his reader-listener in *aporia,* he or she must rediscover the unique structure of a particular dialogue, as well as how it is unresolved and where incomplete.[41] When so doing, we bring Plato's open-ended conversations back to life as we reexperience what it was like to be present when Socrates cross-examined a particular respondent. Hence, what is picked up and continued to be transmitted by us to others is not Platonic dogma but Socrates' oral manner of philosophizing even though his accusers had wished to put a stop to Socrates' conversations and not the idiosyncratic sounds of Plato's own voice.

---

41. Nails (1995), 218–222 offers an analysis of Plato's double open-endedness that is well worth exploring.

8

Not Doctrine but 'Placing in Question'

The "Thrasymachus" (Rep. *I*) *as an* Erôtêsis *of Commercialization*

P. Christopher Smith

> The premise in demonstration, however, differs from the premise in dialectic in that the demonstrative premise is an assumption of one or the other side of a contradiction; for the person demonstrating does not ask about something but rather assumes it to be so. The dialectical premise, on the other hand, is a placing in question of a contradiction *(erôtêsis antiphaseôs)*.
>
> —Aristotle, *Analytica Pr.* 24a 22–25

Taking the "Thrasymachus" or Book I of the *Republic* as an example, this chapter will show that, in fact, Plato's dialectical strategy is not at all to state doctrines or make "claims" and to argue for them by adducing grounds as premises for some sort of demonstration *(apodeixis)*. Rather, in response to any assertion, proposition or assumption *that* "P is Q," he wishes to entertain simultaneously both sides of the contradiction, "P is Q" and "P is not Q"; he wishes to entertain *the question*, that is, *whether* "P is Q or P is not Q."[1] In Plato's dialectic the declarative *logos* is thus subverted by the interrogative *logos*. As Gadamer puts this, "When a question arises, the being of what is asked is disrupted" (*WM* 345). When one *declares* that "P is Q," the "being" of P, namely that it *is* Q, is assumed to be stable; however, if one *asks*, "Is P Q or is P not Q?" P's being Q

---

1. See Hans-Georg Gadamer, *Wahrheit und Methode* (Tübingen: Mohr, 1960), henceforth "WM", 344ff., "The Hermeneutical Priority of the Question": "(a) The Paradigm of Plato's Dialectic" (344–51), and "(b) The Logic of Question and Answer" (351–60). Translations from German and Greek throughout this study are my own.

becomes unsteady and now wavers indefinitely somewhere between the contradictory answers "Yes, P is Q" and "No, P is not Q."

The same thing is said in a different way in *Republic* I, 348a ff., by contrasting adversarial argument, which must be brought before a judge who will decide which of the two opposed claims is best supported, with argument in which "we might see about reaching an understanding with one another" (348b).[2] It is agreed here that despite Thrasymachus's attempts to revert to adversarial argument, the interlocutors will carry on with the investigative kind of argument they had been pursuing. The point is that neither party should make claims or counterclaims and then try to support them with "good" reasons in order, finally, for one claim to prevail definitively over the other. Rather, in placing all claims in question "we might see about" getting clearer about a finite range in the inexhaustible possibilities of their meaning.

In the "Thrasymachus" dialogue, accordingly, claims are made regarding the "being" of justice, namely that justice *is* "giving back what one has received from someone" (331c), or that justice *(dikaiosunê) is* "giving back what is due to each" (331e), or "benefiting one's friends but harming one's enemies" (334c), or that the just *(to dikaion) is* "nothing other than the advantage of the stronger" (338c) or *is* "the good of somebody else" (343c), or that perfect injustice *(adikia) is* "more profitable than perfect justice" (348b). Contrary to what Thrasymachus wants, however, these "assumptions" are not argued for by "giving grounds" for them *(logon didonai),* neither are counterclaims advanced and supported with grounds. Instead, all such "assumptions" are immediately "placed in question" and the "being" and meaning of what they assert becomes unsteady insofar as the proponents of them are made to entertain simultaneously the contradiction that justice, or the just, or injustice, *is* and *is not* what each of these has been assumed to be.

As is obvious, this reading of the *Republic,* Book I, conflicts sharply with the predominant American approach to it as this is capably exemplified, for instance, by Annas and Reeve.[3] In defense of my own reading I would argue that

---

2. ἀνομολογούμενοι πρὸς ἀλλήλους σκοπῶμεν. For the plural participle *anomologoumenoi,* literally, "we, coming to an agreement," or "we, reaching an understanding," Gadamer would say "uns verständigend." See, for instance, WM 363: "A conversation is a process of reaching an understanding *(Das Gespräch ist ein Vorgang der Verständigung)."*

3. See Julia Annas, *An Introduction to Plato's Republic* (Oxford: Clarendon Press, 1981) and C. D. C. Reeve, *Philosopher-Kings: The Argument of Plato's Republic* (Princeton: Princeton University Press, l988). In her account of the *Republic,* Book I, Annas, for example, unquestioningly takes Plato's dialectical argument and counterargument to be demonstration of something, that is, *apodeiksis* or "pointing something out." Hence, contrary to the approach taken here, in her reading the thing supposedly pointed out, that is to say, the answer to the question under investigation, consistently suppresses the question itself. In stating these things supposedly "pointed out," she succumbs, therefore, to the "Plato says ..." syndrome, for example, "Plato does not begin his philosophical arguments about justice in a vacuum" *(Introduction,* 17), or "Later on in the *Republic,* when we find what Plato's own account is, we shall see that he moves away entirely from justice as a state of the agent" (23). She blithely passes over the inconvenient fact that Plato himself is never a speaker in the dialogue, with the all too easy assumption that the "Socrates" character speaks for him, but no justification for saying this is given. In this regard Reeve is somewhat better, for he does make clear that the Socrates of Book I, at least, cannot be making Plato's own arguments (see *Philosopher Kings,* 3–42).

in forcing the always inconclusive zigzag of Plato's interrogative dialectic into the Procrustean bed of conclusive argument by linear demonstration, both Annas and Reeve only cover up the original open-ended, conversational nature of the dialogue. It is no accident, then, that the people most influential in this chapter's attempt to get beneath this interpretive overlay, H.-G. Gadamer above all, but also Jacques Derrida and Herbert Marcuse, are themselves all strongly influenced by Heidegger.[4] For if, in a phenomenological *Destruktion,* this overlay is removed, it can be shown, I contend, that far from demonstrating something, "showing" something, or "pointing" something "out" in some sort of *apo-deiknunai,* Plato's *dialegesthai* opens up questions in "talking" things "through." In trying to penetrate the layers of standard interpretation and to "lay bare" and "lay out" this "original" (Heidegger: *ursprüngliches*) phenomenon of *dialegesthai* I would hope to accomplish for Plato something of what Heidegger's wholly unorthodox interpretations accomplished for Aristotle.[5]

However, the concern here is not just with the form of argumentation in the "Thrasymachus," but also with its specific content, and here too a derivative abstraction needs to be "taken down."[6] In this regard we note that the contradiction in the various assumptions of what justice, the just, and injustice are, is introduced precisely then when the interlocutors, in the dialectic of question and answer into which they are drawn, are "reminded" of forgotten, primary, communal understandings of what is right, beneficial and decent *(to dikaion, to sumpheron, to kalon),* the original meanings of which have been effectively gutted by commercialization and the concomitant erosion of the *philia,* the kin-

---

4. Contrary to those traditional classicists who would dismiss Derrida as reckless and beyond the pale, I consider his "Plato's Pharmacy" [in Jacques Derrida, *Dissemination,* tr. Barbara Johnson (Chicago: University Press, 1981), 65–171] and *Khôra* (Paris: Galilee, 1993) remarkably scholarly, careful, and illuminating rereadings of Plato's *Phaedrus* and *Timaeus,* respectively. Though I have dealt critically with Derrida's "Pharmacy" in *The Hermeneutics of Original Argument* (Evanston, IL: Northwestern University Press, 1998), without the examples of his deconstruction of Plato's texts my own approach to Plato would not have been possible.

5. For Martin Heidegger's *Destruktion* of traditional understandings in order to uncover and interpret phenomenologically the "original" phenomena beneath them, his 1927 *Sein und Zeit* (Tübingen, 1960) remains the paradigm. Heidegger's incomprehension of conversation thwarts his attempts at *Destruktion* of traditional interpretation of Plato's dialogues, but this strategy works beautifully on Aristotle's monological treatises. For an application of his truly astonishing reading of Aristotle's *Rhetoric* in his still unpublished 1924 Marburg lecture course, see my *The Hermeneutics of Original Argument.* Perhaps even more influential in regard to Aristotle, however, were Heidegger's "destructive" interpretations of the *Nicomachean Ethics, Physics* and *Metaphysics* as outlined in his 1922 application for a professorship at Marburg and Göttingen (see Martin Heidegger, "Phänomenologische Interpretationen zu Aristotles" in the *Dilthey-Jahrbuch,* vol. 6, 1989, 237–69). Gadamer reports, "These interpretations had such vital energy that the auditors of the lectures corresponding to them in Freiburg at that time, Leo Strauss and many others, to be sure, were enraptured and were everywhere heard to say that in comparison, not only Werner Jaeger, who was indeed a truly great Aristotle expert, but even Max Weber, who surely represented the most redoubtable scientific temperament at any German lectern then, appeared mere orphan boys" (Gadamer, "Heideggers 'theologische' Jugendschrift" in the *Dilthey-Jahrbuch,* vol. 6, 1989, p. 232).

6. Herbert Marcuse will figure most prominently in the destructive exposition here, in particular his "A Note on Dialectic" included as the preface to the Boston, 1966, edition of his *Reason and Revolution,* pp. vii–xvi. In this essay one can see clearly how Marcuse extends his earlier (1932) correlation of Heidegger's *Destruktion* with Hegel's dialectic in *Hegels Ontologie* (Frankfurt: a.M., 1968), to a dialectical *Destruktion* of commercialized society.

ship, loyalty, affection, that sustains any community of people with each other.[7] Hence, in seeking to penetrate the abstraction of commercial relationships and thereby to "lay bare" beneath it the primary the community of *philia,* we need to highlight the "Thrasymachus'" apparently incidental mention of money, exchange, commercial contracts, and the competition *(agôn)* to "have more" *(pleon echein)* than one's antagonists.[8] We note that even the very procedure of argument favored by the character "Thrasymachus" (see 348a) reflects this abstraction from communal interpersonal relationships to commercial ones: argument for him is no longer a cooperative "taking counsel with" others and "talking things through" *(sumbouleuesthai, dialegesthai);* rather it has devolved to a competitive transaction, an "exchange" carried out, for money, in the self-interest of those engaged in it (see 337d), and in which one of the two antagonists wins and "has the better of it" *(pleon echei)* and the other loses and "fares the worse" *(elatton echei)* (see 343d). In contrast, the kind of interrogative argument and conversation that Socrates pursues presupposes the precommercial community and kinship of those who would participate in it.

It is no accident, then, that the first "assumption" to be placed in question, namely Cephalus'—in Socrates' reformulation of it—that justice *is* "giving back what one has received from someone" (331c), follows closely upon the consideration of what money makes possible. Nor is it an accident that this "bookkeeping" definition in terms of balancing credits and debits is placed in question precisely by introducing the *friend, ho philos,* who, having left weapons on deposit, and having gone mad in the meantime, returns to reclaim them (331c). Cephalus recuses himself and exits, but that he himself also entertains a contradictory noncommercial understanding of human relationships as something more than transactions and exchanges has already been made clear by his declaration of affection for Socrates and by the delight he takes in the prospect of inquiring into arguments, *logoi,* with him (see 328 cd). And indeed, this example of the friend gone mad puts into play just this contradictory possibility that justice *is not* "paying back what one has received from someone." It does this precisely by reminding us that in our relationships with those who are *philos* or dear to us we do not think at all in terms of commercial transactions and that,

---

7. The reference of "reminded" is, of course, to Plato's *anaminêiskô* and *anamnêsis* taken here, however, in the sense of a recovery of received senses of right and wrong, *endoxa,* and not as insight into some idea, *eidos,* of what these are in essence. (See my *Hermeneutics and Human Finitude* (Bronx, NY: Fordham University Press, 1991), 280–81. The *dikaion, sumpheron* and *kalon* are, as Aristotle tells us, the three principal subject matters with which rhetoric's deliberation or "taking counsel" *(bouleusthai, sumbouleusthai)* is concerned (see *Rhet.* I, 3), and, as he also makes clear in *Rhet.* II, 1, we allow ourselves to take counsel about these three matters only with those for whom we feel *philia* and who display good intensions, *eunoia,* for us. Compare Gadamer, WM 306: "Only friends can counsel one another, that is to say that only counsel that is meant in a friendly way is meaningful for the one counseled."

8. With Marcuse (see n. 6), we are, in other words, giving a Marxian twist to the Heideggerian strategy of *Destruktion,* namely "taking down" the derivative and secondary abstraction—in Heidegger's case, the understanding of the being of objects as *res extensae* just lying about on hand for subjective consciousness—and "founding" the abstraction in the original, practical "being-there" of human "being in the world" "with" others and in the midst of things "ready at hand" to be used (see *Sein und Zeit,* pp. 89–114).

in fact, it would be a violation of what is just and right to think this way. Rather, we might better think of justice, as Polemarchus, the "heir" to the argument, now "assumes," in terms of *ta opheilomena*: Justice, he says, *is* "giving back *what is due* to each" (331e).

In one sense, of course, *opheilomena* are "debts" and, as is indicated by the repetition here of the *apodidonai* (giving back, paying back) from the first "assumption" of what justice is, the thinking behind *opheilomena,* too, is still largely commercial. Even so, the questioning, in listening to the multiple resonances of this equivocal *onoma* or word-name, can move easily, via something like the English "what is due" to someone, to "what befits" someone or, in Greek, *to prosêkon* (332 c). Thus, in employing the dialectical-rhetorical topic of "contraries" and a subtle modulation of vocabulary, the question can now be posed whether, assuming that "what is due" *(ho opheiletai)* to friends is to give them back something good, it "befits" *(prosêkei)* enemies to give them back something bad (332b).[9] And now, in a further modulation the new "assumption" emerges: Justice *is* "doing well *(eu poiein)* by one's friends and treating one's enemies badly *(kakôs [poiein])*" (332d). As opposed to a declarative demonstration, which presupposes the univocity of its significant terms *(sêmeia),* in this interrogative *dialegesthai,* or "talking things through" we are, by listening to a range of its equivocations, following the traces of one ambiguous *onoma* or word-name to another by moving via syn*onyms* and ant*onyms,* from *ta opheilomena* to *to prosekon,* and then from *eu poiein* to *kakôs poiein.* We note that, in contrast to demonstrative reasoning by determinate classes of things, genera and species, *genê* and *eidê,* in Plato's actual dialogical, dialectical practice here there is no appeal whatever to some sort of stabilized conceptual structure behind the equivocal *onomata* among which the questioning moves. As we will see momentarily, the paths of these equivocal *onomata* can even be traced via met*onymic* inflections, say, of the *dik* stem, from *dik-aion* to *dik-aiosunê* to *a-dik-ia* to *a-dik-ein.*[10]

With the arrival at "doing well," *eu poiein,* by one's friends it might seem that an underlying sense of community based in *philia* had been disclosed beneath the surface of self-interested commercial transactions that it contradicts. And as a matter of fact, Polemarchus does share in the communal, *philia*-based understanding of justice, and he will soon be "reminded" of this when he agrees that it is never just to do harm to anyone (see 335e). Still, exactly why this understanding of justice contradicts his commercial understanding still eludes him. Indeed, how very commercial his thinking remains becomes obvious when the question is raised next what the occasion for justice—"assuming" that it *is* "doing well by one's friends and treating one's enemies badly"—would be in peacetime when, technically, at least, one has no enemies. Justice, he proposes, would be useful in "contracts," *sumbolaia,* a

---

9. See Aristotle, *Topics,* 113b 15 ff., on the four kinds of dialectical arguments by the topic of "antithesis": contradiction *(antiphasis),* contraries *(enantia),* having/lacking *(sterêsis),* and, 114a 13–26, correlatives *(ta pros allêla).*

10. For an account of dialectical argument by the topic of "inflection" *(ptôsis)* see Aristotle, *Rhet.* 1397a 20–23 and *Topica* 106b 29–38 and 114a 27–b6.

word in which Socrates immediately hears *koinônêmata,* meaning "common
enterprises," and here the communal *koinêi* or "in common," that will figure
so prominently later on, is clearly audible (333a). Indeed, the "assumption"
that justice *is* "useful in *sumbolaia*" is now placed in question precisely by the
inflection of the word *koinônêma* into *koinônia,* meaning "partnership," to be
sure, but also "community" (333b) (see n. 10 on dialectical argument by *ptôsis* or "inflection"): it is now asked in what special kind of *koinônia* justice *is*
useful, for plainly justice *is not* specifically useful in communities of chess
players, builders, and harpists (333b). Justice *is* useful, it is now assumed, in
partnerships "about money *(eis arguriou)*" (333b).

At first glance the questioning of this assumption at 333b–d seems captious
and even facetious, but viewed in terms of an unfolding contradiction between
abstract commercial, and concrete communal understandings of what is right
and wrong, just and unjust, it in fact proves to be significant and serious. Indeed, when it is shown that "justice *is* useful in money partnerships" only when
money is "useless" (left on deposit) and is not being used to buy any concrete
thing, horses, ships, and the like, we could say, with Marcuse and Heidegger,
that a commercialization is displayed in the abstraction from the original community of human beings engaged in the everyday practices of buying and sell-
ing concrete things and using implements "ready at hand," pruning hooks,
shields, lyres (334d), to get things done cooperatively. Justice would then *be*
useful only when human *koinônia,* our actual engagement in practices with others, had become the abstract relationship of money to money. But clearly—and
this is the point of which we are now "reminded"—justice *is not* something useful in this kind of abstract relationship, and thus the "assumption" that it *is* useful there is thereby placed in question.

Throughout all of this "talking things through" or *dialegesthai* it has become
increasingly evident that the tacit commercial "assumption" that the friend *is*
some sort of self-interested partner in one's transactions with inimical competitors must also be called into question. For so conceived, the "just friend,"
which is to say, the one with the *technê* or know-how of keeping your money
safely for you, would also have the opposite know-how of stealing it from you;
if your business partners are only skillful and have no communal sense of right
and wrong, you had better watch out. (The point here foreshadows the concluding arguments about the dysfunctionality of any partnership without a
basis in justice at 353a ff.) Like Odysseus's grandfather Autolykus, the "just
friend" would *be* a thief (334a–b), but obviously, as we are now "reminded,"
the "just friend" *is not* a thief. On the contrary, in some sense still open to
question, the "just friend," it is now "assumed," should *be chrêstos,* meaning
"good" in the sense of reliable and even "good for something" as opposed to
ponêros or "good for nothing" (334c).

The path traced here from *dikaios* or just to this new *onoma chrêstos,* which
is said of things as well as people, is by no means arbitrary, for it provides the
perfect synonymic transition from the commercial understanding of the just
friend as a "useful" partner back to the original communal understanding of the
just friend as "good" person. Indeed, the antonyms *chrêstos* or *ponêros* quickly
lead to *agathos* meaning ethically "good" and its opposite, *kakos,* "bad"

(334c–d), and at 335d the question, "Is the just person good *(agathos)?*" is answered emphatically, "Most assuredly." With that, the original understanding of justice as human *aretê* or excellence in communal relationships has been recalled and disclosed beneath, and in contradiction to, the abstract understanding of justice as the commercial *technê* of "knowing how" to benefit friends and injure enemies in business deals (see 335b). And now the once seemingly stable proposal that justice *is* "benefiting friend and harming enemies" has been shaken. As early as 334b, in fact, we heard Polemarchus allow that "I myself no longer know what I was talking about."

It is no accident, then, that in conclusion to this section of the dialogue, the assumption that justice is benefiting friends and injuring enemies is attributed not to Simonides at all, but more likely to some "rich man" with enough money and power to do whatever he desires (see 336a), attributed, this is to say, to a completely self-interested man who has no community left with anyone, and who has learned to think only of how he might profit in transactions with his competitors. It turns out that instead of having no enemies and only friends in "peacetime," the commercialized human being has no friends and only enemies. For him "peacetime" is a *bellum omnium contra omnes;* or, to continue with Hobbes, *homo homini lupus.* Enter the lupine Thrasymachus, from whom we will never hear the word "friend" at all.[11]

We note that from the start the role of the "Thrasymachus" character in this dialogue is specifically to resist the priority given to the question over the answer in any *dialegesthai* or "talking things through." Indeed, he reviles Socrates for incessantly placing things in question, saying things like "This is that well-known dissembling of Socrates'. I knew it was coming, and I have also said to these people earlier that you would be unwilling to *answer* and you would dissemble and do anything rather than *answer* when someone asks you something" (337a; emphasis added). Then, after feigned reluctance—and once payment is produced—he puts forward his own "answer" or "assumption": "Listen here; I say that what is just *is* nothing other than what is to the advantage of the stronger" (338c; emphasis added).

The definitiveness of this claim is, of course, quickly shaken with the provocatively absurd example of the pancratist whose strength in the violent contest in which he engages is enhanced by eating huge quantities of meat (338cd). However, if one considers that the "Thrasymachus" character treats oratory as some sort of wrestling match with an antagonist, the analogy is not as inapposite it might seem; see his *"biasasthai tôi logôi* (to prevail by force with one's argument)" at 341b. On the contrary, by tangential implication we are *also* supposed to sense the similarity of Polydamas, the pancratist, to Thrasymachus, the orator. In its plays on the allusions of "pancratist" Plato's dialectical logic here once again deviates radically from the single-strand, linear logic of demonstration, and we, for our part, need to listen simultaneously to each of the multiple motifs of his dialectical argumentation.

---

11. See the oblique reference to a wolf at 336e, when the saying is invoked in reaction to Thrasymachus ferocious intrusion, "Had I not seen him before he had seen me, I would have been struck dumb."

Now in the case of the pancratist what is just for the rest of us plainly *is not* what is to the advantage of the stronger. Thus, even if by devious means, this "assumption" has been placed in question, and both sides of the contradiction, "The just *is* what is to the advantage of the stronger" and "The just *is not* what is to the advantage of the stronger," must be entertained simultaneously. Once again the audience is involved in an *erôtêsis antiphaseôs,* and instead of proceeding demonstratively by giving grounds in support of his assumption, this "Thrasymachus" must now "see about" whether the assumption *is* or *is not* true. We note, in this regard, Socrates' "But it is plain that whether what you say is true remains to be seen *(skepteon),*" to which Thrasymachus responds, "Look all you want *(skopei)*" (339b), for *skopein, skepsis, zêtêsis,* "taking a look" at something, "examination" and "inquiry," are always indices of an *erôtêsis* or interrogation that subverts any conclusive declarative sentences and throws them back into question. (Compare above on the *"an skopômen"* ["we might see"] at 348b.)

In the hopes that he can firm up his now shaky assumption, he proposes the first in a series of modifications of it: the just, he now claims, *is* "what is to the advantage of the established ruling power" (339a). The insinuation here of the *onoma* or word-name *archê,* "ruling power," will pave the way for the questioning to introduce, by metonymic inflection *(ptôsis),* the contradictory possibility that the just *is not* what is to the advantage of those who do the ruling, the *arch-ontes,* rather, it *is* what is to the advantage of those who are ruled, the *arch-omenoi.* A first contradiction, however, is now introduced using the dialectical-rhetorical topic of "correlatives": if what the rulers, in their ruling, *order* is just, then *obedience* to what they order is just.[12] But if the rulers order something not in their interest, it would, by the definition of the just as being what is to the advantage of the rulers, then *not be* just to obey their orders: "So by your argument the just is not only doing what *is* to the advantage of the stronger but also the contrary: doing what *is not* to their advantage" (339d; emphasis added). Once again we note that, in contrast to demonstrative, declarative argument, the dialectical, interrogative argument here has moved from *prostattein* to *peithesthai,* from ordering to obeying, without recourse to any stabilized concepts and solely by listening to the equivocal word-names, in this case, hearing in one word-name its correlative contrary. In this way what "the just" *(to dikaion)* means, is placed in question and made to oscillate uncertainly between what *is* to the advantage of the stronger and what *is not.*

The investigation can now proceed to place "ruling" itself in question: "ruling," it is proposed, is the *technê* of the stronger, their "knowing-how" to pursue their own advantage in their transactions with those over whom they rule (340d–341a). Thus the contradiction must be entertained that, maybe, "ruling" *is* a *technê* in the interest of the "rulers" but that, maybe, it *is not.* Here too, there is no logical demonstration by stabilized conceptual classes of things, rather the *dialegesthai* proceeds this time by the dialectical-rhetorical topic of "similarity": the counterproposal is advanced that "knowing-how" to "rule" a

---

12. Cf., *Rhet.* 1397a 23–b 11 on Diomedes the tax collector: "For if it is not shameful for you *sell* [the rights to collect taxes], it is not shameful either for us to *buy* them" (1397a 26–27; emphasis added). See also *Topics,* 114a 13–26.

state *is* like the "know-how" of medicine and *is* like the "know-how" of navigation, but neither of these practices is performed in the interest of the practitioner, rather both are in the interest of those for whom the practice is performed. Thus, by analogy, "ruling" *is not* practiced in the interest of the "rulers." In fact, like any *technê*, "ruling" means something complete in itself that has no needs and interests of its own to be served in the first place (341c–342e).

That communal understandings of practices have in fact been recollected here to contradict, and place in question, commercialized understandings becomes clear in Thrasymachus's vehement response at 343b ff. Indeed, we can see in this character "Thrasymachus" to what grave extent commercialized thinking has displaced not only any communal sense of what is right, any *dikaiosunê*, but all traditional goodness and decency in people's relationships with each other (*epieikeia, kalokagathia*). In the mind of this "Thrasymachus" all *technai* are practiced solely for whatever "profit" the practitioners can "gain" from them for themselves (note the *"lousiteloun"* at 343c and the *"polla kerdainei"* at 343e). All *technai* are thought of, that is, in terms of an *agôn* or contest in which each of the parties contends, in pure self-interest, to "get more" for himself or herself from his or her antagonist (note the *"pleon echonta"* at 343d and *"ton megala dunamenon pleonektein"* at 344a). On this view it is obvious that the "just" will come up short in any kind of "contractual agreements" and "partnerships"—the words, *sumbolaioi* and *koinoniai* are carried over here (343d) from the questioning at 333a. Indeed, the "just" are chumps who in adhering to principles of right and wrong in their transactions with others are, in fact, only doing "what is good for the other guy" (*allotrion agathon*) (343c); "In all matters the just man gets less than the unjust" (343d).

The contradiction that places this commercialized understanding of human relationships in question is introduced precisely by recalling the precommercial, communal understanding of practices. In response to the assumption that shepherds have only their own or their master's interests at heart, not the sheep's (343b), it is now countered that the shepherd so conceived is not a shepherd at all but, significantly, merely a "moneymaker" *(chrêmastês)* (345d), and, like other communal practices such as medicine—the motif of the physician as a "moneymaker" *(chrêmastês)* had already been introduced at 341c—navigation, and housebuilding, shepherding is to be sharply distinguished from moneymaking. For unlike moneymaking these *are not* practiced in the interest of the practitioners (see 346b–d): "Then, O Thrasymachus, this is already plain: that no practice and no rule is concerned to provide for its own benefit, but as we said a while back, it provides and commands for the ones ruled over, and looks out for what is in their interest, they being the weaker ones, and not for what is in the interest of the stronger" (346e). From the communal standpoint of this counterproposal, practices, in other words, are carried out in the service of others and not, as in commercial transactions, in the interest of oneself. Understood communally and prior to commercialism's "What's in it for me?" what is just and right really is "what's good for the other guy."

The collapse of community resulting from "Thrasymachus'" commercialized conception of human relationships is made all the more evident at 348e when he affirms that injustice belongs to the class of excellence and wisdom (*aretê*, *sophia)* and justice, to the opposites of these and, what is even more shocking given the received understandings of the word-names involved, when he says that injustice *is not* shameful *(aischros)*, rather that injustice *is* fine and honorable *(kalos)*. With that, the customary communal values of fairness and decency in one's treatment of others have devolved into predicates of the one thing that counts in commercialized relationships, *pleonektein* and *pleon echein*, "getting the larger part" for oneself in one's exchanges with others by "outdoing" and "having the better" of one's competitors.

Hence, it is not surprising that the counterproposal that places this "assumption" that injustice is fine and honorable in question highlights the fact that when practices such as medicine are understood precommercially, that is, as something other than exchanges for profit, colleagues in these practices *do not* seek "to have the better" of their like: Do the just wish to "have the better" of the just *(tou dikaiou . . . pleon echein)*? No (349c). Do the just try to "out do" their like *(homoiou pleonektei)*? No (349c, 350b, c). Does a musician try to "out do" or "have the better" of another musician in tuning a lyre *(musikou andros . . . pleonektein ê . . . pleon echein)*? No (349e). Does the physician want to "out do another physician *(iatrikou pleonektein)*? No (350a). So the good and the wise will not wish to "out do" their like *(tou homoiou . . . pleonektein)*. So it seems (350b). To be sure, it is allowed here—for the sake of argument—that these practitioners do try to "out do" and "get the better" of ignorant and bad false practitioners of their art, but clearly this is not meant in the commercial sense of besting them to secure a "larger share" of the market for themselves but rather only in the sense that they will seek to exceed them in their service of those for whom their art is practiced. This, of course, is not at all how "Thrasymachus" understands *pleonektein* and *pleon echein:* But, the questioning continues, do the unjust deem themselves fit to "out do" the just? How could they not? They deem themselves fit to "have the better" of everyone *(pantôn pleon echein)* (350c). So the unjust will "outdo" the unjust and "compete that they might themselves get the most of anybody *(hamillêsetai hôs hapantôn pleiston autos labêi)*" (349c).

After one last, and now subdued, demand that he be allowed to argue at length for his doctrine, which is to say, demonstrate it by advancing grounds for it in linear argument, Thrasymachus gives in again to the dialectic of placing a contradiction in question:

> *Thrasymachus:* Either let me speak as much as I wish or, if you wish to ask questions, ask.
> *Socrates:* I shall ask questions.
> *Thrasymachus:* Ask away (350d).

The contradiction placed in question now becomes, *"Is* injustice more powerful and stronger than justice or *is it not?"* (see 351a), and the questioning pursued will put the contradictory second part of this question, "Injustice *is not* stronger than justice," in play against the assumption that it *is.*

This contradiction is yet another variation on the underlying and continuing contradiction we have observed between the abstract commercial understanding of human relationships as transactions between self-interested parties and the original and nearly forgotten understanding of human practices as communities based in *philia*. For it is clear that on the commercial understanding, justice, as an empty vestige of some bygone sense of loyalty and obligation to others, would only be debilitating in transactions with one's competitors. Here, where "Winning isn't everything; it's the only thing," scruples would only hold someone back in seeking to "out do" and "have the better of" his or her antagonists, who, in their own perfect injustice, would be all too ready to take advantage of the "just" person's unwillingness to go for the jugular. In the realm of commercial transactions, obviously, injustice *is* stronger than justice. Thus, to put in play the other side of the contradiction—that injustice *is not* stronger than justice—the audience for the dialogue will need to be "reminded" of the original realm of community based in *philia*, that is, the trust, loyalty, and kinship felt for each other by the participants in common practices.

On the surface, the questioning here (351a ff.) would seem to lead, by analogy with a city, an army, and any clan, even of thieves and bandits (see 351c), to an account of why *dikaiosunê* is excellence or *aretê* in the functioning of the human *psychê*, the human soul, life, self, or personality. Like any analogy, however, this one speaks to both the analogs: what it says about the individual *psychê* tells us something about various kinds of communities as well as vice versa. Thus, in paying attention to the less obvious dimensions of this layered and nonlinear argument, we can apply this passage in clarification to the notion of precommercial community: for us the contradiction placed in question here is not whether injustice makes the soul "stronger," that is, better functioning or worse, but whether it makes a community better functioning or worse. And when it is asked at the end of this section whether "taking care of things and ruling and taking counsel (*epimeleisthai kai archein kai bouleuesthai*)" are the proper function of the soul (353d), and when the question is posed, "It is necessary, is it not, that the bad soul rules and takes care of things badly but the good soul does all these things well" (353e), we can, by reversing the analogy and reading the text from back to front, focus on the tangential civic implications here. For after all, taking care of things, ruling, and taking counsel, are, to begin with, activities of the community and not the individual. Hence, *adikia*, as perfect unscrupulousness, the utter absence of any principles concerning what is right and wrong, decent and despicable, and *pleonexia*, as commercialization's fundamental principle of "having more" for oneself in one's transactions with others, we can consider not primarily as vices of the disordered soul but as vices of the disordered community, as ethical degeneracy in its collective understanding of itself.

Thus the central questions for us, the questions that introduce the communal understanding of human relationships in contradiction to commercialism's transactional understanding of these and that place the transactional understanding in question, are in fact raised at the beginning of this section not the end: in any community of people "Injustice generates rebellions and hatreds and conflicts among each other but justice, concord and kinship *(philia)*, not so?" (351d), and "And if this is the work of injustice, namely to inject hatred in anything in which it is present, will it not, once it has arisen among the free or among slaves, make them hate and rebel against each other and make them be incapable of practicing anything in common with each other *(adunatous einai koinêi met' allêlôn prattein)*?" Just what happens when injustice infects communal practices can be inferred in reading backward from what comes later: any common "taking care" of things in any common endeavor and any "taking counsel" and "ruling" over how it is to be carried out, can succeed only if the participants in communal practices maintain some sort of kinship and care for each other.[13] Conversely, if their relationships devolve to competitive exchanges in which each seeks to "out do" the other and to "have more" for himself or herself, the principles of right and wrong governing and enabling their "common practices" will have become the mere façade for self-aggrandizement, and under those conditions, where *philia* has become enmity, any possibility of communal "taking care" of things, "ruling" and "taking counsel" has been ruined.

Though it is not the province of this chapter to comment on the *Republic* as a whole, we will allow ourselves the observation that the ambiguity in whether the city is an analog for the soul, or the soul for the city, persists throughout the entire work; *the question is never answered* whether we are doing psychology or politics, nor does it need to be given the nonlinear nature of Plato's dialectical, interrogative argumentation. What is more, if, contrary to Annas and Reeve, one treats the entire *Republic* as a "destructive" *erôtêsis antiphaseôs* rather than a constructive argument for particular conclusions, the problem of continuity between Book I and the rest turns out to be only an "apparent problem" (Heidegger: *Scheinproblem*) needing to be dissolved rather than resolved. Contrary to Reeve, for instance, who struggles so earnestly to construct a conclusive linear argument for the whole from the very inconclusiveness of the first book (see *Philosopher Kings*, pp. 3–42), I suggest that one might better read the entire *Republic* with a grain of salt. One should be particularly sensitive to the risible absurdity of its proposals, and things like the botched calculation of the number for the best mating time (546b ff.) should alert us to the continuing *eironeia* of what Socrates is saying even when he seems to be providing answers instead of raising questions.[14] Irony, perhaps meaning not A by saying A, or vice versa, is in fact the perfect dialectical means of disconcerting an audience that might otherwise have taken the matter to be settled, and of bringing them, instead, to entertain both sides of a contradiction: "Is it true, what he is saying? Or is it not true?" Irony is the perfect way, that is, to call things into question, and this not to induce nihilistic skepticism but to recollect, and remind us of, heretofore unseen and forgotten possibilities, in the case of the *Republic* possibilities of valid community.[15]

---

13. Heidegger's word for *epimeleisthai* is *Besorgen* or "taking care": "[H]aving to do with something producing something, putting something in order and tending it, using something, giving something up and losing something, ... these ways of being [in the world] have the kind of being, which we must later characterize more precisely, of taking-care" (*Sein und Zeit*, 56–57).

14. See Hans-Georg Gadamer, *The Idea of the Good in Platonic Aristotelian Philosophy*, tr. P. Christopher Smith (New Haven: Yale University Press, 1986), 72–73, on the mating number.

15. "Surely one must take all of the institutions and structures in this model city as dialectical metaphors.... [T]hey should make truly bad conditions and the dangers for the continued existence of a city visible *e contrario*" (Gadamer, *Idea of the Good*, 71).

The conclusion of the "Thrasymachus" is important for us, then, precisely because of its inconclusiveness: the question what justice is is left open and unanswered. When at 354b it is lamented—apparently—that that the investigation *(to skepsasthai)* has not established "whatever the just is *(hoti pot' estin)*" but has instead concerned itself only with asking things "about it *(peri autou)*," and when at 354c the "Socrates" character is made to say, "For I do not yet know what the just is," we should—*pace* Annas and Reeve—not take this as some sort of deficiency that might be remedied in this dialogue or in any other, when Plato will finally and definitively pronounce what he *assumes* the just is. Rather, it is a declaration of the perpetual priority of the question over any answer and of the inevitable concomitance of *euporia* and *aporia* in our *pathos tôn logôn*, the experience of *both* penetration to clarity *and* impasse that we undergo in tracing where what we say to one another is taking us.[16] If Plato has any "doctrine" to propose to us it is this, and surely none of the characters in his dialogues proposes it but rather the dialogues as such.

---

16. See *Philebus* 15d: τῶν λόγων αὐτῶν ἀθάνατόν τι καὶ ἀγήρων πάθος (the immortal and un-aging experience of the things themselves that we say)" and for *euporia* and *aporia*, 15c.

9

Letting Plato Speak for Himself

Character and Method in the Republic

Ruby Blondell

"Show a little more spirit, my good man . . . and attack my actual statement itself, and refute it, if you can. . . . You keep talking about pigs and baboons; you show the mentality of a pig yourself, in the way you deal with my writings, and you persuade your audience to follow your example. That is not the way to behave" (*Theaetetus* 166c; tr. Levett 1990). Thus Protagoras, in Plato's *Theaetetus*, complains that instead of speaking for himself he has been represented by an inexperienced boy. Ironically, of course, the complaint is put into the dead Protagoras's mouth by Socrates, and into Socrates' mouth by Plato. Protagoras is very far from speaking for himself either here or anywhere else in the dialogue. In typically ironic fashion, the passage evinces Plato's pervasive preoccupation with the problem of responsibility for one's own words and ideas—especially after one is dead. This preoccupation is most strikingly manifested in Plato's own refusal in his own writings to present even the appearance of speaking in his own voice.[1] This refusal leaves us little choice but to behave like pigs in the way we interpret his writings, if we attempt to extract his own views from the speeches he places in the mouths of his characters.

Yet Plato still speaks to us. He does so like Homer or Sophocles, through the deployment of character, speech, style, and incident. In this chapter I shall focus on a central aspect of this authorial voice in a central work, namely Plato's manipulation of dramatic character in the *Republic*. I take the word "character," like the Greek *ethos*, to embrace both moral and intellectual qualities, together with the social and personal features (such as age, social status, gender, way of life, profession, manner of speaking) that help to

---

1. This is fundamental to the interpretation of the dialogues as dialogues. See Press 1995: 134 n. 4.

embody and convey these qualities.[2] As such the concept of character is integral both to the "literary" enterprise of representing human interaction in
spoken dialogue, and the philosophical inquiry into the best form of human
life and behavior. It is therefore the site of an intrinsic and indissoluble connection between aspects of Plato that are still often distinguished as "literary" and "philosophical" respectively.

The *Republic* is a particularly promising work in which to examine this facet
of Plato's writing, because of the marked shifts that occur between Book 1 and
the rest of the work. Book 1 of the *Republic* resembles the 'early' or 'elenctic'
dialogues, and as such deploys dramatic form and character very differently
from the remainder of the work.[3] Since Books 2–10 were clearly composed as
a continuation of Book 1, we may expect the stylistic shifts to tell us something
about Plato's own shifting attitudes towards philosophical method and its literary expression.[4] This chapter will examine the meanings of this marked alteration in literary and philosophical style.

I . CHARACTER AND ELENCHUS IN *REPUBLIC* 1

In the interests of brevity, I shall confine my discussion of Book 1 to Thrasymachus, one of Plato's most vivid and memorable characters.[5] As with many
Platonic characters, his personality, views, and philosophical methods are represented as mutually reinforcing. He is portrayed as a marauding wild beast
who preys on innocent victims (336b; cf. 336d, 341c, 358b). This not only suggests an absence of rational control,[6] but also prefigures Thrasymachus's own
picture of the exploitative relationship between the shepherd—or ruler—and
his flock (343ab). The champion of injustice, with his hostile and uncooperative
manner, bears out, on the level of philosophical practice, Socrates' view that injustice generates hatred and quarrels (351d). As one who glorifies the success-

---

2. Greek conceptions of character have been much discussed. See further Pelling, ed. 1990, Gill
1996, and cf. Blondell 1992a.

3. I prefer the latter designations since it does not prejudge issues of chronology. For recent criticisms of attempts to date the dialogues, see Thesleff 1982, Howland 1991, and further references
in Gonzalez, ed., 1995a: 6 n. 14; Press 1995: 137 n. 20.

4. This is true regardless of the circumstances of its composition. I do not share the view that
Book 1 was written earlier as a separate dialogue (for the history see Giannantoni 1957). But even
if it was, this need not affect interpretation of the mature work as a whole. The same applies to
Thesleff's interesting arguments for the composition of the dialogue over an extended period of
time (1982: 101–10, 137–40, 184–6). For arguments in favor of the unity of the *Republic* see Harrison 1967: 37–9; Sesonske 1969: 66–9; Giannantoni 1957; Bruns 1896: 320–27.

5. I hope to say more about Book 1 elsewhere, along with other matters elided or abbreviated
in this chapter.

6. Later the defender of injustice is said to feed the lion and the many-headed beast representing *thumos* and desire (588b–90c; cf. also the reference to Thrasymachus at 590d). Beast
imagery is used for anything hostile to reason, such as the desires (e.g. 439b, 572b, 573a, 573e),
untamed *thumos* (e.g. 411e), and the unphilosophical many (e.g. 493bcd, 496d, 535e, 590b; cf.
also *Politicus* 309e). Thrasymachus' anger is a manifestation of *thumos* (cf. 440c, and below),
while the taming metaphor allies his intellectual progress with the subjugation of desire (cf.
358b, 501e–502a, 589b, 591b).

ful strong-man, Thrasymachus has nothing but contempt for Socrates and his cooperative method.[7] Instead, he favors the confrontational method of opposed speeches (343b–44c; cf. 350de), relies on intimidating outbursts of abuse (336bc, 340d, 343a), and views argument as a violent battle in which he asks no quarter (341a9–b2, b8–10; cf. 342d2–3). When these methods fail, he refuses to cooperate and abandons both intellectual integrity and consistency rather than face defeat (cf. 345b).[8] These qualities, so essential to effective rational argument, are as alien as common courtesy to the admirer of tyrants. Even his didactic stance, which is both mercenary (337d) and authoritarian (345b), befits the autocratic values that he applauds. His character thus finds expression not only in his ethical views but also in his approach to rational argument that disqualifies him in Socratic terms, both as an effective philosopher and as an appropriate guide for the young. This character is in turn a reflection of the views that he proves unable to defend from the elenchus.

The extent to which Thrasymachus's views are constitutive of his identity emerges at a pivotal moment in the argument. Socrates has forced him to conclude that it is the just man, not the unjust, who is both good and wise (350cd). When Thrasymachus realizes he is losing the battle, he responds with intense physical symptoms of discomfiture. Socrates tells us, as narrator, that he saw the sophist not only break into an amazingly copious sweat, but actually blush—an unprecedented occurrence (350cd). This visceral response to intellectual criticism, as if to an emotional assault or even a physical threat, vividly and concretely displays the sophist's dialectical inadequacy. Anyone so wedded by pride to his convictions will be unable to adapt to the search for truth without destroying his self-image and with it his sense of his own identity.[9] Indeed, it is from this point onwards that Thrasymachus refuses to cooperate with Socrates, except superficially, insincerely, or at best sporadically (cf. 350e, 351d, 352b, 353e, 354ad). The moment of refutation that should theoretically lead to *aporia* and then to new progress leads instead to a divorce between the interlocutor's convictions and his responses.

Thrasymachus's rigidity is further fuelled by his role as a professional teacher. As Plato is careful to remind us, he habitually receives payment for his teaching (337d). Since his very livelihood depends on his persuasiveness and intellectual credibility, he literally cannot afford to admit defeat. Under the circumstances, evasion of an argument he cannot rebut is a prudent maneuver. But the silencing of his true voice constitutes a different kind of refutation, one that shows not the weakness of his arguments so much as the poverty of his intellectual skills, methods and achievements, and the corresponding inadequacy of his character for cooperative and fruitful rational inquiry. His effective withdrawal from the argument therefore helps to undermine further his credibility as a thinker and educator.

---

7. Cf. 336cd, 337a, 337e, 338b, 338d, 340d, 341ab. Socrates, for his part, will condemn the kind of argument that leads to strife (*eris*) (499a).

8. Thrasymachus never explicitly subscribes to the Socratic principle that one should say only what one believes. But he does claim to be serious about the subject under discussion (344e).

9. For the elenchus as a challenge to the ego, cf. Vlastos 1983: 36–8; Patterson 1987: 343–5. The seat of shame is the *thumos*, which is closely related to self-image (cf. 440c and Gill 1985: 8).

This account of Thrasymachus points towards some of the ways in which dramatic characterization is internally related to the philosophical method represented there, namely the Socratic elenchus. Since the elenchus aims to transform its targets' whole way of life, by scrutinizing their particular views and assumptions, it is an intrinsically ad hominem form of argument of a peculiarly personal kind.[10] If its force is to be fully appreciated, the character of each interlocutor, those aspects of their lives and personalities that make them respond as they do, must be made present to the reader. The resources of dramatic characterization enable Plato to accomplish this in a particularly compelling way.

Dramatization thus serves to clarify certain aspects of the Socratic method.[11] At the same time, it invites us to evaluate the philosophical potential of the characters themselves, with their personal qualities and circumstances, as well as their articulated beliefs. It therefore makes us a party to the Socratic search for someone with authentic philosophical talent, who may share his "wisdom" with us or serve as an effective partner in the search for truth. The pressure of elenctic scrutiny brings to light those qualities of character that determine the capacity of each respondent both to profit from Socrates and his method and to contribute to the success of the Socratic mission. Thrasymachus suffers from severe dialectical failings. Above all he is ruled by his passions, including passionate convictions so intimately wedded to his personality that they remain unshaken by Socrates and his arguments, despite his inability to answer those arguments.[12]

II. SONS OF ARISTON

Book 2 of the *Republic* presents us with an unequivocal shift in philosophical method, accompanied by an equally radical change in dramatic style. This transition is marked, among other things, by a change of interlocutors. Socrates' respondents for the rest of the work will be two young men, Glaucon and Adeimantus, who also happen to be Plato's brothers. Socrates speaks of the "sons of Ariston" as a pair, punning on the word *aristos* ("best") as he commends the *phusis* and "divine" lineage that enables them not only to show prowess in battle but to speak so eloquently without believing their own words (367e–68b; cf. also 362d). It is tempting to detect oblique authorial self-reference here. Plato too is a "son of Ariston," who of course has the eloquence to create all these speeches and many others, but is not thereby committed to the views they promulgate.[13]

Glaucon is lightly but clearly characterized. He is an Athenian aristocrat, who disparages Socrates' primitive city as a "city of pigs" (372cd), assumes that a

---

10. Cf. *Apology* 29e, *Laches* 187e–88a, *Gorgias* 472bc, 474a, 475e–476a, *Protagoras* 331c, 333c; Vlastos 1983: 36–8; Merlan 1947: 408; Mittelstrass 1988: 129; Blondell 1992b.

11. Another such aspect is the principle that dialectic should be adapted to the personality and abilities of each respondent. Cf. *Meno* 75d, and for a detailed discussion see Coventry 1990.

12. It is perhaps worth noting that the real Thrasymachus seems to have specialized in swaying the emotions (DK 85 B 5–6).

13. The address "son of Ariston" is only used twice elsewhere in the *Republic*, once for Adeimantus (427c6–d1) and once for Glaucon (580b9), both at pivotal moments in the argument.

citizen-army will be adequate (374a), is well educated in music (398e–99a; cf. 400a, 531a), knows how to breed hunting dogs, birds, and horses (459ab; cf. also 451de), has had (or still has?) an *erastes* (368a), and himself takes an erotic interest in boys (402e, 474d–75a; cf. 468c). By the internal standards of the *Republic,* many of these qualities are potential harbingers of philosophical success. Socrates' political and educational program will transform and endorse the aristocratic idea of inherited excellence (415abc; cf. also 535c), as well as the importance of "music," eugenic breeding, and properly directed *eros* (501d). Glaucon shows signs that he is developing these traits in the right kind of way, for example by his insistence that erotic desire should be aimed at the soul rather than the body (402de), and his lack of musical pedantry (400abc, 531a; cf. 399e). The occasional touch of urbane humor (451b) likewise accords with the philosophical enterprise of "serious play."[14] Even his interest in the spectacle at Peiraeus, shared with Adeimantus and Polemarchus (328ab) may point to a taste that might be directed towards the greater "spectacle" of philosophy (cf. 475de).[15]

Glaucon displays further virtues of character and intellect more explicitly related to fruitful dialectical intercourse. He is portrayed from the opening of the work as good-natured, compliant, and cooperative (e.g., 327bc, 328b, 435d, 451b). He is the peacemaker who undertakes that the company will pay Thrasymachus's fee (337d), and the representative eager bystander who begs Thrasymachus and later Socrates to speak (338a, 368c). He takes Socrates' side against Thrasymachus (347e–48b), but is willing to stand up to Socrates and even criticize him (347ab, 358b, 372d, 432e8, 471cde). He shows occasional touches of impatience with Socrates' hesitations (432e8, 472b, 474c4), but never crosses the line into discourtesy, and accepts Socrates' teasing with good humor (475a). He is dogged, enthusiastic, and encouraging (see references below). He has a persistent desire to learn (517b, 544b) and demands a complete and thorough account (430d, 471c–72b, 509c). He is an attentive listener, who interrupts the argument even in Book 1 when he does not understand (347a), and remains unflaggingly alert as it strays at great length over a wide range of subjects. His philosophical credentials range from an excellent memory (441de, 522ab, 543b–44b), though not a perfect one, to an ability to see the charm in solid geometry (528d).[16] The vigor of his character is manifested in dialectical as well as military courage (e.g. 357a, 472a) and a certain philosophical and conversational initiative (357bcd, 402de, 441a, 445ab, 467b, 468bc, 479bc, 526cd).[17] At the beginning of Book 2 he even takes on the role of questioner, using typically Socratic examples that suggest that he may have learned from the kind of conversations reported in Book 1, putting Socrates himself into the unaccustomed role of docile respondent (e.g., 357b9), and going on to demonstrate the method that Socrates should

---

14. For this theme in Plato's writings, see Guthrie 1975: 56–65.

15. Cf. Clay 1992: 128.

16. 474cd is a trivial example that enables Socrates to tease Glaucon. But he is also capable of forgetting an important point (519e–20a).

17. For more evidence of a bold and impetuous character see Jowett and Campbell, eds., on 357a.

now follow (358d).[18] He sometimes errs through overconfidence (523b, 529a–b), but accepts teasing and even rebukes with equanimity, and learns from his mistakes (527d–28a, 528e, 529c).

Adeimantus is introduced in Book 1 (327c), but says very little there (he speaks only at 328a). As the work continues, however, he displays the same philosophical virtues as the brother whose *phusis* he shares. Like Glaucon, he breaks vigorously into the conversation in Book 2 (362d), is willing to stand up to Socrates (362e1, 449b–50a),[19] and continues to express concern about Socrates' methods (487a–d).[20] His complaint that Socrates has not made the guardians very happy (419a) echoes Glaucon's objection to the "city of pigs" (372d), and betrays an equally conventional view of happiness. He puts pressure on Socrates to provide a full account of what he thinks (449c–50a, 497e, 504e). Socrates both teases and compliments him for his persistence, in particular for not settling for secondhand opinions (506abc). Adeimantus does not underestimate the opposition, or forget about Thrasymachus (498c, 499d). Like Glaucon, he is attentive, encouraging, enthusiastic, brave, persevering, and committed to the argument; he has a good memory (504ab); he knows Socrates' ironic ways (362e1, 487e); he can himself be "playful" (573d) and ironic (487e, 498d5); and he cooperates in a good humored way without any sign of flagging.[21] Though he participates in the discussion less actively than his brother, he does make his own minor contributions, and is quite good at anticipating where Socrates' argument is heading (cf. e.g. 371cd, 381c, 394d, 497c). In particular, he has an inkling in advance of what justice really is (372a).

Glaucon and Adeimantus share one more feature crucial for philosophical success, namely the belief that justice is worthwhile (cf. 347e–48b, 358c, 367a, 368bc). As we shall later discover, firmly grounded right opinion (*orthe doxa*) is a necessary preliminary for the study of dialectic (cf. e.g. 377b, 378d, 429c–30b).[22] Plato's brothers' conviction of the value of justice is sufficiently "deeply dyed" to have passed the test of exposure to Thrasymachus and his arguments (for the metaphor cf. 429c–30b). But right opinion alone is not enough for unshakable virtue. An enthusiasm for spectacle (328ab) may be directed not just towards philosophy, but towards the "sights and sounds" that delight the *philotheamon* (475d–76b). Glaucon and Adeimantus are interested in the views of Thrasymachus (338a), and even Glaucon has been reduced to *aporia* by the words of the sophist and others (358c). Moreover Adeimantus aligns himself with those young men who are in danger of learning that it is more important to *seem* just than to *be* just (365b, 365d–66a; cf. 362a).[23] By praising their Thrasymachean defense of injustice (367e–68a), Socrates suggests that they

---

18. Compare his examples (357c) with e.g. 341c–342e.

19. The two brothers use exactly the same phrase to contradict Socrates (362e1, 427d8).

20. Socrates paradoxically legitimates this concern (487d), and makes Adeimantus his emissary of the truth about philosophers (489ab).

21. For the brothers' philosophical spiritedness, cf. Patterson 1987: 343, 348–9.

22. For the importance of this, see Gill 1996: ch. 4. We see the beginnings of such an interlocutor in Polemarchus, whose friendliness and approval of justice underlie Socrates' successful application of the elenchus.

23. See further Blondell 1993: 32–3.

may be potential Thrasymachi themselves.[24] And indeed, the primary talent that they have displayed here is a gift for rhetoric, the province of Thrasymachus and other sophists. We may also recall Socrates' later claim that the most truly talented natures, when nurtured in a less than ideal state, end up in the most spectacular failure (495ab; cf. 518e–19b).[25] Despite Glaucon and Adeimantus's resistance to Thrasymachus, then, Socrates has not yet completely won the battle for their allegiance. Good character coupled with right opinion must still be fortified by "giving an account" of justice and its opposite through dialectic (cf. 505e–506e, 531e, 532ab, 534b, 535b; *Meno* 98a). Conversely such questions should not be addressed until right opinion has been indelibly established (537cd). Glaucon and Adeimantus are thus poised at a pivotal stage in their moral and philosophical development.

Plato's brothers possess many of the requisite character traits for dialectical success: courage, cooperation, memory, initiative, good humor, enthusiasm for learning, and stamina (see 449a–51b). Many of these qualities echo the qualifications for guardianship, and ultimately for rulership, put forward in the construction of the ideal state.[26] The brothers are engaged in the pursuit of wisdom and virtue; they have sufficiently well-established right opinions and sufficient personal maturity to move forward philosophically; they may even be among the special few who might rise to preeminence in the ideal state. The terms in which he praises their *phusis* (367e–68a), and their "divine" ability to resist the view that injustice is better than justice, echo the "divine *phusis*" to which Adeimantus attributes the rare ability to reject injustice (366c).[27] Plato thus suggests that they not only have the rare and extraordinary talent necessary for true virtue and philosophy, but also have been saved by divine agency from corruption by the damaging education that anyone raised in contemporary Athens must have received (491a–93a).[28] Socrates makes the equivalence explicit when he prescribes the guardians' education for the interlocutors themselves, including himself (402bc; cf. 504b–e).[29] Plato's brothers are even equated with the ruling class of philosophers, in virtue of their role as legislators (cf. 497cd). It remains to be seen, however, whether Glaucon or Adeimantus, or for that matter Socrates, can live up to this most demanding of roles.

Glaucon and Adeimantus are not identical. Of the two, Glaucon is more fully and explicitly characterized. He is Socrates' primary interlocutor. He accompanies Socrates at the opening of the dialogue (327a), and is the explicit addressee

---

24. Cf. Bloom 1968: 345–6. Some editors think that at 368a1 Socrates is calling the two brothers "children" of Thrasymachus. This would link them with Thrasymachus in the same way that Polemarchus "inherited" and developed his father's views. But Socrates may just be alluding to their real parentage.

25. It seems likely that Plato has Alcibiades in mind here (so, e.g., Clay 1988: 30).

26. See 455b, 475bc, 485a–87a, 489e–90c, 503bcd, 504c, 535a–36b.

27. Cf. 518de, where Socrates argues that the power of thought (*phronesis*) is "more divine" than the other virtues, since it cannot be instilled by habituation and practice.

28. This "divine" escape (492a, e) alludes most obviously to Socrates himself, with his *daimonion* (496c). Glaucon and Adeimantus' speeches, and Socrates' detailed knowledge of Homer, give abundant evidence of their exposure to such cultural influences.

29. For the confusion of the interlocutors with the guardians here, see Sider 1976: 346.

of the myth of Er at its close (615a, 618b, 621c). In between, he plays a much larger role than his brother, and participates in many of the most philosophically challenging parts of the discussion.[30] Adeimantus, however, is not so much a different color from his brother as a paler shade of the same hue.[31] They are two more or less well-developed examples of the same character type.

Their similarity is heightened by contrast with the highly varied interlocutors of Book 1. Cephalus and Thrasymachus, in particular, are quite different both from each other and from Glaucon and Adeimantus.[32] Plato's brothers have more in common with the less colorful but more philosophically promising Polemarchus, who embodies a kind of mean between Cephalus, the pusillanimous traditionalist, and the savage innovator Thrasymachus. They do, however, differ from him in certain important respects: their greater youth, their aristocratic lineage, their relative immunity to the "teaching" of the poets,[33] the firmness of their prior convictions, their eloquence, their ability to defend a position, the pressure they bring to bear on Socrates, and their demand for positive, substantial argument. Like Cephalus and Polemarchus they are sympathetic to Socrates, but like Thrasymachus they offer him a real philosophical challenge. Polemarchus, more unreflectively conventional, represents an earlier stage of intellectual development, as befits his earlier place in the dialogue. But his continuing presence as an engaged bystander offers him the promise of further progress (cf. 427d, 449b). And overall, he shares similar qualities of character with them. As with the differences between Glaucon and Adeimantus, Polemarchus differs from Plato's two brothers in degree, rather than kind. The characters of these three also overlap to a certain extent with that of Socrates himself (see further below). Their common aptness for philosophy seems to impose a uniformity that militates against the more developed and individual kind of characterization that we see in both Cephalus and Thrasymachus.[34]

It should not surprise us if dialectically desirable qualities turn out to be less individual than the countless traits leading to failure. This is not merely a manifestation of the familiar literary phenomenon that it is much harder to breathe life into virtuous characters than into flawed or wicked ones.[35] As Socrates says in Book 10, the simple and virtuous *ethos* is harder to represent than the complex and inferior (604e). This difficulty is not insignificant, nor is it merely a matter of literary skill. Plato proves his capacity for portraying a "virtuous" *ethos* with Socrates in many of the dialogues. But the problem of *poikilia* remains.

---

30. He is the interlocutor for about two-thirds of the constructive portion of the dialogue. For the distribution of parts and Glaucon's progressive "encroachment" see Diès 1947: xxiii–vi

31. Others have seen more substantial differences between them. Cf. Diès 1947: xxv–vi; Wilamowitz 1948: 350–1; Jowett and Campbell, eds., on 362e–363e; Brumbaugh 1967: 663 and 1954: 101–2; Strauss 1964: 90–91; Bloom 1968: passim; Sider 1976; Howland 1991: 40–41.

32. See further Blondell 1993.

33. But cf. Blondell 1993: 32–3, where I argue that Adeimantus is more susceptible than Glaucon, that may help to explain his more modest role and performance.

34. Cf. Irwin 1986: 73, who argues that in the *Republic* Socrates moves from arguing with a particular person to "what any rational interlocutor must agree to." Merlan 1947: 409–10 relates the shadowy characterization of Socrates' later interlocutors to their ability to learn.

35. Two notorious examples are Dante's *Paradiso* and Milton's *Paradise Regained*, as contrasted with the *Inferno* and *Paradise Lost* respectively.

The possibility of portraying a wide range of idiosyncratic but virtuous people appears to be ruled out not simply by the literary challenge this presents, but by a theory that views virtue as uniform and vice as variegated. As Socrates will subsequently declare, "there is one form of virtue, but the forms of vice are unlimited" (445c).[36] This means not only that there are many more ways of being bad than being good, and that everyone should be the same (590d), but that within each individual, complexity and variation of character are to be frowned upon, in contrast to the simple and homogeneous.[37] This theoretical perspective compounds the purely literary difficulties of portraying virtue. The theory of character explored and espoused by Socrates within the dialogue is thus reflected in the characterization of the dialogue's own dramatis personae.

III. PLAYING DEVIL'S ADVOCATE

Glaucon and Adeimantus make their most important appearance in the transitional passage that begins Book 2. Perhaps the most striking feature of Plato's double portrait here is his brothers' shared detachment from the case they make with such vehemence, in contrast to the usual requirement of the elenchus that one say only what one sincerely believes.[38] This separation between conviction and argument was foreshadowed in Book 1, when Thrasymachus declined to answer Socrates' questions honestly. The sophist's reactions graphically illustrate how the Socratic method may succeed only verbally, leaving the interlocutors unmoved even in defeat.[39] As with Thrasymachus, Plato often characterizes the interlocutor in a way which suggests that he himself is to blame for this state of affairs. Yet the frequent alienation of Socrates' victims suggests that the situation is more complicated. Socrates' pedagogical failure may result in part from his own method as well as his interlocutor's character flaws. For a method that cannot allow for and surmount such flaws is doomed to failure in practice. The painful sting of the gadfly may be the best teacher for a rare few, but it was not destined to succeed in converting the varied inhabitants of classical Athens to wisdom and virtue.[40]

Any skilful arguer may lead a less-skilled one to agree with his conclusions, whether enthusiastically, like Polemarchus, or grudgingly, like Thrasymachus. Such agreement is obviously not enough to establish either argument or conclusion as sound. The elenchus, which depends on the scrutiny of one individual by another, is thus flawed by its personal character, its reliance on the sincere participation of particular people. Of course any form of discourse is limited by the skills of the participants. But the elenchus is particularly vulnerable, insofar as Socrates' *own* moral and philosophical

---

36. This is echoed by Aristotle, who quotes a line of verse of unknown origin to the same effect (*EN* 1106b27–35).
37. Cf. Annas 1981: 96–8.
38. Cf. 346a, 349a, 350e, 337c. See further Vlastos 1983: 34–8.
39. Cf. Annas 1981: 56–7.
40. Cf. Sesonske 1961: 30–31, 34–6.

progress depends on the refutation of others.[41] If none of Socrates' opponents is a match for him, any insight he acquires through questioning them will be circumscribed by their level of comprehension and critical capacity. This problem is exacerbated by the requirement that the interlocutor say only what he believes. Since the elenchus aims to convince each individual of his own inconsistencies or errors, it is constrained not only by his intellectual capacity but also by his particular interests and convictions. In an important sense, then, it is Socrates' opponent who (at least in principle) controls the elenchus. At the end of Book 1, it is Thrasymachus who has served Socrates his "feast" of arguments (354a). On the level of dramatic representation, of course, it is Plato who controls the argument. He is free to endow Socrates' interlocutors with whatever abilities and interests he pleases, and thus give his protagonist access to a wide range of ideas.[42] He may also give a particular refutation broader significance, by characterizing the interlocutor as representative of a larger class.[43] He may even take the argument far afield from what the interlocutor might in "real life" be expected to understand. But the fact remains that he portrays Socrates himself as committed to the refutation and/or improvement of one respondent at a time.[44] This methodological restriction is reinforced by Plato's use of dialogue form to dramatize each conversation as a confrontation between Socrates and one or a series of individuals.[45] The personal character of the elenchus is thus a serious limitation, unless, of course, Socrates can meet his argumentative match. That he fails to do so in *Republic* 1 is clear from the end of the book, when everyone else has been silenced by Socrates' argument, and only he himself can find fault with it (354ab).

If Socrates is to escape these limitations, and gain access to a broader and more speculative intellectual canvas, he must be given the opportunity to scrutinize ideas not just because a particular interlocutor happens to hold them, but for their own sake. As Thrasymachus points out, the argument must be dealt with in its own right (349a), regardless of who does or does not believe it, or of whether or not a believer happens to be present.[46] Plato tacitly acknowledges this in Book 1 by representing Socrates as uncharacteristically willing to continue the argument without the sincere cooperation of his interlocutor. He concedes that it does not matter to him whether he refutes the speaker or simply the *logos* (349ab), and ignores the respondent's manifest disengagement in

---

41. Cf., e.g., *Apology* 28e, *Charmides* 166cd. For the difficulty of determining how the elenchus can be a means of discovering objective truth, see Vlastos 1983 (with *Afterthoughts*); Irwin 1986.

42. Since most of Plato's characters are based on known historical figures, there were no doubt some historical constraints on his literary practice. But, first, he was free to choose figures that suited his purposes, and second, like the dramatists and even the historians (cf. Hershbell in Gonzalez, ed., 1995: 35), he seems to have shown considerable freedom in his treatment of real individuals.

43. Cf. Blondell 1992b: 165–6. Cf. also Protagoras' role as the spokesman of the many (*Protagoras* 333b).

44. Cf. Griswold, ed., 1988a: 156.

45. Cf. Gonzalez, ed., 1995a: 11–12.

46. For the independence of the truth from individual speakers cf. *Phaedo* 91bc, *Phaedrus* 270c, 275bc, *Symposium* 201c, *Republic* 595c–96a.

order to press on with the argument.[47] Although this disengagement vitiates the educational function of the elenchus, it frees Socrates to take the argument wherever he wishes, winning Thrasymachus's improbable "agreement," for example, to the proposition that justice is the excellence of the soul (353e)—a good example of the kind of thing that is *not* satisfactorily proved by the elenchus.

At the beginning of Book 2, Plato dissociates the arguments to be refuted from the personal character and beliefs of the interlocutors in a different way, by giving Glaucon and Adeimantus the role of devil's advocates.[48] Unlike Thrasymachus, who claimed to care about the question at issue (344e), but withdrew from sincere participation in the argument, Plato's brothers are committed to the argument, but not to the views under scrutiny.[49] By making an eloquent case for a position they do not believe in, they illustrate the positive value of intellectual disengagement. Socrates confesses that his *aporia*, caused by the brothers' dissatisfaction with his elenctic arguments, is exacerbated by their own detachment from the views they have put forward for his refutation (368ab). Since these are not their own views, he cannot refute the interlocutors themselves, in the elenctic manner, but must show what is wrong with these views regardless of who holds them.

In the role of devil's advocates, Glaucon and Adeimantus restate Thrasymachus's most serious charges against Socrates and his method. When Glaucon complains that Thrasymachus was silenced prematurely (358b), he implies that Socrates might have fared less successfully with a different interlocutor; that Socrates' focus on a particular interlocutor has allowed him to get away with arguments that might not survive more rigorous scrutiny. The case for justice must be made not just in a way that silences the interlocutor, but in the most convincing manner possible. This includes refuting not merely the interlocutor's arguments, but the best arguments by the best speakers. Socrates obliquely acknowledges this when he claims to be defeated by Glaucon's case for injustice (362d), applauds the brothers' eloquence (368a), and confesses the magnitude of his task in face of their dissatisfaction with his previous arguments (368bc).

Glaucon and Adeimantus also restate Thrasymachus's other main complaint—that Socrates refuses to give a positive account of his own views (cf. 336cd, 337de, 338b). A convincing defense of justice requires some positive

---

47. Cf. also 350e, 351d, 352b, 354ab. In the *Gorgias*, Socrates becomes his own respondent (cf. also *Protagoras* 354e–56c), and then resorts to continuous discourse (*Gorgias* 505d–509c; cf. the discussion of Irwin 1986: 68–72). *Protagoras* 333c is only an apparent parallel, since Socrates warns Protagoras that examining the views of the many will lead to scrutiny of themselves (see Vlastos 1983: 38–9), though it is unclear how this can be so. Vlastos 1983: 35 n. 24 calls Socrates' acquiescence at 350e a *pis aller* to which Socrates resigns himself, but the very fact that he is willing to continue the argument under these conditions shows that its value does not depend on the interlocutor's sincerity.

48. Socrates explicitly distinguishes their character (*tropos*) from their *logoi* (368b). On their role here, cf. Sesonske 1969: 68–70.

49. Throughout his speech Glaucon makes it clear that he does not agree with the views he is expressing (e.g. 358c, 359b, 360c5, 360c8, 360d2, 360d4, 361e). Adeimantus does likewise (367a).

substitute for Thrasymachus's position, some substantive advice on "how to live the most profitable life" (344e, cf. 352d). They are thus challenging not only the arguments of Book 1, but also the efficacy of Socrates' method generally as a means of discovering and teaching moral truth. The elenctic Socrates is accustomed to scrutinizing the lives of others, but now his own way of life is on trial (367d). This time the jury is composed not of hostile or indifferent fellow citizens, but of men who share his philosophical concerns, including a number of clever and impressionable youths from the governing class, whose own lives may hang in the balance.

Book 1 concluded with Socrates declaring that they must find out what justice is before investigating what it is like (354b). The question and the methodological stricture are both typical of the elenctic Socrates. But after Glaucon and Adeimantus have issued their challenge at the beginning of Book 2, the question is pursued quite differently, and the methodological stricture abandoned.[50] Plato makes Socrates voice positive and sustained ideas concerning the nature of justice, thus tacitly granting some legitimacy not only to Glaucon and Adeimantus's dissatisfaction, but to Thrasymachus's complaints about the negativity of the elenchus. Once Socrates turns to a new method, and starts to develop his own substantial theories, Thrasymachus is converted into an attentive, interested, and even friendly listener (450a and b; cf. 498cd). Positive and successful dialectic requires cooperative interlocutors; conversely, an intransigent interlocutor is more likely to cooperate when his own concerns are addressed.

In their challenge to Socrates, then, Glaucon and Adeimantus not only question the adequacy of his arguments, but also cast doubt on certain aspects of his method. Their admirable *phusis* and firm convictions enhance the significance of this dissatisfaction. That they find Socrates' refutation inadequate poses serious questions about the efficacy of his method. That they adopt Thrasymachus's own method—the long rhetorical discourse—suggests that Socrates' rejection of such methods was at best premature. The gadfly turns out to be an inadequate teacher not only for the ill-tempered sophist, but also for Plato's brothers.

Glaucon and Adeimantus's dissatisfaction with Socrates' methods, combined with Plato's own change of tactics, also suggests another kind of criticism of Book 1. In that book, Plato represents Thrasymachus's response to the slipperiness of Socrates' arguments not as a legitimate uneasiness, but as crass and offensive rudeness that discredits the sophist personally. Plato allows Socrates to exploit his role as narrator and portray Thrasymachus as a contemptible beast, while at the same time subjecting him to an editorial mockery that belittles his objections (336b, d, 344d).[51] Socrates also interprets his interlocutor's motives for us, telling us, for example, that Thrasymachus has been "made angry by the *logos*" (336d)—when otherwise we might be forgiven for supposing that he had been made angry by Socrates. Later he informs us that Thrasymachus's reluc-

---

50. Cf. Annas 1981: 39.

51. Contrast 336b with the way Polemarchus, Cleitophon or Glaucon breaks into the argument (331d, 340a, 347a). Cf. also 337a.

tance to speak was a pretence, since he "clearly" wanted to show off (338a). This kind of editorial interpretation of the sophist's motives undermines the legitimacy of his rage at what he perceives as philosophical sharp practice.

In response to Thrasymachus's other main charge, that his method is too negative, Socrates intimates that he would have given a positive definition of justice if he could, but that Thrasymachus prevented him (337abc, 337e, 339ab). Plato thus deploys Thrasymachus in such a way as to suggest that Socrates does have a positive account to give, even though this sits uneasily with his habitual claim to know nothing (cf. 337e, 354c). Once again Plato uses literary means (a blocking character) to evade a serious methodological challenge. In both cases, the resources of dramatic characterization rather than philosophical argument are mobilized to exonerate Socrates by belittling and discrediting his opponent.

This is a technique more commonly associated with rhetoric than with philosophy, and the intervention of Glaucon and Adeimantus suggests that it is unfair and inappropriate in the present context.[52] Rather, any criticisms of Socrates and his method should be evaluated independently of the character of those who utter them. By introducing his brothers as intelligent, eloquent and good-natured spokesmen for injustice, Plato thus implicitly criticizes not only Socratic practice, but also his own literary practice in representing it. As Glaucon puts it, the silencing of Thrasymachus is merely an appearance of persuasion (357ab), for Plato has allowed him to be prematurely "charmed like a snake" (358b).

It is equally unfair to counter unpalatable ideas by discrediting the personality of the messenger. The literary strategy of Book 1 suggested that Thrasymachus's peculiarly offensive character is inseparable from his ethics. But according to Plato's brothers, it is not just Thrasymachus who holds such views, but all kinds of ordinary people as well. In "renewing" the sophist's argument (358b; cf. 367a, 367c), they represent his ideas not as the views of an idiosyncratic extremist, but as part of a complex of ideas widely held by the general Athenian public, and closely linked with traditional Greek values, as embodied in literature, religion, and the family.[53] Such views therefore cannot be impugned by focusing on the personal unpleasantness of this particular spokesman. Plato—and Socrates, the narrator—must do more than paint him as a villain and dismiss him.

Plato's self-awareness here is suggested by the fact that within the drama itself, this technique is unsuccessful. The presence of Cleitophon shows that Thrasymachus has admirers despite his deplorable manners (cf. *Cleitophon* 410c).[54] Even Glaucon is open to his influence (cf. 337d, 338a, 358c). Plato therefore offers us retrospectively a new way of reading Book 1—and perhaps other dialogues?—one that resists his own prejudicial use of characterization. He makes Glaucon and Adeimantus re-present Thrasymachus's views as powerfully as possible, without ridicule, abuse, or any other attempt to discredit

---

52. Aristotle, *Rhetoric* 1356a1–13, 1366a8–14, 1377b21–31; cf. also Smith 1995: 97, 107.

53. The point is taken by Socrates, if 368a1 means he is calling the two brothers "children" of Thrasymachus (n. 24).

54. He has been defended in modern times, to various degrees, by White 1995.

personally those who hold them.[55] Like Thrasymachus, they pose a real intellectual challenge, but their personalities are closer to that of the cooperative
Polemarchus. Only if the sophist's views are successfully refuted under *these*
conditions can we be sure that his anger at Socrates—as opposed to the argument—is not well founded. Socrates will subsequently maintain that personal
abuse is alien to the philosopher, who should be just, tranquil, and orderly
(500bcd).[56] This admonishment applies not only to Thrasymachus's personal attacks on Socrates, but to the treatment meted out to Thrasymachus himself by
Plato and his narrator, Socrates.

IV. NODDING MANDARINS

Having said their say at the beginning of Book 2, Glaucon and Adeimantus
quickly assume their familiar roles as Plato's Rosencrantz and Guildenstern.
There are corresponding changes in the character of Socrates himself. From
Book 2 onwards, he becomes less ironic, elusive, and provocative in manner
than the familiar figure of the elenctic dialogues, including Book 1. He remains
committed to cooperative dialectic, the atmosphere remains collaborative, and
he still eschews dogmatism (cf. esp. 450a–51b, 506c–507a). But this Socrates is
much more paternalistic and didactic than his earlier counterpart, while his
method has become less personal and more authoritarian and hierarchical. This
is reflected in Plato's use of literary form. Despite the interrogative form of so
many of his speeches, Socrates' style becomes largely expository, punctuated by
expressions of formulaic agreement from his respondents.

These simultaneous changes in Plato's dramatic style and Socrates' dialectical method make sense when understood as a response to the limitations of the
elenchus, some of which emerged in Book 1. One of the most serious problems
with the earlier method was its negativity. A desire to move towards positive exposition doubtless prompted Plato to provide Socrates with a broader canvas on
which to develop his ideas, as many have suggested. But this alone is not
enough to account for the stylistic changes. What made the earlier dramatic
style uniquely appropriate to the Socratic method was the personal character of
the elenchus. As Plato moves his protagonist away from this method, the lively
characterization of the earlier style becomes not only redundant, since Socrates
is no longer engaged in refuting ideas as held by particular persons, but also a
liability. For individual characterization privileges the kind of personal idiosyn-
crasy that interferes with philosophical progress and undermines the universal-
ity of the argument.

The elenctic Socrates' preoccupation with the particular caused at least some
of his methodological and pedagogical problems. His egalitarian search for the
potential wisdom in respondents of all kinds therefore seems doomed to fail-

55. They evince only a general contempt for such for people (363d1–2).
56. Adam 1963 ad loc. suggests that Isocrates is responding to this passage when he declares that
his opponents (such as Plato) have been much more abusive and less "gentle" than himself (*Anti-
dosis* 260). Cf. also *Theaetetus* 173d, 174b–75b, Aristotle *EN* 1125a5–9.

ure.[57] The new kind of dialectic dramatized in Books 2–10 still calls in principle for a sympathetic response to the individual interlocutor. But in practice, as we have seen, it suggests that successful dialectic calls for qualities that militate *against* individuality. If Socrates' respondents have the set of qualities needed for success at dialectic, he no longer has to tailor his method to their particular needs, and Plato no longer has to demonstrate this to us dramatically. We must therefore content ourselves with cardboard renditions of virtually interchangeable philosophy students. That is why the personalities of Glaucon and Adeimantus are so similar. What matters about them is not their idiosyncrasies, but their philosophical receptivity, that differs in degree rather than kind. This is one effect (if not also a cause) of Plato's use in Books 2–10 of two alternating but barely distinguishable interlocutors as opposed to the sharply differentiated serial interlocutors of Book 1.

If Glaucon and Adeimantus are uninteresting, then, it is not because Plato no longer cares about the qualities required for successful philosophizing, but because his dramatic style continues to reproduce the views and methods explored by Socrates within the dialogue. This Socrates views those qualities as essentially uniform, and has become increasingly suspicious of the kind of personal idiosyncrasies with which his former self once wrestled in his opponents. This shifts away from the personal matches—the shift we have already observed in Plato's presentation of the ideas to be refuted. These are not only voiced by detached rather than committed spokesmen, but also generalized and abstracted from the vivid individual who first gave them utterance. It is no longer enough to refute the views of individuals one at a time, in the manner of the early Socrates.

So far I have focused on the benefits—from the point of view of Plato and his Socrates, but also of ourselves—in Plato's transition to a new style and method. But there are also costs, the most striking of which is a newfound harmony that verges on the oppressive. In contrast to earlier Socratic principles (if not practice), the interlocutor displays little if any of the moral or intellectual autonomy that would seem to be needed for real progress. It might be argued that this is simply part of the price to be paid for liberating Socrates from his early method. But the situation is not so simple. For within the *Republic's* own framework, intellectual creativity and even autonomy are prized as an essential aspect of the character of the young guardians. They must learn not only quickly and easily, but *inventively* (455b). Plato seems unable, or unwilling, to dramatize for us an interlocutor who might fill such a role; or an interlocutor who embodies the positive qualities of Glaucon and Adeimantus, *along with* the critical spirit of Thrasymachus, plus an intelligence that can even begin to match up to that of Socrates.

The fact that Glaucon and Adeimantus have so little to contribute may suggest a Platonic pessimism about the natural, social, and educational conditions that may succeed in fostering the growth of a true philosopher. At the same time, there is a tension between their lackluster performance after Book 2 and

---

57. For Socrates' willingness to tackle anyone indiscriminately cf. *Apology* 29d, 30a.

the glowing terms in which Socrates as narrator has characterized them (above). It seems that Plato is once again allowing Socrates to exploit his narrative role, this time to assure us implicitly that despite appearances, and despite any preconceptions to the contrary, this is in fact what a gifted philosophy student looks like.

Few readers have been convinced of this. Yet Plato's sleight of hand here may have a substantive point, connected with the internal educational program of the *Republic*. The young guardians must learn to be steadfast, compliant, and respectful of authority before they are permitted to move on to creative intellectual work. But this raises a potential difficulty. As Annas puts it, "Why should people who are (crudely put) brought up to be moral conformists suddenly turn out to be intellectual pathbreakers in later life?" (1981: 87). In this, as in other ways, Plato's use of characterization echoes the internal structure of the ideal state. The characters of Glaucon and Adeimantus replicate the tension between conformism and creativity encoded in the guardians' curriculum. For the most part, they agree passively with Socrates' ideas, and they clearly have not reached the stage of philosophical creativity. Yet there are *narrative* signs that they have the capacity for greater autonomy and creativity, and are poised to develop it. Plato seems to be trying to assure us that such a person can in fact exist—that some, at least, of the dutiful young guardians may retain the capacity to blossom into creative philosopher-rulers. He uses his portraits of Glaucon and Adeimantus to suggest that this gap can indeed be bridged.

I argued earlier that at the beginning of Book 2 Glaucon and Adeimantus have reached the stage of firmly established *orthe doxa* and are ready to pursue a higher level of understanding. As the work proceeds, there are signs that they are specifically on the brink of understanding about the Forms, though neither of them has yet attained that vision (cf. 475e, 504b–505a, 506b–507a, 517c, 532d, 533a, 596a, 597a), and the present conversation is conceived of as a part of the continuing process that will lead them all to greater understanding. The possibility is thus left open that a creative philosophical role does await Socrates' interlocutors as they strive towards the vision of the Good. Socrates gives us no clear explanation as to how this transition is supposed to occur—the exact nature of the *Republic*'s 'dialectic' is notoriously obscure. But he does argue that it will require rigorous propaedeutic studies in mathematics and astronomy (533a). It is here, during the program for the guardians' higher education, that we can see, in Glaucon in particular, some sign of ability to follow the curriculum that will eventually lead to knowledge of the Good (528d; cf. also 511cd).

The gap between Socrates and Glaucon is also partially bridged from the other side. Despite his extraordinary intellectual and verbal creativity, Socrates himself has not perceived the Forms, but is confined to the level of opinion (cf. 506bcd). Like them, he is not portrayed as the static embodiment of philosophical perfection, but caught in the particularity of a specific moment of development. This lessens the gap in attainment between him and his interlocutors. Nonetheless, the idea that Glaucon might evolve into a creative philosopher remains dramatically asserted, rather than demonstrated. If Plato's dramatic technique is supposed to assure us that a philosophical butterfly may emerge from this dry chrysalis, why does he not dramatize the process directly, by allowing Glaucon to participate creatively in the discussion? Part of the answer to this may lie in his desire to explore, if not advocate, an authoritarian philosophical method, in which Socrates must not be eclipsed (above). But it is also possible that such moments of transition by their very nature cannot be represented or communicated in words.[58] This would help to explain why Plato should redeploy a dramatic technique from Book 1 that he had seemed to eschew for the rest of the work, namely the use of the interlocutor to impose limits on Socrates' philosophizing. The limitations of Glaucon and Adeimantus let both Socrates and Plato off the hook, so that no one is obliged to give a full explanation of the *Republic's* arcane metaphysics. Such an evasion makes sense, however, if that metaphysics, and the educational epiphany through which it is apprehended, are ultimately and in principle ineffable and incommunicable through language. On the dramatic level, the counterpart to this failure of *logoi* is conveyed through Socrates' inability to impart even his "opinion" about such mysteries to those who do not already understand them. What seems like a cheap trick in Book 1 turns out to have intrinsic meaning here, as the only possible way to dramatize the moment at which pedagogical limitation becomes inevitable, and further progress ineffable. The "blocking" use of the interlocutor's character has thus become self-justifying in terms of the theory it is now being used to explore.

The gulf between Socrates and Glaucon is not the only difference in philosophical ability portrayed in the *Republic;* Thrasymachus and Cephalus both fail on account of character deficiencies of very different kinds. Polemarchus, Adeimantus, and Glaucon each in turn show greater promise. The Socrates of Books 2–10 is at a higher level still, instantiating the intellectual autonomy and creativity that must be part of the philosopher's final training. And on the horizon we see the mysterious vision of the philosopher-ruler, the final, abstract model of human excellence towards which we, according to the program of the *Republic,* are to strive. Glaucon praises the image of the philosopher-ruler, as "completely beautiful" (540c; cf. 361d, 472d, 500d–501b).

What is the significance of this for the reader? The theory of *mimesis* explored in Books 2–3 suggests that by reading Plato's drama we will identify with and so come to resemble each character who speaks. After the style and characterization of Book 1 have been discredited, we are offered three models that are all more or less evolved members of the same type. By identifying with each speaker in turn, and above all with Socrates (who plays by far the largest part), we may acquire the characteristics that will enable us to go further. The more skeptical may identify with Adeimantus, the more enthusiastic with Glaucon, and the more creative with Socrates, but like the young guardians in Books 2–3, all will be identifying ultimately with their own desired philosophical character, albeit at different stages of development.[59]

---

58. Like the insight that "catches fire" in the *Seventh Letter* (341c), such moments are ineffable. They are analogous to the transcendent moment when the Forms are glimpsed (cf. 490ab, 511b, 516b, 532a–33d), the moment of arrival at the top of the *Symposium's* erotic ascent (210e–12a).

59. On identifying with one's own character cf. Blondell 1993: 34.

But how are we to move from one level to another ourselves? Above all, how can we hope to make the leap between a Glaucon and a Socrates? Paradoxically, the very acquiescence of Glaucon and Adeimantus is a stimulus to the reader to progress beyond them. Even their most wooden responses invite resistance, by leaving us space to question what they unhesitatingly accept.[60] By offering us both teacher and students as models, Plato displaces onto his dramatic characters the tension between authoritarian dogmatism and creative autonomy that pervades his work.

In a further and more profound paradox, however, mere identification with Socrates cannot accomplish the desired goal of becoming like him. The purposefully provocative nature of his ideas stimulates the reader to disagree and argue. This is the only possible way to bridge the gap between a Glaucon and a Socrates. At the same time it helps to compensate for the alarming lack of opposition experienced by Socrates within the dialogue. Plato gives his Socrates free rein, but by committing his work to writing, continuing to employ dialogue form, making Socrates reiterate the tentative and uncertain nature of his controversial conclusions, and refusing to verbalize the ineffable, he also invites his readers to do a better job than Glaucon and Adeimantus as critics.[61] They have made a promising start, but the argument of the *Republic*, as well as its form, indicates just how far they still have to go. Yet even if they have not yet gained access to the truth, they still exemplify the character needed by one who wishes to work towards it. As such, the reader is invited to identify with them and emulate their philosophical virtues, including the determination to keep on striving for something that may lie forever beyond their reach. Whether any of us will attain it lies beyond the purview of the written word.

---

60. This is emphasized e.g. by Arieti 1991: 232–4; West 1995: 45, 55–60.
61. Cf. Clay 1988.

WORKS CITED

Adam, James. ed. *The Republic of Plato.* 2d ed. Cambridge: Cambridge University Press, 1963.

Annas, J. *An Introduction to Plato's Republic.* Oxford: Clarendon Press, 1981.

Arieti, James A. *Interpreting Plato: The Dialogues as Drama.* Lanham, MD: Rowman & Littlefield, 1991.

Bloom, Allan. *The Republic of Plato: Translated, with Notes and an Interpretive Essay.* New York: Basic Books, 1968.

Blundell, Mary Whitlock. "*Ethos* and *Dianoia* Reconsidered." In *Essays in Aristotle's Poetics,* ed. A. O. Rorty. Princeton: Princeton University Press, 1992: 155–75 (=1992a).

———. "Character and Meaning in Plato's *Hippias Minor.*" In *Methods of Interpreting Plato and his Dialogues,* ed. J. C. Klagge and N. D. Smith. *Oxford Studies in Ancient Philology,* supp. (1992): 131–72 (= 1992b).

———. "Self-Censorship in Plato's *Republic.*" In *Virtue, Love, and Form: Essays in Memory of Gregory Vlastos,* ed. T. Irwin and M C. Nussbaum. *Apeiron* 26 (1993): 17–36.

Brumbaugh, R. S. *Plato's Mathematical Imagination.* Bloomington: Indiana University Press, 1954.

————. "A New Interpretation of Plato's *Republic.*" *Journal of Philosophy* 64 (1967): 661–70.

Bruns, Ivo. *Das literarische Porträt der Griechen.* Berlin: Hertz, 1896; reprinted Hildesheim: Olms, 1961.

Clay, Diskin. "Reading the *Republic.*" In Griswold, ed., 1988: 19–33.

————. "Plato's First Words." *Yale Classical Studies* 29 (1992): 113–29.

Coventry, L. "The Role of the Interlocutor in Plato's Dialogues: Theory and Practice." In Pelling, ed., 1990: 174–96.

Diès, Auguste. Introduction to *Platon: Oeuvres Complètes,* tome VI, *La République: Livres I–III,* Émile Chambry, ed. Paris: Guillaume Budé, 1947.

Giannantoni, G. "Il Primo Libro della *Republica* di Platone." *Rivista Critica di Storia della Filosofia* 12 (1957): 123–45.

Gill, Christopher. "Plato and the Education of Character." *Archiv für Geschichte der Philosophie* 67 (1985): 1–26.

————. *Personality in Greek Epic, Tragedy and Philosophy: The Self in Dialogue.* Oxford: Clarendon Press 1996.

Gonzalez, Francisco J. "A Short History of Platonic Interpretation and the 'Third Way'." In Gonzalez. 1995: 1–22 (= 1995a).

————. ed. *The Third Way: New Directions in Platonic Studies.* Lanham, MD: Rowman & Littlefield, 1995.

Griswold, "Plato's Metaphilosophy: Why Plato Wrote Dialogues." In Griswold, ed., 1988: 143–67 (= 1988a).

————. C. L., ed. *Platonic Writings/Platonic Readings.* New York: Routledge, 1988.

Guthrie, W. K. C. *A History of Greek Philosophy.* Vol. III. Cambridge: Cambridge University Press, 1969.

————. *A History of Greek Philosophy.* Vol. IV. Cambridge: Cambridge University Press, 1975.

Harrison, E. L. "Plato's Manipulation of Thrasymachus." *Phoenix* 21 (1967): 27–39.

Hershbell, Jackson P. "Reflections on the Orality and Literacy of Plato's Dialogues." In Gonzalez 1995: 25–39.

Howland, Jacob. "Re-Reading Plato: The Problem of Platonic Chronology Reconsidered." *Phoenix* 45 (1991): 189–214.

Irwin, T. "Coercion and Objectivity in Plato's Dialectic." *Revue internationale de philosophie* 156–7 (1986): 49–74.

Jowett, B., and L. Campbell, eds. *Plato's Republic.* Oxford: Clarendon Press, 1894.

Levett, M. J., tr., revised by Myles Burnyeat. *The Theaetetus of Plato.* Indianapolis: Hackett, 1990.

Merlan, Philip. "Form and Content in Plato's Philosophy." *Journal of the History of Ideas* 8 (1947): 406–30.

Mittelstrass, Jürgen. "On Socratic Dialogue." In Griswold, ed., 1988: 126–42.

Patterson, R. "Plato on Philosophic Character," *Journal of the History of Philosophy* 25 (1987): 325–50.

Pelling, C., ed. *Characterization and Individuality in Greek Literature.* Oxford: Clarendon Press, 1990.

Pollitt, J. J. *Art and Experience in Classical Greece.* Cambridge: Cambridge University Press, 1972.

Press, Gerald A. "Plato's Dialogues as Enactments." In Gonzalez, ed., 1995: 133–52.

Sesonske, A. "Plato's Apology: *Republic I.*" *Phronesis* 6 (1961): 29–36. Reprinted in *Plato's Republic: Interpretation and Criticism,* ed. A. Sesonske. Belmont, CA: Wadsworth, 1966: 40–47.

————. "Ryle on the *Republic.*" In *The Progress of Plato's Progress,* ed. Richard Freis. *Agon,* supp. 2 (1969): 63–71.

Sider, David. "The Structure of Plato *Republic* VI." *Rivista di Studi Classici* 24 (1976): 336–48.

Smith, P. Christopher. "Plato's Methods of Argument in the *Phaedo*." In Gonzalez, ed., 1995: 95–107.

Strauss, Leo. *The City and Man*. Chicago: University of Chicago Press 1964.

Thesleff, H. *Studies in Platonic Chronology*. Helsinki: Societas Scientiarum Fennica, 1982.

Vlastos, G. "The Socratic Elenchus." *Oxford Studies in Ancient Philology* 1(1983): 27–58.

West, Elinor J. "Plato's Audiences, or How Plato Replies to the Fifth-Century Intellectual Mistrust of Letters." In Gonzalez, ed., 1995: 41–60.

White, Stephen A. "Thrasymachus the Diplomat." *CP* 90 (1995): 307–27.

Wilamowitz, U. von. *Platon: sein Leben und seine Werke*. Nach der 3. vom Verfasser herausgegebenen Aufl., durchgesehen von Bruno Snell. Berlin: Weidmann, 1948.

10

Eros as Messenger in Diotima's Teaching

Gary Alan Scott and William A. Welton

A handful of characters in Plato's dialogues have traditionally been taken as 'mouthpieces' for their author's views. The implicit interpretive assumption of many commentators and readers of Plato generally has been that Plato conveys his own views through these, mostly philosophical, characters: Socrates, Timaeus, Parmenides, the Eleatic Stranger, the Athenian Stranger, and Diotima. Various subsets of the positions taken by these alleged 'mouthpieces' have come to be regarded as Plato's 'doctrines'—'doctrines' convertible into a set of propositions when extracted from their native context. The "Theory of Forms," with the related 'doctrine' of recollection, the account of the ascent of Eros given by Diotima in the *Symposium,* various theses concerning the immortality of the soul, the afterlife and judgment, even the belief in reincarnation, have all been ascribed to Plato and have been taken quite seriously as his 'doctrines' by commentators of diverse persuasions. Plato however, it must be remembered, does not assert any views in his own name in the dialogues; rather he puts these views into the mouths of characters.

In this chapter we will examine the role of one 'mouthpiece' in order to show that taking a character as Plato's mouthpiece often does very little to help understand a Platonic dialogue. We will argue that what makes the task of ascribing 'doctrines' to Plato so difficult, and sometimes impossible, is not just that he chose to present his philosophy in dialogue form; the difficulty stems, upon further analysis, from the *kind* of dialogues he writes.

Different emphases, even outright contradictions, in what various characters say (and do) in the dialogues force interpreters to determine what part of which statements express Plato's own philosophical viewpoints and what parts do not. This problem is exacerbated, and taking a particular character as Plato's mouthpiece is even less helpful, when differences of emphasis or blatant contradictions are expressed by a single character. Then there is the matter of Plato's portrayal of his philosophical characters. For instance, Socrates, although he seems to be privileged by his pervasive role as the protagonist philosopher, is far from an authority figure who claims to have all the answers. He offers his most important or most controversial ideas while claiming not to know what he is talking about or saying he is unsure of the particulars of a case. Professing not to have significant knowledge or wisdom himself, Socrates often presents his ideas in the form of appeals to other sources—myths, dreams (*Theaetetus* 201e), the tales of priests and priestesses (*Meno* 81a–b), and, on one occasion, a mysterious "wise woman" from Mantinea.

Although this feature of Plato's more philosophical characters is most obvious in the case of Socrates, it is by no means unique to him. Most, if not all, of the characters traditionally chosen as the source of clear, unequivocal statements of Plato's 'doctrines' often disclaim their own knowledge and authority. The dialogues contain statements made by the Athenian Stranger, the Eleatic Stranger, Timaeus, and even Plato's Parmenides, that function in similar ways. This is not to say that they all profess Socratic ignorance, but that they say things that in some analogous way undermine their own authority. The Eleatic Stranger, for instance, says that all humans are like dreamers who think that they know something only to awake to realize they do not (*Statesman* 277d). Timaeus admits that the best he can give is a likely story (*Timaeus* 29b–d). The Athenian Stranger at several places throughout the *Laws* makes statements that express skepticism about his own knowledge.[1] Finally, the very structure of the *Parmenides,* with the apparent contradiction at its end, makes it difficult to know what doctrine to attribute either to the character Parmenides or the author of the dialogue. In short, the views scholars have ascribed to Plato as 'doctrines' are, in fact, presented by him through the mouths of characters who do not (or who by the implications of their own claims cannot) attest to their truth. Since interpretation cannot merely accept what these characters say straightforwardly, calling such enigmatic characters 'mouthpieces' for Plato only begs the question: On what grounds can one ascribe views to their author?

The aim of this chapter is not, however, to deny that Plato had 'doctrines' in the sense of views or beliefs[2] but to argue against the view that his dialogues should be understood in terms of a conception of philosophy that takes its primary task to be the defense of doctrines. Plato may have believed many things, and these may even be reflected in the dialogues and relevant to their interpretation, but from this it does not follow that a chief function of the dialogues (or of Plato's conception of philosophy) is to defend these beliefs. We follow Gerald Press in holding that what the dialogues do primarily is to 'enact a vision', creating an occasion for philosophizing by making or showing

---

1. Cf. *Laws* 641d6–9, 732a4–b2, 799c4–e7, and 859c2.

2. The word "doctrine" is ambiguous. On the one hand it suggests those teachings that a philosopher might suppose to be known or rationally justified. But taken more loosely, it could refer to articles of faith, and eventually, any belief at all. But surely the term "doctrine" cannot be stretched to include hypotheses to be examined in a philosophical inquiry. Some of what have been taken to be Plato's doctrines are hypotheses offered to stimulate thinking—hypotheses that engage his thought, but about which he himself has come to no final conclusion.

as much as by asserting.[3] As important as any belief conveyed or defended may be *the way in which* it is conveyed or defended, and because a belief is defended at the level of the drama is no guarantee by itself that Plato's point is to convince his audiences of it. Every dialogue, if it is taken as a coherent whole, seems to be more than a vehicle for doctrine; and the performative effect of the drama appears to be an inseparable part of what Plato *does* want to convey. Only such an assumption seems likely to make sense of the extraordinary harmony between the form and content of the Platonic dialogues, seen in the fact that the "deeds" of the characters in the dialogues are so skillfully and deliberately intertwined with the matters they discuss. A close look at the example of Diotima will provide a case in point.

I.

Diotima's riveting discussion of Eros has traditionally been regarded as the apex of the *Symposium*. Socrates tells of his education in *ta erotika* (201d5) at the feet of a priestess, reputed to be from Mantinea.[4] The first problem an interpretation must face is whether, in offering the character Diotima, Plato is presenting someone who can claim to speak authoritatively (like Parmenides' goddess), or whether he is instead introducing another philosopher-figure like Socrates, who paradoxically speaks about things she cannot claim to know. Or perhaps he intends her to fall outside these categories. If, as we shall argue in this chapter, Plato's chosen way of writing makes it impossible to settle this issue, an interpretation of the *Symposium* must consider the significance of this fact. We will argue against those, such as Reeve, who hold that "Diotima is Plato in disguise."[5] We do not purport to be offering here an interpretation of the *Symposium* as a whole, or even to be providing an interpretation of all the

---

3. See Gerald A. Press, "Plato's Dialogues as Enactments," in *The Third Way: New Directions in Platonic Studies*, ed. Francisco J. Gonzalez (Lanham, MD: Rowman & Littlefield, 1995), 133–52.

4. Mantinea, the name of an actual Greek city, is where the Athenians finally succeeded in defeating the Spartans in 362. That the Greek word here is cognate with the word for "seer" has led several commentators, such as Halperin, to suppose that introducing Diotima is Plato's way of undermining the seriousness of her account. David Halperin, *One Hundred Years of Homosexuality and Other Essays on Greek Love* (New York: Routledge & Kegan Paul, 1990), 121. Dover cites precedent for translating her name as either "honored by Zeus" or "honoring Zeus." K. J. Dover, *Plato: Symposium* (Cambridge: Cambridge University Press, 1980), 137.

5. C. D. C. Reeve, "Telling the Truth about Love: Plato's Symposium," *Proceedings of the Boston Area Colloquium in Ancient Philosophy* 8 (1992): 89–114, and Mary Whitlock Blundell's commentary that follows (115–32). The citation is from p. 101. Reeve is by no means alone in holding this view. Vlastos writes, "This is the grand methodological hypothesis on which my whole interpretation of Socrates-in-Plato is predicated . . . with the qualification that in the *Symposium* and the *Parmenides* Plato creates new voices—Diotima in the former, Parmenides in the latter—to supersede that of Socrates *pro tem.*" Gregory Vlastos, *Socrates: Ironist and Moral Philosopher* (Ithaca: Cornell University Press, 1991), 117, n. 50. See also Dover, *Symposium*, 137. This is not the place to catalog the numerous examples of a less rigorous kind of reading which makes no attempt to consider who is speaking when citing passages from the Platonic dialogues, building an argument against Plato by quoting indiscriminately from any character in any dialogue.

possible tensions, ambiguities, and perceived inconsistencies discernible within Diotima's account of Eros. We hope to show only how content and dramatic context work together to provide one piece of the dialogue's puzzle, a piece that in itself is richer than the one-sided Platonism some would attribute to Plato.

According to Diotima, something analogous to Socratic ignorance is characteristic, not of Socrates alone and specifically, but of the philosopher *as such*. Socrates declares in the *Apology* that his wisdom is not worth very much compared to the wisdom of the gods. His human wisdom consists in not believing that he knows what he does not know; moreover, Socrates thinks this accords him a kind of superiority in wisdom over the other classes of people he examined, for they all believed that they knew when they did not. (Cf. *Apology* 21d–e, 23a–b.) Diotima says that philosophers do not possess wisdom, nor are they entirely ignorant. Rather, they are in-between ignorance and wisdom. They are not so ignorant as to suppose that they know what they do not; yet they lack the wisdom they desire, and thus they are lovers, rather than possessors, of wisdom. The gods are said to possess wisdom and, being wholly free of the lack that produces erotic striving, are not philosophers (204a). Philosophers in general then, by the very nature of philosophy as the striving after wisdom, are in this in-between state of Socratic ignorance, being in-between ignorance and wisdom (204a–b). And yet Diotima is also famous for her remarks about the Beauty which "always is and neither comes to be nor passes away" (211a). Scholars have frequently skirmished over the kind of knowledge implied by the vision of which Diotima speaks, and most have taken Diotima's remark here, and again at 212a, as alluding to Plato's infamous "Theory of Forms." If this is indeed what Diotima is suggesting, what would be the significance of the fact that Socratic ignorance and the vision of a Form appear to be directly juxtaposed?

Diotima's remarks concerning the nature of philosophers are apparently a small illustrative element in the larger discussion of the nature of Eros in general. Eros is depicted as a philosopher, and the image of the philosopher here is Socratic. Although the desire of the philosopher would seem to be only one type of erotic desire, Diotima describes Eros itself, Eros in general, as a philosopher; and what makes the image apt is said to be the fact that both are intermediate, and both long for what they lack.[6] At 203d6–7, Eros is said to be *"kai phronesios epithumetes kai porimos, philosophon dia pantos tou biou"*— "both desirous of wisdom and supplied with it, philosophizing through his whole life." Notice the expression "both desirous of wisdom and supplied with it." This expression suggests that there is a kind of wisdom in the Socratic ignorance of Eros (and this is consistent with Socrates' characterization of himself in the *Apology* as having a human kind of wisdom).

According to the first part of Diotima's account, Eros has a hybrid nature; it is born of Poverty and Plenty, exhibiting characteristics intermediate (*metaxu*) to both. In accord with its intermediate status, Eros bridges two realms or acts

---

6. This seems to be the central thrust of Socrates' cross-examination of Agathon. See 199c–201c and 201d–e.

as their "go-between," functioning as messenger from one to the other. Eros is a *daimon,* and *daimones* are spirits who serve as messengers between gods and mortals, bringing the entreaties of mortals to the gods, and the commands of the gods to mortals (202e–203a).

What does it mean to say that Eros is a messenger? It seems to mean that one gains some insight and inspiration from the very thing one longs for *through* longing for it. Through Eros for what one lacks one gains an intimation of it. Yet such an intimation of the truth never seems to take the form of something one can simply possess; for the best humans seem to attain to is the love of wisdom, not its possession. At least that is the best that philosophers can attain, according to Diotima, as her teaching is related by Socrates. Yet at the apex of the ascent, on the traditional reading, Diotima seems to promise the true lover something that earlier she had reserved for the gods alone.

In the early part of her account, all mortal creatures are said to strive for immortality; but as mortal creatures the closest humans can come to immortality is that gained through the life-preserving act of reproduction. Manifestations of this desire occur at various levels. At the physical level, humans share with all animals an urge to reproduce the species. But this desire also occurs at levels that are unique to humans: the love of honor, for example, is explained by Diotima as a kind of desire for immortality (208c). Both body and soul must continually be renewed (as far as possible). According to this part of her account, humans and all creatures existing in the world of change are capable only of approximating the immortality of the gods through offspring, whether such offspring are biological or the creative works and deeds that are the soul's "children."

It is against this background that Diotima presents the "final mysteries" of Eros. According to these greater mysteries the lover proceeds "from one body to two and from two to all beautiful bodies" until it is possible to know "just what it is to be beautiful" (211c–d). To apprehend the force that animates its striving is the ultimate object of all Eros. In the first part of her account, humans are clearly erotic beings, denizens of the realm of Becoming, who share in the intermediate character of Eros and are thereby denied full possession of what they seek (although they must always have some partial grasp of it at the same time). Commentators have usually understood the last part of her account as referring to a Platonic Form, the Beautiful Itself, and as suggesting that mortal, erotic creatures can actually have a vision of this. Too often these passages are interpreted as eclipsing the intermediate character of Eros and philosophy.

According to the account of Eros as a hybrid, it would seem that the philosopher, as the lover, not possessor, of wisdom, never attains wisdom. Moreover, insofar as one remains mortal, a creature of Eros and Becoming, then, given what Diotima says about the egress and renewal of all knowledge (207e–208a), even if one could experience such a vision, it cannot bring Eros to an end. Philosophers are human and, like Eros itself, are stuck in-between. The immortal, unchanging kind of reality, which lovers (and, therefore, philosophers too) seek, is fully available only to the gods. And yet at the climax of her account, Diotima claims that the vision of beauty will do two things for the one who has it: (1) it will provide true virtues (the implication being that without

this vision, the virtues one may have possessed previously were somehow false
or less secure); and (2) it will make the one who has it immortal, if anyone can
be made immortal.[7]

But what about Diotima and Socrates? Are they gods or philosophers? Let
us suppose for brevity's sake that Socrates is what commentators generally take
him to be, the paradigmatic philosopher.[8] What about the "wise woman" Diotima? Does she possess wisdom, a greater wisdom than the "merely human wisdom" claimed by Socrates in the *Apology*? Clues about Diotima's status may be
found by reflecting on the context within which Socrates introduces her. She
appears only in the *Symposium*. Socrates' recollection of her teaching (that
took place twenty-four years earlier) is, in turn, relayed by Aristodemus (who
drifts off in sleep for part of the dialogue) to Apollodorus, and Apollodorus, the
narrator of the dialogue, relates the whole story (more than ten years later)—
what Aristodemus said that Socrates said that Diotima said—to an unknown
companion.[9] On a temporal level, Socrates' recollection of Diotima's teaching
pushes the dramatic date back to 440; on a narrative level, it adds another layer
of remove to what follows, another reminder of the multiple layers of ambiguity in which the dialogue is framed.[10]

---

7. How seriously are we to take the qualifying phrase, "if anyone ever is" (212a6–7)? Bury notes
a "certain oracular obscurity which veils the clearness of the teaching" but has no doubt that "personal immortality was a doctrine taught and held by Plato." He notes that "the language of the
clause *epier to allo* may be simply an equivalent for "he above all" or "he most certainly." He suggests finally that if we press the matter, the clause may mean that insofar as he is compounded of
body and soul the philosopher is not wholly immortal, but insofar as he is a soul "grasping eternal
objects," he is immortal. Plato, *The Symposium of Plato*, ed. R. G. Bury (Cambridge: W. Heffer and
Sons Ltd., 2nd ed., 1969), xliv–xlv. We would only like to emphasize the fact that the "oracular obscurity" he notes does indeed veil the clarity of the teaching, and is probably designed to do so.

8. Gagarin believes that Socrates is no longer ignorant. Michael Gagarin, "Socrates' Hybris and
Alcibiades' Failure," *Phoenix* 31 (1977): 27–28. Rather than supposing that by the time of his writing of the *Symposium*, Plato no longer intends Socrates to be a philosopher in the required sense,
we would prefer to adopt the alternative rejected by Gagarin: Socrates' knowledge of *ta erotika* can
be reconciled with his ignorance, if the philosophic nature of Eros is stressed. The knowledge of
Eros is the knowledge of fundamental human need and its manifestations and in particular its manifestation as Socratic ignorance. Since Eros, this longing or felt lack, is said to be a messenger communicating to humans from the gods, it is possible that Socratic ignorance has this messenger function too. Somehow the truths for which Socrates seeks are intimated to him by his very desire for
them, but never in such a way as to quell his desire.

9. Commentators generally agree that the dramatic date of the *Symposium* is 416, prior to the
ill-fated Sicilian expedition and the charges against Alcibiades. We know from Thucydides that the
plague struck in 430 (see n. 12), so if Diotima forestalled the plague for ten years (201d), then she
would have visited Athens around 440. There is disagreement about the precise date of Apollodorus's narration of the story, but it could not have occurred before "several years after" 407,
when Agathon left Athens (172c), and it could not have been later than Socrates' trial.

10. Helen Bacon reminds us that "dramatic form is only one of Plato's devices for keeping us at
a distance from the truth," only one way Plato approaches "the truth obliquely, of suggesting what
it is like without saying what it is." Helen Bacon, "Socrates Crowned," *The Virginia Quarterly Review* 35 (1959): 417–18. Bacon stresses the way in which the rules of syntax governing indirect discourse in the Greek language underscore the shift between the "real time" of Apollodorus's narration and the speeches Plato has placed within the frame. The grammar of indirect discourse makes
"it impossible to forget that the speaker is quoting what he has heard from another" (418–19).

One might wonder what other reasons Plato had for making Socrates speak in Diotima's voice. Is it to permit him to distinguish himself from the other symposiasts who have each conceived of Eros in their own image? Or might he expect Socrates to be taken seriously when the philosopher introduces a Sybilline priestess to legitimize his claim to knowledge about *ta erotika*? Does Plato have Socrates intentionally enshroud this "wise woman" in mystery to arouse the suspicion of the audience or to provide himself with a veil of authority?[11] And why is his veil a woman? Is this intended to provoke his audience into regarding Socrates in the same way as they might regard Pericles after learning from the *Menexenus* that Aspasia, his *hetaira,* was also the great statesman's teacher in the art of rhetoric? Or is it designed to interject humor into the homoerotic *Symposium,* as Dover (1980) suggests? Or is Saxonhouse (1984) right when she suggests that fashioning this mask for Socrates is necessary in order to reintroduce the female into the dialogue in order to challenge the "phallocracy" and its barren attempts at generativity? Does Plato have Socrates introduce her as a priestess to tie her to the mystery religions? And, if so, how should one imagine that Plato's Socrates, and Plato himself, regarded the mystery religions? What did Plato want his audience to infer from her use of the language of initiation? The most important point, we would suggest, is that Plato has written the dialogue so as to provoke all these questions, and yet to leave them unresolved, even unresolvable. It seems clear that he did not want to make things easy on his audiences, and we think this is significant.

In his introduction of her, Socrates provides other clues about how Diotima is to be regarded. As proof of her wisdom, he says that she forestalled the great plague for ten years by telling the Athenians what sacrifices to make (201d). But this is a specious claim to authority. Socrates' audience would have known that postponing the plague from 440 to 430 only increased the casualties since, according to Thucydides, the spread of the plague was hastened by the concentration of inhabitants inside the city walls as a result of the war effort.[12]

---

11. In addition to providing Socrates with a veil of authority and allowing him to praise Eros in terms reminiscent of his characteristic features without seeming quite as self-congratulatory as certain other speakers were, speaking through the voice of Diotima accomplishes at least three things for Socrates: (1) it permits him to refute previous interlocutors, especially Agathon, in a less offensive, indirect manner and, by showing that he had to learn what he now knows, to accomplish this refutation without elevating himself as the know-it-all; (2) it permits him to reintroduce a form of his customary question and answer method rather than simply giving a set speech, keeping consistent with his view—implicit throughout the dialogue—of teaching and learning; and (3) it permits him to reintroduce the feminine into the homoerotic gathering, a movement Plato completes by having Alcibiades enter with a second flute-girl.

12. Saxonhouse and Daniel Anderson have noticed this irony, but surprisingly few others have paid attention to it. Arlene Saxonhouse, "Eros and the Female in Greek Political Thought: An Interpretation of Plato's Symposium," *Political Theory* 5 (1984): 5–27, and Daniel E. Anderson, *The Masks of Dionysus: A Commentary on Plato's Symposium* (Albany: State University of New York Press, 1991): 53. Those who make the case that Diotima was an historical figure must, of course, have often overlooked the fact that this "proof" erodes her claim to authority rather than attesting to it. Thucydides discusses the migration into the city in his *History,* particularly in Book II: 13–16 and in the sections expressly devoted to the plague (II: 47–54). See especially I: 13 and I:16, Thucydides, who was himself struck by the plague, attributes its severity to the influx of people and the

Socrates should know that Diotima's authority will be less than convincing on the basis of this dubious boon.

Now suppose she has had the vision, will it not have already slipped away, as she claims human knowledge always does? If one supposes her to be guided by her memory of the vision, this would at best be merely a more vivid form of the sort of "recollection" that Eros as a messenger must be capable of eliciting in everyone. Finally, it is possible that after a long and rigorous initiation process she has indeed had the vision that renders one immortal, and has been so transformed from the mortal state as to never lose her hold on this vision. If so, the mystery in which Socrates enshrouds her might tend to make her seem even more divine to his listeners. One might even suppose that she has become a goddess, until one recalls that her account makes plain that mortals cannot have direct intercourse with the gods, relegated as mortals are to the world of becoming. And if Diotima is a philosopher, her account of the final attainment, like Socrates' account of the Good in the *Republic,* is a supposition, at best a philosophical inspiration, but not knowledge in the strict sense.[13] Yet such inspirations, such dreams, may be an example of how Eros intimates its absent object, articulating the desire for absent Being until it seems to give form to a positive account of Being. In this case, then, both knowledge (in a weaker sense) and ignorance would be present in such a vision.

It may be appropriate for someone who has just been speaking about Eros to illustrate how Eros is a messenger between mortals and gods, knowledge and ignorance, being and becoming. It may be that toward the end of her lesson Diotima is acting as a true mantic or like the Pythian priestess at the Delphic oracle, showing how Eros goes both ways: as a messenger from gods to mortals, Eros issues in inspiration, and as a messenger from mortals to gods, it conveys prayers and entreaties. Across the entire spectrum of human desires, then, these desires, as manifestations of Eros, are acting as messengers in both directions. When philosophers seek to know what is Beauty or Truth or Goodness, their Eros entreats; while, in and through their erotic striving, they receive an adumbration, an intimation, hint, or outline of the object of their desire. Now this discussion of Eros as inspiration suggests that if Diotima's "vision" is inspired by her Eros for the Beautiful or the Good, then the mere fact that she *has* Eros for it rules out the possibility that her grasp of it is fixed and secure: she either longs to possess it and does not have it, or she "has" it somehow, but must keep striving in order to retain it.

---

overcrowded conditions, especially since the plague struck during the hottest time of the year (II: 52). Anderson makes the novel assertion that the Athenians might have been much less hasty to go to war had the plague struck in 440 and lasted for three or four years (as it did when it struck in 430, the second year of war).

13. Anderson (*Masks,* 53) rightly notes that, for the most part, Diotima functions as a philosopher rather than a priestess, taking Socrates through a dialectical examination of Eros. The problem concerning the kind of knowledge at issue here cannot be explored in detail within the scope of this chapter. Suffice it to ask: If the vision of the Beautiful Itself is a kind of inspiration, will it be able to give an account of itself? And, if not, what does this mean for all the passages in the dialogues in which knowledge is said to consist in giving a *logos*?

II.

The key elements in Diotima's account—a description of the nature of philosophy according to which it is Socratically ignorant, an account of existence in time according to which humans can only approximate to the eternal through Eros, and the explanation of the broadening of Eros which holds forth the promise of a vision that will yield true knowledge (securing virtues and facilitating immortality, if anyone ever achieves it)—these elements generate a tension that complicates the problem of interpretation. This is the very same tension that appears on a larger level in the *Republic* as the contrast between philosopher-kings and the Socrates who envisions them.

It is as though Plato's dialogues present two distinct and seemingly incompatible visions: the vision of the philosopher impelled by Eros, and exemplified by the ignorant Socrates, and the vision of Forms.[14] We take the tension between these two visions to be the source of the controversy between doctrinal and nondoctrinal interpretations; and it is to attempt to resolve this fundamental tension that some versions of developmentalism have arisen. Plato's audiences are faced with the task of reconciling the skepticism of his ignorant, self-deprecating Socrates with the doctrinal metaphysics of the "Theory of Forms." According to Vlastos, the same thinker would have to be schizophrenic to hold these two sides together; so Vlastos tries to solve the problem by distinguishing between the views of the historical Socrates and the views of the mature Plato (presented through his mouthpiece "SocratesM").[15] Vlastos's developmentalism sees the *Symposium* as reflecting Plato's transition from an early fidelity to the historical Socrates to his own mature, independent views. Against this theory, we claim that the contrast between what have come to be thought of as "Socratic" and "Platonic" elements in the dialogues is a principal feature of what has recently been termed a contrast between the form and content of Plato's work.[16]

This tension has many manifestations, and we contend that it has less to do with Plato's relation to the historical Socrates than with his characteristic way of thought. The fact that the same sort of tension that exists between the 'doctrines' of Vlastos's "SocratesE" and "SocratesM" can also be found in the two parts of the account of Eros provided by Diotima argues against Vlastos's developmental hypothesis.[17] Hence, regarding Diotima as Plato's 'mouthpiece'

---

14. This tension seems too obvious, especially given that it is Plato we are discussing, to have been created by an oversight or sloppiness. Apparently, then, Plato either thought this tension could be reconciled, or wanted his audience to be aware of it as a problem.

15. Vlastos, *Socrates: Ironist*, 46. For another criticism of Vlastos, see Debra Nails, "Problems with Vlastos's Platonic Developmentalism," *Ancient Philosophy* 13 (1993): 273–91.

16. Francisco J. Gonzalez, "Introduction: A Short History of Platonic Interpretation and the 'Third Way'," in *The Third Way*, ed. Gonzalez, 2–13. Gonzalez shows how the two main traditional alternatives for interpreting Plato leave us with a paradox: "The skeptical interpretation can account for the form of Plato's writings only by minimizing their positive philosophical content, while the 'doctrinal' interpretation can uncover their content only at the cost of considering their form little more than a curiosity and even an embarrassment" (13).

17. Vlastos has to take both SocratesE and SocratesM as appearing in different parts of the *Symposium*, but he does not take account of the fact that Diotima's characterization of philosophy *as*

only pushes the problem of interpretation back one level, since both sides of the tension exist in her account. If such a fundamental phenomenon as Eros must be related to both Socratic ignorance and something like the Forms because Eros itself is characterized by this tension, then it is not something an interpretation can explain away by a theory of Plato's development. Perhaps Plato saw this tension as a feature of all human life and of any discourse meant to awaken the erotic longing for wisdom. We suggest that the dialogues themselves exemplify such discourse. They perform their function of arousing Eros, in part, by posing a contrast between the kind of knowledge Plato's characters can plausibly claim and the kind they are allowed to envision. The tension of which we speak derives from the "in-between" status of human life, a life which, as Diotima makes clear, is immersed in Becoming yet dimly reminiscent of Being. Thus, the tension generated in trying to interpret the dialogue mirrors the tension spoken of in the dialogue, so that Plato has harmonized the form and content of his work.

That the tension in Diotima's account is reflective of the in-between status of Eros is confirmed by the fact that Eros forms the textual link between the two elements under consideration: the discussion of the Socratically ignorant nature of philosophy and the apparent reference to Forms. The in-between, Socratic, status of philosophy is mentioned as part of a discussion of the nature of Eros; and the Form of the Beautiful Itself is presented as the ultimate object of Eros, the reality Eros seeks at every level as it is reflected in various particular worldly manifestations.[18] Whether or not he conceives the transition from particular beauty to universal beauty as a seamless one, Plato seems to stress that Socrates can be Socrates, philosophers can be philosophers, only because *there is* something more desirable than human opinion that is the ultimate object of all desire. Moreover, Socrates is only Socrates, the philosopher is only a philosopher, because this more divine reality never appears before us, and ought never to be mistaken for any opinion or philosophical 'doctrine' a human being can hold. At least while they are here on earth, humans cannot stop striving, because any finite form that Beauty (or Goodness, or Truth,) takes must necessarily be incomplete.

Bearing in mind the in-between nature of Eros yields insight also into the way Plato writes. All creative works spring from Eros, but philosophy is especially aware of itself as erotic, as a longing for something that is lacked. Plato may have

---

such is Socratic (Vlastos, *Socrates: Ironist*, 47, n. 11), Nails ("Problems," 275, n. 5, and 281, n. 13) draws attention to the "indeterminate status" of the *Symposium's* Socrates on Vlastos's view. Although we cannot examine all the details of Vlastos's complex arguments here, we would note that even if there is a "historical Socrates" in various places in Plato's works, Vlastos has not convincingly demonstrated his account of why that Socrates appears there. Plato may have chosen to use more or less "historically accurate" portrayals of Socrates as needed, and done so for a wide variety of purposes. The important issue for Platonic scholarship is not whether an historically accurate Socrates can be found but whether he can be used to impute particular views to an "early" Plato.

18. Pender has stressed the parallel between the language used by Diotima at *Symposium* 212a and the language used by Socrates at *Republic* 490b. Pender follows A. E. Taylor in holding that both in *Symposium* and *Republic* Plato writes his characters' speeches in terms that describe quite graphically how the lover of wisdom engages in a kind of intercourse with "true reality." E. E. Pender, "Spiritual Pregnancy in Plato's *Symposium*," *Classical Quarterly* 42, no. 1 (1992): 72–86. See especially 82–3.

seen his philosophical dialogues as addressing the Eros in his audiences, designed to awaken a longing in them, as Socrates tried to do with his interlocutors.[19] To awaken Eros is to make one aware of a lack, and that is to make one simultaneously aware of Being and the fact that one does not possess it. The dialogues are ambiguous, even contradictory, in part, precisely because they aim to make their audiences experience this in-between position; they must suggest the eternal world while underscoring that neither their protagonists, their audiences, nor their author are in a position to simply reach out and grasp that world.[20]

What has been supposed to be Plato's metaphysical 'doctrine' has another unusual feature: just when one assumes that this 'doctrine' is true, it becomes most questionable whether anyone can "know" that it is true, because this 'doctrine', whatever else it may contain, clearly implies that living humans are not really in a position to know very much. If true knowledge is knowledge of the Forms and Forms are extremely hard to know, if it seems to require an exceptional human even to catch glimpses of them at the end of a long, dialectical journey, and if human life itself seems to be prohibited from any secure access to this realm, then it is unclear who can possess authoritative knowledge. Still, Plato's "metaphysics" might be seen as an explanation of the intermediate position of human beings. It is integral to his attempt to communicate the strange mixture of knowledge and ignorance, Being and Non-Being, that humans experience in their mortal, in-between state. The Eleatic Stranger in the *Statesman* characterizes this experience as follows: "Every one of us is like a man who sees things in a dream and thinks that he knows them perfectly and then wakes up, as it were, to find that he knows nothing." He calls this "our strange human plight where the winning of knowledge is concerned" (*Statesman* 277d). If Plato is offering a "Theory of Forms" to explain the inherent ambiguity of life at metaphysical and epistemic levels, that would still seem to give the metaphysics it implies a far different sense than the rationalism of Descartes. And it would imply, further, that the tension of which we speak is not only a tension between the two parts of Diotima's account; it is also limned in each part considered separately. This is due to the hybrid nature of Eros. Diotima suggests that the lover, always intermediate between Need and Resource, somehow moves from a state in which Need is greater than Resource to one in which Resource predominates over Need. And yet both Resource and Need are always there, as inseparable ingredients in the nature of Eros.

What can we say to someone who claims that Philosophers do get out of the Cave eventually, and that the vision of the Beautiful Itself does indeed put one outside of, or above, the predicament of other mortals who are characterized by

---

19. And as Diotima, in Socrates' recollection of her teaching to him, tried to do with Socrates.

20. Press puts this point nicely: "What the dialogues create in us is the *experience* of this as philosophy, and of Plato's vision: of human life as lived in a reality through which we catch enrapturing glimpses of the ideal; but frustratingly, the ideal remains beyond our grasp just because we live in time and space. Precisely because of their disconcerting combinations of the eternal and the ephemeral, the ideal and the real, the dialogues actually *embody* (what some of them try to articulate) how the eternal and ideal is glimpsed but never really grasped in the ephemeral real world in which alone we philosophize." Gerald A. Press, "Plato's Dialogues" in *The Third Way*, ed. Gonzalez (1995), 148.

ordinary, not Socratic, ignorance? Diotima does say that if any human ever becomes immortal, it is the one who has this vision (212a). But, looked at critically, this is almost a truism, for it simply makes clear that such a vision is not an experience available to mortal, embodied beings. (Recall why Socrates in the *Phaedo* claims to look forward to death.[21]) And Plato's audiences need only ask again: Do Socrates and Diotima qualify for this? Whether or not one supposes that Diotima does, the fact that she told Socrates about it does not seem to be sufficient to secure for him either knowledge or immortality. The vision Diotima depicts cannot be conferred upon others simply by persuading them to believe it as a doctrine.

Philosophical Eros, likewise, can neither rule out the grasping of Forms nor expect to grasp them easily. Both alternatives seem to be essential to Eros: one must know one does not have whatever one lacks, and one must believe that grasping it is possible. By conveying this in his dialogues, Plato leaves his audiences pregnant with desire. Hence the dialogues are erotic too in that they communicate like *daimones* from the divine region to the mortal region. To say that Eros is a messenger and to describe the progress of knowledge in terms of a broadening of Eros, as Diotima does, implies that desire of a certain kind leads to knowledge. Ignorance, when it is felt as a lack, becomes curiosity and the desire for wisdom. By reflecting on this desire for wisdom, progress can be made toward knowledge and excellence. This is one way that the dialogues function: They reflect the Eros embodied in Socrates, the longing for wisdom that is part of the Socratic awareness of ignorance, and the activities that arise from it. Plato shows Socrates conversing with others but never arriving at final solutions. His apparent and provisional conclusions turn out, upon examination, to assert little, if anything, that is dogmatic. Charles Griswold puts the point nicely when he says, "Plato structures the dialogues so as to cast doubt on any claims to completeness."[22] By portraying Socrates' quest for wisdom in contrast

---

21. See, for example, *Phaedo* 66e–67a. The *Symposium* gives ample reason for holding that human desire may not overlook embodied existence without becoming a caricature of itself. As inbetween, Eros cannot overlook its Resourceful side without becoming tragic; and it cannot forget its Needful side without becoming comical. In a recent article, Rojcewicz argues that Plato here presents Socrates as even more rarified than in Aristophanes' caricature of the philosopher suspended in a basket. Rojcewicz follows Sallis in suggesting that Plato wants his audience to see that Socrates is practically disembodied, so much so that he has even lost his shadow, Aristodemus, who may as well be invisible to the other symposiasts. Having Socrates bathe before and after the drinking party, according to Rojcewicz, provides a kind of purification to go with the rarification. He takes these dramatic clues as intended to announce how far the dialogue allows the Apollonian forces to exclude the Dionysian elements. That Socrates is wearing slippers and that he veers off in thought on the neighbor's porch prior to entering the party, confirms how exceptional this gathering will be. The banishment of the flute-girl, the decision to exercise moderation in the consumption of wine, and the homoerotic framework of the first three speeches completes the one-sided context in which Socrates is forced to speak. Dionysus will not fully return until Alcibiades crashes the party, draped in ivy, inebriated, and followed by a second flute-girl. Richard Rojcewicz, "Platonic Love: Dasein's Urge Toward Being," *Research in Phenomenology* 27 (1997): 103–20.

22. Charles Griswold, "Response to Kenneth Sayre," *Proceedings of the Boston Area Colloquium in Ancient Philosophy* IX (1993), ed. John J. Cleary and William Wians (Lanham, MD: University Press of America, 1995): 194–211. The passage cited is from p. 201. See also p. 200, where Griswold writes, "Not only the aporetic dialogues are aporetic; superficially non-aporetic dialogues such as the *Statesman* and the *Republic* are also aporetic in that they raise important questions to which they provide no answers or at least no satisfactory answers."

to the tendencies of his various interlocutors, Plato is able both to examine and exemplify Socratic Eros. He uses this approach to illuminate and to clarify the most far-reaching possibilities of human life, displaying the relations between philosophy, political life, religion, poetry, the arts, the various excellences, law, education, language, writing, and love in its various forms, including the love of gain and the love of honor. It is as though the "forms" of all these things emerge in sharp relief, but their emergence results simply from paying closer attention to the search for knowledge itself and the conditions of the search.

It might seem that we have had to interpret Diotima as Plato's 'mouthpiece' in order to apply her account of Eros to our understanding of how Plato writes his dialogues. But when Diotima is taken as Plato's mouthpiece it is usually in order to ascribe to Plato the views associated with traditional Platonism as conventionally understood. It should be noticed that the effect of our interpretation, by contrast, is not to leave us with a clear conception of what Plato believes; or if it is taken to give some indication of what Plato believes, that belief does not seem to be a belief in textbook Platonism. Plato is not a modern rationalist confident in the powers of unaided reason to win indubitable truths, but a philosopher who seems profoundly aware of the obstacles to knowledge. He gives his thought a highly enigmatic form befitting its content. The form of Diotima's account of Eros, as we have seen, produces a tension rather than resolving it. Like Socrates, Plato does not teach by giving answers, but by stimulating questions.

The way of reading the *Symposium* we have proposed here requires grasping that Plato deliberately juxtaposes the dogmatic and skeptical elements in the dialogues, and that it is necessary to read each in relation to the other in order to grasp a dialogue's full meaning. We only understand Eros fully when we see how Socrates both personifies and replaces it in the action of the dialogue; and we only understand Socrates as the lover when we understand what he loves most of all. Likewise, we only understand Diotima's vision of Beauty when we see that Socrates is as close as Plato ever takes us to it. This may suggest that the Forms hold the greatest significance for Plato as objects of human striving; they may be most significant for philosophy precisely as something that is lacked. This implies not only the skeptical assertion that humans cannot know Forms now, but the more "Platonist" assertion that being human means striving to know them. If, as it were, one can find the Form of the Good or of Beauty by reflecting on the in-between position of Socrates in the dialogues, then we would have a "third way" of reading Plato, a way between dogmatism and skepticism that integrates the two poles in the dialogues. Erotic striving cannot utterly preclude the possibility of grasping its object—in fact, the possibility may be necessary to inspire Eros; but neither is it the case that Eros is rendered worthless if it never succeeds in grasping what it seeks. For if the quest to know Forms fails, one is still left with the in-between Socrates, the most erotic man in the *Symposium*.

11

The Eleatic Stranger

His Master's Voice?

Francisco J. Gonzalez

Interpreters of the *Sophist* and the *Statesman* almost universally assume that the Eleatic Stranger speaks for Plato.[1] This is surprising, given how little speaks in favor of this assumption and even how intuitively implausible it is. The same interpreters take *Socrates* to be Plato's mouthpiece in most other dialogues, even the one immediately preceding the *Sophist* in dramatic time: the *Theaetetus*.[2] Is it plausible that Socrates, while speaking for Plato in the *Theaetetus*, should suddenly cease to be Plato's mouthpiece when the discussion continues the next day in the *Sophist* and the *Statesman*, even though he is still present and speaks? And is it plausible that the function of mouthpiece should be transferred from Socrates, Plato's teacher and close associate, to a character who is introduced as a foreigner and a member of a rival philosophical school?[3]

Yet, interpreters are apparently willing to live with some implausibility here because they consider it even *more implausible* that the Stranger should *not*

---

1. The mouthpiece paradigm has become so entrenched that two recent papers devoted to the question of why the *Sophist* and the *Statesman* were written as *dialogues*, Frede 1996 and Rowe 1996, simply assume that what the Stranger says is what Plato says (though Rowe in a note [172n48] surprisingly backs away from the equation "Plato-ES" dogmatically maintained throughout the rest of his paper: see 158). Among interpretations that have rejected this assumption are Scodel 1987, Brumbaugh 1989, and Rosen 1995. For general comments on the latter two, see below. While sharing some of Scodel's conclusions, I find his arguments unconvincing, since they rest mostly on extremely obscure and tenuous textual allusions, and word-plays.

2. Though in the "early" dialogues Socrates is thought by some scholars to speak for himself.

3. Friedländer suggests that the art of division is particularly suited to an Eleatic, given the tendency of Parmenides, Zeno and Melissus to make rigid distinctions, starting with that between being and not-being (1969, 250). The Stranger of course attempts to overcome these rigid Eleatic dichotomies, but ironically in the end he fails to do so. He proves unable to escape his heritage. Scodel offers another explanation of the Stranger's Eleatic background (1987, 166), but it is successfully rebutted by Rowe (1995a, 11).

speak for Plato. Their argument, insofar as it can be reconstructed, assumes that the only positive assertions made in the two dialogues are the Stranger's and that therefore one could, without losing anything essential, eliminate the dialogue form by putting what the Stranger says into the form of a treatise authored by Plato.[4] The aim of the present chapter is to refute this specific assumption and therefore the interpretation that depends on it. Socrates *does* speak in both dialogues, and what he says is of extraordinary importance; furthermore, a major, perhaps *the* major event of Socrates' life, namely, his trial, forms the dramatic context. These words and deeds of Socrates are not peripheral curiosities added to relieve the tedium of an otherwise highly abstract discussion. Instead, as I will show, what Socrates says and who he is, even his silence in the dialogue, expose serious problems in what the Stranger says. If Plato in this way uses Socrates against the Stranger, the assumption that the Stranger speaks for Plato, already implausible on the surface, is rendered untenable. On the other hand, we are not thereby required to conclude that Plato rejects everything the Stranger says and chooses *Socrates* instead as his mouthpiece. What we have here, as elsewhere, is not a disguised author expounding doctrines in a disguised treatise, but rather a *drama* in which two opposed and limited perspectives confront each other and in that confrontation leave us with a *problem*.

I. SOCRATES VERSUS THE STRANGER IN THE *SOPHIST*

The importance of what Socrates says is not in proportion to the amount of speaking he does. His few words at the beginning of the *Sophist* determine the course of both that dialogue and the *Statesman*. These words are the following: "These men—those, that is, who are not counterfeit but genuine philosophers—appear in many different guises, thanks to the ignorance of others, as they visit cities, observing from above the life below, and they seem to some to be of no worth, and to others to be worth everything. And sometimes they appear as statesmen, sometimes as sophists, and sometimes there are those to whom they give the impression of being completely mad" (216c4–d2). Socrates in this way introduces and defines the problem that will occupy the Stranger in the next two dialogues: that of distinguishing among philosopher, statesman, and sophist. But why does this problem concern Socrates? The answer is provided by the dramatic context. As we learn at the end of the *Theaetetus*, the charges that will eventually lead to Socrates' condemnation and death have already been formally brought against him when the *Sophist* opens. To answer these charges in the upcoming trial Socrates, misrepresented by Aristophanes and others, will need to distinguish himself from the sophists and show that his philosophical activity does not undermine the *polis* by rejecting its gods or corrupting its youth. Nothing, therefore, could concern Socrates more at this time than the relations between philosopher, sophist, and statesman. And his words

---

4. Friedländer was among the first to oppose this assumption, as he recognized (1969, 524n55). Unfortunately, Friedländer's interpretations overlook most of the specific dramatic tensions noted in the present chapter.

show what is really at stake here: the *worth* of philosophy that is the fundamental dispute behind his trial. Socrates therefore does not want the Stranger
to make distinctions for their own sake. He wants him to defend the *worth* of
the philosopher vis-à-vis the sophist and the statesman. In other words,
Socrates seeks from the Stranger a defense against his Athenian accusers and
we must judge the Stranger's results in these terms.[5]

Unfortunately, we are led to suspect early on that the Stranger will not come
to Socrates' rescue. He instead appears utterly unsympathetic to philosophy as
Socrates practices it. When Theodorus first introduces the Stranger as "a very
philosophical man" (μάλα δὲ ἄνδρα φιλόσοφον, 216a4), Socrates attempts to
see in him a kindred spirit, suggesting that he is a "god of refutation" (θεὸς ὤν
τις ἐλεγκτικός) come to expose their worthlessness in argument, like that
Homeric god of strangers who comes to judge human ὕβρις and justice
(216a5–b6). Socrates is clearly alluding here to his own philosophical mission as
he describes it in the *Apology*. Yet Theodorus, with no protest from the
Stranger, rejects Socrates' suggestion, replying that the Stranger is not one of
those who devote themselves to disputations (τὰς ἔριδας, 216b7–8). He thus
ignores the difference between elenchus and eristic, as the Stranger himself
will later.[6] Theodorus also ignores Socrates' implied attribution of an ethical
mission to the Stranger. As we will see, there is good reason for this: the ethical dimension of Socrates' philosophizing is also foreign to the Stranger.

As the discussion proceeds, we learn why the Stranger is not devoted to
elenchus. According to Theodorus, the Stranger is qualified to address the
problem Socrates has posed because he "admits he has been thoroughly instructed and has not forgotten what he has heard" (217b8–9).[7] Thus in what follows the Stranger will simply be recalling what he has already committed to
memory. What need has he for examining and refuting the opinions of others?
He has been instructed and now he will instruct others in turn. This characteristic of the Stranger's method becomes only more evident when Socrates asks
him whether he prefers "to discourse at length by yourself (αὐτὸς ἐπὶ σαυτοῦ
μακρῷ λόγῳ διεξιέναι) on any matter you wish to make clear, or to use the
method of asking questions" (217c3–4). Socrates offers his earlier discussion
with Parmenides (λόγους παγκάλους, 217c5) as an example of the latter
method. His intention is clearly to get the Stranger, who is from the school of
Parmenides, to follow that philosopher's example. Yet, the Stranger is not willing to do more than *seem* to follow it. Because of his shyness before the present
company (217d8), he is willing to present his views in the question-and-answer
format, but only on the condition that he be given an untroublesome and
tractable respondent (217d1–2). Two points need to be made here. First, the
Stranger clearly would prefer giving a long speech: he believes that only this approach would be fully adequate to the difficulty of the subject matter (217e3–5).
His willingness to adopt the other approach is a polite favor (χαρίζεσθαι,

---

5. Cf. Sallis, 1996, 464, and Miller 1980, 2 & 11.

6. Cf. Rosen, 1983, 64, and Miller 1980, 11.

7. As Rosen points out, it is hard to square the suggestion that the Stranger will be repeating
Eleatic doctrine with the view that he is Plato's mouthpiece (1983, 67).

217e5). Second, the Stranger adopts Socrates' question-and-answer method in semblance only. Socrates' model is his conversation with Parmenides in which he was anything but a tractable respondent.[8] The Stranger's favor is simply to veil his monologue as a dialogue, *not* genuinely to engage in the kind of dialogue favored by Socrates.[9] The introductory discussion thus reveals a fundamental methodological rift between Socrates' dialogical and explorative elenchus, on the one hand, and the Stranger's monological exposition of what he has already committed to memory, on the other.[10]

We find out more about what the Stranger thinks of Socrates' method in the divisions he makes for the fifth definition of the sophist. Beginning with the general class of fighting (as opposed to hunting), the Stranger divides his way towards an art of verbal warfare conducted in private through question-and-answer and having as its subject matter the just and the unjust in themselves (225a–c). The Stranger calls this art "eristic," failing to recognize, like Theodorus earlier, the existence of an elenctic method that, while conducted in a similar way and concerned with the same subject matter, is yet distinct from eristic. Then the Stranger divides this art between a part that aims at making money, which is the art of the sophist, and a part that is mere garrulousness (τὸ ἀδολεσχικόν, 225d10–11). The garrulous person is described as taking pleasure in disputation for its own sake, while neglecting his own affairs and causing most of his hearers no pleasure at all. As we know from the *Apology* (23b7–c1), Socrates at his trial will emphasize the extent to which his disinterested pursuit of the *elenchus* has both impoverished him and been greatly resented by others. The popular perception of Socrates, reinforced by the comic poets, accordingly saw him as an ἀδολέσχης, an idle and annoying chatterbox.[11] In a passage from the *Statesman* that clearly refers to Socrates' trial, the Stranger tells us that the accused will be called an ἀδολέσχην τινὰ σοφιστήν (299b8). The type of eristic distinguished from sophistry here is therefore to be seen as a reference to Socrates' own method.[12] But then what the Stranger's divisions imply is that Socrates' method of disputing about the

---

8. Yet, as Rosen points out, for the second half of the dialogue Parmenides desired a tractable respondent and received one in the young Aristotle: "It looks as though Eleatics are not fond of contradiction" (1983, 68).

9. The Stranger's method accordingly abstracts from differences between interlocutors (cf. Rosen 1995, 12). The only reason for the change of interlocutors at the beginning of the *Statesman* is *fatigue*. And the role of the interlocutor does not change there: Rowe (1996, 173–4) emphasizes the extent to which Young Socrates is passive, subordinate and uncritical.

10. *Pace* Cornford, who thought that the Stranger "understands dialectic as the cooperative search for truth, and, once the conversation is started, his manner is distinguished by no individual trait from that of the Platonic Socrates" (1935, 170).

11. At *Phaedo* 70b10–c1 Socrates observes: "I do not think that anyone listening now, not even if he were a comic poet, would say that I babble (ἀδολέσχω)." According to Socrates' ship analogy in the *Republic*, the sailors would call the true pilot an ἀδολέσχης (488e3–489a2). See also *Theaetetus* 195b10 and *Phaedrus* 270a1. For the accusation in the comic poets themselves, see Eupolis 352, as well as Aristophanes' *Clouds* 1485 and *Tagenistai*, fr. 490 Kock.

12. Cf. Sallis 1996, 472, and Rosen 1983, 114. Cornford objects that "This would make the true philosopher a species of Eristic, arguing for fame or victory" (1935, 176). Precisely: that is just what the Stranger takes Socrates to be.

just and the unjust in themselves is a form of eristic differing from sophistry only in its garrulous impracticality.[13] In the next definition of the sophist the Stranger again makes a clear reference to Socrates' elenchus, but now assigns it the positive function of purifying the soul of ignorance. Unfortunately, he proves unable to distinguish elenchus as thus characterized from sophistry. The first division in the definition is one between two forms of discrimination: that of better from worse and that of like from like (226d1–3). The former is called purification and is then divided into purification of the soul and purification of bodies (226e–227c). Purification of the soul is further divided into purifying the soul of ignorance, or instruction (ἡ διδασκαλικὴ τέχνη) and purifying the soul of vice, or chastisement (ἡ κολαστικὴ τέχνη, 227c–229a). Through further divisions of the former, the Stranger defines a type of purification practiced by those who have convinced themselves that all ignorance is involuntary (230a5–8): this purification exposes inconsistencies in the beliefs of others through refutation *(elenchos)* and thereby purifies them of the ignorance of thinking that they know what they do not know (229c–230e). This is, of course, the way in which Socrates characterizes his own elenchus in the *Apology*. There is, however, one very important difference. By sharply distinguishing between ignorance and vice and asserting that elenchus corrects only the former while the latter is corrected by "chastisement," the Stranger rids the elenchus of any ethical import.[14] In doing so he renders it vacuous.[15] If elenchus does not purify one of the ignorance of wrongly thinking that one knows what is good or virtuous, what kind of ignorance *does* it eliminate? The ignorance of wrongly thinking that one knows how to build a house? When the Stranger suggests that vice is corrected through chastisement, Theaetetus significantly replies: "That is plausible, if we are to speak according to the opinion of mankind" (κατξ τὴν ἀνθροπίνην δόὰαν, 229a7–8). This reply points to an important characteristic of the Stranger: his understanding of ethical issues never transcends ordinary common sense. The reason is that philosophy is for him a purely theoretical enterprise no more concerned with ethical questions than is mathematics.[16] As we will see, this view is what most distances him from Socrates and explains his failure to understand the Socratic method.

But what is most striking about the present passage is the Stranger's identification of the elenchus he has described with *sophistry* and thus his failure to distinguish Socrates from the sophist. The identification is made only more striking by the Stranger's *hesitation* in making it. He fears, he tells us, that it would grant the sophist *too much honor* (γέρας, 231a3). But then why does he nevertheless proceed to make it? Why does he not deny the sophist this honor, reserving it for

---

13. Significantly, in attempting to recollect the definition later, the Stranger forgets even this difference (231d12–e2). See Rosen 1983, 314.

14. Cf. Sallis 1996, 475.

15. At 230c4–d4 the Stranger characterizes the purifying elenchus as purely preliminary to positive teaching, a teaching Socrates denies he can provide (*Apology* 19d–20b, 33a–c). Howland sees here the Stranger's condemnation of Socrates as a sophist (1993, 20–21).

16. See Plochmann 1954, 227. This is confirmed by the Stranger's classification of statesmanship under theoretical knowledge: see *Statesman* 258bff.

the philosopher? Plato takes care to show us that the answer lies in the very nature of the Stranger's method. Only three pages of the Greek text earlier, Plato
has the Stranger characterize his method as one that, seeking to know what is and
is not kindred in all the arts for the sake of acquiring insight (νοῦς), "honors them
all alike" (τιμᾷ πρὸς τοῦτο ἐξ ἴσου πάσας, 227b2–6). It does not, for instance,
rank the general's art any higher than that of the pest exterminator as forms of
hunting. But in this case the question of the honor due to sophist or philosopher
cannot have any relevance for the Stranger. His method *forbids* him to retract a
definition of the sophist simply because it grants him too much honor.

The Stranger's methodological aside reveals something even more important.
As we have seen, the general class with which the present definition of the
sophist begins is the art of discrimination. Since the Stranger's method of division is clearly itself an art of discriminating, we must ask under which of the two
types it falls: discrimination of like from like, or discrimination of better from
worse (purification)? The Stranger's own description of his method as one that
honors all things alike reveals that it does not discriminate better from worse,
but only like from like.[17] The Stranger's sympathies are not with the Socratic
method of elenctic purification because his own method is fundamentally different. Socrates' method is concerned with questions of better and worse,
honor and worth, and therefore has ethical import; the Stranger's method does
not seek to show that one thing is better or more honorable than another because it claims for itself the ethical neutrality of a theoretical science.[18]

The serious consequences of this fundamental rift become fully apparent
only if we recall that what Socrates desires is a demonstration of the *worth* of
the philosopher vis-à-vis the sophist and statesman. We now see that this is exactly what the Stranger's method cannot provide. But if the Stranger cannot
make a distinction *of worth* between the philosopher and the sophist, he cannot
in the end really distinguish between them,[19] as is suggested by his failure to
keep them distinct not only in the sixth definition of the sophist discussed
above, but also in the concluding definition of the dialogue, to which I now turn.

This definition attributes to the sophist the following characteristics: (1) he
produces images rather than originals; (2) the images he produces are semblances rather than likenesses (266d–e); (3) he imitates by means of his own
person, rather than by means of tools (and therefore practices *mimēsis*, 276a);
(4) his imitation is based on opinion, not knowledge (267c–e); (5) he is "ironic,"
i.e., suspects that the knowledge he is thought by others to possess is really ignorance (268a); (6) rather than giving long speeches in public, he proceeds by
means of short questions in private, forcing others to contradict themselves
(268b–c). It is immediately striking that this definition does not apply to most
of the sophists we encounter in Plato's dialogues. Gorgias and Protagoras, for

---

17. Cf. Scodel 1987, 126, and Rosen 1983, 119–21.

18. Though, as Rosen shows, this claim of neutrality is self-deceiving (1983, 121; see also 135–7,
317, 326). Rosen also shows that the Stranger violates his methodological principle in the *Statesman*: see 261c9, 262e3–5, 281c7–d4, 286d4–9 and, for Rosen's comments, 1995: 25, 30, 110, and
138, respectively. Similarly Scodel 1987: 47, 70, 81 n8, 114, 130, 159–60, 167. See also Howland
1993, 20.

19. Rosen asks a similar question (1983, 120–1).

example, prefer to give long speeches in public and it is unlikely that they are "ironic." The definition describes only those sophists who most resemble *Socrates* in their practice, such as Euthydemus and Dionysodorus (though can even they be said to be "ironic?"). Moreover, careful examination of the above characteristics reveals that none of them distinguishes the sophist they define from Socrates. Socrates imitates, rather than produces reality in his *logoi*. He claims to have no *knowledge* of the virtues he discusses. He forces others to contradict themselves by means of questions. Finally, not only is he ironic, but this appears to be his most distinctive trait. The only division that looks promising for distinguishing Socrates from the sophists is that between semblances and likenesses. One could argue that Socrates imitates things in his discourse in such a way as to reproduce their true character, while the sophist distorts the things he talks about to make them seem more plausible to his audience. In this case, Socrates would be a maker of likenesses, while the sophist is a maker of semblances. However, the *Stranger* repeatedly expresses his uncertainty about whether the sophist should be classified under likenesses or semblances (236c–d, 264c). When he finally does place the sophist under semblances, he does so without argument or explanation (266d–267a).

As can only be suggested here, this oversight is no accident. According to the conclusion of the ontological digression that occupies a large part of the dialogue, an image *is not* the original only in the sense of being *other than* (ἕτερον) the original. But if both likenesses and semblances, as images, are simply *other* than the original, what could be the difference between them? Is one "more other" than the other?[20] The Stranger appears to think that by showing that falsehood exists he has demonstrated the distinction between semblances and likenesses (266d–e). But if a semblance is false simply in the sense of being *other* than the true original, then must we not also say that the likeness is false? The Stranger's account of not-being seems unable to explain the *greater negativity* involved in *distorting* the original (semblance) as opposed to simply being *distinct* from the original (likeness). To make the same point concerning the issue at stake here, the sophist is not simply *other* than the philosopher, but is the *negation* of the philosopher and in this sense indeed *worse* and *less honorable*. But the Stranger's method, with its leveling tendency, cannot account for this negation nor, as we have seen, can it address the issues of goodness and worth that, as we learn from the *Gorgias*, are the issues *Socrates* considers decisive in the clash between the sophist and the philosopher.

Yet another very important reason for the Stranger's failure to distinguish Socrates from the sophist is evident in a curious question he asks at the completion of his final divisions: he asks Theaetetus whether the person who has been marked off by these divisions is *sophon* or *sophistikon* (268b10). Theaetetus replies that this person cannot be wise, since he was characterized as lacking knowledge; therefore, he must be the sophist they have been looking for.

---

20. Rosen has argued that the Stranger even fails to distinguish between image and *original* (see, for example, 1983: 115, 120, 311) and that this failure is rooted in the Stranger's method as one that can distinguish only like from like (120). For Rosen's most recent critique of the Stranger's account of not-being as "otherness," see 1995: 127–30.

This discussion shows that the Stranger's divisions do recognize a distinction between *wisdom* and sophistry. The problem is that this distinction is of no help in showing that Socrates, who confesses ignorance, is not a sophist. Nor can it distinguish between the sophist and the philosopher as described in the *Symposium*. For the Stranger philosophy is not only value-neutral; as dwelling in the pure light of being (254a8–10), it is also wisdom. From this perspective, images, ignorance, and irony all belong to sophistry. But this is to say that *Socrates* belongs to sophistry.[21]

II. SOCRATES' CRITIQUE
OF THE STRANGER IN THE *STATESMAN*

But how, one might ask, can Socrates listen to all this in silence? If the Stranger has failed at his task, why does Socrates not point this out? The answer is that *he does*. At the very beginning of the *Statesman*, which immediately follows the *Sophist*, he presents a devastating critique of what the Stranger has done, disguised as a critique of the Stranger's advocate, Theodorus.[22] At first Socrates appears pleased with the outcome of the preceding discussion, since he thanks Theodorus for having introduced him to both Theaetetus and the Stranger. However, when Theodorus proudly replies that Socrates will owe him three times as much thanks after the statesman and the philosopher have been defined, Socrates can keep silent no longer. I hope that we are now prepared to *hear* what Socrates says: "My dear Theodorus, are we to say that we heard our greatest mathematician and geometer say *that*? ... Are we to say that we heard you counting as being of equal worth (τῆς ἴσης ἀξίας) these men who are so distant from one another in honor (τῇ τιμῇ) as to defy any of your mathematical proportions!" (257b2–4). Socrates sees the differences between philosopher, sophist, and statesman as differences of worth and honor so great as to defy any proportion. But then the Stranger's method, as one that honors all arts alike, must be completely unable to explain or even acknowledge these differences. If Socrates is mostly silent, that is because he here says all that needs to be said. In just a few words he exposes the fundamental flaw of the Stranger's method and thus the source of its inadequate conclusions. In case one is tempted to fault Socrates for not expressing his objection more directly and to the Stranger himself, one should recall that by demanding a tractable interlocutor, the Stranger is the one who refuses to converse with Socrates, not vice versa. As Socrates pointedly observes, the Stranger is conversing with only likenesses of Socrates: Theaetetus, who resembles Socrates in physical appearance, and the young Socrates, who shares his name (257d–258a).

Socrates' comments also indicate an important kinship between the Stranger's method and mathematics. Mathematics can reckon only with equal, homoge-

---

21. Cf. Sallis 1996, 532. Rosen has commented in detail on the differences between Socrates and the Stranger (1983, 20–28; 1995, 2–4, 41–2, 50, 91, 154).

22. Also recognized by Howland (1993, 23) and Scodel (1987, 23, 24n11, 44); but Howland's explanation differs from mine and Scodel's explanation, while much more like mine, does not work out the implications in any detail.

nous units. To the extent that things are fundamentally heterogeneous, they cannot be counted or measured in relation to each other. This is why a fundamental disparity of worth, like that between the sophist and the philosopher, must, as Socrates says, defy any mathematical proportion.[23] No amount or degree of the one can equal any amount or degree of the other. Furthermore, as Socrates suggests in the *Euthyphro* (7b6–d6), things such as the noble and the base, good and bad are not amenable to precise measurement in the way that the objects of mathematics are. The Stranger's method resembles mathematics in treating everything as on the same level, recognizing no hierarchical distinctions between better and worse, more honorable and less honorable.[24] It does not allow for fundamental heterogeneity because its divisions must always proceed from a common genus. Finally, it arrives at definite, unambiguous conclusions. We can now understand why it is *Theodorus* who introduces and champions the Stranger.

Socrates' critique looks forward as well as backward, since the limitations of the Stranger's method will be as evident in the discussion of the statesman as they were in the discussion of the sophist.[25] Indeed, in the *Statesman* the Stranger once again describes the fundamental characteristic of his method, and now in a context in which its consequences are especially striking. The Stranger's first account of the statesman begins with the classification of statesmanship under theoretical (μόνον γνωριστική) as opposed to practical/productive (πρακτική) knowledge (258b–259d). This odd classification, which renders the possession, manner, and objects of rule completely irrelevant to statesmanship (so that both a private citizen and a slavemaster can be statesmen no less than the actual king), reveals once again the Stranger's tendency to sever the theoretical from the practical. By repeatedly dividing this theoretical knowledge, the Stranger eventually arrives at the definition of the statesman as the person who issues his own directives for the nurture of walking, hornless,

---

23. Rosen assumes that Socrates is here denying only that philosopher, sophist, and statesman are of equal worth. He therefore cannot make sense of Socrates' reference to *analogia* (1995, 10–11).

24. Plochmann distinguishes between vertical and horizontal distinctions (1954, 226; see also 228). The Stranger's method cannot make vertical distinctions, while the distinctions between philosopher and sophist, original and image, likeness and semblance, are necessarily vertical. Scodel distinguishes between Socrates' "vertical orientation" to reality and the Stranger's "horizontal orientation" (1987, 46).

25. In 1983, Rosen suggests that the Stranger's procedure undergoes a radical change between the *Sophist* and the *Statesman* (25–8), even calling the latter a "recantation" of the refutation of Socrates in the former (28). Howland sees a "partial recantation" in the *Statesman* (1993, 21–7, 30n15). Both, apparently see the change as coming with the Stranger's use of the cosmic myth to expose the limitations of his initial diaireses. In 1995, Rosen still appears to defend this thesis (39 & 51), though his account of the myth sees it as sharing at least some of the deficiencies of diaeresis (41). The Stranger's motives for turning to the cosmic myth are beyond the scope of this chapter, but, for reasons presented below, I do not see the turn as overcoming the fundamental limitations of the method of diaeresis. Specifically, I see no evidence for Rosen's claim that the Stranger comes to *explicitly identify* as an error his earlier abstraction from the distinction between humans and brutes (1995, 87). Scodel claims that the Stranger's method is transformed after the seven-fold division of the contributory arts (287b–289c), with the result that the Stranger becomes more "Socratic" in the concluding part of the dialogue (1987, 151, 159–60). Yet, Scodel recognizes that the "Socratic" features of the Stranger's concluding discussion exist alongside contradictory "unSocratic" features: how, then, does this differ from the self-contradiction that, on Scodel's view, characterizes the Stranger's method throughout the whole dialogue?

cloven-hoofed, two-footed animals, i.e., the statesman is the shepherd of the human herd. As the Stranger notes, this definition has two startling results: the statesman becomes nearest neighbor to the swineherd, since they find themselves on the same side of all the divisions, except the final one, where the swineherd is classified as the shepherd of *four-footed* animals; furthermore, their "herds," humans and pigs, are thereby also revealed to be nearest neighbors, differing only in their number of feet. The Stranger himself points out that this latter result is of interest to comic poets (266c). The comic interest clearly lies in the collapse of the distinction between noble and base. But then how can the Stranger justify this "comical" conclusion? He does so in the following words: "Things that possess greater dignity are of no more concern to this method of definition than things that do not (τῇ τοιᾷδε μεθόδῳ τῶν λόγων οὔτε σεμνοτέρου μᾶλλον ἐμέλησεν ᾖ μή). It does not dishonor what is petty in favor of what is greater, but always abiding by its own procedure it attains what is most true" (266d7–9).[26] The Stranger's characterization of his method here is the same as the one he provided in the *Sophist*. But now we see the consequence of such a method for our understanding of human nature: unable to make distinctions of worth, it deprives human beings of their proper dignity.[27]

Young Socrates tried at one point to preserve this dignity. When he was first asked by the Stranger to divide the nurturing of living herds, he made a division between the nurturing of humans and the nurturing of beasts (262a). The Stranger, however, objected. The objection is explained in a long methodological digression, the main point of which is that there is a difference between a mere part of a class (μέρος) and a real form or species of it (εἶδος or γένος) and that we should divide along the cleavage between the real forms or species. For example, it would be wrong to divide the human race into Greeks and Barbarians, because the word "Barbarian," while indeed describing a *part* of the human race, does not name a real form or species: it lumps together people who have no intercourse with each other and speak different languages. On the other hand, a division of the human race into "male" and "female" divides between real and distinct forms. The Stranger's objection to young Socrates' division is that it is like the division between Greeks and Barbarians: it arbitrarily puts human beings to one side and then lumps together all of the remaining animals under the term "beasts."[28]

But one could reply to this objection that young Socrates' division is perfectly legitimate *as a division between rational and nonrational animals.* The word

---

26. Rosen (1995, 18–35) refutes the Stranger's claim that his method "always abiding by its own position ... attains what is most true."

27. The Stranger does provide an alternative set of divisions that make us humans nearest of kin to chickens and other fowl. But this is not much of an improvement.

28. Miller gives a positive twist to the Stranger's criticism by seeing it as an argument against partisanship (1980, 22–4). But is a sense of our uniqueness vis-à-vis other animals "partisanship"? And is loving one's own truly incompatible with philosophical discussion? Miller acknowledges that what the Stranger says here appears to contradict *Republic* 470aff., where Socrates even supports a distinction between Greeks and barbarians like the one rejected here, though Miller questions Socrates' sincerity (23). On whether or not the criticism of the distinction between Greeks and barbarians is "Platonic," see also Friedländer 1969, 287–8.

"beast" would in this case name something common to the animals to which it refers and something that distinguishes these animals as a group from humans, namely, the lack of reason. If such a division is not possible because "irrationality" is not a positive form, then does not this impossibility of arriving at rationality through the method of division reveal a serious limitation of this method?[29] In any case, the Stranger, while capable of distinguishing between two-footed and four-footed, appears utterly blind to this other much more important distinction between humans and pigs. Plato brilliantly draws our attention to this blindness in a very curious passage (263d3–e2). The Stranger tries to show the absurdity of young Socrates' division by comparing it to what *cranes* would do if they decided to invest themselves with "a unique and proper dignity" (σεμνῦνον αὐτὸ ἑαυτό, 263d7, tr. Skemp) by distinguishing themselves from all other animals, humans included. *Yet this comparison rests on the assumption, explicitly made by the Stranger, that cranes and other animals are capable of rational thought and thus of making divisions* (εἴ που φρόνιμόν ἐστί τι ζῷον ἕτερον 263d).[30] This unfounded and undefended assumption ignores what in fact may be an essential and real difference dividing the *genos* of human beings from the *genos* of all other animals. But the Stranger's example reveals another, even more significant consequence of his refusal to divide in this way: in not allowing that humans can distinguish themselves from all other animals as a whole, he is denying humans "a unique and proper dignity." This of course is to be expected, since the Stranger's method does not make distinctions of worth or honor.[31]

The extraordinary insight of Socrates' implicit criticism of the Stranger at the beginning of the dialogue should now be apparent: the Stranger does indeed count all things as being of equal worth. Consequently, he not only deprives philosophy of its proper dignity vis-à-vis sophistry, but also deprives human nature of its proper dignity vis-à-vis beasts. In case the reader does not immediately see the relevance of Socrates' criticism to the conclusion of the Stranger's first set of divisions, Plato does something extremely odd to make this relevance as evident as possible: he has the Stranger express the final division between humans and pigs *as a mathematical proportion* (266a5–b9)! Humans, the Stranger says, have the potency (δύναμις) of two feet or the square root of two; the other class, which turns out to be pigs, has the potency of four feet or the square root of four (266b1–7). The Stranger then expresses a proportion between these two classes by identifying humans with the *diagonal* and pigs with the *diagonal of the diagonal:* in other words, the square root of four feet is the diagonal of a square with sides measuring the square root of two; the square root of two feet is in turn the diagonal of a square with sides measuring one foot; thus, the square root of four is the diagonal of a diagonal.

---

29. See Miller (1980, 31–2), who implausibly assumes that the Stranger recognizes the limitation.

30. Miller misses this point (1980, 25). Rowe, whose assumption that the Stranger = Plato commits him to finding no criticism of the Stranger in the dialogue, sees Plato here as casting doubt on "the rationality of human beings as contrasted with the irrationality of the brutes" (1995a, 183)!

31. Yet even the Stranger cannot consistently deny a distinction of worth between humans and other animals. E.g., 271e5–7and 289b8 (Rosen 1995, 143). Yet in neither passage does the Stranger explain what makes humans superior. Scodel notes that the distinction between man and beasts is made at *Philebus* 16a and *Laws* 653e (1987, 57).

The Stranger here appeals to a specialty of Theodorus and his pupils: the use of diagonals to identify and commensurate incommensurables such as the square root of two.[32] This obscure mathematical joke reveals that, like his mathematician friends, the Stranger through his method of division commensurates things that are in fact incommensurable: humans and pigs.[33] The affinity of the Stranger's method with mathematics subjects it to the same limitation Socrates sees and criticizes in mathematics at the beginning of the dialogue: in their desire to render all things commensurable and thus analyzable, the Stranger and his friend Theodorus are blind to questions of worth and nobility that defy such commensurability and analysis. The suggestion here again is that the Stranger's mathematical, theoretical method cannot comprehend human nature nor even, therefore, the nature of human reason. It is, after all, striking that the Stranger's mathematical analogy renders humans "irrational" (the square root of two) and pigs "rational" (the square root of four).[34]

In this part of the dialogue Plato also once again exhibits the antagonism between the Stranger's method and ethics. As noted above, the Stranger's conclusion makes the statesman and the swineherd nearest neighbors. This is troubling because, as the Stranger himself points out, the swineherd was proverbially identified with "easy living" (τὸν εὐχερῆ βίον, 266d1–2). Thus, the conclusion puts the virtuous, rational life of the king on a level with the easygoing, grossly physical life of the swineherd. This can no longer surprise us: the Stranger's method must of necessity level all ethical distinctions.[35] This is the price it pays for being "scientific."

III. THE STRANGER'S
POLITICAL THEORY CONDEMNS SOCRATES

The dialogue of course does not end with this initial account of statesmanship, since the Stranger himself recognizes problems in it, though *not* the fundamental ones identified above. The Stranger's final account cannot be discussed in any detail here, but I wish to indicate some of the ways in which it renders

---

32. See Miller 1980, 31.

33. For the negative consequences of this attempt to "commensurate" humans and pigs, see Miller 1980, 31. Miller exonerates the Stranger, blaming instead *young Socrates'* failure to see the difference between partisanship and "the philosophical distinction of uniquely intelligent mankind from other animals" (32). Yet *the Stranger* appears not to see this difference, since the methodological principle he asserts at 266d7–9 rules out both. Nor does Miller relate the mathematical joke to Socrates' words at the beginning of the *Statesman*.

34. Cf. Scodel 1987, 65, and Rosen 1995, 34. Rowe (1995a, 185), like others who identify the Stranger with Plato, dismisses the absurdity of the Stranger's results as "incidental," hence not showing any limitation in his method. I claim that the absurdity is not at all incidental.

35. When the Stranger later turns to a discussion of the fundamental presupposition of his scientific method as well as of the art of statesmanship, i.e., the doctrine of the "mean," he does not take the opportunity to give this doctrine any explicit moral or ethical content, though, as Scodel points out (1987, 130), he cannot escape entirely its implicit moral connotations. Rosen observes that the Stranger "is concerned primarily with efficacy rather than with moral virtue" (1995, 127). However, Rosen later argues that the Stranger's account of the ideal statesman sharply distinguishes between *techne* and *phronesis* and therefore supposedly between efficacy and goodness (182). I find no such distinction in the text.

politics inimical to philosophy as practiced by Socrates. In this way, the antagonism between Socrates and the Stranger, which has already been highlighted, will be shown to reach its ultimate crisis.

The Stranger's account as a whole tends to characterize the statesman as a godlike individual capable of ruling the city on the basis of unshakable knowledge. One of the purposes of the Stranger's famous cosmic myth is to show that his initial characterization of the statesman as the shepherd of the human herd fails to distinguish between the divine shepherd, who provided for all of our needs during the reign of Kronus, and the human shepherd, whose "caring" (θεραπεύειν, 275e4) is much more limited in scope (275a–276d). Yet the characterization of the statesman at the end of the dialogue as an ideal ruler capable of ruling without laws again appears to grant him a godlike stature. This ideal statesman rules entirely based on knowledge and, like the doctor, is not confined to general prescriptions, but can do what is best for each individual under his care. The Stranger himself tells us that the state ruled by such a statesman would be exalted above every other state "like a god (θεὸν) among mortals" (303b4).

Socratic philosophizing, however, would be at home neither in the Age of Kronus nor in the ideal state as the Stranger describes it. At one point (272b8–d4) the Stranger claims that the Age of Kronus can be judged happier than our own age only if the men of that time used their leisure to philosophize, that is, if they used their ability to converse with animals for the purpose of discovering what the special faculties of each animal could contribute to "the common treasure store of wisdom" (εἰς συναγυρμὸν φρονήσεως, 272c4–5, tr. Skemp). The description of this bizarre scenario can only have the aim of showing its absurdity. Living lives like those of the citizens of the City of Pigs Socrates describes in the *Republic,* the people of the Age of Kronus are no more likely to have used their leisure in the pursuit of wisdom.[36] Nor would greater communion with animals have encouraged such a pursuit. Here we should recall that the human beings herded by the divine shepherd are the nearest of kin to pigs.[37]

An ideal ruler above the law would clearly not be a lover of wisdom in the Socratic sense, but rather someone in possession of wisdom. Nor would such a ruler encourage philosophy in his subjects. The Stranger's account of the statesman's "weaving" demonstrates this. The statesman's task is to "interweave" the antagonistic virtues of moderation and courage in his citizens, since either virtue, if left unchecked by the other, would result in great evil (306a–311b). The Stranger can claim that moderation and courage are opposed to one another and thus need to be interwoven only because he identifies them with gentleness and aggressiveness, respectively (306e2–307b3). We thus see that the Stranger's conception of virtue does not go beyond that of the young Charmides, who defines *sophrosune* as gentleness or quietness, only to be refuted by Socrates (*Charmides* 159b–160d). As already suggested by the

---

36. Cf. Scodel 1987, 81n9; Griswold 1989, 151, and 1995, 177–8; Howland 1993, 26; Rosen 1995, 55–61. Scodel points out that the Stranger does not even mention philosophy in his description of the reign of Zeus (83n11).

37. Cf. Rosen 1995, 61.

Sophist, the Stranger's "ethics" remains on the level of "common sense."[38] He therefore describes the statesman, not as providing or encouraging a philosophical understanding of the virtues, but simply as seeking a balance of the virtues as they are commonly understood. The Stranger indeed proceeds to claim that the statesman requires a "bond" (δεσμός) by which to join the aggressive and gentle natures among his subjects. But what is this bond? The Stranger describes two. The "human" way of bonding the opposed natures is interbreeding; the statesman will therefore need to regulate marriages (310a7–e4). This strategy appears to reduce the virtues to facts of biology.[39] However, the Stranger also describes a "divine bond," which he identifies with "both types of character sharing one belief (δόξα) about the good and the noble" (310e6–7). In other words, one way of bonding gentle and aggressive people is to make them have the same beliefs. Yet, as the Stranger's words make clear, this "divine bond" consists of nothing more than "a genuinely true and unshakable *opinion* (ἀληθὲς δόξα μετὰ βεβαιώσεως) concerning what is good, just, and profitable, as well as their opposites" (309c5–7).[40] There is no question of the statesman encouraging the pursuit of *knowledge* among his subjects; all that is required to harmonize and keep in check aggressiveness and gentleness is the right *indoctrination*.[41]

In this context it is important to note another general feature of the Stranger's discussion: its failure to keep the statesman distinct from the tyrant. The Stranger himself acknowledges this fault in his first definition of the statesman and can correct it only by adding the condition that the statesman's rule must be willingly accepted by his subjects (276d8–e13). However, this condition is later explicitly dropped when the Stranger maintains that the *only* requirement for being a statesman is that one rule on the basis of knowledge (ἐπιστήμη) of how to make the subjects better; whether or not the subjects

---

38. Mishima (1995:311) sees this but does not see that the Stranger's method and objective are purely theoretical throughout and that it is *for precisely this reason* that he has nothing insightful to say about *ethics.* He is like a brilliant mathematician whose moral concepts are completely commonplace. Miller (1980, 107) also notes the difference between the Stranger's way of inquiring into virtue and Socrates' but sees the Stranger as sharing Socrates' view that the virtues can become one by being founded on insight (107–8). The "divine bond" the Stranger describes, however, is not philosophical insight, but mere true opinion (a point Miller later acknowledges: see below). Nor is there any suggestion that through this bond the courageous become equally temperate or the temperate equally courageous: the two temperaments remain distinct and opposed (see Scodel 1987, 161–3, and Rowe's comment on 309b6–7 [1995a, 96]); the divine bond only keeps them from the extremes of madness and indolence, belligerence and appeasement.

39. Mishima rightly draws attention to the "quasi-biological view of virtue" behind the Stranger's idea of intermarriage (1995, 308–9). This view explains why people apparently retain their opposed virtues even after the ruler has imposed upon them shared beliefs about the good: if these virtues are part of one's physiological makeup, beliefs can keep them in check, but not change them.

40. Cf. Miller 1980, 110. Lane (1995, 282n24) argues that beliefs are accorded an elevated status at 309c5–7. But Friedländer correctly observes: "Socrates who is listening might well ask whether 'right opinion' is enough, even though the stranger underscores its 'unshakability' . . . — or whether we should rather look toward a kind of knowledge that rises high above right opinion" (1969, 303; see also 304).

41. Scodel cites the word ἐμποιεῖν at 309d3 to make the point that the divine bond is *imposed* by the statesman (1987, 163).

accept this rule is irrelevant (292a–293e).[42] The statesman thus turns out to be an enlightened despot. As such, he is not one to encourage or even allow philosophical inquiry, with its tendency to undermine authority, among his subjects.

The tendency of the Stranger's discussion to make the statesman more than human is counterbalanced by an opposed tendency towards skepticism. Not only does the Stranger correct his first definition of the statesman by distinguishing the human from the divine shepherd, but his final account gives voice to the doubts people have that anyone could rule on the basis of knowledge alone and could transcend the general guidelines of the laws in providing for the specific good of each individual: people "refused to believe that there would ever come to be anyone who deserved to rule in such a way, so as to be willing and able to rule with virtue and expert knowledge (μετ' ἀρετῆς καὶ ἐπιστήμης) distributing what is just and right correctly to all" (301c10–d3, tr. Rowe). This refusal is not without justification, and the Stranger himself appears to grant as much. Though he proceeds to say that the ideal ruler would be prized if he appeared on earth, he adds: "But as things are, when it is not the case—as we say—that a king comes to be in cities as a king-bee is born in a hive, one individual immediately superior in mind and body . . ." (301d8–e2, tr. Rowe). While this passage does not explicitly deny that such a king could *ever* come to be, in its context it certainly casts serious doubt on such a possibility.[43] Furthermore, as noted above, the Stranger elsewhere describes the rule of the ideal statesman as exalted like a god above mortals (303b4). But if this statesman is in fact no more a possibility during our age than is the divine shepherd, then what is the second-best alternative?[44] *Rule according to law*—which can take a number of forms, some better and some worse, depending on the number of rulers and the manner of their rule. The Stranger's point is that, in the absence of knowledge capable of transcending the laws, the only curb against anarchy and the lust for power is absolute and unquestioning respect for the laws.

---

42. The Stranger tells us that the expert rulers "ἐκ χείρονος βελτίω ποιῶσι κατὰ δύναμιν" the state (293d9–e1). This implies that the art of the statesman, like that of Socrates, but unlike that of the Stranger, is an art of purification. But the comparison of statesmanship to weaving implies the opposite, since *Sophist* 226b–d appears to classify weaving under the arts that discriminate *like from like*, rather than *better from worse*. Cf. Rosen 1995, 109.

43. Vlastos (1957, 234–7) argued against reading any pessimism into this passage, followed recently by Lane 1995, 290–1, and Gill 1995, 295–6. According to Vlastos, the passage asserts only that there is presently no such person to be found. Yet the context tells us that even if the ideal statesman should arise, he would not be recognized as such, but would be put to death for questioning the laws. Rowe insists that the difference between the human city and the beehive is compatible with true statesmen being "actually available, even if not in power" (1995a, 233). But the passage also gives us no confidence that such statesmen are available and the context suggests that the rule of blind law would never let them come into power. This view may not be *as* pessimistic as a firm denial that a true statesman could ever exist, but it is very pessimistic nevertheless.

44. See Griswold (1989, 156–7) and Rosen (1995, 149, 155, 162, 176–9). Significantly, the shepherd analogy, which is the paradigm for the god's rule during the age of Kronus, returns in the final account of the statesman with the description of the ruler's subjects as "flocks" (ἀγέλαι) at 294e9–10 and 295e6. Miller discounts the significance of this (1980, 94–5). Rowe argues that the characterization of statesmanship as dealing with herds is preserved throughout the dialogue (1996, 162n23 & 164n29).

Could Socrates and his philosophizing thrive in one of these second-best forms of government in which law reigns supreme? The Stranger's answer is clear: such a government can not allow any inquiry that would question or threaten its laws. It can recognize no claim to wisdom greater than the wisdom of the laws (οὐδὲν γὰρ δεῖν τῶν νόμων εἶναι σοφώτερον, 299c5–6).[45] So that we cannot fail to see the connection to Socrates' imminent trial, Plato, as it were, hits us over the head with it. He has the Stranger make an extensive analogy between the second-best form of government and a state in which medicine and seamanship are practiced according to laws enacted by a general assembly of mostly unqualified citizens and in which therefore private inquiry into these arts is strictly forbidden (297e8–299e10). Anyone who pursued such private inquiry, the Stranger tells us, would be denied the name of "doctor" or "seaman" and would instead be called "a man with his head in the clouds (μετεςρολόγον), one of these chattering Sophists (ἀδολέσχην τινὰ σοφιστήν)" (299b7–8, tr. Skemp). It would be legal for any citizen to indict such a man "on the charge of corrupting the younger men and influencing them to go in for seamanship and medicine in an illegal manner by setting up as doctors or captains on their own authority" (299b8–c3, tr. Skemp). The allusion to Socrates' indictment on the previous day could not be clearer.[46] But what is its point? It shows that the second-best government the Stranger describes is one that would *necessarily* sentence Socrates to death. Such a government depends on the absolute authority of it laws concerning what is good and what is bad; philosophical inquiry into the good is *incompatible* with such authority.[47] The price that must be paid by rule according to law is the sacrifice of philosophy. If this is the only form of government possible for us, Socrates' execution is not only necessary, but *justified*.[48]

---

45. But this also implies that rule by law must prevent the emergence of true statesmanship. As the Stranger points out, those who question and seek to alter the laws are doing what the statesman would do (300d4–7); however, these are precisely the people who would be persecuted. How, then, can the second-best constitutions even approximate the best? Rowe's solution is that what they imitate is the fact that even the best state does not change its laws in the absence of the statesman (1995a, 17 & 232; 1995b, 27; 1996, 169). Rowe recognizes that this is a highly inadequate imitation and rightly claims, against Skemp's translation, that 300c4–6 cannot refer to the laws of the second-best constitutions, since these laws are *not* based on expert knowledge and therefore cannot be imitations of the truth (1995, 15–7, 230–1). Lane (1995, 287–89) and Gill (1995, 300) characterize the second-best constitutions as open to and awaiting the advent of the true statesman. But if these states renounce and even outlaw change in the laws, as the Stranger claims, they will clearly put the true statesman to death if he ever appears, just as Athens put Socrates to death. (Significantly, Gill does not even mention Socrates' fate.) Rowe's more pessimistic interpretation seems unavoidable.

46. Though the allusion to Socrates in this passage is generally recognized, its significance is almost as often left unexplored. This is surprisingly true even of Rosen's book, despite the careful attention it otherwise gives to dramatic details: Rosen dismisses the whole of this passage as a diatribe, excessive, and question-begging (1995, 172–3). Exceptions are Friedländer 1969, 298; Scodel 1987, 155; and Dueso 1993. Dueso's account, however, is extremely unclear and throughout speaks of "Plato" instead of the "Stranger."

47. That the rule of law is in this sense *tyranny* is suggested by the Stranger's comparison of the law to "a self-willed, ignorant man who lets no one do anything but what he has ordered and forbids all subsequent questioning of his orders even if the situation has shown some marked improvement on the one for which he originally legislated" (294c1–4; tr. Skemp). Cf. Miller 1980, 92.

48. Griswold's claim that rule according to law, especially in the form of democracy, allows for greater freedom among the citizens than does the ideal government (1989, 161–2; 1995, 181) does

Yet, even if the ideal state were possible, we have seen that it too would exclude Socrates! The Stranger's discussion recognizes only two alternatives for the philosopher: either he must attain a knowledge that will enable him to rule the city always for the best, something that apparently only a god could do, or he must stop philosophizing and allow the laws to rule. Neither alternative represents Socrates. It is significant that after ranking the different forms of second-best governments, from monarchy to democracy to tyranny, the Stranger identifies the leaders of *all of them* with "the greatest sophists among sophists" (τῶν σοφιστῶν σοφιστάς, 303c5; tr. Rowe).[49] The Stranger therefore recognizes only two possibilities: ideal statesman or sophist, just as in the *Sophist* he recognized only wiseman *(sophos)* or sophist. In either case, there is no place for Socrates. As the silent, or rather *silenced* Socrates must recognize, he has already been sentenced to death by what the Stranger has said.[50]

But the Stranger's discourse fails to do justice to Socrates because it fails to do justice to the proper dignity of human beings. It is indeed hard to recognize *ourselves* in what the Stranger says. The ideal statesman is more like a god than a human; the people in his "herd" are more like animals or, to be precise, pigs than humans. The ideal statesman possesses a knowledge that seems simply unattainable; his subjects seem hardly capable of rational inquiry, their behavior being determined instead by controlled interbreeding and indoctrination. What is completely absent from the Stranger's discourse is the both erotic and rational pursuit of the good that most distinguishes us as humans. It is therefore no wonder that the Socratic philosopher finds no place there.[51]

---

not take sufficiently seriously the Stranger's insistence that such rule depends on recognizing no wisdom greater than that of the laws and therefore on prohibiting private inquiry. The kind of inquiry that will be prohibited is, of course, not medical research; both Griswold (1989, 167n28; 1995, 180) and Lane (1995, 284–6) apparently fail to see that this is only an analogy for what rule by law must suppress: philosophy. Griswold surprisingly ignores the glaring counterexample to his view provided by the dramatic context and by the Stranger's clear allusion at 299b–c: a *democracy* condemning a philosopher to death. Therefore, unlike Griswold, I see no similarity between the Stranger's discourse and "la vision socratique" (1995, 181n54), but only antagonism.

49. Even in ranking the different constitutions, the Stranger characterizes *all* of them as hard to live with (302b6). What, then, is the meaning of the ranking? Gill correctly concludes that "the argument of 291–301 is irrelevant to this ranking; and that the relevant criteria are derived rather from the kind of conventional thinking about constitutions (as a necessary constraint on unchecked power) referred to in 301c6–d6" (1995, 300). Gill proceeds to qualify this conclusion slightly, but I find strange his suggestion that a smaller number of rulers makes it more likely that they will be able to *copy* knowledge-based ruling (301).

50. Schleiermacher attributed the final words of the dialogue, which express approval for what the Stranger has done, to the elder Socrates. Friedländer, however, rightly points out that both Theaetetus in the *Sophist* and young Aristotle in the *Parmenides* conclude the discussion with an affirmation of the conclusion; we should therefore expect a similar affirmation from young Socrates at the end of the *Statesman* (304). The editors of the new Oxford text, which unfortunately departs from Burnet's in adopting Schleiermacher's reading, conjecture that a reply by the young Socrates has dropped out. But then why not take the easier and more plausible course of attributing the words already in the text to the young Socrates? Robinson's account of the emendations provides no answer (1995, 41). Rowe (1995, 245) also attributes the final words to the elder Socrates, as does Miller, whose interpretation depends on the assumption that Socrates *approves* of what the Stranger does (1980, 112–3). Mishima observes (1995, 312n22) that even if this attribution was necessary, the words could still be ironic. However, this is one case where I think that silence would be even more effective than irony.

51. In wondering about the place of the philosopher in the Stranger's city (1995, 181), Rosen fails to see that the philosopher *has no place there*.

IV. IMPLICATIONS FOR THE INTERPRETATION
OF THE *SOPHIST* AND THE *STATESMAN*

The above does not constitute an interpretation of the *Sophist* and the *Statesman,* but obviously has important implications for their interpretation. If the Stranger does not speak for Plato, then his words cannot be directly translated into Plato's ontology or political theory. One must reckon with the possibility that Plato stands at a critical distance from the Stranger's positions and therefore from what are often taken to be 'Platonic doctrines'. Some interpreters, fearing the consequences of such a possibility for their readings, might be tempted to retain the identification of the Stranger with Plato by invoking the ever-handy "developmental hypothesis," suggesting that Plato in his old age became completely disillusioned with Socrates and used the character of the Stranger to express this disillusionment. This suggestion, however, apart from being purely speculative, is made untenable by the trouble Plato takes to expose the problems with the Stranger's own method. He does this both by putting an implicit but devastating critique into Socrates' words at the beginning of the *Statesman* and by doing everything possible to bring to our attention the inadequacies of the Stranger's conclusions. If one of the interlocutors is portrayed in a negative light, it is the Stranger.[52]

Should we then see Plato as completely rejecting and only ridiculing what the Stranger does? Certainly not. That Plato should have devoted two lengthy and complex dialogues to the Stranger and his method solely for the purpose of parody is not credible.[53] Furthermore, it is intuitively obvious that a monological,

---

52. Miller (1980) recognizes the inadequacies of the Stranger's account and the tension between this account and Socrates. However, he attributes all this to the Stranger's need to adapt what he says to Theodorus and his students who, in Miller's view, are the ones opposed to Socrates' philosophizing (see especially 3–10, 73–4 and 81–2, but also 26–7, 29–30, 32–5, 55, 60, 69, 86–7, 96–7, 106, 111). By thus shifting the blame to the Stranger's interlocutors, Miller is free to identify the Stranger with Plato (and even with a disguised Socrates, 12), as he clearly does, even though he rightly points out that such an identification cannot be assumed (xi–xii): Miller describes the cosmic myth as *Plato's* (40ff.), identifies the Stranger's reticence with *Plato's* (81) and, most importantly, sees the indirect communication between the Stranger and the young Socrates as "an act of indirect communication between Plato and the youngest generation of Academicians" (5; see also 115–7). Two general objections can be made: (1) the inadequacies and unsocratic features of the Stranger's account are a result of *his own* methodological principle of honoring all things alike, a principle which even Miller apparently takes to be sincere. (2) Miller's interpretation sees the Stranger as mediating between the philosophical standpoint of Socrates and the nonphilosophical standpoint of Theodorus' circle and the many (12, 14–5, 73–4, 89, 91, 112–3), but the Stranger does no such thing. His account of the second-best government, or rule according to law, makes it completely incompatible with, and hostile to, philosophical inquiry. Therefore, contra Miller, it is not the case that the goals of this government "fall short of the best *in a way which preserves its ultimate possibility*" (112, my emphasis). Miller himself recognizes that the many will not be able to distinguish between the true statesman and the imposter and therefore might put both to death (103); I do not see how, in Miller's view, the Stranger's "pleasing image" of the statesman can solve *this* problem (103–11). Significantly, Miller's concluding consideration of the possibility of a true statesman emerging from the ranks of the young members of the Academy completely forgets Socrates' impending execution (177–8). This forgetfulness is common among interpreters who seek to give an optimistic reading of the Stranger's proposals (e.g., Griswold and Gill, as noted above).

53. Rowe (1995a, 10) makes a similar objection against Scodel, who interprets the *Statesman* as mere parody (1987: see especially 148–9 & 167).

value-neutral, and theoretical method such as the Stranger's can have results that Socrates' dialogical, practical and indirect method never could. Specifically, the Stranger's method can address serious problems in ontology that are clearly beyond the purview of Socratic elenchus. The Stranger also attempts to give the distinction between sophist and philosopher an ontological and theoretical foundation, while for Socrates the distinction is strictly practical and revealed only indirectly through his discussions with individual sophists. In addition, the Stranger's ideal of the expert statesman enables him to explain by contrast the nature and deficiencies of the rule of law in a way unequaled by Socrates elsewhere. The Stranger may be blind to the limitations of what he says, which is why Socrates must be present to both embody and voice these limitations, but that does not discount the value of what he says within these limitations.

I maintain, therefore, not that the Stranger's method and its results are worthless, but rather that Plato takes great care to distance himself from them. He does not completely reject the method because he has found no other that does what it does better. He may even believe that the method's limitations are unavoidable, i.e., that being and not-being cannot be adequately defined, that a purely theoretical distinction between the sophist and the philosopher is impossible,[54] and that no politics can be fully reconciled with philosophy. On the other hand, Plato cannot fully endorse the method because, while perhaps the best at what it does, there is a whole dimension of human existence to which it is utterly blind and to which only Socrates' way of philosophizing can do justice. And the very demonstration of the method's blindness can be highly instructive: it can show, for example, the impossibility of applying a mathematical model of science to questions of worth, that in turn shows what *philosophy* cannot be (or cannot *only* be) if it is to address such questions.

The conclusions of this chapter therefore do not require the identification of Plato with *Socrates*.[55] While Plato uses Socrates to expose the inadequacies of the Stranger's method, he clearly understands and even sympathizes with this

---

54. Cf. Rosen 1983, 325. However, Rosen seems to go too far in suggesting, if I understand him correctly, that the distinction between philosopher and sophist simply cannot be validated philosophically (326, 328). It cannot be validated theoretically in definitions, but it can be validated by Socrates' *practice* of philosophy, a practice that is itself a separation of the noble from the base.

55. A major virtue of Rosen's interpretation of the *Statesman* is his insistence that Plato is to be identified with neither Socrates nor the Stranger (1995, 70 & 77). Unfortunately, however, Socrates eventually drops out of Rosen's interpretation, to the extent that Rosen *makes nothing of* the allusion to Socrates' condemnation in the Stranger's account of rule by law (174). Since Rosen as a result comes to interpret what is said entirely from the Stranger's perspective, we can suspect that Plato is in the end identified with the Stranger. Brumbaugh on the *Sophist* (1989) avoids identifying Plato with either the Stranger or Socrates. He characterizes the Stranger as someone "able, as Aristotle was later, to disconnect problems of semantics and syntax from questions of ethics, or physics, or metaphysics" (107). Therefore, Brumbaugh sees Plato as creating the Stranger for the purpose of refuting the sophist without question-begging, i.e., "in an ordinary language, non-Platonic enough so that even the Sophist cannot object that he does not accept or understand its technicalities" (110; see also 111). The Stranger must therefore not be Plato in order to serve his function. Yet it is by no means clear that the Stranger's method completely avoids metaphysical presuppositions (after all, the discussion of not-being is not simply about semantics). Furthermore, a refutation of the sophist through logic alone seems impossible, as Rosen has successfully shown (see n. 54). Scodel claims to remain agnostic about whether Socrates or any other character speaks for Plato (1987, 14), though he adds that if there is a mouthpiece, Socrates is the most likely candidate (16).

method in a way Socrates could not. In short, what is required by the rejection of the view that the Stranger speaks for Plato is simply that we finally read the *Sophist* and the *Statesman* as *dialogues*: i.e., that we see the author not as expounding his doctrines through some 'mouthpiece', but rather as using his characters to play positions against each other in a dramatic context that reveals both the virtues and the limitations of these positions. This is not to say that the dialogues, like the *Dissoi Logoi*, have no unified teaching or conclusion, but rather that, as in a great play, the "message" is not to be found in the words of one character, but rather in the interaction of all the characters.

WORKS CITED

Brumbaugh, Robert S. "Diction and Dialectic: A Note on the *Sophist*." In *Platonic Studies of Greek Philosophy: Form, Arts, Gadgets, and Hemlock,* 103–111. Albany: State University of New York Press, 1989.

Cornford, F. M. *Plato's Theory of Knowledge.* London: Routledge & Kegan Paul, 1935.

Dueso, José Solana. "*Statesman* (299B–D) and the Condemnation of Socrates." *Polis* 12 (1993): 52–63.

Frede, Michael. "The Literary Form of the *Sophist*." In *Form and Argument in Late Plato*, ed. Christopher Gill and Mary Margaret McCabe, 135–151. Oxford: Clarendon Press, 1996.

Friedländer, Paul. *Plato.* Vol. 3, tr. Hans Meyerhoff. Princeton: Princeton University Press, 1969.

Gill, Christopher. "Rethinking Constitutionalism in *Statesman* 291–303." In *Reading the Statesman: Proceedings of the Third Symposium Platonicum*, ed. Christopher J. Rowe, 292–305. Sankt Augustin: Academia Verlag, 1995.

Griswold, Charles L. "Politikê Epistêmê in Plato's *Statesman*." In *Essays in Ancient Greek Philosophy*, vol. 3, ed. John Anton and Anthony Preus, 141–67. Albany: State University of New York Press, 1989.

———. "Le libéralisme platonicien: de la perfection individuelle come fondement d'une theorie politique." In *Le Platonisme Renversé*, ed. Monique Dixsaut, 155–95. Paris: J. Vrin, 1995.

Howland, Jacob. "The Eleatic Stranger's Socratic Condemnation of Socrates." *Polis* 12 (1993):15–36.

Lane, Melissa. "A New Angle on Utopia: The Political Theory of the *Statesman*." In *Reading the Statesman: Proceedings of the Third Symposium Platonicum*, ed. Christopher J. Rowe, 276–91. Sankt Augustin: Academia Verlag, 1995.

Miller, Mitchell H. *The Philosopher in Plato's* Statesman. The Hague: Martinus Nijhoff, 1980.

Mishima, Teruo. "Courage and Moderation in the *Statesman*." In *Reading the Statesman: Proceedings of the Third Symposium Platonicum*, ed. Christopher J. Rowe, 306–312. Sankt Augustin: Academia Verlag, 1995.

Plochmann, G. K. "Socrates, the Stranger from Elea, and Some Others." *Classical Philology* 49 (1954): 223–231.

Robinson, D. B. "The New *Oxford Text* of Plato's *Statesman*: Editor's Comments." In *Reading the Statesman: Proceedings of the Third Symposium Platonicum*, ed. Christopher J. Rowe, 37–46. Sankt Augustin: Academia Verlag, 1995.

Rosen, Stanley. *Plato's* Sophist: *The Drama of Original and Image.* New Haven: Yale University Press, 1983.

————. *Plato's* Statesman: *The Web of Politics.* New Haven: Yale University Press, 1995.

Rowe, Christopher. *Plato: Statesman.* Warminster, England: Aris and Phillips LTD, 1995a.

————. "The *Politicus:* Structure and Form." In *Form and Argument in Late Plato,* ed. Christopher Gill and Mary Margaret McCabe, 153–178. Oxford: Clarendon Press, 1996.

————, ed. *Reading the Statesman: Proceedings of the Third Symposium Platonicum.* Sankt Augustin: Academia Verlag, 1995b.

Sallis, John. *Being and Logos: Reading the Platonic Dialogues.* 3d ed. Bloomington: Indiana University Press, 1996.

Scodel, Harvey Ronald. *Diaeresis and Myth in Plato's Statesman.* Göttingen: Vandenhoeck & Ruprecht, 1987.

Vlastos, Gregory. "Socratic Knowledge and Platonic Pessimism." *Philosophical Review* 66 (1957): 226–38.

12

Who Speaks for Whom in the *Timaeus-Critias*?

Hayden W. Ausland

Plato's dialogues are different from other dialogues, not only from treatises. Within an ancient diversity, Plato's version is *sui generis*. Xenophon and Aristotle appeared in *propria persona,* and most later dialogues were designed for doctrinal instruction, rather than for philosophical inquiry. In comparison with all, Plato's dialogues remain genuinely dramatic compositions.[1] The implications of this fact for reading the dialogues are somewhat blurred by the most common premise of his literary dramas. In the paradigmatic case, Plato's own supposed teacher, Socrates, converses with someone apparently in need of instruction, reproof, or the like. But Plato's preference for such fictions does not mean that one *persona* speaks for the author. It may mean that he prefers depicting a dialectical relationship to imparting any philosophical doctrines. Where other writers make the dialogue a vehicle for teachings, Plato uses teachings as topical elements within a given dialogue's literary economy.

Scholars have long regarded the apparent protagonist in a Platonic dialogue as stand-in for the author himself. Where Socrates for some reason lacks this status, it devolves upon some other such as Timaeus, who presumably replaces Socrates specially to convey Plato's physical teachings. This way of reading the dialogues is quite inadequate, because it fails to appreciate them as artistic wholes. Platonic "physics" has been extracted from the *Timaeus* for centuries; but for many of these same centuries, such doctrines were also located in the poems of Homer and Hesiod. As recently as the nineteenth century the statements of characters in Attic dramas were selectively mined in an effort to expose a hypothetical movement's presumed philosophical position; in the case of Euripides, one scholar even sought to derive the playwright's own esoteric

---

1. See Hermann Schlottmann, *Ars Dialogorum quas Vicissitudines apud Graecos et Romanos Subierit Commentatio* (Rostoch: Adler, 1889), 12–16.

doctrine.[2] Students of Greek literature have arrived at a better appreciation, but Plato's role in the history of philosophy has retarded this development for most of his interpreters.

A complementary problem occurs in some literary readings of the dialogues, whether traditional aesthetic appreciations, or those arising out of newly theoretical methods of reading imaginative literature. A common example will serve to illustrate both. As mentioned already, the role of Platonic spokesman has been most readily accorded to Socrates. But already in antiquity, four dialogues were grouped together to tell a single story about Socrates' final crisis (Diogenes Laertius 3.56f.). A related modern view is that Plato's philosophical spokesman here also functions as his "tragic hero." Viewed against this romance, the defendant's rhetorical appeal to Achilles in the *Apology* offers a welcome alternative to comparing him with Jesus: his fictional *persona* becomes a new, philosophical hero.[3] This further invites a literary treatment of the dialogues in tune with avant-garde philosophical treatments of Greek literature.[4]

All this confuses our understanding of the dialogues. That Socrates is a tragic hero fits ill with his status as the author's spokesman. Does Oedipus, or rather Teiresias, speak for Sophocles?[5] Surely Sophocles does not himself speak at all, except via the entire drama. It here seems noteworthy that the most popular way of understanding Socrates as both spokesman and hero is to hold both character and author as in some doctrinal sense fatally flawed.[6] This shows how important it is not to correct overly analytical readings of the dialogues by resorting to literary readings mired in later theories or fashions.[7] While the dia-

---

2. See Ferdinand Dümmler, *Prolegomena zu Platon's Staat und der Platonischen und Aristotelischen Staatlehre* (Basel Univ. Prog., 1891)[=id., *Kleine Schriften* vol I. (Leipzig: S. Hirzel, 1901), 150–228] and A. W. Verrall, *Euripides the Rationalist: A Study in the History of Art and Religion* (Cambridge: Cambridge University Press, 1895), especially 231f. and 259f.

3. For Socrates' heroism, see Erwin Wolff, *Platos Apologie* (Berlin: Weidmann, 1929), chapters 4 & 5; cf. Gregory Vlastos, *Socrates. Ironist and Moral Philosopher* (Ithaca: Cornell University Press, 1991), 233–5. For variations, see Richard E. Walton, "Socrates' Alleged Suicide," *Journal of Value Inquiry* 14 (1980): 287–299; Robert Eisner, "Socrates as Hero," *Philosophy and Literature* 6 (1982): 106–118; and Kenneth Seeskin, "Socratic Philosophy and the Dialogue Form," *Philosophy and Literature* 8 (1984): 181–194, especially 189–192.

4. See T. H. Irwin, "Socrates and the Tragic Hero," in *Language and the Tragic Hero. Essays in Honor of Gorden M. Kirkwood*, ed. Pietro Pucci (Atlanta: Scholar's Press, 1988), 55–83.

5. See Wolff, *Platos Apologie*, 75–83. Cf. Diskin Clay, "Socrates' Mulishness and Heroism," *Phronesis* 17 (1972): 53–60.

6. For the Platonic Socrates' failure by Christian standards, see Gregory Vlastos, *Platonic Studies* (Princeton: Princeton University Press, 1973), 30 and id., *The Philosophy of Socrates. A Collection of Critical Essays* (Garden City: Anchor Books, 1971), vi and 16f., comparing the fuller antecedent statement in Leo Strauss, *The City and Man* (Chicago: Rand McNally, 1964), 60f. Derivative recent discussion takes up Nietzsche's radical criticism, according to which Socrates' flaw is his failure to be tragic in a modern sense; see Martha Nussbaum, *The Fragility of Goodness. Luck and Ethics in Greek Tragedy and Philosophy* (Cambridge: Cambridge University Press, 1986), 122–35; cf. Vlastos, *The Philosophy of Socrates*, 17 n.8.

7. Defenders needlessly seek to rehabilitate Socrates as truly tragic; see David L. Roochnik, "The Tragic Philosopher: A Critique of Martha Nussbaum," *Ancient Philosophy* 8 (1988): 285–295. Cf. the partly analogous criticism of Derrida by Stanley Rosen, "Platonic Hermeneutics: On the Interpretation of a Platonic Dialogue," *Proceedings of the Boston Area Colloquium on Ancient Philosophy* 1 (1986): 271–97, especially 296.

logues' contents look different to specialists in philosophy and scholars of literature, it is doubtful what is to be gained by replacing one professional apparatus with another. We might better begin by viewing dialogues in terms familiar to the ancients themselves. After preliminary reflections on Plato's use of characters and his groupings of certain dialogues, this chapter attempts this for certain elements of the *Timaeus* and *Critias*.

I. *DRAMATIS PERSONAE*

The view that Socrates is Plato's philosophical spokesman quickly encounters several interconnected problems—some general but others clearer in specific contexts. Plato preserves verisimilitude in depicting Socrates' conversations with different interlocutors under differing circumstances. But his Socrates is also a reticent ironist; often it is his interlocutors who put forward a dialogue's key theses. Things can be said even by Socrates' most vehement antagonists that must have been contemplated by Plato himself (see Aulus Gellius, *Noctes Atticae* 10.22).

Basics are complicated when several parties are involved. An illustrative Socratic case, the *Philebus* begins just as the argument has reached a stage ripe for Protarchus to become Socrates' interlocutor. Socrates now speaks with Philebus indirectly, just as he clearly has already spoken with Protarchus by conversing with Philebus. We begin already part way through the greater drama.[8] If Socrates speaks for Plato in the *Philebus,* he does so also for the sake of two distinct characters, and without our knowing the boundaries of the greater discussion. Socrates' words are thus conditioned in ways left deliberately unspecified. Characterizations of Plato's doctrine in terms of Socrates' statements here are therefore highly problematic; but we must also wonder how best otherwise to proceed.[9]

Enigmatic hints about Plato's management of his characters are found in analogous relationships he depicts within the dialogues.[10] In the *Symposium,* Socrates purports to convey the doctrines of a Mantinean alien named Diotima (cf. 201d2 with 211d1f.). Did such a woman really exist, or did Plato invent her? If the latter, is she supposed to be real within the terms of the dialogue or is she there invented by Socrates? Perhaps Plato (and/or his hypothetical

---

8. Cf. the *Gorgias* and *Republic 1*, where fresh volunteers replace interlocutors overcome by Socrates. The *Philebus* rushes us *in medias res.*

9. See Dion. Hal. *In Dem.* 23. Scholars today generally respect a Victorian view in which understanding Plato depends on a conjectural chronology of the dialogues that isolates the *Philebus* within a "late" group significantly lacking Socrates in his authoritative role (see Lewis Campbell, *The Sophistes and Politicus of Plato* [Oxford: Oxford University Press, 1868], xix–xxiv. For the difference between Philebus's and Protarchus's characters, see *Plato. Philebus and Epinomis,* tr. A. E. Taylor, ed. Raymond Klibansky et al. (London: Thomas Nelson & Sons, 1956), 11f. For the incompleteness of the conversation represented, see Seth Benardete, *The Tragedy and Comedy of Life. Plato's Philebus* (Chicago: University of Chicago Press, 1993), 87–91.

10. Homer likewise hints at his relation with his audience by way of the paradigms of Demodocus, Phemius, and Odysseus. Cf. Aristotle, *Poetics* 1460a18–26.

Socrates) knew of a real Diotima, but depicted her in a fictional light (see *Epistle* 2, 314c1–4).[11] Whatever we may decide, a question remains: Why did Plato attribute important statements in the dialogue to her rather than to Socrates? Here ingenious answers are proposed.[12] In the *Phaedrus*, Socrates listens as Phaedrus reads a written speech he attributes to Lysias. Did Lysias write these words, or are they Plato's? If the latter, are we to understand that Phaedrus himself wrote the speech but attributes it to Lysias in order to impress Socrates?[13] Why does Plato involve the person of Lysias in the dialogue at all, especially in this ambiguous way? The two problems just illustrated converge in the *Menexenus*, where Socrates himself recites a "Periclean" speech in praise of Athens for which he assigns authorial responsibility to Pericles' lady friend Aspasia. No one supposes this speech more historical than that in Thucydides; no one takes the attribution to Aspasia literally.[14] If Socrates speaks for Plato in the *Menexenus*, then, why does he use this strange means of praising Athens? Why does he (or Plato) praise Athens at all? Is Athens truly praised? No one has answered these questions in a satisfactory way.[15]

---

11. Diotima's fictionality is a modern development. Ancient writers speak of her as real: testimonia in *Platonis Symposium*, ed. Otto Jahn, 2nd ed. (Bonn: Marcum, 1875), 16–18. F. A. Wolf held that Socrates clothed his thoughts as those of an actual wise woman of the times; see id., *Platons Gastmahl* (Leipzig: Schwickert, 1782), xlvi [2nd ed. (1828), lxiv]. Friedrich Ast brought her actuality into question; see id., *Platons Leben und Schriften* (Leipzig: Weidmann, 1816), 312, and K. F. Hermann would settle this in the negative; see id., *De Socratis Magistris et Disciplina Iuvenili* (Marburg Univ. Prog., 1837): 11–19. In a monograph devoted to Platonic *personae*, G. Groen van Prinsterer argued on literary grounds that she was not likely mere invention: Plato regularly used historical personae for greater verisimilitude, so it is likely that his own literary Socrates did the same. See id., *Prosopographia Platonica* (Leiden: Hazenberg, 1823), 125. R. G. Bury later urged the opposite inference on doctrinal considerations: to place an original teaching in the mouth of an actual person would be to confess it derivative. See id., *The Symposium of Plato*, 2nd ed. (Cambridge: W. Heffer, 1923), xxxix. For later references, see J. A. Arieti, *Interpreting Plato. The Dialogues as Drama* (Lanham, MD: Rowman & Littlefield, 1991), 115 n.24.

12. Ast (*Platons Leben und Schriften*, 312) was sure that Plato wanted to have a woman instruct Greek pederasts about metaphysical love. K. F. Hermann saw a device indicating that what was said in her speech went beyond the doctrines of the historical Socrates; see id., *Geschichte und System der platonischen Philosophie*, I (Heidelberg: Winter, 1839), 523. For recent discussion, see R. G. Rutherford, *The Art of Plato* (Cambridge, MA: Harvard University Press, 1995), 191f.

13. Ancients speak of the speech as the orator's own (*Diogenes Laertius* 3.25; cf. Hermeius, *In Phaedrus* 35.20). Moderns again first raised a question. For older discussion, see K. F. Hermann, "Die Rede des Lysias in Plato's Phaedrus" in id., *Gesammelte Abhandlungen* (Göttingen: Dieter, 1849): 1–21, and A. B. Krische, *Über Platon's Phaedros* (Göttingen: Vandenhoeck & Ruprecht, 1848), 26–28; for newer, see R. Hackforth, *Plato's Phaedrus* (Cambridge: Cambridge University Press, 1952), 16–18, and K. J. Dover, *Lysias and the Corpus Lysiacum* (Berkeley: University of California Press, 1968), 69–71.

14. Citing Cicero (*Epist. ad Fam.* IX.viii), Hans Gottleber understood Socrates' invocation of Aspasia in terms of literary license peculiar to dialogue; see id., *Platonis Menexenus et Periclis Thuydidei Oratio Funebris* (Leipzig: Schwickert, 1772), 1. Consistently, he rejected an ancient view that the Periclean funeral speech in Thucydides' historical work was the author's invention (Gottleber, *Menexenus*, 67; cf. Dion. Hal., *De Thuc.* 18). Ancient anecdotes have Plato's dialogues branded inaccurate by persons like Gorgias, Phaedo (Athenaeus *Deipn.* 9, 505e), and even Socrates himself (Diogenes Laertius 3.35 and *Anon. Prol.* I. 3. 28–31).

15. Gottfried Stallbaum held the entire work satirical; see id., *Platonis Opera Omnia* IV.ii (Gothae: Hennings, 1833), 9–11. George Grote viewed the satire as concluded with the end of the opening dialogue; see id., *Plato and the Other Companions of Sokrates*, 3rd ed. (London: Murray

More puzzling still are contexts in which a speaker attributes statements to persons left unidentified. In the *Crito,* Socrates silences Crito with arguments he attributes abstractly to "the laws"; in the *Euthydemus,* Crito urges objections of a critic he leaves unnamed. In the *Hippias Major,* Socrates attributes key points to an unspecified "someone." What are we to make of these (whether Socrates' rhetorical, or Plato's literary) devices?[16] The answer to such a question may not be that simple, but two results seem clear. Consideration shows that Plato (a) speaks properly only through an entire drama, which he (b) playfully leaves incomplete or ambiguous in some crucial regard.

Such problems arise in particular dialogues even where Socrates is ostensibly the principal character. A general problem for the view that he is Plato's spokesman is posed by the way in which in other dialogues he fades in the presence of a novel authority. Later writers would ask whether Plato was a skeptical, or dogmatical, philosopher. Some identified a third way: Plato held views on some matters but withheld judgment on others; thus one could understand why he seems to spell out definite doctrines in some places but elsewhere confines himself to refuting every position put forward.[17] Diogenes Laertius explains that four persons—Socrates, Timaeus, and the Eleatic and Athenian aliens—have the role of conveying the Platonic *placita* in the dialogues, whereas Thrasymachus, Callicles, Polus, Gorgias, Protagoras, Hippias, Euthydemus, "and other such persons" are included only for refutation (3.52). He does not say why Plato uses spokesmen besides Socrates, or why in each such case Socrates himself is retained in some subordinate or implicit way. Diogenes fails to mention the eponymous speaker of the *Parmenides.* Is Parmenides a Platonic spokesman?[18] A simple pedagogical relationship is again precluded by

---

1875), III, 9–11 [four volume edition (1889): III 409–411]. The *Menexenus* would presumably have been dismissed universally as spurious, were it not for an inconvenient citation in Aristotle (*Rhet.* 1415b31; the *Hippias Minor* appears similarly at *Metaph.* 1025a6). Aspasia figured in the writings of other Socratics; see M. M. Henry, *Prisoner of History. Aspasia of Miletus and her Biographical Tradition* (Oxford: Oxford University Press, 1995), 29–56.

16. On Socrates' "laws," see Leo Strauss, "Plato's *Apology of Socrates* and *Crito*" in *Essays in Honor of Jacob Klein,* ed. R. B. Williamson & E. Zuckeman (Annapolis: St. John's College Press, 1976), 155–70 [= id., *Studies in Platonic Political Philosophy* (Chicago: University of Chicago Press, 1983), 38–66]. Confusion of Socrates with his personified laws has occasioned an extensive literature on a supposed contradiction between the *Crito* and the *Apology;* see e.g. Richard Kraut, *Socrates and the State* (Princeton: Princeton University Press, 1984). On the nameless someone of the *Hippias Major,* see Plato, *Hippias Major,* tr. Paul Woodruff (Indianapolis: Hackett, 1972), 43f. n.47 and 107f. Most assume that he must be the inner (i.e. fictional, but unironic) Socrates decorously disguised. But then why he does not surface in more dialogues? By contrast, the anonymous critic of the *Euthydemus* is regularly identified with some historical person (Wilamowitz-Moellendorff first viewed him as a fictional type). See Paul Friedländer, *Plato II,* tr. Hans Meyerhoff (New York: Pantheon 1964), 338 n.25.

17. See Cicero, *Acad.* I.12 (46) and *Lucullus* 23 (74); Plutarch, *Adv. Colot.* 1121e–1122a; Sextus Empiricus, *PH* I.221–25; Diogenes Laertius 3.51f. and IX.72; Elias, *In Arist. Categ.* 110.12–30; Photius, *Bibl.* 212 *ad fin.*

18. Maximus of Tyre (26.5 Hobein [16.5 vulg.]) includes Parmenides with Timaeus et al. as one whom Socrates treats with respect (he opposes to these Thrasymachus, Polus, Callicles, et al.). Contrast Athenaeus's partisan source (*Deipn* 11, 505c–d) who names Parmenides with Thrasymachus et al. as one disparaged by Plato.

Zeno's interested participation: if Plato means to approve of Parmenides' statements, he can do this only in the complex sense that he approves views expressed by Socrates in the *Philebus*. But here Parmenides' initial interlocutor is a youth who is the senior character elsewhere. The *Parmenides* is a particularly troublesome case.

Assuming that one can explain as Plato's spokesman the historical Parmenides discoursing by a historical impossibility with a less-experienced Socrates, one still has to wonder about his enigmatically anonymous foreigners. Who are these persons even supposed to be? Diogenes says that some thought the Eleatic alien was Parmenides, as the Athenian Plato. But Diogenes himself calls both "nameless fictions." "For," he adds, "Plato dogmatizes in recounting both what Socrates and what Timaeus says" (3.52). Plato cannot, that is, have meant anyone's anonymity merely in this way, since he exposes his own views elsewhere through spokesmen of definite personality. If Plato's employment of non-Socratic spokesmen is in fact exceptional, this is a fair inference. But Diogenes does not explain the literary or philosophical need even for identifiable alternative spokesmen, much less that for mysterious foreigners.[19] Related questions arise when potentially authoritative types are present who say little or nothing (e.g., Niceratus in the *Republic*), or where other such persons are invoked though absent (e.g., Protagoras in the *Theaetetus*). One potentially main speaker is even characterized as authoritative and absent, but left anonymous. Even assuming, therefore, that Plato expresses certain doctrines through the speeches of Socrates, we confront at least three further questions: (a) Why does Plato sometimes feature non-Socratic main speakers? (b) Why does he sometimes keep other authorities out of the action? And (c) Why are only certain alternative authorities left anonymous?

In the same way that Socrates' statements occur relative to the characters of his interlocutors, their own questions and responses normally reflect their appreciation that they are conversing with Socrates. Without identifying any Platonic spokesmen, Basilius of Caesarea says that Plato uses indefinite characters, as in the *Laws*, when he wants to place the subject matter into relief for the interlocutors, free of any particular authority (*Epistle* 135, 1. 20–32). This implies that normally Plato deliberately confuses issues with definite personalities. It is not quite the same as the idea, rejected by Diogenes, that the Athenian alien is simply Plato, but it could suggest that Socrates, especially when in the presence of other such authorities, may himself speak less than directly for the author. In a modified form, this is the inference of students of Plato who believe that he moved philosophically away from his teacher's critical method toward a positive position of his own: while young and still somewhat tentative in his views, Plato

---

19. Like its dramatic time and location, a dialogue's characters are a part (and the most important part) of its "matter" (*Anon. Prol.* V. 16.7f. and 17.1). Their concreteness is thus relative to the dialogues' educational purposes (IV 15.20–29). For modern attempts to understand indefinite characters, see H. G. Gadamer, *Platons dialectische Ethik* 2nd ed. (Hamburg: Meiner, 1968), 83f.; Leo Strauss, *The Argument and Action of Plato's Laws* (Chicago: University of Chicago Press, 1975), 1f.; and Jacob Klein, *Plato's Trilogy: Theaetetus, The Sophist and The Statesman* (Chicago: University of Chicago Press, 1977), 7–9.

could speak skeptically through the enigmatic Socrates, but then later, establishing more determinate views, he dogmatized through less definite main speakers. This is essentially Diogenes' view with a developmental twist.[20] Neither Diogenes nor Basilius explains why Plato makes one main speaker an obscure non-Athenian named "Timaeus" whose very existence is doubtful.[21] One might depict a historical Parmenides criticizing a young Socrates, while having only anonymous experts lecture him in his old age, but then why is Timaeus not simply cast as a "Locrian alien"? If he existed, the imaginative reader would evidently be free to identify him with this anonymous person. If he did not, why did Plato name him? (Philebus at least bears a suggestive name.) Critias is a recognizable Athenian (if of ambiguous generation), but the sense in which he speaks for Plato is unclear. Diogenes classified the *Timaeus* and the *Critias* as "magisterial" (vs. "investigative") dialogues; both should be relatively dogmatic. But they are, respectively, "theoretical" and "practical," more particularly, the *Timaeus* is "physical" while the *Critias*, along with the *Republic, Laws, Minos,* and *Epinomis,* is "political" (3.49–51). In the others of this list, either Socrates or the anonymous Athenian alien is principal speaker. But Diogenes for some reason does not seem to think that Plato "dogmatizes" through Critias. Why is this?

Socrates begins the *Timaeus* by counting his three interlocutors and then asking, "Where is the fourth?" Kept away by illness, he is informed. This anonymous, absent person says nothing, of course: the others present will "make up for" him. If he is Plato himself, as some think, we here have an answer to the question, Who speaks for the author? Timaeus, Critias, and Hermocrates do so together. Paradoxically, on this view Socrates alone of those present fails to speak for Plato. Of course, as on other occasions when he is replaced as principal speaker, he can still qualify what is said by his presence (or his absence). Why else place him there (or, in the single exception, not there)? Here, Socrates has actually set the other three their joint task; he is the architect of what they will say. In this broader sense all speak for Plato, but Socrates most authoritatively. The device of an anonymous fourth person is curious, if a signal of this. But if the mysterious fourth is not Plato himself, why keep him absent in a way so reminiscent of the *Phaedo*?

Timaeus is the first main speaker in a series that includes Critias and Hermocrates. Critias never gets going; just as the action of his story is about to commence, the dialogue breaks off. This has occasioned much speculation, but a careful reading reveals that Plato has contrived to include the substance of Critias's speech in the opening of the *Timaeus*. Hermocrates is barely identified, but he is present and speaks twice. We never hear his main contribution; indeed, it is never specified what he is supposed to say if we do. He is to follow

---

20. Hence embarrassment accounting for Socrates' apparent comeback in the "late" *Philebus*; see Dorothea Frede, "The Hedonist's Conversion. Socrates' Role in the *Philebus*," in *Form and Argument in Late Plato,* ed. Christopher Gill and Mary Margaret McCabe (Oxford: Oxford University Press, 1996), 213–48, especially 213–17. For a careful approach to the Eleatic alien, see H. Ronald Scodel, *Diaeresis and Myth in Plato's Statesman* (Göttingen: Vandenhoeck & Ruprecht, 1987), 14–19.

21. Ancients seem to take his existence for granted.

Timaeus and Critias; but, given Socrates' assignment and what these two announce as their undertakings, there seems nothing left for a third speaker—
much less for a fourth. Are their roles in some way unspecialized? Critias's
speech is prooemial, and Hermocrates' seems designed so as to remain mere
enthusiasm. The fourth person's contribution is left a question mark, so that the
whole series seems carefully designed to make us ask about something missing,
just as Socrates does as he sets the entire action into motion.

Perhaps there is a way out of the labyrinth. Often it is said or assumed that
Plato speaks directly and authoritatively in his letters.[22] But this involves problems
greater than mere authenticity. The Plato who speaks in the Platonic epistles is
himself a literary character whose statements need express their factual author's
thoughts no more directly than Socrates and Protagoras in Plato's *Protagoras* pro-
pound views of the historical Socrates and Protagoras. When the *Phaedrus's*
Socrates and the *Seventh Letter's* Plato concur that anything written down is not
to be taken too seriously, we must listen for *both* statements' playful tone.[23] If the
Definitions are not Plato's own, then, there seems no way simply to identify Plato's
views with statements made anywhere within the *Corpus Platonicum.*

As mentioned earlier, Plato suggests certain things by way of paradigms like
Socrates' relationship with Diotima. Several dialogues subordinate their main
contents in this way, framing a thematic dialogue within a subsequent narration
of some kind. Diogenes dismisses the distinction between performed and narrated dialogues as more "tragic" than "philosophical" (3.50). But, one might
reasonably ask, if Socrates speaks directly for Plato in a performed dialogue like
the *Meno*, then for whom does the narrator speak in the *Phaedo*? Socrates is at
the center of the conversation recalled, but Phaedo's own contribution is crucial to the dialogue's success. This is given an ironic twist in dialogues where
Socrates himself is the narrator of an earlier conversation in which he himself
has participated; in the *Euthydemus*, for instance, he describes his encounter
with a sophistical duo comically, even though highly serious matters are at
stake. No one finds the *Phaedo* comical, even though it is not without playful
humor. If Plato is speaking hereby, he does so via various interpretations offered by different intervening narrators.

The *Republic* is an unusually complex case. The Socrates who disputed with
Cephalus, Polemarchus, and Thrasymachus earlier yesterday (call him
Socrates-E) apparently regarded the conversation concluded at the end of our
first book. But the Socrates who meditates on the entire argument the next day
(*Socrates-M*) now knows otherwise. If Plato speaks through Socrates in the *Republic*, then, he speaks with at least two voices, of which at most one can represent completely the author's viewpoint.[24] There are places in lesser dialogues
where Socrates remarks that the argument proceeds otherwise than he would

---

22. Gunnar Rudberg derives some remarkable conclusions from this assumption; see "Plato in
the First Person," in id., *Platonica Selecta* (Stockholm: Almquist & Wiksell, 1956), 72–108.

23. See Aryeh Kosman, "Silence and Imitation in the Platonic Dialogues," in *Methods of Interpreting Plato and His Dialogues*, ed. J. C. Klagge, and N. D. Smith (Oxford: Oxford University
Press, 1992 [*Oxford Studies in Ancient Philology*, Suppl. Vol.]), 73–92.

24. The view according to which Book 1 is an "early" dialogue originates in a certain appreciation of this difference; see Friedrich Schleiermacher, *Platons Werke*, III.i (Berlin: Realschulbuch-
handlung, 1828), 9f. But this has been generally forgotten.

have liked or expected. In some of these cases, he has his way and gets control of the argument, but in others he seems not to. Plato uses this device on several occasions to organize the argument of the *Republic*, perhaps most importantly at the beginning of Book 5. Socrates is about to continue with a discussion of the degenerative departures from the standard he has established in Books 2–4, when he is forced by the others to discuss instead whether his hypothetical city can in fact be realized. His treatment of the question occupies Books 5–7. Plato himself was under no such compulsion, so that there must also be a difference between the original intention he attributes to a developed Socrates-E, who seeks to meet the joint challenge of Adeimantus and Glaucon with the discourses of 2–4 and 8–10, and the greater intention reflected in the dramatic interaction that Socrates-M describes ironically on the next day as having borne Socrates-E willy-nilly into the central discussion of 5–7. It is Adeimantus and Glaucon who set out Socrates-E's general task and who discipline him in accordance with their understanding of it. Throughout Books 2–10 they may speak for Plato in a way that even Socrates-M does not. The digression of Books 5–7 in particular comes about with Polemarchus's and Thrasymachus's momentarily renewed participation in the dialogue (449b1–7 and 450a5–7). One way to study what Plato is saying is therefore to see how different characters' speeches are conditioned dramatically, rather than only what one or another of them may say.

II. GROUPINGS OF DIALOGUES

Since antiquity, Plato's writings have been organized according to various principles in one way or another intended to reveal an underlying philosophical unity. But they have also been compared with several nonphilosophical literary genres, mostly drama.[25] According to Diogenes Laertius, Aristophanes of Byzantium, among others, brought fourteen dialogues and the letters into five "trilogies," which were then ordered in a numerical series and followed by other dialogues in no particular order. The first trilogy so formed included the *Republic, Timaeus,* and *Critias;* the others seem more arbitrary.[26] Diogenes has just explained that the scholar Thrasyllus organized thirty-five dialogues with the letters into nine "tetralogies," claiming that Plato himself had arranged, or published his dialogues in this form. Thrasyllus formed the eighth of his groups by prefixing the *Cleitophon* to the three dialogues just mentioned (3.56–61). Diogenes' discussion implies that these attempts to bring the dialogues into some order were designed to reflect the way Plato's dialogues imitate or respond to Attic tragedy. Indeed some modern scholars have held that Plato is following an established dramatic practice with certain groupings of his dia-

---

25. See Jacob Klein, *A Commentary on Plato's Meno* (Chapel Hill: University of North Carolina Press, 1965), 3f.

26. Diogenes Laertius 3.61f. Aristophanes's remaining four trilogies were: *Sophist-Politicus-Cratylus; Laws-Minos-Epinomis; Theaetetus-Euthyphro-Apology;* and *Crito-Phaedo-Letters.* See A. Nauck, *Aristophanis Byzantii Grammatici Alexandrini Fragmenta* (Halle: Lippert & Schmidt, 1848), 250, and Wilhelm Christ, *Platonische Studien* (München: 1885 [*Bayer. Akad. Abhandlungen* 17 (2)]), 466f.

logues.[27] The notion of dramatic tetralogies is itself historically problematic, and it is possible that trilogies and tetralogies were first seen in works like those of Plato rather than in Attic drama.[28] But the idea provides a useful new beginning for the present inquiry since, although it is influenced by modern philosophy, it remains fundamentally free of the assumption that a doctrinal unity underlies the dialogues. It is in this connection important to establish at the outset what is and what is not a Platonic trilogy or tetralogy.[29]

The arrangements of Aristophanes and Thrasyllus are two among a number devised over the centuries.[30] Most modern scholars have ignored dramatic or thematic interconnections except when convenient for developmental hypotheses—prudently so, given the difficulties.[31] Scholars normally dissociate

---

27. Thus, e.g., Wilhelm Christ, *Geschichte der griechischen Literatur*, 2nd ed. (Munchen: Beck, 1890), 390 [5th. ed. (1908)], 623. More cautious is Rudolf Hirzel, *Der Dialog. Ein Literärhistorische Versuch* (Leipzig: S. Hirzel, 1895), 253–55.

28. See Peter Wiesmann, *Das Problem der tragischen Tetralogie* (Zurich: Leemann, 1929), 28. Cf. Hirzel, *Dialog*, 253 n.3. Herbert Richards looks to the rhetorical practice exemplified in Antiphon's tetralogies; see id., "On the History of the Words τετραλογία and τριλογία" *Journal of Philology* 11 (1882): 64–74. Christ thinks that Plato's dialogues may have been the first works so denominated (*Platonische Studien*, 465). Harold Tarrant revives evidence of origins in the writings of the earlier Stoics and perhaps certain Socratics; see id., *Thrasyllan Platonism* (Ithaca: Cornell University Press, 1993), 14f.

29. No ancient source countenances dramatic composition in trilogies according to abstract "principles." Contrast A. W. Schlegel, who explained the trilogy as "Satz, Gegensatz, und Vermittlung"; see id., *Vorlesungen über dramatische Kunst und Literatur* (Stuttgart: Kohlhammer, 1966), 74f. F. M. Cornford interprets the *Timaeus* in this way; see id., *Plato's Cosmology* (London: Routledge & Kegan Paul, 1937), 361–64. Cornford's idea is partly seminal for the treatment by Helmut Kuhn; see id., "The True Tragedy: On the Relationship between Greek Tragedy and Plato," *Harvard Studies in Classical Philology* 52 (1941): 1–41 and 53; (1942): 37–88 [German original in Konrad Gaiser, ed. *Das Platonbild. Zehn Beiträge zum Platonverständnis* (Hildesheim: Olms, 1969), 231–323)]. Kuhn makes the same triadic scheme the basis of his reconstruction of the projected trilogy ; see id., "True Tragedy" (1941) 33–40, especially 38f.

A complementary strain of speculation finds a "Satyr play" in the *Euthydemus*. The idea is seminally present in Diogenes Laertius 3.56; cf. Jaap Mansfeld, *Prolegomena. Questions to be studied before the Study of an Author, or a Text* (Leiden: Brill, 1994), 63. In modern times, Samuel Petit reorganized the dialogues in new tetralogies he held must have existed at the conclusion of Plato's literary activity; see id., *Miscellaneorum Libri Novem* (Paris: Morellum, 1630), IV. ii—usefully excerpted in *Platonis Scripta Graeca Omnia* I, ed. I. Bekker (London: Priestley, 1826), cxliii–cxlvi. These tetralogies include three significant dialogues followed by some less consequential piece (e.g., the third: *Cratylus, Gorgias, Ion, Sophist*). The idea made its way via Aeschylean scholarship to A. W. Winkelmann, who asserted that this dialogue's comic effect depended on its being restored to its proper role within its tetralogy. Cf. id., *Platonis Euthydemus* (Leipzig: Guether, 1833), xliv, with F. G. Welcker, *Die Aeschyleische Trilogie Prometheus* (Darmstadt: Leske, 1824), 528 and id., "Prodikos der Vorgönger des Sokrates," *Rheinisches Museum* 1 (1832): 1–39, 533–643, and 4 (1836), 355–56; see especially 544–53 [= id., *Kl. Schr.* II (Bonn: Weber, 1845), 393–541; see especially 439–47]. Cf. further Christ, *Gesch. gr. Lit.* (1908), 638 n.2. Recently, T. H. Chance takes notice of the tendencies continuing into the present century; see id., *Plato's Euthydemus. Analysis of What Is and Is Not Philosophy* (Berkeley: University of California Press, 1992), 13.

30. C. V. Tchorzewski, *De Politia Timaeo Critia Ultimo Platonico Ternione* (Kazani Diss., 1847), 1–66 reviews various methods. For more on some ancient arrangements, see Mansfeld, *Prolegomena*, 62–107 and Tarrant, *Thrasyllan Platonism*, 31–68.

31. In order to claim Thrasyllus's first tetralogy as Platonic, Christ has to fashion a tale according to which Plato composed it gradually over a number of years (*Platonische Studien*, 462–64). For

the *Phaedo* from the remaining dialogues of Thrasyllus's first tetralogy on the supposition that it belongs to a subsequent period of Plato's philosophical development—legitimately, to the extent that Plato has failed to connect these dialogues by properly dramatic means.[32] The remaining Thrasyllan tetralogies exhibit even less such interconnection (like most of Aristophanes' incompatible trilogies). Leaving these and modern constructions aside,[33] we are left with two sets of dialogues with a strong claim to constituting together a greater dramatic whole: one beginning with the *Sophist* and continuing with the *Politicus,* and a second beginning with the *Timaeus* and continuing with the *Critias.*[34] In both cases, the two discourses so conjoined anticipate explicitly an additional further discourse (we may call these the "Philosopher" and the "Hermocrates," respectively). An additional discourse would make a literary trilogy.[35] But not only is this mysteriously lacking in both cases, but the first discourse always recalls a previous discourse of "yesterday" (the *Theaetetus* and the *Republic* [?], respectively). Thus, both groupings imply a greater whole that is in principle simultaneously tripartite and quadripartite in form:

(Greater tetralogy)	1st	2nd	3rd	4th
(Nominal trilogy)		1	2	3
(Actual trilogy)	i	ii	iii	
	[Republic]	Timaeus	Critias	{Hermocrates}
	[Theaetetus]	Sophist	Statesman	{Philosopher}

the idea that he only late concentrated on certain formal features of the genre, see Hirzel, *Dialog,* 252f. and Ivo Bruns, *Das literärischer Porträt der Griechen im funften und vierten Jahrhundert vor Christi Geburt* (Berlin: Hertz, 1896), 271–80.

32. See Hirzel's criticisms of Christ (Hirzel, *Dialog,* 257f.). If merely being set during this time were crucial, then the *Theaetetus,* et al. would need to be worked in as well. Joseph Cropsey pursues this path, treating both sets of dramas set between Socrates' notification of his indictment and his execution as a single series; see id., *Plato's World. Man's Place in the Cosmos* (Chicago: University of Chicago Press, 1995), ixf. At an extremity, this allows for an ordering of all the dialogues beginning with the *Parmenides* and ending with the *Laws;* one study of Plato; Eduard Munk, *Die naturliche Ordnung der platonische Schriften* (Berlin: Dümmler, 1857), attempted just this.

33. Adducing various doctrinal considerations, nineteenth-century scholars discerned trilogies in such groupings as (a) *Charmides-Laches-Lysis,* (b) *Phaedrus-Symposium-Phaedo,* (c) *Gorgias-Meno-Protagoras* (see Christ, *Platonische Studien,* 460–65). Recently, Charles Kahn likewise finds yet another in the *Apology-Crito-Gorgias;* see id., "Drama and Dialectic in Plato's *Gorgias,*" *Oxford Studies in Classical Philosophy* 1 (1983), 75–121, *ad fin.*

34. See Hermann Usener, "Unser Platontext," *Göttingen Nachrichten* (1892 [6]) 209–14. While it is conceivable that the *Timaeus* and *Critias* were originally published as one continuous text in a single book-roll, one would want to know why this was cut where it was. See M. W. Haslam, "A Note on Plato's Unfinished Dialogues," *American Journal of Philology* 97 (1976): 336–39. The question does not particularly affect consideration of a series of *discourses* quite possibly all internal to a single book (see Richards, "On the History of the Words," 65–68 and Hirzel, *Dialog,* 253 n.3). Something different might be said of the view that the *Sophist* and *Politicus* should be understood as still subordinated to the narrative framework at the beginning of the *Theaetetus;* see Munk, *Die naturliche Ordnung,* 421f. and Hermann Schöne, *Platons unvollendete Tetralogien* (Berlin MS, 1900), 18–20.

35. See G. Hermann, *De Aeschyli Trilogiis Thebanis* (Leipzig: Staritzii, 1835), 5 [=*Opuscula* VII, 193]: "Videtur autem ipsa trilogiae natura postulare, ut argumentum sit unum, iustoque ab initio profectum finem quoque habeat iustum, nec tam quae res tempore sese deinceps exceperunt, quam quae ita cohaerent, ut una actio absolvatur, tribus sint partibus aptae scriptae." Cf. Plato, *Phaedrus,* 264c and 268d.

In both cases, the nominally first and second dialogues (1 and 2) establish a connection with an earlier conversation (i); but this antecedent discourse does not anticipate things to come in the same systematic way that the first discourse of the nominal trilogy (1) does.[36] The first dialogue of the actual trilogy (i) is thus not formally part of the nominal trilogy, which is to be completed by a missing fourth member (3) that in both instances never actually appears: in the nominal trilogy two have to make do for three (and in the tetralogy, three for four). For some reason, Plato uses this curious general form twice. There has been much speculation about the missing fourth members in these series. Some have sought to identify one of the extant dialogues with the "Philosopher" or "Hermocrates"; but this will not complete a literary trilogy. Others hold that some further writing has been lost or revised for inclusion in other dialogues, or else that it was for some reason never completed as projected.[37] A better approach, perhaps, is to try to see whether Plato might not have deliberately constructed these groups just as they exist.

Beyond the common form noted already, the *Sophist-Statesman* and the *Timaeus-Critias* tetralogies differ in noticeable ways. The former includes a trilogy to be made up entirely of dialectical exchanges, while the latter is designed as a series of speeches. In the one case, the hypothetical pairings of main speakers with interlocutors (see *Politicus* 258a4–6) exhibit an interesting pattern:

Theaetetus	*Sophist*	*Statesman*	*[Philosopher]*
Socrates–Theaetetus	Eleatic alien–Theaetetus	Eleatic alien–Young Socrates	Socrates–Young Socrates

The pattern, as well as the coincidence of names, could be taken to mean that the missing material of the "Philosopher" is to be sought in a synthesis of materials already present in the existing trilogy, which would imply the remarkable

---

36. Bruns (*Das literärischer Porträt,* 273–76) holds that, with such "fictional" connections, Plato can invoke dialogues he completed much earlier. Cf. Hirzel, *Dialog,* 258 n.2.

37. Cf. Bion Borysth. apud Stob. *Anth* 3.4 with Diogenes Laertius 2.27. Some ancients located a "Philosopher" in the *Epinomis* (Diogenes Laertius 3.60, Nicomachus, *Intr. Arithm.* 1.3.5); Friedrich Ast and Eduard Zeller found it in the *Parmenides* (cf. Christ, *Plat. Stud.* 468–70). For the notion that an actual dialogue has been lost, see Adolf Dyroff, "Über einen angeblichen Philosophus des Platon," *Blätter für das Gymnasial-Schulwesen* 32 (1896), 18–21. On earlier attempts to account for the incomplete state of the *Critias,* see Theodorus Bach, *Meletemata Platonica* (Warsaw: Lindner, 1858). For subsequent treatments, see Hans Herter, "Urathen der Idealstaat," in *Politeia und Res Publica. Dem Andenken Rudolf Starks gewidmet,* ed. Peter Steinmetz (Wiesbaden: Steiner, 1969), 108–34 [= id., *Kleine Schriften* (München: Fink, 1975), 279–304]. Last century, G. B. Hussey located the ruins of both the "Philosopher" and the "Hermocrates" submerged within the *Republic;* see id., "The Incorporation of Several Dialogues in Plato's *Republic,*" *Classical Review* 10 (1896): 81–85. Recently, Gerard Naddaf rediscovered the older view that the *Laws* are the remains of the "Hermocrates;" see id., "The Atlantis Myth: An Introduction to Plato's Later Philosophy of History," *Phoenix* 48 (1994): 189–209; cf. Edmund Pfleiderer, *Sokrates und Plato* (Tübingen: Laupp, 1896), 689–715. For literal understandings of Atlantis and the *Critias* in antiquity, cf. Strabo *Geogr.* II.3.6 with Plutarch, *Vit. Sol.* 32. For modern variants, see Christopher Gill, *Plato: The Atlantis Story* (Bristol: Bristol Classical Press, 1980), vii–xxiv.

conclusion that supplying the missing dialogue is something for which the reader is intended to assume responsibility in some way.[38] The other grouping shows no such pattern, but the trio sophist-statesman-philosopher is in a way made again thematic at its outset, where Socrates discusses the philosophico-political qualifications of the three speakers in terms of a synthesis of talents found separated in sophists and poets (see *Timaeus* 19c8–20b7). Seeing how this might inform the tetralogy is made more difficult by the fact that the connection between the *Timaeus-Critias* and a supposedly antecedent *Republic* is left comparatively ambiguous; moreover, no hypothetical subject matter for the missing "Hermocrates" is ever specified in the way it is for the "Philosopher," and the *Critias*, unlike the Politicus, seems itself to have been left incomplete. But these phenomena may at the same time signal special features somehow important for an understanding of the *Timaeus-Critias* series.[39] We can begin by recalling the opening of the *Timaeus,* which provides indications that these dialogues form a tetralogy with the *Republic.*

III. THE *TIMAEUS* AND *CRITIAS*

At the opening of the *Timaeus,*[40] Socrates alludes to a feast he hosted yesterday.[41] The three others present undertake to entertain Socrates today. Both feasts are verbal in nature: yesterday's was a discourse by Socrates, and today the others are to repay him in kind.[42] Timaeus asks Socrates to remind them briefly what they are to do (17a1–c1). Socrates summarizes his own account before reiterating his earlier instructions. His summary reveals that he yesterday outlined a polity quite like the hypothetical city of Plato's *Republic* (17c1–19b2). This outline formed the basis for the task he assigned the others for today, viz., to describe how this city will comport itself, in both speech and action, while engaged in controversy with other cities (19b3–20b7).

---

38. Klein speculates to this effect, but also thinks there is a sense in which it may be found in other existing works of Plato (*Trilog.,* 4f. and 200). On the idea that the reader is meant to move matters beyond the dialogue, see Kenneth Dorter, *Form and Good in Plato's Eleatic Dialogues* (Berkeley: University of California Press, 1994), 235f.

39. Hirzel (*Dialog,* 255–56) sees them as indications that it is less a trilogy than the other grouping.

40. The contents of the proem to the *Timaeus* (and therewith also the *Critias*) have received the usual varying degrees of attention from antiquity onwards. See Proclus *in Timaeus* 26c (I. 83.19–30) and 63a–b (I. 204.16–29 D.); Chalcidius *in Timaeus* 71.

41. Ancient and modern commentators alike have sought to identify the absent fourth *persona* with someone specific (whether a Platonic character or some other historical personage). In antiquity, Dercyllides held that he was Plato himself. Others thought him Theaetetus (Porphyry) or Cleitophon ("Ptolemy the Platonist"); see Proclus *In Tim.* 7a–8b (I. 19.30–23.16 Diehl). Moderns have identified him with Plato (P. W. Van Heusde), Philebus (Edmund Pfleiderer), or Philolaos (Constantine Ritter); see *Platon Oeuvres Complétes X, Timée—Critias . . . par* A. Rivaud (Paris: Les Belles Lettres, 1925), 18f. and Friedländer, *Plato III,* 546 n7. Such speculations led Hirzel to deny that Plato himself knew whom he meant (*Dialog,* 240 and 257). Bruns is more cautious (*Das literärischer Porträt,* 279).

42. For the metaphor, see Fritz Muthmann, *Untersuchungen zur "Einkleidung" einiger platonischer Dialoge* (Bonn Diss., 1961), 73f. See further Klein, *Meno,* 193 and Joseph Cropsey, "The Whole as a Setting for Man: On Plato's *Timaeus,*" *Interpretation* 17 (1989–90): 165–91.

In considering Socrates' summary, one must recognize both the limits and extent of the literary relationship implied with the *Republic*. The *Republic* nowhere dramatically anticipates the *Timaeus-Critias* in the way the *Theaetetus* does the *Sophist-Politicus*. But the *Timaeus* and *Critias* presuppose a conversation unlike any other than what we find in Plato's *Republic*. Socrates' discourse was political and addressed chiefly the question of the best polity, with its constituent citizens. In his résumé, he lists political institutions quite like those in the *Republic* but apparently omits mentioning that city's key institution of philosophical rule. The Socrates who will now listen to the other three (Socrates-L) recalls only the institutions developed in *Republic* II.369b5–V.466d5.[43] Yet, at the end of his summary, Timaeus agrees that no principal topic has been omitted.

The *Timaeus* and *Critias* thus both do and do not recall the *Republic*.[44] The *Timaeus* does not require us to imagine the conversation presupposed as identical with Socrates-M's narration on the day after the conversation in the Peiraeus. If it did, his indefinite audience on that day would now stand revealed as having been Timaeus, Critias, Hermocrates, and the anonymous fourth guest.[45] Indeed, they seem to preclude this interpretation by agreeing explicitly that nothing of importance has been omitted from the summary.[46] But neither may one conclude that "the design of the present trilogy is thus completely independent of the *Republic*,"[47] or, worse still, pursue scholarly fictions about earlier versions or planned revisions of the *Republic* as it now stands.[48]

---

43. For the correlations with the text of the *Republic*, see August Boeckh, *Specimen editionis Timaei Platonis dialogi* (Heidelberg: Mohr, 1807) [=*Kl. Schr.* III, 181–203], 15–25 and G. F. Rettig, *Prolegomena ad Platonis Republicam* (Bern: Huber, 1845), 3–7; and the notes to 17c1–19a5 in *The Timaeus of Plato*, ed. R. D. Archer-Hind, London 1888, and Rivaud, *Timée—Critias*. For the rational city, cf. 26c7f, 19a7f, c2, 20b2, 25e2, and *Critias* 110d3f. with *Republic* 369c9 (cf. *Laws* 702e1f.) and 592a10–b1.

44. See U. von Wilamowitz-Moellendorff, *Platon*, 2nd edition II (Berlin: Weidmann, 1920), 257.

45. This was Proclus's inference (*in Timaeus* 3d–e [I. 8.30–9.13 D.]), followed by many moderns; thus Karl Morgenstern, *De Platonis republica commentationes tres* (Halle: Hemmerde & Schwetschke, 1794), 33; August Boeckh, *Progr. Berl.* 1838–1839 [=*Kl. Schr.* IV, 437–92], 438; Schleiermacher, *Platons Werke* III.1, 68; Hermann, *Geschichte und System*, 537f; Archer-Hind, ed., *Timaeus of Plato*, 54f; Otto Apelt, *Archiv für Geschichte der Philosophie* 14 (1901): 409–411; A. E. Taylor, *A Commentary on Plato's Timaeus* (Oxford: Oxford University Press, 1928), 13; Paul Shorey, *What Plato Said* (Chicago: University of Chicago Press, 1933), 330.

46. The summary's incompleteness was noticed by Morgenstern, *De Platonis republica*, 31–34; cf. Rettig, *Prolegomena*, 4–6.

47. Cornford, *Plato's Cosmology*, 5.

48. The first suggestion has a confused history. A speculation voiced during the 1880s by Hermann Usener had been mentioned in print by Paul Brandt (*Zur Entwicklung der platonischen Lehre von den Seelenteilen*, Leipzig 1890, 6), but Hirzel first brought it into prominence by wondering that August Krohn and his fellow hypercritics had not used the idea in arguing for the existence of an earlier edition of the *Republic* (*Dialog*, 456 n1). Erwin Rohde had in fact lately availed himself of the suggestion; see id., *Psyche* (Freiburg: Mohr, 1894), 557 n1. A generation later, a then stale idea would be credited to Krohn and Pfleiderer (Friedländer, *Platon III*, 545 n.4; cf. Muthmann, *Untersuchungen*, 80). Generally forgotten was that Ch. H. Weisse had some time back suggested an earlier version of the *Republic*; see id., *Zeitschrift für Philosophie und philosophische Kritik*, NF 47 (1865): 176; cf. Schöne, *Platons unvollendete Tetralogien*, 16f.). On problems with the entire general approach, see Karl Joël, "Zur Entstehung von Platons 'Staat'," *Festschrift zur 49.*

That such expedients are otiose is plain, once we notice that the elements of the *Republic* passed over in the *Timaeus* all represent considerations external to the task of describing the hypothetical city that, in the *Republic*, serves as a paradigm for the sake of an inquiry into justice.[49] As Socrates reminds Glaucon in book 5, it is sufficient for that purpose if a way is found in which a real city might approach as nearly as possible to the paradigm. This way turns out to be the coincidence of political power with philosophy, which (with its prerequisite education) is therefore to be understood as extraneous to the hypothetical city as such. This city, by the time Socrates looks to its realization, has been fully set out.[50] To this extent it is identical with the hypothetical city Socrates-L described "yesterday"—if without features developed in the *Republic* for the sake of the question of justice.[51] The polity recalled at the beginning of the *Timaeus* is thus occasionally distinct from, but formally identical with, the one constructed hypothetically in the *Republic*. And it is recalled in such a way that we cannot fail to recognize that it is this polity (versus, e.g., that in the *Laws*), which is meant. The *Timaeus* and *Critias* build upon it in abstraction from the particular answer given in the *Republic* to the distinct problem of its realization.[52] This does not mean that Plato somehow altered his views about this problem or the likelihood of its ever being solved. On the contrary, the precise way in which the *Timaeus* and *Critias* invoke the *Republic*'s hypothetical city distinctly suggests that they contemplate the very same question.[53]

Socrates describes the feeling that his own discourse has engendered in him. It is akin to what one feels when one conceives the desire, at having seen beautiful living things (whether represented in painting, or actually alive but at rest),

---

Versammlung Deutscher Philologen und Schulmänner (Basel: Birkhauser, 1907), 295–323, especially 316–23 (cf. Bruns, *Das literärischer Porträt*, 276).

The later hypothesis that Plato either planned, began, or executed a revision of the *Republic* as we have it is connected with the still popular notion that the author eventually "gave up" the work's perceived idealism, pioneered by Henry Jackson, "Plato's Later Theory of Ideas," *Journal of Philology* 10 (1881): 253–98, 11 (1882): 287–331, 13 (1884): 1–40 and 242–72, 14 (1885): 173–230. For criticism, see Eduard Zeller, "Über die Unterscheidung einer doppelten Gestalt der Ideenlehre in der platonischen Scriften," *Berlin S.-B. hist.-phil. Kl.* (1887 [13]), 197–220.

49. Contrast Polybius 6.47.7–10 and cf. Athenaeus, *Deipn.* 9, 507d.

50. Herter (*op. cit.*) goes to unusual lengths to locate the polity of the *Republic*—philosophical rule and all—in primeval Athens. Contrast Muthmann, *Untersuchungen*, 72–97, but see also Strauss, *City and Man*, 122. Herter's and others' inability to see why Socrates' recollection of the *Republic*'s hypothetical city does not require mention of philosophical rule is similar to attempts to reconcile directly the natural and applied orders of the disciplines in *Republic* 7. Thus Cornford takes refuge in the conventional biographical hypothesis that Plato in his "later" work was reacting to the personal disappointments in Syracuse, etc. (*Plato's Cosmology*, 5f.). The geneticist's romanticizing tendency relies in turn on the systematist's assumption that the *Timaeus* is essentially a treatise on physical science. For the former, see an unusually candid admission by Constantin Ritter, *Neue Untersuchungen*, 178. On the dialogue's primarily political nature, see H. G. Brücker, *Politicorum quae Docuerunt Platon et Aristoteles Comparatio* (Leipzig: C.H. Reclam, 1824), 27–30 (cf. Diogenes Laertius 9.15).

51. Cf. the references to having gone through the polity's institutions at *Timaeus* 19a7, 20b2 and 26c8 with those at *Republic* 473e2 and 543c7–d1, comparing the summary at 543a1–c6.

52. See Hirzel, *Dialog*, 256n. and (with less clarity) Schleiermacher, *Platons Werke* III.i, 68ff. And G. Stallbaum, *Platonis Opera Omnia* VII (Gothae: Hennings, 1838), 31–35.

53. See Eric Voegelin, *Plato* (Baton Rouge: Louisiana State University Press, 1966), 181.

of seeing these animals moving on their own and engaged in some competition befitting their physique (cf. 19b5–c1 with *Republic* 472d4–e5). Likewise, he wishes to hear described fully their city of yesterday engaged competitively with other cities, and in the course of this both militarily and diplomatically rendering due return for its citizens' nurture and education (19b3–c8). What Socrates-L tells Timaeus he wants is quite similar to what Socrates-E begged Glaucon *not* to demand of him in *Republic* 5, viz., actual life breathed into his theoretical city. As he explains to Critias and Hermocrates, he himself could never perform this encomiastic task sufficiently; but neither could any of the poets (who lack knowledge) or sophists (who lack experience). This leaves men like them, who are peculiarly qualified in virtue of practical experience combined with philosophical understanding. This is why he obliged them as he did yesterday. Hermocrates here speaks one of his two times in the trilogy, manifesting his eager readiness. He and the rest now submit their proposal, which Socrates approves (19c9–20d6).

One, two, three, but where is the fourth? That was Socrates' question at the outset. This opening can be read figuratively, as alluding to the elliptical structure of the tetralogy as a whole. But if we think of this structure in the light of the higher themes of the *Timaeus*, Socrates' words can evoke the idea of mathematical growth in three dimensions stopping short of a fourth stage by which solids come into motion.[54] And this is just what Socrates wants: to contemplate his motionless city come to life. The city of the *Republic*, without the considerations Socrates develops in Books 5–7, remains a static ideal. On the more fundamental plane of his question about justice, Socrates eventually articulates its realization not in the terms of a fantasy of philosophical political rule, but rather as the attention paid to the lifeless paradigm by an individual, living man (592a10–b6). In the *Timaeus* and *Critias*, he adopts a more leisurely approach to this problem. A heavenly paradigm is developed first in detail as a model for a hypothetically true historical precedent for actual political life. Only real living people like Hermocrates, and others indirectly present to this conversation and able to invoke Memory to recall this tradition, can carry out the poetic and practical work left undone by him and Critias.[55]

---

54. See Klein, *Meno*, 191–202.
55. Cf. Cicero, *De Republica* I.8 (13) with II.1 (3)

Part III
Criticisms and Alternatives

13

Plato *Absconditus*

Lloyd P. Gerson

One traditional and reasonable way of reading Plato, endorsed explicitly and implicitly by countless scholars, is this: Plato began writing his dialogues under the inspiration of his teacher, Socrates. His earliest works articulate that inspiration in a methodology of inquiry and a number of specific claims conveniently labeled "Socratic paradoxes." As Plato began to reflect on the presuppositions of both the methodology and the claims, he began to take bold and original steps in metaphysical and epistemological construction. The world-view expressing these steps is contained basically in what are termed his 'middle dialogues', including the *Symposium, Republic, Phaedrus,* and *Cratylus.* At some point or points along the way, Plato began to reflect critically on this world-view. The distillation of this self-criticism is contained in the first part of his dialogue *Parmenides.* Subsequently, Plato began a sort of reconstruction project, retaining both the original Socratic inspiration and the basic principles of the middle-period constructive phase, but also including some bold and complex new moves.

I offer this intentionally bland sketch of a family of views with many varieties in order to get at their common assumptions. The first assumption is that over a philosophical career spanning perhaps fifty years, Plato's thinking developed or changed in some ways and that this development is reflected in the dialogues. That there should be *some* development in Plato's thinking is of course prima facie plausible. Nevertheless, this assumption has been doubted. The second assumption is that Plato's developing philosophy is expressed through the principal character in each dialogue. This is of course usually Socrates, although the list of Platonic 'mouthpieces' includes also the characters Parmenides and Timaeus in the dialogues named after them, The Eleatic Stranger in the *Sophist,* and the Athenian Stranger in the *Laws.*

The antimouthpiece school of interpretation, as I understand it, questions both assumptions. It evinces skepticism about development in Plato's thinking or in our ability to read off a development within the dialogues. It also denies that there are grounds or conclusive grounds for inferring from the words of any character in any dialogue what their author thinks. Of course, it is not enough to make the uncontentious points that development is not provable and that, logically speaking, there is no direct inference from the words of the character Socrates to the mind of Plato. One must provide reasons for thinking that these claims are not so.

There are two pieces of evidence typically adduced to bolster the position of the antimouthpiece theorists. These are the passages in the *Phaedrus* in which writing is criticized and the passage in the *Seventh Letter* in which Plato, presumably here speaking *in propria persona*, appears to undercut any inclination we might have to take the dialogues as truly representing his views. I think both passages have been seriously misused by antimouthpiece theorists and others.

In the *Phaedrus* passage (274c–277a), Socrates recounts in a myth the discovery of writing by the god Theuth of Egypt. The god praises writing for its ability to improve the memory and to make us wise. The king of Egypt in reply denies that writing has these benefits. In fact, he says, it will promote forgetfulness not memory. Writing is in fact an aid to reminding (ὑπομνήσεως) not remembering (μνήμης). It promotes the appearance of wisdom and not wisdom itself. Socrates proceeds to gloss this criticism in the following way. Writing something down can only remind us of what we already know. It does not itself communicate or contain knowledge. Further, writing cannot defend or explain itself. It is constantly in need of its "father's" support. Writing is compared with a superior form of λόγος, namely, "living, breathing" discourse or speech, "written down" with knowledge in the soul of the hearer (276a5–6). Writing, it is said, is an image (εἴδωλον) of speech.

Socrates then compares the one who knows the just, noble, and the good with the prudent farmer. Like the farmer, who will plant where and when it is appropriate and will refrain from useless activities, the one who knows will not take writing seriously (οὐκ σπουδῇ) because words cannot speak in their own defense and they cannot teach the truth adequately. When he does write, it will be for amusement (παιδιᾶς χάριν), storing up reminders for old age.

That writing should be an image of speech is somewhat puzzling. In addition, it is puzzling what it means to say that speech is written down "with knowledge" in the soul of the learner. Is the knowledge in the teacher or in the learner? A moment's reflection should incline us to the view that it is the former, for spoken words cannot be the knowledge itself and accordingly it is difficult to see how knowledge would be communicated in addition to the spoken words.[1] Two points about the claim that writing is an image of speech are particularly relevant. First, this cannot mean that everything that is written is based upon a previous spoken bit of discourse. Second, if writing is an image of speech, it also must be true that speech is an image, presumably, of the knowledge that is in the soul of the teacher. I shall return to this in due course.

For the moment, however, the main point is how characterizing writing as amusement or play in relation to speech should affect our reading of Plato's di-

---

1. Charles L. Griswold, *Self-Knowledge in Plato's Phaedrus* (New Haven and London: Yale University Press, 1986), 210–11, seems to take the knowledge as being in the learner.

alogues. It goes without saying that if Socrates, in making this critique of writing, is *not* expressing the view of the author of the dialogue, then the antimouthpiece theorist can hardly infer from these words that Plato does not take writing seriously. There does not in fact seem to be any nonquestion-begging way of taking seriously the denigration of writing on the basis of antimouthpiece theory. On the other hand, if we wish to take the passage seriously, it is obviously important to try to understand its implications for our interpretation of Plato's own writings.

I take it that the claim that written words cannot speak in their own defense does not compromise even slightly the truth-value of statements. The claim that they cannot teach the truth adequately is, I presume, essentially equivalent to the claim that writing does not communicate or contain knowledge. But if, as Plato says in the *Republic,* knowledge is an infallible state of immediate cognition of Forms, then the truth-value of statements made with words is untouched even if we agree that they do not communicate knowledge. In the multilayered hierarchical Platonic universe, it is simply a *nonsequitur* to claim that if knowledge does not follow from hearing words, then the words have no meaning or even that the words, when put together in statements, do not have a truth-value. I am here for the moment leaving aside the numerous forms of discourse that are not assertoric statements, such as the stories, questions, exhortations, and so on in the dialogues. I am not claiming that, whereas statements have truth-value, these have no meaning at all or that there are not statements that might be extracted from them. I do not, in other words, wish to hold that everything said, even by the principal mouthpiece in any dialogue, can be straightforwardly read as representing a specific doctrine of Plato.

The claim by Socrates that one who knows will not take written words seriously should be read in this context. He will not expect words to communicate knowledge and for the reasons just given, this has nothing to do with the truth-value of the words. I conclude, therefore, without gainsaying the superiority of spoken to written discourse for Plato, that the *Phaedrus* passage does not warrant us in holding that Plato does not mean what Socrates says in the dialogues.

The *Seventh Letter* presents a slightly different issue. In the famous philosophical passage of the letter (341b ff.) Plato complains that those who claim to know the matters to which he, Plato, is now devoting himself (σπουδάζω) are mistaken. Whether they claim to have gained this knowledge directly from him or indirectly, they understand nothing. Plato then claims that he has written no treatise (σύγγραμμα) on these matters, because, unlike other studies (μαθήματα), it cannot be put into words (ῥητόν).

A number of points need to be stressed regarding this passage. First, the present tense in the verb σπουδάζω at the very least allows the interpretation that Plato is referring to his "current research interests" as opposed to previous interests that, so far as we know from what he says, may have been the subject of extensive writings. Second, Plato says he has written no treatise on these matters. It is clear neither that the word σύγγραμμα can refer to dialogues nor what "these matters" indicate. But there is simply no warrant for assuming that "these matters" refers to philosophy in general or to everything included in the dialogues.[2] Third, Plato says that the matters that he is studying cannot even be put into words, but can be grasped only after a long period of instruction when all of a sudden, like a spark, the knowledge leaps into the soul of the hearer where it is then self-sustaining. The word ῥητόν normally indicates spoken words, although it could have the general sense of "expressible in words" in which case it *could* include written words. But there is no meaning for this word in fourth-century Greek so far as I know that implies *only* written words. It is far more likely, given that the clause in which the word is contained explains the reason (γάρ) Plato wrote no treatise, that he is referring to the fact that the matter under discussion is not or ought not to be communicated in words at all. In that case, this passage cannot be used to denigrate the written word *as opposed to* the spoken word as a vehicle for Platonic philosophy. Thus, it would be reasonable to suppose that the matter of current research and on which there is no treatise is very esoteric and narrow. And it would be unreasonable to suppose that the subject that cannot be put into words is philosophy itself.

Plato then proceeds to make some puzzling statements (341d ff.). He says that if there ever were to be something written or said (γραφέντα ἢ λεχθέντα) about these matters, he would be the best to do it. For one thing, this confirms the above interpretation that Plato is not here favoring spoken over written communication. For another, these words make it implausible in the extreme that he is talking about philosophy in general. But then Plato qualifies his reluctance to communicate, saying in effect that it would be useless to try to express his thoughts "to the many" (πρὸς τοὺς πολλούς). There would only be a point in expressing them to "some few" (τισιν ὀλίγοις), namely, those who, with a little "guidance" (ἐνδείξεως), are able to find out the truth themselves. Assuming that the qualification "to the many" should be understood in the previous, implicitly blanket repudiation, that leaves open the possibility that Plato is willing either to write or to speak to "some few." It is on the assumption that the dialogues belong to communication for the "many" that it is inferred that they do not contain Plato's own thinking. Such an interpretation, however, is a monumental *non sequitur* for Plato is presumably here still talking about his "current research interests."

Next, Plato offers to speak to his interlocutor at greater length about the subject (342a ff.). He says that there is a "true doctrine" (τις λόγος ἀληθής) which is enunciated many times before that "stands before" (ἐναντίος) anyone who dares to write about "these matters." The true doctrine is, briefly, that in addition to things knowable, there is knowledge, a name, a description, and an image. There is much that needs to be said about this account and examples used to illustrate it. For my purposes, it suffices to point out that the fivefold distinction here made is neither esoteric nor can it be said to be unknown to readers of the dialogues. That is, Plato is not now saying in a private letter what he declined to say in his public writings. Then what is the point of saying it and why does this distinction "stand before" anyone who dares to write about "these matters"? I would suggest that the 'true doctrine' is a

---

2. This is what Kenneth Sayre, *Plato's Literary Garden* (London and Notre Dame: Notre Dame University Press, 1995), xiii, takes the passage to mean.

propaedeutic to a more advanced or esoteric doctrine of "the first and highest principles of nature" (τῶν φύσεως ἄκρων καὶ πρώτων), as Plato later calls it (344d4). In addition to the true doctrine being familiar from the dialogues, Plato here explicitly indicates it as a necessary step to the more advanced one. In short, the true doctrine explained here is neither the highest doctrine nor irrelevant to the highest. Therefore, on the basis of the *Seventh Letter*, we may insist that the dialogues do not express the advanced doctrine. But far from indicating that the dialogues do not express Plato's own thoughts, the letter suggests that the dialogues contain information necessary to understanding the subject of Plato's current interest.

If neither the *Phaedrus* nor the *Seventh Letter* provides evidence that we should not regard Socrates and the others as mouthpieces for Plato, what other sorts of considerations might be adduced in favor of the antimouthpiece view? One sort of argument, not based upon particular texts, relies upon an analogy between the dialogues and dramas. According to this line, just as we cannot infer the views of the author of a drama from what the characters in the drama do and say so we cannot infer the views of Plato from what the characters in the dialogue do and say.

I believe the analogy is misleading. One cannot infer the views of the author of a drama from the drama itself basically because representation is not argument. I mean that a dramatist writes a script in which characters are represented as saying things or holding certain views. What the character says is, normally, a function of the character. For example, Hedda Gabler speaks as the character Hedda Gabler would, in Ibsen's mind, speak. Is it not the same for the character Socrates? Yes and no. It is true that Socrates the character says things that the character Socrates would, in Plato's mind, say. But Socrates, as well as the other leading interlocutors in the dialogues, also produces arguments. Arguments have a life of their own. Of course, they are in a sense Socrates' arguments. But they are Socrates' arguments in the same sense that if I argued that "if A is greater than B, and B is greater than C, then A is greater than C" it would be *my* argument. Just because an argument has a life of its own, it is not character bound.[3]

Freeing the argument from the character who expresses it does not mean that we have to take arguments "out of context." But there are contexts and there are contexts. Two egregious examples of taking arguments out of context are in the *Phaedo* and in the *Parmenides*. I think it can rather easily be shown that the individual arguments for the immortality of the soul in the *Phaedo* and the individual arguments against the theory of Forms in the first part of the *Parmenides* cannot adequately be viewed in isolation from their argumentative context. Thus, in the *Phaedo* an implicit premise in one argument is a conclusion in another. And in the *Parmenides* one argument has to be combined with another to produce a destructive dilemma. The complexity or scope of an argument is not gainsaid by detaching it from the characters who express it. By contrast,

---

3. The best example of Plato's intense awareness of the independent life of an argument is the *Phaedo* where the vicissitudes of the λόγος are closely followed and where μισολογία is the constant temptation.

what some mean when they say that an argument in a dialogue cannot be taken out of context is "dramatic context." In my view, this amounts to an attempt to rebind the argument to character so as to compromise its independence. But this is as if in the case of the logical argument cited above, one were to retort, "but he is only saying that to make you think he is smart." A moment's reflection should lead us to see that the purpose for enunciating an argument is quite independent of the validity of the argument or the truth value of the premises.

Perhaps it will be replied in this regard that arguments in themselves do not amount to claims, including the conclusions of arguments. That is, Plato might endorse the validity of an argument without committing himself to the truth of its premises. Two things need to be said here. First, endorsing the validity of an argument constitutes a claim itself. Second, the premises of some of the arguments in the dialogues are fraught with ambiguity. A relatively simple example is in the *Meno*. There Socrates argues that if virtue is knowledge, then it is teachable. If it is teachable, then there are teachers of it. But there do not seem to be teachers of it. So, it does not seem to be teachable and so it does not seem to be knowledge. There are at least two ambiguities evident here, the meaning of "teachable" and the meaning of "knowledge." In this case, we need to pay close attention to the text to see in what sense of "teach," if any, Socrates is claiming that virtue is teachable, and in what sense not. Sorting these out leaves us with two consistent claims, not without any claims. But these are Socrates' claims, it will be urged, not necessarily those of Plato. Here we come to the heart of the mouthpiece dispute.

It seems clear enough that the question of whether the claims of Socrates are claims of Plato is inextricably bound up with the question of why Plato wrote dialogues. Certainly, Plato could have written treatises in which it was clear that he was expressing his own views. Since he did not, both mouthpiece and antimouthpiece theorists should supply an account of the relation of the contents of the dialogues to the purposes of their author. It is obviously question-begging for me to assume an account that makes the dialogues a means to Plato's goal of expressing doctrine. On the other hand, there is *no* account that entails, or even makes likely, the claim that Plato does not hold the doctrines argued for by the principal interlocutors in the dialogues. So, what I shall do is just assume the correctness of the antimouthpiece account of the purpose of the dialogues and show that this is not inconsistent with what the mouthpiece theorist holds. I think that is all that needs to be shown.

The task I set for myself may appear too easy. It will only appear so if one supposes a version of the mouthpiece view that no one I believe holds. After all, as we have seen, developmentalism is a natural adjunct to the mouthpiece theory. So, the mouthpiece theorist is bound to agree that many of the claims made in the dialogues are such that Plato was not so wedded to them that he was unwilling to change them. Relatedly, there is obviously an infinite gradation of strength of commitment that a philosopher may have to a particular claim or argument. Who would presume to know what the precise degree was for Plato in each case?

There is yet a deeper point that both should moderate the mouthpiece theorist's position and also insulate it from captious criticism. No λόγος in any dialogue is equivalent to ἐπιστήμη. I do not think anyone, on the basis of the dialogues, can suppose that Plato is communicating knowledge to his readers by words. After all, that is exactly what Socrates says cannot be done. It is what the *Phaedrus* disparages and the *Seventh Letter* implies is impossible. To hold otherwise would not merely open one to attack by antimouthpiece theorists but would, in my opinion, make hopeless any explanation of the motive for using the dialogue form. So, at best, the claims in the dialogues do not constitute or express the knowledge that Plato supposes he possesses. For example, we are not warranted in inferring from the argument for the tripartition of the soul in the *Republic* that Plato thinks he knows, that is, has ἐπιστήμη, that the soul has three parts. There is no such thing. On the other hand, there is no evidence I know of, including, as we have seen, the *Phaedrus* passage and the *Seventh Letter* passage, to lead us to doubt that Plato thought that "the soul has three parts" is true. But this is the truth of a true δόξα, not the truth of ἐπιστήμη.

The antimouthpiece theorist holds that the dialogues have a protreptic function. I agree. Where we evidently disagree is on the issue of whether having a protreptic function is inconsistent with expressing doctrine. I think it will be conceded that there is no inconsistency in having a protreptic motive and expressing doctrine. But I think that we can plausibly say more. To begin, a protreptic motive is inseparable from *some* doctrine, such as that, to put it generally, philosophy is valuable or worth doing. Is it the position of the antimouthpiece theorist that we cannot from the dialogues themselves infer that their author believes *that*? Perhaps it is. But in that case, we either have to withdraw adherence to the protreptic motive and settle for complete skepticism about the purpose of the dialogues, or else we have to attribute another motive to Plato for writing the dialogues, namely, the futility of philosophical argument. The latter might just be plausible if all the dialogues were like the second part of the *Parmenides*, consisting of apparently perfectly poised counterarguments. But they are not. There are many, many arguments and claims made in the dialogues that are not refuted or gainsaid or undercut by the mouthpiece or by anyone else. It seems difficult to square the expression of these with an invitation to assume what would be, in effect, a Pyrrhonian stance by Plato.

Supposing, more reasonably, that the antimouthpiece theorist adheres to the view that the dialogues have a protreptic function, then Plato wishes to write dialogues that will lead readers to regard the unexamined life as not worth living or, to put it less tendentiously, to pursue philosophy. But if Plato thinks philosophy is worth pursuing, then Plato also must have some view about what philosophy is and why it is worth pursuing by human beings. The antimouthpiece theorist who accepts the protreptic function of the dialogues must say that there is no reason to believe that any character in any dialogue expresses Plato's views about these matters. I think it must be recognized how strange a position this is. I am not here referring to specific doctrines about, say, what a definition of a Form is supposed to be or about how knowledge differs from belief, but about more general doctrines regarding the sort of things that must be true if philosophy really is the best sort of activity for human beings. If we agree on the protreptic function and we can infer these general doctrines from the claims in the dialogues, what possible reason could one give to divert us from taking the next step, namely, that, in all probability, these are their author's beliefs? I can think of none. In addition, the natural tendency to take this next step should be strengthened by recognizing that attributing such beliefs to the author need not amount to attributing to him claims to know that these beliefs are true.

It will perhaps be said in reply that the main thrust of the antimouthpiece argument is not to deny the legitimate attribution of very broad philosophical views to Plato, but rather to deny attributing to him the specific and contentious claims made in the dialogues, such as those regarding the nature and ultimate disposition of the human soul, the Forms, love, knowledge and belief, language, virtue and the good life, the best society, and so on. According to the antimouthpiece proponent, on the basis of the dialogues alone there is no more reason to think that Plato believed in the immortality of the soul than that he did not.

I think it is a salutary first step in evaluating this startling position to ask the following question. If Plato was not intending to reveal his own mind in having his central character, Socrates, argue for the immortality of the soul, then what was he doing? Let us not forget that in the *Apology* Socrates expresses an agnostic position with regard to the ultimate disposition of the soul. Then, in the *Phaedo,* the *Republic,* and the *Phaedrus* he argues for its immortality. And in the *Statesman,* the *Timaeus,* and the *Laws* we find other principal interlocutors expressing beliefs in the soul's immortality. Now one might hold that the arguments used—where there are arguments—are not good ones. But that is question-begging unless one can show that Plato realized they were not good. It is as if one were to take the absurd position that we can only attribute a belief to Plato if it is the conclusion of a demonstrative argument. If we reject such a stringent requirement, then we are left with the situation of an author, writing dialogues to draw people to philosophy, who has Socrates give reasons for believing in the immortality of the soul. If he does not wish his readers to accept these reasons, then it is either because he thinks there are no reasons or that they are bad ones. But in either case that would constitute an intentional misdirection that is, also on the evidence of the dialogues, the essence of sophistry, and the antithesis of the view that philosophy is a rational activity. Either we have Plato giving what he thinks are good reasons for believing in the immortality of the soul without himself adhering to that belief, or giving bad reasons for believing in the immortality of the soul and tempting people to accept these reasons. Both of these positions seem to me to be, without strong supporting evidence, intrinsically implausible. It is true that a radically antidevelopmentalist position would provide some support, but then there is no reason to take such a position other than that it supports the antimouthpiece theory.

Indeed, I would claim that the antidevelopmentalist position is a positive hindrance to the philosophical appreciation of the dialogues. When, for example, the dialogues do say manifestly contrary things, the antidevelopmentalist position urges us not to probe for the philosophical reasons for the contrariety. It discourages us from trying to know the mind of the philosopher who wrote the dialogues. In effect, it cuts off the dialogue between author and reader that should, I think, be the principal dialogue of interest to philosophers. If, by contrast, one asks, as is natural, why the character (not the historical figure) *Socrates* holds the things he does, then I fail to see how one could continue to distinguish the answer to such questions from the views of the author of the dialogues.

Once we recognize that it is not necessary to take the claims made in the dialogues as claims to knowledge by Plato, such initial plausibility as the antimouthpiece theory possesses simply evaporates. We do not have to insist that Plato believes that he knows that pleasure is not the good or that a person is essentially a soul or that Forms are the objects of knowledge in order to hold that, minimally, he believes that these propositions are more likely to be true than not. We can surely say that if Plato did not intend for his readers to attribute to him belief in the truth of these and many other propositions then he failed miserably. If he did intend for his readers to be "Platonists" though he himself was not one, then "sophist" is the most polite term that one could honestly use for Plato.

Even if Plato believed that he knew the truth about such matters, we need not insist that he thought he was communicating knowledge in the λόγοι of the dialogues.[4] Relevant here is the passage from the *Seventh Letter* (342d) in which Plato distinguishes knowledge and cognition generally from λόγος. But even if the objects of knowledge are not λόγοι, we can still recognize the latter as including propositions to which we can assign truth-values. It may well be the case that if we assume that Plato believed that "x is f" is true, that he believed this only with or according to a suitable interpretation of the meaning of "x" and the meaning of "f," and only under certain circumstances, and so on. Holding that Socrates is, generally, a Platonic mouthpiece does not commit us to ignoring the need to interpret the literal claims made in the dialogues. After interpretation, however, comes the philosophical work of criticism and judgment. In my view, the impossible burden borne by the antimouthpiece theorist is holding that, on the basis of the dialogues alone, Plato must be accounted indifferent to the conclusions arrived at by his readers. They must hold that the dialogues do not intend to move the readers in any direction that can be described in terms of adherence to propositional claims. If Plato was *not* indifferent, then that was because he himself did adhere to certain propositional claims. We should recognize that even if we wanted to show that, in some case, Plato did not believe that "x is f" but rather that "it is good or useful for people to believe that 'x is f'," then *that*, too, is a propositional claim.[5]

---

4. Michael Frede, "The Literary Form of the *Sophist*," in *Form and Argument in Late Plato*, ed. Christopher Gill and Mary Margaret McCabe (Oxford: Clarendon Press, 1996), 135–151, makes a similar point. He argues that Plato used the dialogue form in order to avoid authoritarian pronouncements on philosophical matters. But making claims and arguments is not equivalent to claiming authority.

5. I have in mind here, for example, the tenets of the civic theology in Book 10 of the *Laws*. Even if Plato himself did not believe these, it seems very difficult to deny that he thought it useful that citizens believe these. If it is held that he did not believe even this much, then one wonders what sort of account of the *Laws* would follow.

The antimouthpiece camp must hold that the history of Platonism rests upon a colossal mistake. Within this supposed mistaken history I include the testimony of Aristotle. The only point I wish to make in this regard is that Aristotle attributes many views to Plato, some based on the dialogues and some based on the "unwritten teachings," some possibly on both. I do not wish to argue here that Aristotle is an unchallengeable interpreter of Plato. I only point out that Aristotle takes the dialogues as an expression of Plato's views. This is, I believe, particularly significant given that Aristotle claims to have an additional source for Plato's views, namely, his oral teaching. The fact that the oral teaching is different, though consistent, with the doctrines attributed to Plato on the basis of the dialogues indicates the irreducible status of the latter as evidence.

Regarding Platonists after Aristotle, it is obvious that the same argument would have less force, since the Aristotelian testimony itself becomes evidence for Plato's teachings. A very different sort of argument can, however, be made. It is that "dogmatic" Platonism contains an impressively coherent set of beliefs. These are largely derived from the dialogues. Therefore, if Plato intended to promulgate ἀπορία or suspension of belief based upon balanced opposite assertions, he was a spectacular failure. He wrote dialogues in which a thousand-year tradition found a positive philosophy. I hope it will not be thought captious or irrelevant to mention here that, for example, this is exactly what neither Dr. Johnson nor any other interpreter has ever found in Shakespeare.

The antimouthpiece theory gives us a Plato *absconditus*, a Plato hidden from view behind the dialogues. The theory is based on no evidence that is not question-begging about Plato's intentions. If, nevertheless, Plato is intentionally hiding himself, he is a philosopher either with no views or with views diverging from those easily derived from the dialogues. I find the former alternative frankly preposterous; I find the latter perverse. I do not claim that Plato thought that knowledge was equivalent to belief in the propositions expressed in the dialogues. I do not even claim that Plato was a Platonist, especially a "dogmatic" Platonist. But I do hold that, in all probability, Socrates and the other principal interlocutors of the dialogues express opinions Plato himself endorsed at the time of writing. No doubt, at the end of his life Plato revised or even repudiated much that he had earlier thought was true. But in order to revise or repudiate one's own views, one must have views in the first place.

14

Who Speaks for Plato? Everyone!

Erik Ostenfeld

I.

It seems to be a widespread, if not general, opinion these days that Plato has no spokesman among the interlocutors of his dialogues.[1] Edelstein was one of the early advocates of this view: Plato cannot be identified with any of his characters and always preserves his anonymity.[2] And, of course, Plato had no high opinion of the written word: it is naive to write manuals with the intent of offering "something clear and permanent," and if the moral philosopher does write, it is not with serious intent, but by way of pastime and as a reminder (*Phdr.* 275c, 276d, *Rep.* 536c). Indeed, if the *Seventh Letter* is genuine, or to be believed, Plato never has committed his serious philosophy to writing (*Epistle* vii 341c4–6, 344c, cf. perhaps *Republic* 599a).[3]

We have witnessed a shift in Platonic exegesis that has until recently been based on the almost unquestioned premise that Socrates and, perhaps, Parmenides, the Eleatic Stranger and the Athenian Stranger were mouthpieces for Plato. This seemed a natural inference from the fact that Socrates was the admired teacher of Plato and, indeed, generally the hero of the early and middle dialogues. In the later dialogues he is replaced by literary characters that lead

1. E.g., Griswold (1986), 12. Cf. also G. Press's useful synopsis in *The Southern Journal of Philosophy* 34 (1996), 507–32.

2. *American Journal of Philology* 83 (1962), 1–22.

3. *Republic*, for instance, could be viewed as play. Thus its form undermines what is said by its hero, Socrates: it belongs to a genre (*mimesis*) that is to be banned in the ideal society (Kosman), it does not instantiate the philosophical method prescribed in the Line and elsewhere in the *Republic*. The reason, it may be suggested, is that Plato uses not only arguments but also habituation and praise to persuade (cf. *Laws* 663c), to which one might add play (*Paidia* 536c1, 602b8, cf. *Parmenides* 137b, *Timaeus* 59d, *Laws* 685a, 769a). The *Republic* itself is a likely myth as the *Timaeus* (*Republic* 501e, 376d, *Timaeus* 26c8) and *qua* likely myth also play (*Timaeus* 59cd). Though the one is a utopia, the other popular science, both are about probable truths of generation. As Plato says, it is a question of finding a suitable *logos* as a basis for what one wants to say (*Timaeus* 26a5–6, 26d7–27a1). Hence, we find him playing with, e.g., *eikones* in the *Republic*.

the conversation in a way that makes it difficult not to hear Plato's voice. However, the recent discovery (or rediscovery) of the importance of literary form for the philosophical content has swung the pendulum back to Schleiermacher.[4] Or perhaps, we have come round full circle with a deeper insight, based on the intervening analytical experiences.

We are now no longer just studying the arguments in isolation, but are aware that it is relevant to an appreciation of their meaning and intention to see them in their context: literary, psychological, social, political, etc. Hence, the following (historical) questions are now fundamentally important: What was Socrates (the Platonic Socrates) doing? What was Plato aiming at? Do they differ in their aims?

I shall attempt to defend a third kind of answer to the question, Who is Plato's spokesman? It is neither Socrates (nor any other hero) nor is it none of the characters, but it is everyone.[5] I argue that this is the case in: the early antilogical aporetic dialogues, the narrated middle dialogues and the direct conversation of the late dialogues and finally in the nearly monologous *Timaeus*, *Critias* and the *Laws*. What we have, I shall argue, is Plato debating with himself (synchronically) and criticizing himself (diachronically).

Fundamentally, the reason for this view is that the dialogues are not treatises but works of art, which means that the characters, though generally inspired by historical persons, are, after all, creations of Plato's art and imagination. Hence, I think that the question, What did Plato mean? (as opposed to, What did Plato say?) is just as difficult to answer as, What did Aeschylus, Sophocles or Aristophanes mean?[6] Moreover, the special dialectical character of Plato's work and his scattered remarks about it makes it highly questionable to seek Plato's "meaning," if that means what it normally means, i.e., specific message. Of course, it is not denied that Plato may have intended something by writing what he did, but it is arguably not a specific dogma but of quite another order: to set the reader off thinking him/herself. He does not, as Socrates did not, see any point in offering his "meaning" ready as "take away" food. However, he does present alternative ways of thinking, ways that have various degrees of plausibility and that may stimulate our own thinking. This, it appears from the evidence, is the "message" which is really best viewed as the intention of the work. Hence, 'mouthpiece' and "spokesman" are perhaps awkward categories in this connection. If Plato is not communicating his views *via personae dramatis*, but making us think for ourselves *by means of* the *personae dramatis* should we not drop all talk of "spokesmen"?

I suggest that we keep the terminology of spokesman in spite of the slight oddity of not having a spokesman for exactly one specific view. The alternative, that Plato has no spokesman in the dialogues, seems much less attractive. In

---

4. *Introduction to the Dialogues of Plato*, tr.. W. Dobson (New York: Garland, 1973), 14.

5. I note that A. Bowen sees this as a possible alternative. However, he does not pursue it because of doubts as to the meaning of "mouthpiece": Plato does not say what the characters say (Griswold [1988], 59).

6. It is now realized that this question is much more difficult to solve than has previously been assumed. For instance it is now answered with scepticism or vaguely: the meaning is the whole play, etc. I shall return to the issue below.

that case it remains a total mystery what Plato meant, that is, in what direction and for what reason his thought went in a certain direction and not in others. Plato is not that "distant" and does not in general think that he should not write philosophy.[7] Also, and more specifically, Plato does not seem to have had any motive for concealing his thoughts.[8] Hence, I do think it is less absurd, and more in keeping with Plato's project, to maintain that what we have in the dialogues *as a whole* is Plato's meaning.

Considering that the dialogues can plausibly be viewed as art, there is a fairly close and interesting parallel in the interpretation of drama. It is today realized that the "meaning" of a tragedy by Sophocles or Euripides is not to be read off easily, say, from choral songs or elsewhere. This genre is in fact more problem-raising than problem-solving.[9] The characters have traditionally been taken too much as heroes or heroic, in spite of their "ruthless fixity of purpose." Hence, we now see a tendency to look to action rather than character. The latter is not a modern "personality" but a "mask." Also, irony understood as a gap between the apparent and the real is basic to Sophocles and not absent in Euripides.[10]

II.

Plato's dialogues are, formally, dialectical conversations. This means that we must understand them as such. The best source of help for assessing this genre is Aristotle, who describes several varieties of dialogic conversations in *Sophistic Refutations* 2, 9, and 11 and in *Topics* 8.5. He distinguishes four kinds: didactic, dialectical, examination, and eristic arguments. However, it is not easy to fit the dialogues into this framework, and it certainly requires that we specify the dialogue or at least the category of dialogue we are trying to square with Aristotle's kinds. The dialogues exhibit at least four distinct types of conversation: the antilogic of the early aporetic dialogues that is similar to but not identical with peirastic, the narrated and rather didactic but still dramatic dialogue of the middle dialogues, the didactic dialogue of the late dialogues, and finally the all-but-monologous *Timaeus, Critias,* and *Laws*.[11]

If we follow Aristotle and take it that peirastic is found in the antilogical (early) dialogues, we must not assume that the questioner is committed to the argument.[12] The argument belongs to the respondent personally. It is he who is being examined. Hence, it is not Socrates' argument. It has been argued that *a fortiori* it is not Plato's argument either. Also, knowledge being a personal mat-

---

7. The *Seventh Letter* (344d) deals with certain principles. See also Morrow 112 f.

8. The remarks of the *Twelfth Letter* (probably not genuine) and *Second Letter* (also of doubtful authencity) are contradicted by *Seventh Letter*.

9. H. Friis Johansen, 'Den attiske tragedie', in Thomsen I, 95–7, 114. The same scholar also concludes that the choruses are never mouthpieces for the author (*Aischylos* 10).

10. Buxton 12 ff. and 16–9.

11. Cf n.16 below.

12. See Aristotle *Sophistical Refutations,* 183a37–183b8 and *Top.* viii (ch. 5 esp.). I have discussed the peirastic character of Socrates' dialectic "Socrates' Argument Strategies and Aristotle's *Topics* and *Sophistical Refutations*" in *Methexis* 9, 1996.

ter, it would be pointless for Plato to state his own views.[13] All this has some truth in it. However, although Socrates refutes others, he also at the same time refutes himself (*Euthyphro* 11e, *Menexenus* 80c–d) or tests himself (*Charmides* 166d). Moreover, Socrates and his interlocutors do the investigation in common.[14] The dialogues are aporetic (fail in reaching definitions), but whose view is it that: "one must never harm anyone," "it is better to suffer harm than do it," "virtue is knowledge," "the virtues are one," "nobody does wrong willingly," or, for that matter, "pleasure is the good," etc.? Insofar as such propositions are proved they are *homologiai* of the parties to the discussion, i.e. both interlocutor and Socrates. In that case it would be fair to conclude that we have Plato's discussion with himself, perhaps with some emphasis on certain lines of thought, the dialogue being an artistic whole, composed by him. The *Laches* gives us a good example of the progression of a dialogue.

However, Socrates also offers (what seems, in some cases, to be intentional) fallacious arguments, in the later early dialogues (*Hippias Major* 295a ff., *Protagoras, Republic* I, *Gorgias*).[15] This could, among other things, indicate that Plato gradually saw the limitations of what began as his hero, an interpretation that fits in with the view of the dialogues presented in this chapter.

The fact is that the middle dialogues (*Symposium, Phaedo, Republic,* and *Parmenides*) are narrated. They are not elenctic but use the method of hypothesis.[16] Socrates still has interlocutors that resist his questioning and obviously hold opposite views to Socrates. In the *Parmenides* Socrates is even reduced to silence himself. Plato, the author of these dialogues, clearly thinks that Aristophanes, Eryximachos, Simmias, Cebes, Thrasymachus and Parmenides all have some good points that must be considered before an answer can be reached on the subjects at hand. Hence, again, these dialogues may fairly be said to be Plato's conversation with himself. He is thinking aloud. Everybody

---

13. Cf. M. Frede (1992).

14. E.g., *Protagoras* 358a, *Laches* 189c, *Charmides* 175b.

15. Let me refer to an inspiring article by G. Klosko in *Classical Quarterly* ns 33 (1983) in which I find useful distinctions, though I cannot quite agree with the use made of them. Thus he distinguishes helpfully, first between Plato the author and Socrates the character, and hence we get the meaning for Plato and the meaning for Socrates (367). Secondly, if I understand him correctly, we are offered another distinction between Socrates' point of view and that of his interlocutor (equivalent to the "meaning within the context of the dialogue as a whole?"). Anyhow, I assume that Klosko identifies three angles from which a given Socratic proof can be seen: i.e., from the point of view of Plato, of Socrates or of the interlocutor. However, when Klosko goes on to argue that the interlocutor's point of view is criterial for deciding whether Socrates argues fallaciously and sophistically (with intent), then one must disagree. Although the *elenchus* is person-directed it cannot solely be the interlocutor's conception of what is said by Socrates that decides whether Socrates deceives. A given suspicious argument may equally fool Socrates and the interlocutor. Hence, we cannot use the fact, if it is one, that a respondent takes an argument in a different (fallacious) sense from that intended by Socrates to accuse Socrates of arguing fallaciously and unfairly. We seem forced to look for parallels when we encounter suspicious arguments to see whether Socrates can be assumed to know that a train of thought is defective.

16. I assume here Brandwood's chronology, i.e., the order but not the grouping of the dialogues. Methodologically, the *Symposium* ascent mirrors, in part, the *Republic* Line and Cave. However, the deductive part of dialectic is not in focus in the *Symposium*. Also, Socrates uses *elenchus* in the conversation with Agathon (199c–201c).

speaks for Plato. However, there are new elements such as long speeches, monologous myths and in the *Republic* II–X the dialogue is very didactic, the respondents being to a large extent "yes men," although they are not entirely without character.[17]

The late dialogues are all direct conversation.[18] Again the conversation is now very didactic and with large stretches of monologous stuff, virtually lectures, and myths (*Phaedrus, Politicus, Critias,* and *Timaeus*). Socrates no longer monopolizes the main part but gives way to the Eleatic Stranger, the Athenian Stranger, Timaeus and Parmenides. Who speaks for Plato here? Aristotle notes in connection with didactic dialogue that the reasoning is not from opinions of the respondent, who in this case must take things on trust, but from principles appropriate to each subject.[19] This does seem a fair description of the situation of the late dialogues, and it leaves us with the main part as the undisputed mouthpiece.[20] He is, of course, assisted by the "respondent," who never seriously questions anything said. However, insofar as there is virtually only one opinion advanced it seems arguable that, in a sense, everybody is Plato's mouthpiece at this stage, although that role is strictly speaking taken by the main speaker. This, of course, means that Timaeus in the *Timaeus* is Plato's voice.

III.

So far we have considered an answer to the question of this chapter in terms of the constraints of the particular dialogical genre that is at work in the dialogues. However, there are more general considerations that have already been mentioned above: insofar as the dialogues are pieces of art (even mimetic art[21]) we are led to assume that Plato subscribes to all he has written in a stronger sense than that involved by the simple fact that he is the author. Plato may be *sympathetic* to Socrates, but so he is to Protagoras, Cebes, Eryximachus, Timaeus, the Eleatic Stranger, and the Athenian, rather as Sophocles may be sympathetic to not only Oedipus, but also to Iocasta and even Creon. Moreover, it cannot be denied that Plato is interested also in Thrasymachus and Callicles. The characters of the dialogues pursue various lines of thought that Plato thought it worthwhile to pursue. In this sense all the views are Plato's views, even the false and fallacious ones.

---

17. Thus Glaucon is described as enterprising (357a), erotic (468b, 474d) and competitive (548e). Adeimantus, being a subsidiary figure, is not characterized directly, only through what he says. Actually, he seems less philosophical (all the meatier parts are left to Glaucon). His first contribution, the speech in Book 2 (362e–367e), bears the marks of being a sophistic *logos* and in fact he is the one that throughout the dialogue advances common sense (sophistic?) objections, e.g., to the community of children and women (449c ff.), to the happiness of the elite (419a ff.), to philosophy (487b ff.), and the question whether the ideal state is at all possible (471c ff.). He also corrects Socrates (e.g., 497c).

18. Again, Brandwood with some modifications. Cf. my *Forms, Matter and Mind*, 281–3.

19. Aristotle. *Sophistical Refutations* 165b1–4.

20. Cf. also *Phaedrus* 278a2–5.

21. As argued by Kosman (1992).

Thus if Socrates the character is arguing fallaciously, it may be either *bona fide* or *mala fide*.[22] In either case Plato must have had some purpose in letting him do this. If Socrates is innocently arguing fallaciously, we may be witnessing an intellectual limitation of the character.[23] Most of the characters in the dialogues have limitations. If, on the other hand Socrates elsewhere, in the same dialogue or earlier (if that can be established), argues correctly and we must assume that he is consciously arguing fallaciously, then we appear to have a choice between taking this either as a pedagogical device, or as a moral limitation.

However, whatever the explanation, as Plato as the author has chosen to let the characters act in the way they do, it is in the last resort Plato's responsibility. That is, at one level we have to take as Plato's even the arguments that are (consciously or otherwise) inconclusive, unsound or that rest on assumptions that seem un-Platonic or inconsistent with other views elsewhere ("nobody does wrong willingly" [*Protagoras*] rests on "pleasure is the good")—a situation most often met with in the early dialogues. This is, of course, frequently denied by the new Plato exegesis that claims that Plato hides behind the characters, irony, play, etc.

In fact, a contemporary author, like Aristotle, refers to the dialogues as (containing) Plato's views. This applies to all dialogues, early, middle, and late.[24] Hence, even monologous 'dialogues' where Socrates is passive or even absent like the *Timaeus* and the *Laws* are referred to when dealing with Plato's views. All characters are in a way the mouthpiece of Plato (not none or some or one), not in the sense that the views of every character are identical with Plato's views, but rather in the sense that Plato thought that the arguments advanced by each and every character deserved consideration in various degrees.[25] Just like a playwright who includes exactly the characters necessary for the "message" of his play. There is a further similarity with drama: the spectator or reader often knows more than the participants in the play or dialogue do. E.g., when a fallacious argument is advanced the reader may realize this even if it is unknown to the respondent or even the questioner.

IV.

One might object to the above interpretation that it is too generous, i.e., allowing Plato so many views that we are utterly at a loss as to what he really meant.

---

22. Judging from parallel arguments in the Corpus.

23. Not of course to be understood as a limitation of his moral character.

24. Thus Aristotle in his *Politics* refers to and discusses the *Republic* and the *Laws* on the assumption that they represent Plato's point of view (*Politicus* ii, 1–5, 6). But there are references to many other dialogues elsewhere. The following list is a selection: *Hippias Minor* 365–9 (1025a6 ff.), *Phaedo* 100b–e (991b3, cf. 1080a2), *Theaetetus* 178b–179a (1010b12), *Theaetetus* 181d (122b25 ff.), *Phaedrus* 245e (140b4), *Sophist* 237a, 254a (1026b14 f.), *Philebus* 60b–e (1172b28 f.), *Timaeus* 34b (1071b38–1072a3), *Timaeus* 53c ff. (325b20 ff.), *Republic* 511b (1095a31–33), *Republic* 401e–402a, *Laws* 653a ff. (1104b12), *Phaedrus* 245c and *Laws* 894e (1072a2).

One could imagine an objection that Aristotle is not the greatest humorist in the world and in addition or perhaps as a consequence, an outspoken enemy of metaphorical flourish, and that he could therefore conceivably have missed Plato's subtle reservations. Personally, I find this unbelievable in a man of Aristotle's calibre, who had been with Plato for 20 years.

25. Tigerstedt (100) rightly points out that one character, mostly Socrates, has the role of a leader.

He cannot, surely, entertain, say, both the opinion of Thrasymachus and that of Socrates? Either he is simply (too obviously) inconsistent or just a cynical skeptic? A plausible answer to this seems to be that Plato is neither, but that he is dialectically weighing the pros and cons, for, say, hedonism, the advantage of morality, or the nature and the immortality of the soul. However, it must be admitted that from the *Phaedo* and the *Republic* on he begins to feel more certain about these specific topics at any rate. Others are still in the oven. Plato does have his heroes or voices or perhaps a hierarchy of voices.[26]

It has already appeared that I am basically unhappy about ascribing "views" to Plato and I have also given some formal reasons for this based on genre and art in general. I would now like to return to the question why I would be disinclined to ascribe views or 'doctrines' to Plato on the basis of the content of his written work. The written word, we are told, is of little value for communicating important truths and we are warned of taking too seriously what is written (*Epistle vii* 341b–e, 344cd and *Phaedrus* 274–8, 275d). All of this is an antidote against being too dogmatic about Plato's views. However, we do have general and genuine warnings in the *Phaedrus* that the living speech with knowledge (dialectic) is *more excellent* than the written discourse, which is a kind of image (276), though even the living word does not constitute truth. Thus in *Epistle vii* we are told that true wisdom and understanding can only come by long study and reflection, aided normally by a teacher, who is himself still learning, a guide rather than an authoritative exponent. Then "like light flashing forth when a fire is kindled, it is born in the soul" (341cd). In brief, we should find out for ourselves, with a little guidance from a philosopher, whose words are sown like seeds. This was also the impression left on the audience at the lecture on the Good (Aristox. *Harm.* 2.20.16–31.3). Could and should we then take Plato's *written* work as containing a seed whence *new* words or arguments grow up in us (cf. *Phaedrus* 277a)? This seems to be the natural reading of the texts, but we must realize that we are one remove further from truth: "no sensible man will venture to express his deepest thoughts in words, especially in a form which is unchangeable, as is true of written characters" (*Epistle vii* 343a). They are at most reminders (*hypomnemata, Phaedrus* 276d). Words or arguments (*logoi*), spoken or written, are both weak, i.e., unsatisfactory (*Epistle vii* 343a1), but spoken words are less so. This weakness may then be interpreted generally as involvement in sense experience (Sayre 96) or more precisely as the vagueness of words and their conventional application (Morrow 69–70).

However, it is still a fact that Plato does not appear in the dialogues and does not have an easily identifiable mouthpiece. Interestingly, Kierkegaard similarly, perhaps inspired by Plato (*Epistle ii* 314c and *Epistle vii* 341c), writes in an afterword ("A first and final explanation") to *Concluding Unscientific Postscript:* "My pseudonymity or polyonymity has had no casual ground in my personality . . . but an essential one in the production itself. . . . The written word is, you may say, mine, but only in so far as I put the creative poetic-real individuality in the mouth of the character's view of life by the audibility of the dialogue."[27]

---

26. As the Middle Platonists formulated it, Plato is not *polydox* but *polyphone* (Stob. *Ecl.* 2.49/50 Wachsmuth).

27. Kierkegaard, *Samlede Værker* vol. vii. The translations are mine.

Kierkegaard then tells us that he is even further from his own work than a poet who is the author of the foreword, and then concludes: "Hence, there is not one word by me in the pseudonymous books." Also, in "On my literary activity" from 1851 Kierkegaard describes how he has set out in the maieutic mode, with aesthetic products, the whole pseudonymous productivity being maieutic. And in *The point of my literary activity* Kierkegaard reveals that "the aesthetic production is a deceit and in this lies the deeper meaning of pseudonymity" and "one can, with reference to old Socrates, deceive a man into truth . . . [i.e.] . . . you begin by accepting the conceit of the other at its face value."[28]

I am, in fact, suggesting that this strategy has sufficient similarities with Plato's reservations about his own production to be a fair description of what is going on in Plato too. However, even if this should be convincing, where does it leave us? Do we not end up in utter skepticism? How can we ever decide whether a given view is Plato's? Elsewhere and long ago I have argued that in the middle period and in the late period we have to look for *recurring patterns* of thought that we can be fairly sure have Plato's sympathy. The theory of forms and the priority of the soul over matter are surely, we feel, central Platonic tenets. Consistency must be applied here as a principle of interpretation. But this approach is limited by Plato's development. Hence it must be used within the three or four groups of dialogues identified by stylometric method.[29]

However, there is still a considerable element of play and irony (for instance in the myths) that has to be accounted for. What has been called "Platonic irony" is based on the authorial distance from the characters or the tension between surface meaning and deeper contextual meaning.[30] "Platonic irony" is of course not a term found in the Corpus but an authorial attitude towards the reader, displayed, I would argue, basically in the element of play (*paidia*), which is so pervasive in Plato's writings. Kierkegaard's irony is mixed: Platonic in its text-transcending, reader-oriented drive, Socratic insofar as it is his ambition to deceive the reader into truth by means of his aesthetic work. Whether Plato has exactly this purpose, i.e., to *deceive* his readers into truth, I doubt. Whatever Platonic irony, as opposed to Socratic irony, turns out to be, I expect it to be consonant with the interpretation of the dialogue as art that has been discussed above: it involves play and "distance" but not, as far as I can see, deception. This is not at all to deny that Plato's dialogues, e.g., the myths, have a charm that may carry us away. But this is something different from Socratic deception. In other words, I do not think that the Platonic irony, i.e., the "dis-

28. Kierkegaard, *Samlede Værker* vol. xiii 495 f. and 540 f.

29. *Forms, Matter and Mind* 5–6. We cannot, I think, use the criterion: attribution to Plato of most plausible intellectual development (Crombie I, 23). Who is to say what is "a plausible intellectual development?" What are we to do with, e.g., the *Protagoras* or the *Parmenides*? Also their relative chronology is a matter of dispute and thus of no help in serving as a basis for determining Plato's development. There are, of course, those who are unwilling to consider development at all.

30. See, e.g., Tigerstedt 95f. Cf. also his *Plato's Idea of Poetical Inspiration* 11ff. Another scholar dealing with this is Griswold (1986) 12–3. He rightly distinguishes this *reader* dependent irony from *Socratic* irony that is intradialogical, in the text so to speak. I would add that this irony is typically connected with a disavowal of knowledge and with heaping of praise on the interlocutor (*Republic* 336e f.) and indeed with play (*Symposium* 216e), though play is a feature shared with *Platonic* irony. (The reader should be warned that the Socratic-Platonic distinction is kept in the sequel.)

tance" of the author means that we cannot "rely on" the dialogue *as a whole.*
What Plato says about his work (e.g., in the *Phaedrus* and *Epistle vii*) does not
support such a claim; it seems on the contrary to go against it. Hence, insofar
as we base ourselves on this evidence, it does not seem that play and irony necessarily controvert the claim that Plato's mouthpiece is everyone appearing in
the dialogues. That is, everyone appearing in a dialogue offers "a little guidance," is a seed in the reader's mind, provoking him/her to reach a personal answer to problems raised by Plato.[31]

31. Cf. *Phaedrus* 276d, 278ab, *Epistle* vii 341c,e, 344b.

WORKS CITED

Brandwood, L. *The Chronology of Plato's Dialogues.* Cambridge: Cambridge University
    Press, 1990.
Buxton, R. G. A. *Sophocles.* Greece and Rome, New Surveys in the Classics, no. 16, Ox-
    ford: Clarendon, 1984.
Crombie, I. M. *Plato's Doctrines I–II.* London: Routledge and Kegan Paul, 1962.
Frede, M. "Plato's Arguments and the Dialogue Form." *Oxford Studies of Ancient
    Philology,* Suppl. Vol. (1992): 201–219.
Friis Johansen, H. "Den attiske tragedie" and "Den gamle komedie," in Thomsen.
———. *Aischylos.* Hjørring: Klassikerforeningen, 1989.
Griswold, C. *Self-knowledge in Plato's Phaedrus.* New Haven: Yale University Press, 1986.
———. ed. *Platonic Writings, Platonic Readings,* New York: Routledge, 1988.
Kierkegaard, S. *Samlede Værker.* Ed. A. B. Drachmann, J. L. Heiberg, and H. O. Lange,
    København: Gyldendal, 1901–06.
Klosko, G. "Fallacy and Sophistry in Plato." *Classical Quarterly* NS 33 (1983): 363–374.
Kosman, L. A. "Silence and Imitation in the Platonic Dialogue." *Oxford Studies in An-
    cient Philosophy* Suppl. Vol. (1992): 73–92.
Merlan, P. "Form and Content in Plato's Philosophy." *Journal of the History of Ideas*
    (1947): 406–430.
Morrow, G. R. *Plato. Epistles.* New York: Bobbs-Merrill, 1962.
Ostenfeld, E. N. *Forms, Matter and Mind. Three Strands of Plato's Metaphysics,* The
    Hague: Nijhoff, 1982.
———. "Socrates' Argument Strategies and Aristotle's *Topics* and *Sophistical Refuta-
    tions.*" *Methexis* 9 (1996): 43–57.
Press, G. "The State of the Question in the Study of Plato." *The Southern Journal of Phi-
    losophy* 34 (1996), 507–532.
———, ed. *Plato's Dialogues: New Studies and Interpretations.* Lanham, MD: Rowman
    & Littlefield, 1993.
Sayre, K. "Plato's Dialogues in the Light of the Seventh Letter," in Griswold, 1988.
Thomsen, R., ed. *Det Athenske Demokrati* I–II. Aarhus: Aarhus Universitets Forlag,
    1986.
Tigerstedt, E. N. *Interpreting Plato.* Stockholm: Almquist & Wiksell, 1977.

15

Interpreting the Platonic Dialogues

What Can One Say?

J. J. Mulhern

The issue of interpretative technique became newly urgent in Platonic scholarship during the third quarter of this century as different writers claimed incompatible Platos for themselves on the basis of identical evidence. Not that they had not done so in other ages; this time, though, the evidence was being characterized more exactly, some thought, than ever before. Yet Platonic scholarship had come to an impasse.

Did the impasse derive from some common but insupportable lines of reasoning? I came to believe in the late 1960s that I had found two such lines of reasoning in the Plato Says Fallacy and the Plato's Mouthpiece Fallacy. My conclusion was that scholars who committed these fallacies had lost their way because they had gone beyond what they were entitled to say about the dialogues. In this chapter I revisit my earlier criticisms, sample current work, ask whether there has been any important change, and sketch a modest program for improvement.

I. THE SITUATION THEN

The postwar decades were exciting years in Platonic scholarship. They appeared to promise advances more remarkable than any since the decades preceding World War I. Unlike those of the late Victorians and Edwardians, however, these advances were not to be primarily philological; instead, they were to be mainly logical, reflecting the penetration of modern logical analysis into the interpretation of the Platonic dialogues after a long period of dominance by idealists and their heirs who showed little interest in an exact construal of the dialogue's arguments.

This penetration occurred in two ways. For one, scholars of classical philosophy, in their university courses at Vienna, Warsaw, Oxford, and Cambridge, and at their counterpart centers in the United States and elsewhere had begun to be influenced by the logical analysis that had developed between the wars. Often, this logical analysis was focused on the meaning of ordinary language. Logical analysis at Cornell, say, was bound to mold the outlook of students of classical philosophy who took degrees there.[1]

At the same time, the modern historians of logic had broken new ground by rewriting key texts of ancient authors in the languages of modern mathematical logic. The practical effect of their work was that the materials for the analysis of ancient logical texts were enriched and the level of discussion was elevated. By 1970, this effort was well-advanced and still making progress.[2]

Thus, a combination of analytic training and the examples of scholars such as Lukasiewicz and Mates helped to attract Platonic scholars to undertake fresh interpretations of the dialogues, especially of the logical dialogues.[3] Instead of the progress that rewarded the historians of Aristotelian and Stoic logic, however, Platonic scholars at first found something approaching incoherence. While Lukasiewicz could make sense of a large part of the syllogistic in Aristotle's *Analytica Priora* with the aid of the Polish notation, for example, the students of Plato found themselves dealing with logical anomalies in the dialogues, perhaps even with logical mistakes or incompetence. They had not expected this kind of outcome. Had they missed something? The answer took a while to emerge.

Several pointers that, if noticed more widely, might have helped had been provided by Richard Robinson in *Plato's Earlier Dialectic*, especially by the second edition which appeared in 1953. In 1962, Rosamond Sprague advanced the ball a bit further in her *Plato's Use of Fallacy*. Robinson asked how explicit an author had to be to get credit for understanding a point of logic; his answer was that the author should be very explicit indeed. Mrs. Sprague did Robinson one better. She asked, in principle, how explicitness operated in works of different genres; her answer was, in short, that it depends.

These were questions of immense importance from the standpoint of intellectual history because they threatened to call into question the traditional approaches to the Platonic foundations of Western thought and thus its subsequent development. Across the ages, assumptions had been made about the Theory of Ideas that affected orthodoxies in disciplines ranging from mathematics and epistemology to theology and politics. If the traditional interpretations of Plato were contested, what would happen to these orthodoxies?

It seemed to me at the time that the Platonic scholars had not achieved the progress or the corrigibility of the Aristotelians or the Stoicists because they were overly concerned with trying to divine what Plato believed or believed in. The Aristotelians and the Stoicists had worked very carefully to find out what

---

1. Not that ordinary language analysis didn't have classical roots. See, for example, "The Philosophers that Sophie Skipped," *The Economist* 341, no. 7995 (December 7th–13th 1996): 79–82.

2. See my "Modern Notations and Ancient Logic," in *Ancient Logic and Its Modern Interpretations*, ed. John Corcoran (Dordrecht and Boston: D. Reidel Publishing Company, 1974), 71.

3. Jan Lukasiewicz, *Aristotle's Syllogistic from the Standpoint of Modern Formal Logic* (Oxford: Clarendon Press, 1951). Benson Mates, *Stoic Logic* (Berkeley: University of California Press, 1953).

Aristotle and Diodorus, for example, knew how to do. But many Platonic scholars seemed unwilling or unable to isolate the question what Plato knew how to do from the question what Plato believed or believed in; they were confusing competence with conviction. Would it be interesting and valuable to know what Plato believed? Of course it would. Could his beliefs be gathered up in any straightforward way from his writings? Hardly. These points were developed in a paper in *The Monist's* issue on the philosophy of the history of philosophy in 1969 and in a 1971 paper in *Systematics*—a journal that specialized in comparative methodology.

The first paper, dealing broadly with the interpretation of philosophical writings, compared Robinson's work on Plato with G. H. R. Parkinson's work on Leibniz, both of which took the relation between meaning and saying as the focus of interpretation. The paper summarized their views as follows: "Parkinson advises the interpreter to assume that an author means what he says—all that he says, presumably; while Robinson advises him to assume that an author says all he means. Thus, while Parkinson's canon should lead one to infer that an author did not say anything that he did not mean, Robinson's would lead one to infer that an author did not mean anything he did not say."[4]

Both of these canons, I argued, were misguided. Robinson's canon, in particular, depended upon an argument from the philosophy of history whose weakness Moore had pointed out a half-century before (1903) in criticizing Spencer; and his canon prescinded entirely from considerations of literary genre. The *Monist* paper thus attempted to adjudicate the claims of genre criticism against those of philosophy of history in the work of interpretation.

The *Systematics* paper built on the observations about genre to identify two fallacies that would not be found in the interpretation of treatises but might be found in the interpretation of dialogues.[5] These slips were given names—'Plato Says Fallacy' and 'Plato's Mouthpiece Fallacy'—so that instances of them would be easier to identify and therefore, I hoped, harder to overlook. The one consists in substituting the name 'Plato' tacitly for the name of an interlocutor in a sentence which reports what the interlocutor says and then asserting that Plato meant what the interlocutor says. The other is an open move which justifies the transition from a sentence reporting what an interlocutor says to a similar sentence reporting what Plato says by stating that the interlocutor is Plato's mouthpiece. While the definitions of these fallacies might be improved, the difficulties that they highlight have been shown to be substantive for the Platonic scholarship of the mid-century.[6]

---

4. J. J. Mulhern, "Treatises, Dialogues, and Interpretation," *The Monist* 53, no. 4 (October 1969): 634.

5. J. J. Mulhern, "Two Interpretative Fallacies," *Systematics* 9, no. 3 (December 1971): 168–172. I should point out that, while my work took issue with Robinson's, it also built upon his. Robinson had the virtue of stating his positions in an honest and forthright way. This feature of his work deserves the greatest respect since it opens the way to constructive criticism. It is far better than interpretative tentativeness, coyness, or mystification.

6. Press's comments in "The Logic of Attributing Characters' Views to Plato," pp. 27–38, are on the mark in recognizing that my approach was at bottom a logical one and that the other features of my position derived from its logic. The moves that I identified as fallacious were moves that I

It is not as easy to describe the situation in Platonic scholarship today since we lack the advantage of hindsight and cannot tell for sure what will be the mainstream that will endure to connect the present with the future in Platonic scholarship.[7] Failing hindsight, we can surmise that the bridge from past to future is likely to be built by the most robust publishers, since they will be able to keep their books in print and thus to determine the content of student reading lists. Volumes such as *The Cambridge Companion to Plato* may represent this robustness. I have selected a paper from the *Companion* to illustrate the situation in what appears to be the mainstream today.

At the same time, scholars both inside and outside the apparent mainstream have begun to develop interpretations that on the whole are more sensitive to interpretative issues and more explicit about them. Their studies reflect concern not only for the mouthpiece question but also for the reexamination of stylometric results previewed by Holger Thesleff's 1967 *Studies in the Styles of Plato* and since developed much further. Both the apparent mainstream and the alternatives need to be included in a complete account of current Platonic interpretation, and my treatment of the mainstream is balanced toward the end by a few notes on the alternatives.

---

considered fallacious. I would agree also that recognizing Robinson's "Misinterpretation by Inference," *Plato's Earlier Dialectic*, 2nd ed. (Oxford: Oxford University Press, 1953), p. 2 could be useful in reading accounts of Socratic philosophy where those accounts are sophisticated enough to avoid the two interpretative fallacies. My observation that Robinson's claims "grant too much when dialogues are the matter" did not address that kind of case. In fact, I restricted my description of the fallacy closely: "In the case of the latter [dialogues], a sentence of the form 'a says p' will be false, where p ranges over sentences occurring in a dialogue, *whenever a is replaced by the name of the dialogue's author*" (italics added).

In general, I think that Press has made a fuller case than I made in the 1971 paper. There are just a couple of points on which I should comment. With respect to Misinterpretation by Inference (1), I agree that there may be a third deficiency that comes out when people talk this way—the very sort of equivocation that Press points out. In my presentation, however, I was following what I believed to be Robinson's intent in addressing formal issues and assuming that names would be substituted for variables uniformly. If, when we replace 'c' by 'Socrates,' we intend 'Socrates [of the *Phaedo*]' for the first 'c' and '[historical] Socrates' for the second 'c,' the inference of course will not go through by reason of equivocation.

Secondly, I believe that Press and I are making different points about the *petitio* schema (3). His point is, and rightly so, that where there is no question, that question cannot be begged. He is focusing on the awareness of the individual interpreter (as he says, "they have probably proceeded in ignorance"). My point is the logical one that justifying the second line of (3)—'c is Plato's mouthpiece'—by committing the Plato Says Fallacy—tacitly replacing the name of an interlocutor by 'Plato' in 'c says p'—does beg the question in a logical sense. I don't think that we are very far apart here.

Press's last point is that to say, as I did, that a mouthpiece maxim cannot be justified, may go beyond the evidence. 'Cannot,' of course, is a strong word. I am not holding that the mouthpiece maxim might not be justified in the case of some other writer of dialogues who names his mouthpiece; I am holding it only for writers who in fact do not name their mouthpieces. Again, while I appreciate the possibility that some epigraphical or archaeological evidence might provide new information on the way the dialogues were presented, my point is a logical one rather than an empirical one—not simply that the premiss cannot be justified, but that, as I wrote, the premiss cannot be justified "without committing either a Plato Says Fallacy or a *petitio principii*" in the present state of our knowledge.

7. See, however, Gerald Press, "The State of the Question in the Study of Plato," *The Southern Journal of Philosophy* 34, no. 4 (1996): 507–532.

II. THE MAINSTREAM:
MEINWALD'S APPROACH TO THE THIRD MAN ARGUMENT

Constance C. Meinwald's paper "Good-bye to the Third Man" not only is illustrative of the apparent mainstream but also is especially appropriate for our purposes.[8] For one thing, it addresses the most analyzed lines in the Platonic

---

8. In preparing this chapter, I have begun from the Meinwald paper in *The Cambridge Companion to Plato*, ed. Richard Kraut (Cambridge: Cambridge University Press, 1992), 365–396, because of its accessibility and the likelihood that accessibility will lead to use. My page references in the notes are to this chapter. At the same time, since the *Companion* paper clearly derives from Meinwald's monograph *Plato's "Parmenides"* (New York and Oxford: Oxford University Press, 1991), I have consulted that work freely for a more extensive presentation of her method.

Kraut's "Introduction to the Study of Plato," which opens the *Cambridge Companion*, is explicit in arguing in a new way for a position related to the one that I rejected. He assumes that the grounds for objecting to mouthpieceism are derived from "an analogy between a dramatic work and a Platonic dialogue" (page 25) and that, if this analogy can be shown not to be applicable, the objections will disappear. In his words: "if Plato's aims differ from those of a dramatist, then he will have a reason that the dramatist lacks for using his main speakers as a mouthpiece for his own convictions." One can sympathize with Kraut's insistence (about the dialogues, presumably) that "Plato's works were not written to be entered into competition and performed at civic religious festivals, as were the plays of the Greek tragedians and comedians. Plato is not assigning lines to his speakers in order to win a competition or to compose a work that will be considered beautiful or satisfying by official judges or an immense audience." But his argument is weaker than it may appear, for these reasons:

First, an author such as Plato might write a dramatic work, or a work with dramatic elements, that differed in some respects but not in all from the plays of the Greek tragedians and comedians. When we deal with the Greeks, after all, we are dealing with the people who invented some of our basic genres, Plato among them. They were not constrained as we are by genre history. Plato's dialogues can be dramatic without being "entered into competition" and so on.

Second, Plato might have had aims that differed from those of Sophocles, say, while still using the genre of tragedy. Not only did Plato write tragedies (plural), according to Diogenes Laertius, but his competition for a prize with one of them apparently was forestalled by a meeting with Socrates. Authorial aims and genre choices do not always align in the same way.

Third and most important, Kraut's conditional—"if Plato's aims differ... then he will have a reason"—itself addresses aims and reasons, not the matters of fact required for interpretation. In order to get to Plato's Mouthpiece—PM 2 in my schema (see note 5)—via Kraut's route, one would have to have a license for asserting that, if Plato *has a reason for using* his main speakers as a mouthpiece for his own conclusions, then Plato *actually uses* his main speakers as a mouthpiece for his own conclusions. And it seems obvious that, as a matter of intentional logic, having a reason for doing something is no guarantee that one actually will do that something.

Kraut does not need this weak argument to make the point that the dialogues "are vehicles for the articulation and defense of certain theses and the defeat of others" (p. 26). But he does need it for his slide into "the assumption that in each dialogue he [Plato] uses his principal interlocutors to support or oppose certain conclusions by means of certain arguments *because he, Plato, supports or opposes those conclusions for those reasons*" (italics mine, p. 29). The unitalicized portion is easy to justify from common sources; the italicized portion is no more than the unjustified Plato's Mouthpiece once again.

Still and all, the fact that Kraut included thoughts on interpretation in his introduction suggests that interpretative technique is garnering broader attention. Two other introductory essays tend to confirm this view—the "Editor's Prologue" in *Methods of Interpreting Plato and His Dialogues, Oxford Studies in Ancient Philosophy*, Supplementary Volume, ed. James C. Klagge and Nicholas D. Smith (Oxford: Clarendon Press, 1992); and Francisco J. Gonzalez's "Introduction: A Short History of Platonic Interpretation and the 'Third Way'" in his collection *The Third Way: New Directions in Platonic Studies* (Lanham, MD: Rowman & Littlefield Publishers, Inc., 1995).

scholarship of this century's third quarter—those that make up the Third Man Argument. For another, it is critical of others' interpretative methods. Finally, it is explicit, sometimes, about its own rules of interpretation.

Meinwald sets out in "Good-bye" to save the Theory of Ideas from Aristotle and Gregory Vlastos by showing that the Third Man Argument is not damaging to it. Part of her approach is to argue that self predication in the Third Man Argument is something other than it has been taken to be.

Meinwald argues that certain expressions in the dialogues that have been thought to attribute same-order predicates to same-order predicates $(F^1F^1$, or more generally $F^nF^n)$, actually are all right because they are attributing higher order predicates to lower order predicates $(F^{>n}F^n)$ in a way that reveals their natures; she calls this arrangement tree-predication. Her tree-predications are analytic sentences, having to do with relations of ideas. She goes on to argue that predications that do not reveal the natures of their subjects, though ordinary predications for most people, actually are qualified predications. On this reading, sentences of the Fa form are reinterpreted as sentences of the qualified Fa form: Fa really means that a is F with respect to some qualification. These ordinary predications are synthetic sentences, having to do with matters of fact and existence. Using this distinction, she argues that the Third Man Argument does not go through since, in it, Ideas are predicated of Ideas in the first way $(F^{>n}F^n)$ and of particulars in the second (Fa).

The substance of Meinwald's argument, which is ingenious in its way and contains more twists and turns than I have represented, is not my subject here. Mine is the more modest subject of asking whether Meinwald's interpretative technique makes an important advance over its forerunners in avoiding the two interpretative fallacies. In answering this question, I shall deal with her outcome and her interpretative assumptions.

III. THE OUTCOME

Meinwald's outcome is presented in her last section, which is titled "Three Stories of Plato's Development" (389–391). She rejects the first or traditional story, according to which Plato went through a Socratic period, a fruitful middle period, a crisis marked by the *Parmenides,* and a "barren final period." She rejects also the "second and completely opposite story" that recognizes approximately the same periods but evaluates them differently. According to the second story, Plato's middle period was not fruitful but, after the crisis, the last period was. The first and second stories are "completely opposite," we find, in that, while they present a common view of the Socratic period, they reverse their evaluations of the middle and final periods.

Meinwald's third story, also recognizing the three periods, sees the middle period as an incipient response to issues surfaced in the Socratic period. She views "these passages [on metaphysics in the middle dialogues] as indicating the motivations and outlines of views that it is not their purpose fully to develop." And again: "these passages underdetermine the 'theory' to be attributed to their author."[9] According to her, the *Parmenides* represents much more than a crisis over the Theory of Ideas. Indeed, the crisis is confined to the first part of the dialogue, and it is a controlled crisis at that, since "Plato composed the first part of the *Parmenides* in order to exhibit where his middle period description of Forms needed development." According to Meinwald: "The *Parmenides* as a whole gives the best possible evidence for Plato's response to the problems it introduces . . . the dialogue shows that his response was successful. As the late period began, the theory of Forms was in new leaf." Thus Meinwald's outcome is another three-period-plus-crisis story of Plato's development, and in this respect it retains comparability with the better known stories. It is the same kind of story as the others. But it is a different story, since it evaluates the second and third periods and the crisis in a different way.

There is much to be said for trying to see the argument of a dialogue as a whole as well as for looking at the argument piece by piece. Meinwald adopts something like this rule of comprehensiveness, at least for the *Parmenides,* when she writes: "The natural starting point for answering this question [about the first part of the dialogue] is to study the rest of the dialogue to see whether it addresses the problems raised in the first part."[10] The third story thus results in part from looking at the argument of the *Parmenides* as a whole on principle.

On this point I find myself in greater sympathy with Meinwald than with scholars who object to the focus on arguments in the dialogues and especially to what they sometimes describe as taking the arguments out of their context—presumably, the dramatic context of the dialogues. While my motivation for this sympathy is given programmatically below, there are three points that it is best to make here:

First, as a practical matter, where the dialogues present arguments, which they do only in some places, one has to focus on the arguments as arguments or miss the opportunity to deal with them as what they are. The usual alternative to dealing with them as arguments is to deal with their parts individually—that is, to take the sentential parts out of their argumentative context. In some cases, where the dramatic context is in part an argumentative context, removing sentences from their argumentative context is removing them from their dramatic context as well. To take individual sentences out of their argumentative context for the purpose of making a single point or of stringing them together to construct a theory may be useful in some cases, but it is a chancy procedure.[11]

Second, one value of focusing on arguments is that arguments help make clear what their sentential parts mean by showing what they follow from and what follows from them. Arguments have this much objectivity to them. Thus,

---

9. Meinwald, "Good-bye," 391.

10. Meinwald, "Good-bye," 366.

11. Anders Wedberg took an informative theory-construction approach to the Theory of Ideas in *Plato's Philosophy of Mathematics* (Stockholm: Almquist & Wiksell, 1955), chap. 3, "The Theory of Ideas"; reprinted in *Plato: A Collection of Critical Essays,* ed. G. Vlastos (Garden City: Doubleday and Company, Inc., 1971), I, 25–30. See my comments in "Professor Wedberg's Theory of Ideas: Suggestions for Modification," *Apeiron* 9, no.1 (1975): 25–29.

two people of quite different views on the truth of sentences in an argument still can appreciate the argument itself in much the same way. One sometimes can examine a sentence most usefully when one sees it in the context of its function in an argument, whether or not one is sure that one believes in the sentence or would assert it oneself. Readers of Plato should be able to progress toward a common view of the arguments of the dialogues even if they cannot agree on the truth of their several sentential parts.

Third, arguments that one finds in the text are good evidence of what an author knew how to do. Not that everyone can read these arguments off; some cannot do so. Yet, the possibility of reading off an argument is presupposed in the project of understanding philosophical dialogues, even though dramatic elements in the dialogues may interrupt or throw off the ordinary or expected way of stating the argument. It is presupposed just as surely as is the possibility of reading off statements of belief—a very different exercise—from systematic treatises. In the history of thought, knowing that an author knew how to argue and being able to follow the argument may lead eventually to insights of other kinds as arguments are developed for or against important positions.

Meinwald's approach to the hypotheses of the *Parmenides* is consistent with this view of the importance of focusing on arguments in the dialogues. One of her interpretative rules, however, could obstruct argumentative analysis—to wit, the rule that "A premise that does not appear in the text can *a fortiori* not be marked as the target of the exercise." This rule calls for careful testing.

IV. INTERPRETATIVE ASSUMPTIONS:
MEINWALD'S RULE ON THE STATEMENT OF ARGUMENTS

The reconstruction of arguments is not an uncommon process in historical work, in philosophical work, or elsewhere. What thoughtful person has not asked a friend, "How did you come to that conclusion?" Situations of this kind turn out in different ways. Sometimes, the suggestion, once stated, is perfectly obvious to all parties. In other cases, the interlocutors may have difficulty agreeing on what it was. "Oh no; wasn't your reason that *S*?" The way it turns out often depends on the extent to which recognized conventions govern the situation. There is a good chance that conventions familiar in the Academy can be helpful in reconstructing the arguments of the dialogues where those arguments are not obviously complete.

Meinwald, I believe, comes close to overlooking the role of school convention in her treatment of what she calls "*reductio*-oriented readers."[12] She is at pains to overthrow the view that "each argument in the passage [of the hypotheses] should be treated as a *reductio ad absurdum*";[13] indeed, she must overthrow this view to make room for her own. Her interest here pushes her in the direction of an interpretative rule that probably goes too far. The rule, cited above, is, "A premise that does not appear in the text can *a fortiori* not be

---

12. Meinwald, "Good-bye," 371.
13. Meinwald, "Good-bye," 369.

marked as the target of the exercise."[14] This rule brings her close to Robinson's unsatisfactory advice to assume that an author says all he means or, to put it another way, that an author did not mean anything he did not say.

Her rule raises again the far-reaching question about how arguments are stated in works of different genres. The scholars of the mid-century and even earlier[15] who devoted so much effort to understanding and explaining the arguments of the Platonic dialogues found on more than one occasion that these arguments were stated only in part by a principal speaker, part being left for the respondents and interlocutors—and, after them, the reader—to supply. This sort of abbreviation is no more than is to be expected in a dialogue. Some writers have looked for fallacies where gaps occur in these arguments. And of course there are well-attested fallacies in the dialogues. But as Professor Demos pointed out, a gap is merely a lacuna, and a lacuna is not *ea ipsa* a fallacy.[16] Indeed, even mathematicians frequently omit lines in their inferences, thinking them too obvious to mention. One must be on one's guard against finding fallacies where there are only expository lacunae.

Of especial importance in appraising the need for supplying parts of arguments when these are not supplied in the text is the doctrine of enthymeme, which is mentioned very early in his career by Aristotle,[17] perhaps within a decade of Plato's preoccupation with the *Parmenides, Theaetetus,* and *Sophist.*[18] At about the same time or shortly thereafter, Aristotle would have been composing his first work on rhetoric—the *Grylus,* while teaching in the Academy.[19] As presented in the *Rhetorica,* enthymeme provides for omitting parts of an argument whose inclusion would be otiose: an enthymeme may consist of fewer propositions than those of the normal syllogism, according to Aristotle, since, if any of these propositions is familiar, "there is no need to mention it; the hearer adds it himself."[20] Presumably, the omitted material that the hearer would add himself frequently would be in the nature of a commonplace.[21]

---

14. Meinwald, "Good-bye," 371.

15. See, for example, John H. Brown, "The Logic of the *Euthyphro* 10A–11B," *Philosophical Quarterly* 14 (1964): 1–14, especially the programmatic remarks on page 2. Edwin Black provides an explanation of the fragmentary nature of argumentative discourse such as that in the Platonic dialogues in *Rhetorical Criticism: A Study in Method* (New York: The Macmillan Company, 1965), 149–150.

16. R. Demos, "A Fallacy in Plato's *Republic*?" *Philosophical Review*, 73 (1964): 395.

17. *Top.* 164a7.

18. P.M. Huby, "The Date of Aristotle's *Topics* and its Treatment of the Theory of Ideas," *Classical Quarterly*, 12 (1962): 75.

19. Sir David Ross, article "Aristotle," *Oxford Classical Dictionary*, p. 95.

20. *Rhetorica* 1357a16–19; tr. Roberts. M. F. Burnyeat recently has argued that the supposed definition of enthymeme as incomplete syllogism which appears at *An. Pri.*70a10 is not Aristotelian since *ateles* was added by a later hand and since, even with the insertion removed, it is not a definition. See "Enthymeme: Aristotle on the Logic of Persuasion," *Aristotle's "Rhetoric": Philosophical Essays,* ed. David J. Furley and Alexander Nehamas (Princeton: Princeton University Press, 1994), 6–8. Aside from his view on the definition, Burnyeat discusses brevity in enthymeme in a manner that is not inconsistent with my argument; see pp. 21–24.

21. For parallels of the earlier *Topica* with the later *Rhetorica,* see W. A. de Pater, *Les Topiques d'Aristote et la dialectique platonicienne* (Fribourg: Éditions St. Paul, 1965), 101–111. I should suggest that these correspondences indicate the incorporation into the *Rhetorica* of much material drawn from Aristotle's earliest rhetorical teaching. The relevance of commonplaces is reserved for treatment in another paper.

There is more to this matter of reconstructing arguments in a dialogue than there is in a treatise because of the complications introduced by character portrayal. As one finds in other dialogues, there are presuppositions of arguments that the sponsors of these arguments may not want to admit: admitting them may damage their positions. The interpreter who is to understand these arguments, however, like the Platonic Socrates, must recognize and come to grips with the presuppositions. Further, not only may an interlocutor wish not to admit one of his beliefs; he may go so far as to profess convictions which he does not possess. Unfortunately, as Aristotle intimates, the Greeks were no more candid than ourselves.[22] This is a factor which the successful composer or interpreter of dialogues must take into account.

The likelihood is, then, that one will find a high incidence of abbreviated enthymematic arguments in the dialogues. Since this is the case, one should adopt canons that recognize this likelihood. One has little choice but to assume that abbreviated arguments will appear in the dialogues by design and that parts of arguments will be left unstated for dramatic or rhetorical or some other effect as well as through inadvertence. Canons devised on the basis of these considerations will be very different, of course, from Richard Robinson's or the one of Meinwald's that recalls it; but there is every reason to believe that they will accord better with the conventions of literary composition and interpretation that Plato could have expected to be applied to his own work.[23]

V. CONCLUSIONS ABOUT THE MAINSTREAM

All three mainstream stories of the dialogues, not only Meinwald's, are stories about "Plato's own theories," as she calls them. In all three stories, the dialogues are viewed as doctrinal documents, valuable primarily as stating Plato's beliefs. Again, all three stories are developmental stories; and all three stories typically embody the Plato Says Fallacy and the Plato's Mouthpiece Fallacy. Moves of this fallacious kind are simply assumed to be proper or, perhaps, remain below the authors' thresholds of explicit awareness.

Further, being developmental, none of the three stories addresses the genre issue in a fundamental way. The genre issue is that Plato wrote dialogues in which he was not an interlocutor, thereby giving up the opportunity to speak for himself, rather than writing works of another sort, in which he might have spoken for himself. This issue can be addressed in a fundamental way either by accommodating interpretative technique to it or by giving a reason for not addressing it. The three developmental stories do neither.

Why is it that the three stories make common interpretative assumptions yet are incompatible? Part of the answer is that succumbing to the two interpretative fallacies makes the story-level interpretation difficult to control. Once one

---

22. See *Metaph.* 1005b25–26 and 1011a3–4. But see also David Ross, *Aristotle's "Metaphysics."* A revised text with Introduction and Commentary, 2 vols. (Oxford: Oxford University Press, 1966) *ad* 1005b25, who does not think Heraclitus's sincerity is in point.

23. See T. de Laguna, "The Interpretation of the *Apology*," *Philosophical Review* 18 (1909): 28.

agrees to let an interlocutor's remark count for Plato's belief or to let an interlocutor count for Plato, much of the rest depends on the remarks and interlocutors one picks; and there is no secure rule for making the pick.

With respect to the assumptions associated with the two interpretative fallacies, then, little has changed in twenty-five years in the mainstream. But there is more to be said, for, in other respects, Platonic scholarship has moved forward, especially where analytic work has been done that has not depended upon addressing the question whether the dialogues present the development of Plato's own beliefs. This independence is found where authors consider what Plato knew how to do rather than what he believed. Meinwald has taken a step in this direction by laying out an analysis of the argument of the *Parmenides* that can be followed, checked, and, if necessary, modified. But more can be done.

VI. ALTERNATIVES TO THE MAINSTREAM

Some of this more has been attempted by scholars whose work is not included in the *Cambridge Companion* but does attempt to address the impasse of the mid-century.

Kenneth Sayre, for example, has tried an ingenious end run around the mouthpiece issue by arguing that positions that Aristotle and others attribute to Plato as "unwritten teachings" in fact are equivalent to positions in the *Philebus*.[24] On this view, the "unwritten teachings" were written after all. Mitchell Miller follows this approach closely.[25] To the extent that their view is correct, it enriches our second-hand glimpse of the Lecture on the Good and gives us an opportunity to see an interlocutor in one of the dialogues who restates doctrines from the Lecture as Plato's mouthpiece.

This approach remains to be evaluated in a comprehensive way. If, for example, it justifies the statement 'Protarchus is Plato's mouthpiece', it may provide grounds for a whole series of inferences about Plato's doctrine as well as a perspective on his use of mouthpieces. At the same time, it raises a new set of interpretative questions. Where, for example, does it leave all the material in the *Philebus* that is not included in reports of the Lecture on the Good? Is everything that Protarchus says authentically Platonic? What happens to developmentalism? What about the other dialogues? Does the coincidence of the Lecture on the Good and the *Philebus* change our way of reading the other dialogues?

VII. A MODEST PROGRAM FOR IMPROVEMENT

I have written above of "the conventions of literary composition and interpretation that Plato could have expected to be applied to his own work." Think for

---

24. Kenneth M. Sayre, *Plato's Late Ontology: A Riddle Resolved* (Princeton: Princeton University Press, 1983).

25. Mitchell Miller, "The Choice between the Dialogues and the 'Unwritten Teachings': A Scylla and Charybdis for the Interpreter?" in *The Third Way*, ed. Gonzalez, 225–243.

a moment of what the author of the dialogues has done. At the very least, he has done three notable things. He has deployed a certain amount of argumentative material in the dialogues, sometimes trotting out the same argument, or something close to it, more than once.[26] Again, he has broken up the arguments so that their parts are assigned to different individuals who propose a sentence for consideration, assert it, or deny it in the course of question and answer or extended speech. Further, in some cases, the author has presented the assignees in a very lively way as independently attested historical individuals whose characters are developed in the dialogues against a background that lends them verisimilitude. Doubtless, the author revisited each of these three notable things numerous times in the writing of each argumentative passage—a perspective consistent with Thesleff's view of the revision of the dialogues. Each of these three compositional operations says something about how the dialogues might be read.

Use of Arguments

Arguments not only are used in the dialogues; they are drawn from inventory and reused. The notion of an inventory of arguments is not one that needs a lot of fresh support, but it does need more attention for the light that it sheds on the composition of dialogues. In particular, the reuse or repetition of arguments and argumentative moves shows that these argumentative elements have a certain independence of their contexts, as arguments typically do. They are ingredients of each dialogue in which they occur, but they can be ingredients of more than one dialogue and they can be ingredients of works other than these or any other dialogues. They can be repeated, for example, in Aristotelian treatises or in other works. Indeed, the same argument can be repeated, or varied in form, indefinitely.

From the author's standpoint, the availability of a supply of arguments presents a range of choices. Once the decision is made to use an argument, the author can present it in a fairly complete way or can present parts of it. Also, the author can recast it. In any case, the vehicle for presenting an argument in a dialogue is the speech of the interlocutors, and the author has to decide how to present it through the interlocutors' speech.

Assignments of Parts

There is a parallel here to the composition of music for a mixed group of instruments. The composer works with a supply of melodic or serial elements, some of which may be new and original, some of which may have been used before. Putting them together successfully is not a merely mechanical process; but at some point in writing the score, the composer must accomplish the mechanical chore of marking the lines with the voices to which parts will be assigned. Plato had to perform a similar operation.

---

26. See Ausland, "Who Speaks for Whom in the *Timaeus-Critias*?" pp. 183–198.

The music can be rescored; one can arrange a piano or organ transcription of a symphonic work or an orchestral transcription of operatic arias. Each one of these exercises represents a distinct assignment of parts, guided in the best case by good musical sense, which is not merely mechanical but has a mechanical element—touching pen to paper or moving a trackball.

The parallel can be extended in an informative way. In musical composition, the different structural parts—a theme, say, or a coda—may be assigned to different instrumental parts from time to time. The theme may be stated in one section; it may be restated or varied in another. New thematic material may be introduced in a new movement. Individual chords or groups of chords may provide punctuation. In all of these cases, the supply of musical material is distributed in a more or less deliberate way to designated instruments or groups of instruments that are used in different ways for different purposes.

In the dialogues, especially where the speeches are broken up into small pieces, the parts of arguments are assigned to different characters through the medium of question and answer. Through this medium, signals are given that, to speak in Fregean terms, a sentence is being proposed for consideration, when an interlocutor asks a question *(Satzfrage)*, or that it is being asserted or denied, when another interlocutor responds in a definitive way. Given the result of the argument, if it is completed, and as with a musical score, one may go back to the basic material and reassign roles, as Plato sometimes does.

This assignment of parts is of the essence in the presentation of arguments in the dialogues, and so it should be retained in translating and interpreting them. The assignment of successive parts to interlocutors provides the action of the dialogues—moves them forward—just as the assignment of successive notes and phrases to instruments provides the action of the musical piece. Much has been made of Cornford's rendering of the *Republic* because it dispenses with some of the question and answer, giving passages of the dialogue more of an expository tone.[27] Cornford's translation thus fails to translate Plato, whatever else it does, because it obscures the signs that indicate whether a sentence, in the context of some argument, is being considered, asserted, or denied.

Setting the Stage

Insofar as Cornford's translation omits assignments of parts, it presents the further flaw of weakening the author's association of certain speeches with interlocutors whose characters have been developed or are being developed in defined settings.

The dramatic elements of the dialogues are presented through the settings and the interlocutors, who are known for their character as well as for their actions. The settings and the character development are distinct and separate from the use of argumentative material and the assignment of parts, though the elements are woven together in an apparently seamless way in some of the dialogues—perhaps in those that underwent the most extensive revision.

---

27. *The Republic of Plato*, tr. Francis MacDonald Cornford (New York and London: Oxford University Press, 1945).

The author Plato has taken great pains to provide settings and to portray the characters of the interlocutors. The settings, whether verifiably historical or not, help the reader understand the interactions of the interlocutors, especially their argumentative interactions; so does their character portrayal. These dramatic elements overlay the use of argumentative material and the assignment of parts.

Thus, though separate in principle, the dramatic elements are linked intimately to the use of arguments and the assignment of parts in the finished dialogue. One can see the effect of the overlay, for example, when an interlocutor refuses to continue an argument. For dramatic reasons, one needs to know who is breaking off an argument or doing something else with it. One often needs to know the setting as well to understand the whole.

Conclusions on the Program

If Plato, as I have suggested, actually went through these operations in composing the dialogues, he might well have expected readers to pay attention to arguments, part assignments, and dramatic elements when they read the dialogues. In fact, he might have expected that these features would receive the main attention from at least some readers. If so, one might reasonably adopt the following approach to interpreting the dialogues.

- Identify the arguments.
- Note the way the interlocutors state them—what questions are considered, what asserted, what denied.
- Note the setting and the characters of the interlocutors to identify the motives that they might have in considering, asserting, or denying.

None of these is easy to do. Arguments may not be easy to identify. They may need to be approached from both ends—from conclusions and the support given to them, and from their apparent starting points. Some reconstruction may be required. The assignments to interlocutors will shed light on the arguments, both in the way they speak and in the way their characters are portrayed. But this light will not be full light in every case. At the very least, this approach, if accepted, will provide a framework that sets certain standards for interpretation while allowing great latitude in the range of information that may be brought forward.

VIII. SUMMARY

If the foregoing account is approximately accurate, the last quarter of this century has seen some improvement in the technique of Platonic interpretation. This improvement is visible mainly outside the mainstream, and it depends in part on avoiding the Plato Says Fallacy and the Plato's Mouthpiece Fallacy. It depends as well in part on avoiding the seductions of developmental stylometry. Constructive efforts can go forward most efficiently, I suggest, if interpreters get a grip on some main features of the composition of the Platonic dialogues and so on the way they might, profitably, be read.

General Index

Achilles, 85, 184
Adkins, A. W. H., 95
Aeschylus, 212
Aischines of Sphettus, 18
Ajax, 88, 95
Albinus (Alcinus), 1, 72
Alden, John, 99
Alexamenos, 69
Anaximander, 43
Anglo-American philosophy, 41
Annas, Julia, 27, 115, 125, 126, 142
Anonymous Commentary on the Theaetetus, 8, 77–79
Antilogism (antilogy), 58, 59
Arcesilaus, 2
Archilochus, 85, 86
Aristophanes, 17, 21, 212; of Byzantium, 70, 71, 191, 192
Aristotle, 1, 40, 47, 51, 52, 54, 110, 113, 183, 210, 213, 215, 222, 223, 226, 230, 232
Aristoxenus, 217
Aspasia, 153, 186
Aulus Gellius, 8, 74–76, 77, 185
Austen, Jane, 15
Autolykus, 119

Bacon, Helen, 104
Basilius of Caesarea, 188, 189
Biography, 15
Burger, Ronna, 106, 107

Cambridge, 222
Carneades, 2
Cicero, 2, 8
Clay, Diskin, 47
Communication, 29
Cornford, F. M., 234
Creon, 215
Crete, 69

David, Jacques Louis, 100, 106, 109
Demos, Rafael, 229
Derrida, Jacques, 115
Descartes, Rene, 157
Detienne, Marcel, 44, 45, 48
Diodorus, 223
Diogenes Laertius, 1, 68, 69, 70, 71, 72, 74, 187–189, 191
Diomedes, 52
Dissoi Logoi, 58, 180
Dover, K. J., 153
Drama, 63

Edelstein, Ludwig, 211
Edwardian, 221
Epic, 63
Eristics, 58
Euripides, 39, 183, 213

Fiction, 15
Fields, W. C., 109

235

Platonic Index

About the Contributors

Hayden W. Ausland is associate professor of classics at the University of Montana. His publications include "On the Moral Origin of the Pyrrhonian Philosophy" in *Elenchos* and "On Reading Plato Mimetically" in the *American Journal of Philology*. He is writing a book on Plato's *Republic*.

Eugenio Benitez is a senior lecturer in the department of traditional and modern philosophy at the University of Sydney. His publications include *Dialogues with Plato* (ed. 1996) and *Forms in Plato's Philebus* (1989), as well as several articles in ancient philosophy in *The Review of Metaphysics*, *Philosophy and Rhetoric*, and *Apeiron*. He is editor of the journal *Literature and Aesthetics*.

Ruby Blondell is a professor of classics at the University of Washington. She is the author, under the name Mary Whitlock Blundell, of *Helping Friends and Harming Enemies: A Study in Sophocles and Greek Ethics* (Cambridge, 1989), annotated translations of Sophocles' *Oedipus at Colonus* and *Antigone* for the Focus Classical Library, and articles on Greek tragedy and philosophy. Under the name Ruby Blondell, she has translated Euripides' *Medea*, with introduction and commentary, for *Women on the Edge: Four Plays by Euripides* (Routledge, 1999).

Lloyd P. Gerson is a professor of philosophy at the University of Toronto. His books include *The Cambridge Companion to Plotinus* (ed., 1996), *Plotinus* (1994), *God and Greek Philosophy* (1990), *Hellenistic Philosophy* (with Brad Inwood, 1988), *The Epicurus Reader* (with Brad Inwood, 1994), *Aristotle's Politics* (with H. G. Apostle, 1986), *Aristotle: Selected Works* (with H. G. Apostle, 1984), *Graceful Reason* (ed., 1983), and *Knowledge and the Self in the Platonic Tradition* (forthcoming). He has published more than forty articles in various Anglo-American and European philosophy journals. Gerson is editor of *Aristotle: Critical Assessments* (four volumes, forthcoming).

Francisco J. Gonzalez is an associate professor of philosophy at Skidmore College. He is editor of *The Third Way: New Directions in Platonic Studies* (Lanham, MD: Rowman & Littlefield, 1995) and author of *Dialectic and Dialogue: Plato's Practice of Philosophical Inquiry* (Evanston, IL: Northwestern

University Press, 1998). He has also contributed articles on Plato, Aristotle, and Heidegger to a number of journals and collections. He is currently writing a book entitled *Kin, Rivals, Lovers: A Reading of Plato's* Lysis.

J. J. Mulhern is the director of the Fels Center of Government at the University of Pennsylvania. He edited *Population Policy in Plato and Aristotle* (1975) and has published articles that appeared in *Journal of the History of Ideas, Phoenix, The Monist, Classica et Mediaevalia, Apeiron, Systematics, Phronesis, Logique et Analyse, Classical Philology, Teorema, Arethusa,* and *The International Journal of Applied Philosophy.*

Debra Nails is an associate professor in the department of classics, philosophy, and religion at Mary Washington College. In September 2000, she will become an associate professor in the department of philosophy at Michigan State University. She is the author of *Agora, Academy, and the Conduct of Philosophy* (1995), and coeditor with Abner Shimony of *Naturalistic Epistemology: A Symposium for Two Decades* (1987) and with Marjorie Grene of *Spinoza and the Sciences* (1986). She has published articles in *Ancient Philosophy, Phoenix, Bryn Mawr Classical Review, Teaching Philosophy, The South African Journal of Philosophy, The Southwestern Journal of Philosophy,* and several collections.

Erik Ostenfeld is head of the Center for the Study of Antiquity and a member of the classics department at the University of Aarhus, Denmark. He is the author of *Forms, Matter and Mind* (1982), *Three Strands in Plato's Metaphysics* (1982) and *Ancient Greek Psychology and the Modern Mind-Body Debate* (1986). He has contributed articles to *Classica et Mediaevalia, Agora, Philosophy and Medicine, Hellenismestudier,* and *Rivista di Filosofia* (Argentina).

Gerald A. Press is a professor of philosophy at Hunter College, City University of New York and is a member of the graduate faculty. He is the author of *The Development of the Idea of History in Antiquity* (1982), and editor of *Plato's Dialogues: New Studies and Interpretations* (1993). He was coeditor for "Ancient Philosophy" of *The Columbia History of Western Philosophy* (1998). His articles have appeared in *History and Theory, Southern Journal of Philosophy, International Studies in Philosophy, Journal of Neoplatonic Studies, Augustinian Studies, Augustiniana,* and *Philosophy and Rhetoric.* He serves as editor of the *Journal of the History of Philosophy.*

Gary Alan Scott teaches philosophy at Saint Peter's College in New Jersey. He is the author of *Plato's Socrates as Educator* (Albany: SUNY Press, Forthcoming), and he is currently editing a collection of essays on *Rethinking Socratic Method.* His several articles and book reviews on Plato's *Symposium, Lysis,* and *Phaedo,* have been published in the *Journal of Neoplatonic Studies, The Southern Journal of Philosophy, Interpretation* and *Ancient Philosophy.* The article included in this volume is the second paper he and William Welton have coauthored. They are presently at work on a commentary on the *Symposium.*

P. Christopher Smith is a professor in the department of philosophy at The University of Massachusetts at Lowell, and the translator of H.G. Gadamer's *Hegel's Dialectic* (1976), *Dialog and Dialectic* (1980), and *The Idea of the Good* *in Platonic-Aristotelian Philosophy* (1986). He is the author of *Hermeneutics and Human Finitude* (1991) and *The Hermeneutics of Original Argument: Demonstration, Dialectic, Rhetoric* (1998). His articles have appeared in *Philosophy and Literature, Modern Schoolman, International Philosophical Quarterly, Southern Journal of Philosophy, Heidelberger Jahrbuecher,* and *The New Scholasticism.* He has contributed to a dozen books, most recently *The Philosophy of Hans-Georg Gadamer* (1997).

Harold Tarrant worked for twenty years in the area of Greek studies at the University of Sydney, and currently is professor and head of the department of classics at the University of Newcastle in New South Wales, Australia. He is the author of *Scepticism or Platonism?* (1985); *Thrasyllan Platonism* (1993); with H. Tredennick, *Plato: The Last Days of Socrates* (1993); and with K. Lycos and K. R. Jackson, *Olympiodorus: Commentary on Plato's Gorgias* (1998). Tarrant's articles have appeared in *Phronesis, Apeiron,* and *Classical Quarterly,* among other journals. He serves as an executive member, International Plato Society and is a fellow of the Australian Academy for the Humanities. His *Plato's First Interpreteres* is forthcoming.

Holger Thesleff is an emeritus professor of Greek at University of Helsinki and is the author of *An Introduction to the Pythagorean Writings of the Hellenistic Period* (1961), *Studies in the Styles of Plato* (1967), *Studies in Platonic Chronology* (1982), *Platon* (1989), and *Studies in Plato's Two-Level Model* (1999). He edited *The Pythagorean Writings of the Hellenistic Period* (1965). He is currently completing a monograph entitled *Studies in Plato's Two-Level Model.* He has contributed articles to *Arctos, Phronesis,* and the *Bulletin of the Institute for Classical Studies.*

Joanne Waugh is an associate professor of philosophy at the University of South Florida in Tampa. She was one of the editors of *Hypatia: A Journal of Feminist Philosophy* from 1995–1998. Her work has appeared in *The Monist, The Journal of Aesthetics and Art Criticism, The Journal of Aesthetic Education,* and *Art Criticism.* She has contributed chapters to a number of collections; three were published in 1995, one in 1997, and several appeared in 1999.

William A. Welton teaches philosophy at Xavier University. He is the author of articles that have appeared in *Apeiron, Polis, Philosophy and Rhetoric,* and *Interpretation.*

Elinor J. M. West is a professor emeritus of philosophy at Long Island University. She has taught at Sarah Lawrence, Rutgers, Queens College, and Columbia University and contributed essays on Nietzsche, Euripides, Plato, Socrates, and Arcesilaus to *Arethusa, The Journal of Critical Analysis, Thesis Eleven* and in several collections of scholarly articles. Presently, she is working on a book on Plato and Aristophanes as witnesses for Socrates and composing chapters on the ancient religions of Greece and Rome for a book on world religions.